PAUL AND THE TORAH

PAUL
AND THE TORAH

Lloyd Gaston

UNIVERSITY OF BRITISH COLUMBIA PRESS
Vancouver
1987

PAUL AND THE TORAH

This book has been published with the assistance of a grant from the Canada Council.

CANADIAN CATALOGUING IN PUBLICATION DATA

Gaston, Lloyd, 1929-
Paul and the Torah

Includes bibliographical references and index.
ISBN 0-7748-0284-7

1. Paul, the Apostle, Saint - Contributions in the theology of law. 2. Paul, the Apostle, Saint - Views on Judaism. 3. Law (Theology) - Biblical teaching. 4. Judaism (Christian theology). 5. Bible. N.T. Epistles of Paul - Criticism, interpretation, etc. I. Title.
BS2655.L35G38 1987 241′.2 C87-091380-8

ISBN 0-7748-0284-7

Printed in Canada

CONTENTS

ACKNOWLEDGEMENTS

Gratitude is expressed for permission to reprint the following essays in slightly modified form:

1. "Paul and the Torah." Essay originally published in *Anti-Semitism and the Foundations of Christianity* edited by Alan T. Davies. Copyright © by Alan T. Davies. Used by permission of the Paulist Press.

2. "Abraham and the Righteousness of God," *Horizons in Biblical Theology* 2 (1980) 39-68, published by the Clifford E. Barbour Library, Pittsburgh Theological Seminary.

3. "Israel's Enemies in Pauline Theology," *New Testament Studies* 28 (1982) 400-423, published by Cambridge University Press.

4. "Angels and Gentiles in Early Judaism and in Paul," *Studies in Religion/Sciences Religieuses* 11 (1982) 65-75, published at Wilfrid Laurier University Press.

5. "Works of Law as a Subjective Genitive," *Studies in Religion/Sciences Religieuses* 13 (1984) 39-46, published at Wilfrid Laurier University Press.

6. Paul and Jerusalem," *From Jesus to Paul; Studies in Honour of Francis Wright Beare* (eds. P. Richardson and J. C. Hurd; Waterloo: Wilfrid Laurier Univeristy Press) 61-72.

7. "Paul and the Law in Galatians Two and Three," *Anti-Judaism in Early Christianity; Vol 1, Paul and the Gospels* (ed. P. Richardson with D. Granskou; Waterloo: Wilfrid Laurier University Press) 37-57.

A RETROSPECTIVE INTRODUCTION

Introductions come at the beginning because they help the reader set what follows into a wider context. They are usually written last because only at the end of the road can the author look back on the journey and see something of what that context has been. This introduction consists then of an inextricable mixture of what have been presuppositions for the following chapters and what are conclusions drawn from them. What will be presented here are not arguments meant to persuade the reader but only a description of the context to enable the reader to understand better why the following chapters argue in the way they do.

The essays contained in this book were written at various times and are presented here in chronological order. The first one had its origins in a paper presented to the first meeting of the Anti-Judaism Seminar of the Canadian Society of Biblical Studies in 1977. That seminar continued to be an important context for working out many of the subsequent studies. It has seemed advisable to let the essays stand in more or less unrevised form, in order that the reader might follow the progress of the research. Discoveries which are still only questions in one often become the subject of a fuller investigation in a subsequent one. If this procedure sometimes results in repetitions concerning method, they are repetitions which seem to be important to reiterate. In the author's mind, at any rate, the result is not a collection of essays on discrete and unrelated themes but a unity whose growth can still be traced.

Hermeneutical Context

First, I write in the context of the second half of the twentieth century in the firm conviction that things which happened in the first half must mean a radical and irrevocable change in the way Christians do theology. Nevertheless, the present book is in no sense meant to be understood only as part of a "theology after Auschwitz."[1] Recognition of the consequences of the church's centuries-long "teaching of contempt" [2] should indeed lead to repentance and a resolve to do theology better in the future, but it should not inspire an apologetic revision of texts written in the past. On the contrary, it is the task of exegesis after Auschwitz precisely to expose the explicit or implicit anti-Judaism inherent in the Christian tradition, including the New Testament itself. It is a task in which I have willingly participated,[3] and when I began I expected to find anti-Judaism particularly present in Paul. That is not, however, the conclusion to which my own studies have led me.

Just as important as Auschwitz as a context for Christian theology is the refounding of the state of Israel. Very central is the recognition that Judaism is a living reality and that the covenant between God and Israel continues. Such a recognition is even more important than the Auschwitz context for how Christians do theology, and it can also open exegetical eyes and make it possible to see texts in a new way and perhaps understand them better, once traditional anti-Jewish blinders have been removed. The aim of the present study is then not apologetic, for it has been written not out of guilt toward Israel but of gratitude to Israel that a new perspective allows us to pose questions in a new way. It deals not with how Paul can be understood in a post-Auschwitz situation but with how the recognition of living Israel might help us to a better understanding of Paul in his own situation.

Exegesis ought to be done without theological presuppositions, but the reader has the right to be suspicious of any interpreter who claims to have achieved that goal. While it is hard for authors to identify their own unconscious theological context, readers have the right to know that the only person with whom I have formally studied systematic theology was Karl Barth, that most of my New Testament study was done with Oscar Cullmann, and that the contemporary theologian for whom I have the greatest respect is Paul Van Buren.[4] Whenever I am aware of the influence of unconscious assumptions I will try to view them critically. Such influences may account for a rather "high" Christology and an even higher "theology," a tendency to want to think in terms of *Heilsgeschichte* rather than existentialism, and a desire to do contemporary theology rather than simply to pass on the tradition. It is also well known that the Reformed tradition has an especially high regard for the so-called "Old Testament" as an essential part of Holy Scripture. It perhaps should also be noted that I teach in the context of a school of theology and am therefore especially wary of the desire to want to bring personal religious questions to the text. All of this is not part of my own conscious context but only hints for readers to make of what they may.

The following chapters were written with a strong commitment to the historical-critical method, understood as the radical criticism of the assumptions of the interpreter. While it remains true that a conclusion is worth no more than the evidence and arguments on which it is based, it is also true that unstated assumptions often govern the selection of the evidence and the questions asked of it. The result is that anyone who tries to challenge too many of these assumptions is put into a precarious situation and risks not being taken seriously. Such an undertaking involves what could be called a hermeneutic of experimentation. What if one were to look at the matter from this perspective? Can all the evidence still be accounted for? Is the resultant picture plausible in itself? It is worth reopening old questions. A hermeneutic of experimentation invites the reader to an initial suspension of disbelief and a serious playfulness.

One important critical principle has been curiously neglected in the history of Christian scholarship, and that has to do with the picture that has been developed of what was often called "late Judaism." The history of this misrepresentation has been well documented,[5] and now after the work of Sanders and Gager,[6] surely it can no longer be repeated. Insofar as the Pauline interpreter finds it necessary to speak about Judaism, what is said must be based exclusively on Jewish sources and understood as far as possible from the perspective of those sources. This principle is hardly new, even if seldom applied in this area. The scholarly maxim underlying this injunction is *ad fontes* (back to the original sources), and the Biblical commandment which applies is the prohibition not to bear false witness against one's neighbour.

Related to this misrepresentation is the deeply held assumption that Paul's theology must stand in direct antithesis to that of Judaism. Typical is Käsemann's aphorism, "The real opponent of the Apostle Paul is the pious Jew."[7] Indeed, the misrepresentation arises because of a kind of mirror reading of Paul (and the gospels). Whatever Paul (or Jesus) affirms, Judaism must have said the opposite. To be sure, Paul's gospel was controversial, he had problems with "opponents," and "polemic" against them is reflected in some of his letters. But the opponents seem to be in every case rival Christian missionaries, and it is not at all sure either that they represent a united front,[8] or that all of them are Jewish Christians.[9] The one place where the opponents can most clearly be identified as Jewish-Christian missionaries is 2 Corinthians, and the fact that Torah or Judaizing are not at all at issue in this letter ought to give pause.[10] In fact, even if some of Paul's argumentation should be directed against individual (Christian) Jews, Judaism as such is never attacked. Paul's letters cannot be used either to derive information about Judaism or as evidence that he opposes Judaism as such.

If, on the other hand, one were to assume that Paul's statements about the Torah were intended to be directed against the understanding of Judaism, then in accordance with the principles enunciated the conclusion would have to be that in this respect at least Paul was simply wrong. This has often been the position of those who know early Judaism best. For example, in his well-written study of Pauline theology from a Jewish perspective, H. J. Schoeps has to entitle the conclusion of his chapter on Paul's teaching about the law "Paul's Fundamental Misapprehension."[11] If Paul does not perceive the relation between covenant and commandment, then he does not understand anything at all about Torah, and nothing he says about it should be taken seriously. Indeed, even to say "fundamental" misapprehension may be to give Paul too much credit. Much more likely is the view Räisänen expressed in his recent important book on *Paul and the Law* that Paul is simply inconsistent and confused.[12] Before coming to such a conclusion, however, it might be advisable to try a different starting point. Unless there are clear indications to the contrary, I shall assume that Paul understood "covenantal nomism"[13] very well indeed and that he is to be interpreted within the context of early Judaism rather than that the Christian concept of Judaism is to be derived from what Paul denies. It may well be that when Paul says something seemingly quite different, it is because he is asking a different question,[14] or even more because he is addressing a different audience. For example, when he speaks about the curse of the law in Galatians, might it not be because he *does* understand covenant as the context for commandments, which makes the situation of Gentiles outside that covenant all the bleaker. A priori, one would not expect the Apostle to the Gentiles to be engaged in a dialogue with Judaism[15] but rather with Gentile Christians, explaining how such central concepts as Torah relate to them.

One final basic hermeneutical assumption needs to be mentioned. Perhaps because of the misleading designations "Old Testament" and "New Testament," interpreters are prone to apply a hermeneutic of antithesis not only to Paul and Judaism but also to Paul and the Old Testament.[16] Some interpreters not only assume that Paul cites Holy Scripture as an antithetical foil to his own gospel but that he does so in an arbitrary and unintelligent manner.[17] Paul himself claims, however, that his gospel was "proclaimed beforehand to Abraham" because "Scripture knew beforehand that God would justify the Gentiles from faithfulness" (Gal

3:8), that "the gospel of God concerning his Son was promised beforehand through his prophets in Holy Scripture" (Rom 1:2), and that "the Law and the Prophets testified to the righteousness of God through the faithfulness of Jesus Christ" (Rom 3:21f). This dilemma is overcome by the important concept called canonical criticism, with its necessary aftermath called comparative midrash, especially as practised by James A. Sanders and his students.[18] The Hebrew Bible is the starting point, and there then begins a tradition of midrashic interpretation of the Scriptural text. The task of the Pauline interpreter is not to contrast Paul and the Old Testament itself but to try to reconstruct something of the history of interpretation of the text and to locate Paul with respect to these midrashic traditions. Insofar as this can be done, Paul's own midrash, while creative, is not at all arbitrary and outlandish. In any case, unless there are compelling reasons to the contrary, it seems best to assume that Paul stands in continuity with the midrashic traditions of Judaism rather than in antithesis to them.

Shared Exegetical Method

It might be helpful to refer to certain aspects of current Pauline studies which are not explicitly discussed in the following essays but which are simply assumed in company with many other scholars. The first is that Paul is to be interpreted strictly from his own writings and that the portrait of Paul to be found in Acts and the Pastoral Epistles is to be put resolutely to one side.[19] That is not to disparage the importance of the latter in their own right but only to adhere to the methodological principle that a primary source is always to be preferred to a secondary source. The discussion is therefore restricted to the seven letters about which there is little disagreement: 1 Thessalonians, 1 Corinthians, 2 Corinthians, Philippians, Philemon, Galatians, and Romans. It may well be that both 2 Corinthians and Philippians contain fragments of more than one Pauline letter, but that does not affect any of the arguments here.

Second, Paul's missionary actions are even more important than his theological thoughts. His commissioning as Apostle to the Gentiles is the context in which he conceives "his" gospel and in which he says what he says to his congregations. Indeed, a statement of Paul's gospel in a creedal formula comparable to the Islamic Shahada (There is no God but God, and Mohammed is his prophet) might run: Jesus is Lord and Paul is his Apostle to the Gentiles. This commissioning and mission situation are to be taken most seriously.[20] In particular, justification is not a central Pauline *doctrine* but language which is used whenever the legitimacy of the status of his Gentile converts is being discussed.[21] Paul is not the first Christian dogmatic theologian, writing timeless truths about God and the world. He is rather a pastoral theologian, saying what he thinks needs to be said in very concrete missionary situations.[22] One task of the interpreter is therefore to try to understand the situation as well as possible. Needless to say, it makes a difference whether the Christians addressed are Gentiles or Jews.

Third, there has developed a fair amount of consensus that Paul is writing about the objective situation of Gentiles before God and not about individuals as such.[23] The traditional eschatology of the prophets and Jesus and the Jerusalem church envisaged the influx of the Gentiles only at the end,[24] and it required a special revelation of God to call Paul to the Apostolate to the Gentiles before that time. Given the newness of his situation, it naturally occupied much of his thought and writing. Paul's major theological concern I take to be the justification of the legitimacy of the Gentile mission now before the end. "Is God the God of Jews only? Is he not the God of Gentiles also?" (Rom 3:29). Also, Paul seldom writes autobiography, and a psychological approach has in the past led to serious misrepresentations. Nowhere is this consideration more important than when speaking of Paul's "conversion." It has become more and more clear that it is totally inappropriate to speak of a transition from one religion to another.[25] As Paul himself describes it, typically in a subordinate clause, "when it pleased him who had called me through his grace to reveal his Son through me, in order that I might preach him among the Gentiles." That is not the language of a conversion but of a prophetic call, and it is not so much a statement about Paul personally as it is about the God who calls and the Gentiles who are the beneficiaries of the call. Although it is not part of the consensus, perhaps it is worth mentioning how I conceive the circumstances of the call, in accordance with what has been said above about the importance of Scripture for Paul. His call and commissioning as a revelation from God came while he was living in Damascus, not with the Lucan conversion fireworks but while quietly pondering the text of Isaiah 49, the second servant song.

Finally, two lexicographical matters have not been the subject of a special investigation by me but are important for the following discussions. First, as Richardson has shown, Paul (and the whole Christian movement before Justin Martyr) continues the Biblical distinction between Jews and non-Jews, Israel and Gentiles.[26] The word *ta ethnē* in Paul always means "the Gentiles," some of whom have become Christian. (Of course, Paul does not know the word "Christian" but uses such phrases as "belonging to Christ," "the believers," and the like.) "Israel," on the other hand, means the Jewish people in all its fullness, past and present. Paul never uses a phrase like "new Israel" or "spiritual Israel," and he never applies the name "Israel" to the church. Second, Dahl and Kramer have convincingly demonstrated that *Christos* is for Paul a proper name and is not to be translated "Messiah."[27] Kramer finds no more than a stylistic distinction among the words Christ, Jesus, Christ Jesus, or Jesus Christ. There nowhere appears a sentence in which Jesus is the subject and Christ part of the predicate, and Christ is never followed by a genitive (e.g. "the Anointed of God"). When Paul uses a title, the person of Jesus or Christ is given the title "Lord" or the like. Jesus is then for Paul not the Messiah. He is neither the climax of the history of Israel nor the fulfilment of the covenant, and therefore Jesus is not seen in relation to David or Moses. For Paul, Jesus is the new act of the righteousness of God in the inclusion of the Gentiles, and therefore he is seen in negative relationship with Adam and positive relationship with Abraham.

Congruent Conclusions

The conclusions of the following studies can be outlined briefly, together with an indication of the chapters where they are principally discussed. The intention is to provide the reader with a kind of road map: the larger picture into which the discussions of specific texts are meant to fit. Such a map can, of course, only be drawn in retrospect, for I was often not aware in the beginning of where the study of specific texts would lead. If there is now a clarity and consistency in the resultant picture, that does not mean that the picture is true. That question can be resolved, if at all, only on the basis of the specific arguments concerning specific texts which are contained in the following essays. It is also to be noted that most of these essays deal with what were from my perspective "problem texts." If it appears that a thesis is stated in Chapter 1 and that the rest of the chapters deal with specific texts which could be cited against the thesis, that is at least partly true. Other, less problematical texts should be easier to incorporate into the final picture. In general terms, then, here are the results of my study of Paul.

Gentiles as Addressees. Insofar as this reading of Paul had a starting point, it came with the conviction that one ought to take more seriously than is usually the case Paul's description of himself as Apostle to the Gentiles. He refers to his commissioning explicitly that way, he cites his solemn promise at the Jerusalem Council to confine his missionary activity to Gentiles, and his letters are all addressed explicitly to Gentiles. He himself impressively describes his calling as "the grace given to me by God to be a [priestly] minister of Christ Jesus to the Gentiles, acting as priest for the gospel of God, in order that the sacrifice consisting of Gentiles might be acceptable [to God], sanctified by the Holy Spirit" (Rom 15:16). This starting point was set out in Chapter 1, the first of these essays to be written, and has continued ever since. I there rather unwisely referred to Paul's converts as "former God-fearers," as if the term referred to a quasi-technical class of "semi-proselytes" and as if I were after all following the picture of Acts.[28] I only meant to refer to the fact that Judaism was well known and respected in much of the Hellenistic world,[29] and that Paul can presuppose in some of his letters (Romans) considerable knowledge of Scripture and its Jewish interpretation and in others (1 Thessalonians) almost none. There has since appeared a very good description of Paul's missionary practice, with which I concur wholeheartedly.[30] It is in any case clear that Paul's converts were all Gentiles.

Why letters specifically addressed to Gentiles should have been understood as opposing Judaism is not hard to explain. It developed as part of the displacement theory, whereby the early church thought it could claim its own legitimacy only by denying that of Judaism. Already Tertullian agrees with Marcion when he says, "we too claim that the primary epistle against Judaism is that addressed to the Galatians."[31] Beyond that concern there are the desire to universalize the letters of Paul and the modern Romantic notion of the unity of the primitive church, the "church of Jews and Gentiles." While that ultimate unity is of theological importance for Paul, there is very little evidence for its sociological reality in the early church. Apart from the first generation in Antioch, mixed congregations are not really known, whatever may be commonly assumed about their existence. The church in Jerusalem and later Jewish-Christian churches in Transjordan were apparently made up exclusively of Christian Jews, although there is little direct evidence. Paul's churches and their successors were exclusively Gentile (with the possible exception of some Jewish apostates). "Judaizing" was a recurrent phenomenon in the early church,[32] but I always use the term with its ancient meaning, referring to the adoption by Gentiles of specific Jewish practices. Paul, of course, was not the only Jew to preach the Christian gospel to Gentiles, for such people are among his friends and fellow-workers (e.g. Romans 16) and enemies and rivals (e.g. 2 Corinthians 10-13), but it was to Gentiles that they all preached. One of the reasons, then, for thinking that Paul may have been addressing Jews is based on a false assumption concerning the composition of the early churches.

One of the ways of seeing Paul's gospel to the uncircumcised in clearer perspective is to compare and contrast it with that of the Jerusalem church. Chapter 7 is an attempt to do this. Even if the distinctions there made between "the gospel to the circumcised" and "the gospel to the uncircumcised" are clearer in retrospect than they would have been to the original apostles, they are quite significant. Certain "omissions" in Paul were quite puzzling to earlier interpreters, who thought that he was speaking universal theological truths. For example, Paul never speaks of repentance, a concept central not only to prophets and rabbis but also to the teaching of Jesus. Not only that, he also never speaks of forgiveness. (The necessary qualifications to these general statements will be found in Chapter 7 below.) If the church likes to say that Jesus died for our sins, Paul always says that Jesus died for us, for you, for persons, and never "for our sins." Indeed, he does not speak of sins at all, as acts which people do and for which they are guilty before God. He speaks rather of Sin, in the singular and probably to be written with a capital "S," as a power which oppresses and from which one cannot escape. But all of this can be explained from the situation addressed, for what Gentiles need first is not guilt but liberation, not repentance but life from the dead, not a turning back (*tšbh*) but a "turning *to* God from idols" (1 Thess 1:9). Understanding the situation addressed as a Gentile one is very crucial to my understanding of Paul.

The Gentile Predicament. Even to set down conclusions briefly will distort Paul. He did not begin with an objective analysis of the Gentile situation, and he thought mythologically rather than systematically about it. Nevertheless, it might be helpful to oversimplify here in order to make clear what is at issue. Chapter 1 raises the question of how the law relates to Gentiles in early Jewish thought. Chapter 2 carries the argument further by discussing in particular the apocalyptic conception of the angels of the nations. Since these two essays were written, there has appeared a significant study of Paul's theology advocating apocalyptic as the matrix for all of Paul's thought.[33] An even more recent book revives the "principalities and powers" as part of Paul's background.[34] It is to be hoped that these two works will provide the stimulus for renewed attention to these important aspects of first-century thought.

The basic myth can be baldly stated. If early Judaism thought that God ruled over Israel directly, his rule over the Gentile nations was indirect and impersonal, through an agent something like a Persian satrap, if one will. The most common way of imagining these agents is in terms of the "angels of the nations." A more Hellenistic way of putting the matter is to say that God's rule, especially over nature, is administered by the "elements of the world," that is, earth, water, air, and fire, or by the gods, especially the national gods. All of these are to be found in Paul along with much more general language concerning "the powers." If in principle the rule of the angels or elements or gods was intended to be benevolent, for most people of this period it was experienced as oppressive. None of this is stated explicitly by Paul, but the basic pattern must be presupposed as part of the first century world-view.

Soteriology in such a perspective would mean liberation from the tyrannical rule of the powers. One could imagine a redeemer figure sent from God to dethrone the powers by destroying them, or imprisoning them, or taming them and calling them back into the service of God. While all of these aspects are to be found in early Christian writings,[35] they are much too triumphalist for Paul. Instead of Christ the Redeemer killing the tyrannical powers, it is people who die, by participation in his death. E. P. Sanders characterizes the heart of Paul's soteriology appropriately as "change of Lordship."[36] By "dying" in baptism people lose as it were their old citizenship and acquire a new one ("Our commonwealth is in heaven, and from it we await a Saviour, the Lord Jesus Christ," Phil 3:20). They still live in the country of the tyrant but as resident aliens no longer subject to his laws, and with the hope of his eventual dethronement.

There is a peculiarly Pauline version of this whole conception of "the powers." He emphasizes the function of God's law in the administration of the angels or elements to the extent that he can use "law" as a power which oppresses Gentiles and from which they need to be redeemed. It is not just that the law will function as a criterion in the final judgment; it also operates within history. As in the Wisdom of Solomon, the law punishes evildoers outside the covenant by visiting them with the inevitable consequences of their acts. This is a retributive process within history which Paul, drawing on Biblical concepts, can call "the Wrath."[37] Once he even refers to "the curse of the law," meaning nothing different (Gal 3:13). The powers administer the law, and "the law works wrath" (Rom 4:15). The "law" then is not just something which people do; it does something to people, as I hope to show in Chapter 6. There is a further usage, the most important of all, when Paul also speaks of Sin and Death as personified powers. They are really not to be put in the same category as "angels of the nations" or the like, and to distinguish them perhaps they should be called "the Superpowers." If the angel administers the law, and the law works wrath, then Sin uses the whole process. Sin uses the process to produce more sin (Romans 1), so that sin is a corporate concept for Paul, and Sin does so in order to pay wages, namely death (Romans 5-6). Indeed, both Sin and Death can be said to reign over all humanity outside the covenant, and it is the importance of these Superpowers which has kept Paul from spelling out more clearly the role of angels or elements as powers. Those outside the covenant are completely subject to the Lordship of Sin and Death, who use the process of the powers administering the law. This is the Gentile predicament.

Gentiles and the Law. Paul uses the word *nomos*, law, in disparate and strange ways indeed. He can say, for example, that "I myself serve with the mind God's *law* but with the flesh Sin's *law*. For the *law* of the Spirit, of life, has set you free in Christ Jesus from the *law* of Sin and Death . . . so that the decree of the *law* might be fulfilled in us, who walk . . . according to the Spirit" (Rom 8:2-4). Like most interpreters,[38] I conclude that this richness of usage parallels the variety of meanings found in the Hebrew word *Torah*. I have already referred to the concept of the law as it relates to Gentiles. This concept, which is not recognized by many interpreters, is discussed mostly in Chapters 1, 2, and 6. Chapter 4 deals also with other uses of the word *nomos*, as it occurs in the central section of Galatians. Like the Hebrew *Torah*, *nomos* is often used for Scripture, either in the narrower sense (Pentateuch) or wider sense (Torah, Prophets, and Writings). Parallel to the development in Rabbinic writings,[39] in Paul *nomos* occasionally means "covenant," but the reference is to the covenant made on Sinai with Israel and only with Israel. Also, in certain contexts Paul can speak of Gentile Christians keeping the commandments (1 Cor 7:19) or fulfilling the law (Gal 5:14, Rom 13:8-10), a concept about which he speaks firmly but vaguely.

If it is true that the word *nomos* is used in such different senses, ought this not to be indicated in translation? I once thought so, and in most of what follows, *nomos* is translated by "law" when it is used in the bad sense of what Gentiles need to be redeemed from and by "Torah" when used in the good sense of that which redeems both Gentiles and Jews. That may be important in alerting the reader the first time through the material to the various senses in which Paul uses the word, and therefore the distinction has been maintained in the following essays and translations. Nevertheless, it is ultimately not satisfactory for the following reasons. First, it obscures the fact that, as it is axiomatic for Paul that God is one, so it is equally true that God's *nomos* is one. To be sure, it makes a great difference if that *nomos* is experienced in the context of covenant or in the context of creation and the angels of the nations, but there are not two different laws operative here. Second, to distinguish accurately all the ways in which Paul uses the word *nomos*, more than two words would be necessary in English, as when covenant is distinguished from Scripture in Rom 3:21. Third, Paul is aware of the ambiguity of his usage, and the sharpness of some of his deliberately paradoxical statements would not be clear if the same word were not used, as in: "I through the *nomos* died to the *nomos*" (Gal 2:19). In the future, then, one ought to use a single English word to translate *nomos*; perhaps the word "Law" can be rehabilitated to serve this purpose.

The Righteousness and Faithfulness of God. Most of the following essays were begun as experiments, which means that the outcome was not known at the beginning. One way to begin an experiment is to try to state explicitly what have been the more or less unconscious assumptions of the traditional interpretation, and that has often been done in the following. If there is one attitude which underlies all of these assumptions, it would be the religious attitude which predisposes a certain way of construing the Greek when it is ambiguous, particularly with respect to certain genitives. The religious attitude assumes that when the text speaks of faith or righteousness or the law, it intends to answer the question: what ought we to believe or be or do? The ambiguity of the genitive can be shown by the English phrase "love of God": does it mean God's love for us or our love for God? That is, is the genitive objective or subjective (there are, of course, other kinds)? I have already referred to the possibility (cf. Chapter 6) that "works of law" refers not to something which people do or fail to do and thereby become guilty but to something an objective power, the law, does to them and from which they need liberation. I now turn to two further, less ambiguous genitives.

The correctness of the translation of *pistis Iēsou Christou* as the "faith or faithfulness *of* Jesus Christ" has by now been too well established to need any further support.[40] I believe that something similar can be said with respect to "the righteousness *of* God" for *dikaiosynē tou theou*. But, if recognition of the proper translation of these two genitives was part of the starting point for the studies presented here, further examination of the texts has led to unanticipated conclusions. The word *pistis*, which in any case should be translated as "faithfulness" rather than "faith,"[41] was found in many contexts to refer to the faithfulness of Christ or God, even without an accompanying genitive.[42] The word "righteousness," even without an accompanying genitive, was found in many contexts to refer not to a human quality but to God's saving activity. This is not always the case, but it tends to be so in those passages dealing with the inclusion of the Gentiles in the people of God, the question of "getting in," as Sanders puts it.[43] Words from the *dik*- and *pist*- roots are statistically concentrated in certain sections of Galatians and Romans,[44] and these are the sections that speak not of human activity but of God's activity in Christ. Chapters 4 and 8 discuss these passages in more detail; here I emphasize how the concept of justification *by faith* has completely disappeared from the Pauline texts. I list below all passages where the verb *dikaioō*, to justify, appears with an indication of means. There are also some which state how one is not justified, namely by law or works of law, but these are all the positive ones:

> We are justified as a free gift by his grace. (Rom 3:24)
>
> Since then we have now been justified by his blood. (Rom 5:9)
>
> You were justified by the name of the Lord Jesus Christ. (1 Cor 6:11)
>
> To be justified in Christ. (Gal 2:17)
>
> God justifies the one who lives out of the faithfulness of Jesus. (Rom 3:26)

> God is one, who will justify the circumcised out of [his] faithfulness and the uncircumcised through the same faithfulness. (Rom 3:30)
>
> Since then we have been justified out of [his] faithfulness. (Rom 5:1)
>
> Now Scripture, knowing beforehand that God would justify the Gentiles from faithfulness. (Gal 3:8)
>
> In order that we might be justified from faithfulness. (Gal 3:24)
>
> We maintain that a human being is justified by means of [God's] faithfulness. (Rom 3:28)
>
> A human being is justified through the faithfulness of Christ Jesus. (Gal 2:16)

What then is the centre of Paul's gospel, which, as he says, "I preach among the Gentiles" (Gal 2:2, etc.)? He says it is contained in Holy Scripture (Gal 3:8; Rom 1:2), and a figure of prime importance to him is Abraham. Chapter 3 is very important for the development of my understanding of Paul. God made promises to Abraham concerning Gentiles which he fulfilled in the death and resurrection of Jesus Christ. God is faithful to his promise, whereby he expresses his "righteousness" as his power for salvation, now extended also to Gentiles. Or, to put it in terms of the person in whom the promise has been fulfilled, it is through the faithfulness of Christ that the blessing of Abraham has been extended to the Gentiles. Gentile inclusion into the elect people of God is through incorporation into Christ. By a change of Lordship, Gentiles become servants of Christ and are thereby liberated from the tyrants Sin and Death. Chapter 8 directly argues the thesis that the inclusion of Gentiles does not mean the displacement of Israel. This oversimplified statement may provide a road map to the following essays.

Israel and the Gentiles. A work with a title like the present one will of necessity concentrate on Romans and Galatians, and one would expect a lengthy section dealing with Romans 9-11. As it turned out, I dealt with each of the sections separately, Romans 9 in Chapter 5, Romans 10 in Chapter 8, and Romans 11 in Chapter 9, each in connection with a wider topic. In retrospect that was a fortunate way of proceeding, for it led me to an understanding of Romans 9-11 that I would not have attained in any other way. If there is one discovery which underlies all three chapters, it is that Jewish Christianity is never on Paul's horizon in Romans 9-11. He speaks rather of Israel as a whole and how the Roman Gentile Christians, or by extension Gentile Christians in general, should understand themselves in relationship to Israel. Chapter 8 contains in my opinion the most important conclusions of all the essays. Chapter 9 is in many ways only a corollary. Paul's quarrel with his fellow Jews is never about Judaism as such but rather about a Jewish understanding of Gentiles. In particular, he has no quarrel with the Jewish understanding of Torah as it applies to Israel. That conclusion can be supported, if at all, only by the thesis that most of Paul's statements about *Torah/nomos* refer to how it relates specifically to Gentiles; that is, only by the cumulative effect of all the essays.

Paul and Scripture. If one begins with the initial statement of theses in Chapter 1, there remain a number of problem texts that cry out for further discussion. Many of the following essays deal with such texts: Gal 2:15-21 (Chapter 4), Galatians 3 and Romans 4 (Chapters 3,4,8), Gal 3:19-20 (Chapter 2), Gal 4:21-31 (Chapter 5), Rom 2:1-16 (Chapters 6,8), Rom 2:17-29 (Chapter 9), Romans 9 (Chapter 5), Rom 9:30-10:4 (Chapter 8), and Rom 11:13-24 (Chapter 9). There remains one more such problem text with respect to Paul's use of Scripture. I hope that many of the essays will show Paul's respect for the Torah of Israel as Scripture and as the source of his gospel. I hope to show also that one can understand Paul's use of the "Old Testament" only in continuity with the tradition of Jewish interpretation, a procedure which is often complex but always necessary. Nevertheless, there is always the nagging thought, in my mind if not the reader's, "Yes, but what about 2 Corinthians 3?" Chapter 10 deals not with Paul's relation to Torah as a whole (that would be too large a topic) but with some of the problems of understanding this specific text.

The Appendix. Translations of Romans and Galatians have been appended to provide a kind of summary. All translations are, of course, in themselves interpretations, often the distillation of longstanding exegetical traditions. These fresh translations are meant to show how the individual passages discussed in some detail in the earlier chapters might fit into the sweep of the letter as a whole.[45] Justification for the translation has been provided for only some of the passages, and the reader will have to forgive the lack of a complete commentary. The text translated is usually that of the twenty-sixth edition of Nestle-Aland, but a few text-critical judgments which depart from it underlie certain passages. The translation is as literal as possible, sometimes at the expense of good English, in order to remind readers of the Greek text.[46] When, on the other hand, it was felt necessary to add words to bring out the meaning, they have been enclosed in square brackets. Because of the importance of Paul's use of Scripture, particularly in Galatians and Romans, citations are identified by double quotation marks and source. The translations ought not to be taken more seriously than they deserve, but they do represent real conclusions.

1

PAUL AND THE TORAH

James Parkes has devoted his life to the issue of Christian antisemitism, often as a rather lonely voice in the wilderness. The Holocaust and the refounding of the state of Israel have opened some startled theological eyes, but in general theology has gone on as if nothing had happened. Now Rosemary Ruether has posed in all its sharpness what must surely become *the* theological question for Christians in our generation. "Possibly anti-Judaism is too deeply embedded in the foundations of Christianity to be rooted out entirely without destroying the whole structure."[1] It may be that the church will survive if we fail to deal adequately with that question, but more serious is the question whether the church ought to survive. A Christian church with an antisemitic New Testament is abominable, but a Christian church without a New Testament is inconceivable. Many would add that a New Testament without the Christ-event as its material centre and the Pauline corpus as its formal centre would not be the New Testament at all. And yet, whatever the general effect of the gospels, it is Paul who has provided the theoretical structure for Christian anti-Judaism from Marcion through Luther and F. C. Baur down to Bultmann, in a manner even more serious than Ruether indicates in her brief discussion of Paul. Here then is the dilemma.

For me as a Calvinistic Protestant, the dilemma is posed from a slightly different perspective than it is for Ruether. It has been said that Protestants tend to study movements from the perspective of origins and Catholics from the perspective of development. In any case, Ruether's Paul is quite patristic. The insight that Platonic dualism replaced eschatological dualism

(95) is exceedingly fruitful, but surely this is a post-Pauline development. The view that the Mosaic covenant belongs to "a people who were apostate from the beginning" (104, cf. 76) sounds more like *Barnabas* than Paul, and I wonder if there really is that much of an "affinity between Marcionite and Pauline thinking" (50). "The Christological midrash and its anti-Judaic left hand" are characteristic of Justin[2] and the *adversos Judaeos* literature, but is it really the "foundation" on which Paul builds (95)? Pauline anti-Judaism seems not to be through the left hand as an implication of his Christology; rather his teaching on the law appears to be a spear in his right hand aimed straight at the heart of Judaism, that is, Torah. To be sure, there is a close relationship between Christology and Paul's teaching on the law, but his midrash seems to be halakhic and direct rather than haggadic and Christological. As important as her general thesis is, when it comes to Paul I am going to shift the discussion from Ruether's Paul to Luther's Paul. The shift is only one of emphasis, but it allows me to deal with the specific issue which has most offended Jewish readers of Paul.

Paul seems to speak not incidentally but fundamentally about the nature of Judaism. He does not disagree with individual Jews but with Judaism itself, saying that Christianity has replaced it. By attacking the law as such, Paul appears to attack not abuses and personal failings but the very essence of Israel, and he does so from a position of knowledge. Paul the Pharisee, the disciple of Rabban Gamaliel, has apparently experienced the best that Judaism has to offer and rejected it completely, so much so that Wellhausen could call him "the great pathologist of Judaism."[3] Paul seems able to proclaim his gospel of grace only against the dark foil of Jewish legalism. The Judaism which many see reflected in Paul's polemics is thus a joyless, hypocritical, nationalistic means of earning salvation by mechanically doing the works of the law. The God of the Jews is seen as a remote, gloomy tyrant who lays the burden of the law on people, and their response is twofold: they either become proud and self-righteous hypocrites who are scrupulous about food but ignore justice, or they are plunged into guilt and anxiety, thinking themselves accursed for breaking a single commandment. Schürer speaks of "the fearful burden which a spurious legalism had laid upon the shoulders of the people."[4] Against this background, the gospel of freedom from the law would be good news indeed, and it could only be stiff-necked stubbornness which kept the Jews from welcoming it.

From the top of one mountain peak it is possible to look over to the brilliance of another peak and then down into the cloud-covered valley between them. From the perspective of Luther's rediscovery of the gospel of grace, it was possible to look back to the Pauline proclamation he had revived and to see in between the dark valley which from this time forth was to be called the "Middle Ages." Similarly, Paul's gospel of justification by faith alone could be seen as a revival of the faith of Abraham, who "believed and it was reckoned to him as righteousness," who became the father of Jews and proselytes, and who lived 430 years before the law. In between lay the dark middle ages of the Torah, which had intruded into human history in order to increase sin (Gal 3:19, Rom 5:20), which was given not by God but only by angels (Gal 3:19f), and which functioned at the best as a pedagogue and at the worst as a jail-keeper (Gal 3:24) until Christ should come to revive Abraham's life of faith. Even if the law were to be seen positively as a means of salvation whereby one might be justified, it had failed, for "by the law no one is justified before God" (Gal 3:11, Rom 3:20), and now "Christ is the end of the law" (Rom 10:4). It seems that Paul's view of history, like Luther's, was determined by his personal past, the contrast between the old and new life of the convert. This interpretation remains the common understanding of Paul in relationship to Judaism in most Christian circles, implying that the ultimate goal of the church is the complete elimination of an Israel faithful to Torah. Is it then inevitable that a Pauline Christian be essentially antisemitic?

Perhaps I should make clear what I mean when I speak of antisemitism or anti-Judaism in this connection. Just as individuals can be relatively free of personal prejudice and still participate actively in a system of racism, so anti-Judaism has to do with the objective effect of the words used, whether or not the people who speak them subjectively hate Jews. This underlines the seriousness of Ruether's point that theological anti-Judaism is the fundamental root of later cultural and political antisemitism. (Philosemitism, in other words, is no excuse.) If the three pillars on which Judaism stands are God, Torah, and Israel, then a fundamental attack on any of the three would be anti-Judaism, a denial of the right of Jews to exist in terms of their own self-understanding. Is Paul guilty? Although many of his interpreters from Marcion to Harnack make a distinction between the God of the Old Testament and the God of the New, this surely does not hold for Paul himself. Yet with respect to Torah, did not Paul declare that "Christ is the end of the law" (Rom 10:4), so that one can say, "Saint Paul . . . now feels that he has a superior revelation in whose light the Jewish Torah becomes reduced to a demonized revelation and negative power on the level of those evil Powers and Principalities which reign over the imprisoned cosmos?"[5] With respect to Israel, does not the logic of Paul's position mean that it has surely been replaced by the Christian church, called from Jews and Gentiles, who appropriate Israel's responsibilities and privileges and Scriptures and name? Although Paul explicitly denies these charges ("Do we then overthrow the law by this faith? By no means" [Rom 3:31]; "Has God rejected his people? By no means" [Rom 11:1]), it is typical that C. H. Dodd, for example, has to scold Paul for inconsistency in his commentary on those passages.[6] According to the almost universal interpretation of Paul, he is plainly guilty of the last two charges, and in view of his central position with respect to Christian understanding of both Judaism and the gospel, he has become, wittingly or unwittingly, the chief source of Christian anti-Judaism.

From the second century, it has been the displacement theory, which says that the church has supplanted Israel as the people of God, that has been the greatest obstacle to the Christian understanding of Jews. To be sure, Paul does not cite the standard rejection texts (Isa 6, Ps 118, etc.); he never applies the honoured name of Israel to the church;[7] the phrase "Israel according to the flesh" is not used negatively,[8] and in spite of many interpreters, it is never counterbalanced by the phrase "Israel according to the Spirit"; and he seems to affirm the continued election of Israel (Rom 3:1; 9:3-5; 11:28f, etc.). Nevertheless, it is very salutary for Ruether to point out that the interpretations of Romans 9-11 offered to date continue to deny to Israel any positive significance according to its own self-understanding for the period between resurrection and paraousia.[9] The displacement theory is so bound up with the understanding of the continuing validity of the Torah that for Bultmann and his followers the end of the history of Israel as the people of God is paradigmatically expressed in Rom 10:4, "Christ is the end of the law." Again, the Pauline concept of *Torah-nomos* is the heart of the matter.

It is Paul's abrogation of the law which most disturbs Jewish interpreters and those who know something of the concept of Torah in Jewish writings. It is not Paul's invective which disturbs them so much as his ignorance. For anyone who understands Rabbinic Judaism, Paul's attacks are not merely unfair, they miss the mark completely. The Rabbis never speak of Torah as the means to salvation, and when they speak of salvation at all, the way of Torah, "which is your life" (Deut 32:47), *is* that salvation. The ethical earnestness of the Rabbis becomes all the more impassioned because of their belief that the commandments express God's will for Israel's good, but they can never in all fairness be called legalists. Faith and works could never be seen as opposites, for each would be meaningless without the other. The law is not felt to be burdensome (when it is, it is modified), and the characteristic phrase is "the joy of the commandments." Far from being an inducement to sin or the curse of condemnation, the law is God's gracious means of helping people to conquer their "evil impulse." There is no indication that Paul is aware that many of the laws concern the means of atonement, which presuppose human sin, but which also proclaim the divine forgiveness. It is most significant that the concept of repentance, so central to both rabbinic theology and the teaching of Jesus, never occurs in Paul. As G. F. Moore says: "How a Jew of Paul's antecedents could ignore, and by implication deny, the great prophetic doctrine of Judaism, namely, that God, out of love, freely forgives the sincerely penitent sinner and restores him to his favour—that seems from the Jewish point of view inexplicable."[10] One of the best recent books on Paul's theology, that by H. J. Schoeps, has to entitle the conclusion to the chapter on Paul's teaching about the law "Paul's Fundamental Misapprehension." He says, "Paul did not perceive and for various reasons was perhaps unable to perceive, that in the Biblical view the law is integral to the covenant. . . . The law was no longer a living possession, and this for the obvious reason that he had ceased to understand the totality and continuity of the Berith-Torah."[11] How is Paul's fundamental ignorance to be explained? Various suggestions have been offered.

1. The traditional answer to the problem is to deny its existence. Most Christian scholars have drawn their primary understanding of the Jewish concept of Torah not from Jewish sources but from the pages of the New Testament. This understanding could then be "discovered" in the pseudepigrapha (Bousset-Gressmann) or in Talmud and midrash (Weber, Billerbeck). The fundamental ignorance, not of Paul but of his interpreters, has been documented for earlier works by G. F. Moore among others,[12] but it is still very prevalent, as in the only book on Pauline theology cited by Ruether.[13] This is not done out of sheer malice. Most of the great interpreters of Paul have identified Paul's opponents with their own. Particularly impressive is the recent commentary on Romans by Käsemann, which identifies the "Jew" with the universal type of *homo religosus* (read: the Church establishment). But can profound theology be bought at the price of historical inaccuracy and the slander of a sister religion?

2. Why should the apostle to the Gentiles devote so much of his energy to attacking Judaism? Still the most influential answer to this problem is the one provided by F. C. Baur in the middle of the last century: Paul's opponents are Jewish Christians from Jerusalem who assert the necessity for salvation of keeping the whole law. Baur derives his concept of Jewish Christianity from the pseudo-Clementine literature, which he thought was quite early, from the caricature of Judaism held by most Christians, and from his own fertile Hegelian imagination. According to Baur, the Jerusalem Christians were not only legalists of the worst sort but also fierce opponents of Paul, violently jealous of his Gentile converts. Following him all over the cities of the East and attempting to subject his congregations to Jerusalem were emissaries of James and Peter, whom Paul has to denounce as the party of Cephas (1 Cor 1:12), super apostles, servants of Satan (2 Cor 11:5, 13f), so-called pillars who are false brethren, who intruded to rob us of our liberty (Gal 2:4), dogs and evil-workers who mutilate the flesh (Phil 3:2). The most important work opposing Baur's reconstruction, one which

for all its weaknesses is the foundation of the new look in Pauline studies, is Johannes Munck, *Paul and the Salvation of Mankind.*[14] According to Munck, Paul was interested not in isolated individuals but in the place of Jews and Gentiles in God's *Heilsgeschichte*, and his basic theological position did not differ from that of the Jerusalem Christians.

3. If Paul's opponents were not Jewish Christians, perhaps they were Jews after all. In its attempt to present Christianity as the true Judaism, Acts perhaps inadvertently presents Paul as a frustrated missionary to the Jews who constantly met stubborn resistance from the synagogues and then turned in resentment to the Gentiles. Such is the situation in Salamis (Acts 13:5), Pisidian Antioch (13:14), Iconium (14:1), Thessalonica (17:1), Beroea (17:10), Athens (17:17), Corinth (18:4), Ephesus (18:19, 19:8), and, as a climax, at Rome (28:17). Typical is the conclusion reached in Antioch, "It was necessary that the work of God should be spoken first to you. Since you thrust it from you and judge yourselves unworthy of eternal life, behold we turn to the Gentiles" (13:46). If this picture were true, it could explain Paul's polemic even without recourse to the Tübingen hypothesis of opposition from Jerusalem. Paul's frustration would account for the bitterness of his attacks, and his few successes could account for enough Jewish Christians in his congregations to provide an object for the attacks. But because a primary source is always preferable to a secondary one, the letters should provide the basic framework of an understanding of Paul's life and thought, to which certain statements in Acts can provide at the most supplementary evidence.

4. If, then, Paul is attacking neither Jewish Christians nor the synagogues of the Diaspora who refused to listen to him, perhaps the battle is within himself, and as a typical convert he has come to hate what he once adored. The psychological approach, particularly popular among pietists, makes a great deal of Paul's "conversion" as his personal release from an anguished conscience in bondage to the works of the law. But Paul does not repudiate his own past in this negative way (Gal 2:13f, Phil 3:5f), Romans 7 is not to be interpreted autobiographically,[15] and Munck has demonstrated that one should speak of Paul's call as a prophetic commissioning (Gal 1:15f) rather than a conversion from a repudiated past.[16] Paul's central theological concern is not salvation from his own past, not authentic existence, not even justification by faith of the individual, but rather the legitimacy of including Gentiles at this time as full-fledged members of the people of God. Krister Stendahl has spoken to this point in a seminal article, "The Apostle Paul and the Introspective Conscience of the West."[17] It would, perhaps, not be necessary to mention this approach except for its recent revival in an extreme form in a book that, however moving as a personal testimony, is quite misleading with respect to Paul: Richard Rubenstein's *My Brother Paul.* If

one had to choose, a Marxist interpretation of Paul (as in F. W. Marquardt, *Die Juden im Römerbrief*) is much more appropriate than a Freudian one.

5. Those who know Rabbinic Judaism best sometimes want to understand Paul against the background of Hellenistic Judaism. The word *nomos*, they say, is so different from the word *torah* that Hellenistic Jewish conceptions, which were "poorer, colder, less satisfying and more pessimistic than Rabbinic Judaism," must have provided the impoverished understanding against which Paul's polemic was directed.[18] Or, it may be that the Diaspora was exceptionally lax[19] and that Paul has only perfected what was already a tendency within Hellenistic Judaism to subordinate the particularistic law of Sinai to the universalistic law of nature.[20] But the dichotomy between Hellenistic and Palestinian Judaism is false; there are too many Hellenistic elements among the Rabbis and too many Palestinian loyalties in the Diaspora, with constant intercourse between the two. This attempt to find a background for Paul's apparent rejection of the Torah can be considered to have failed, and the explanation must lie elsewhere.

6. Perhaps Paul should be understood as a theologian of the messianic age, in which there will be no more Torah.[21] Particularly impressive is the parallelism which can be drawn with the antinomianism of some of the followers of Shabbatai Zvi.[22] Ultimately, however, this solution too fails. The texts are all very late and do not really speak of the abolition of Torah.[23] Even if this concept could be presupposed for a first century situation, it would still have to fall under the accusation of being a fundamental misunderstanding of Torah within the context of Israel.

Torah and Christ are for Paul mutually exclusive categories, even if it is not clear why this is so. Whether his enthusiasm caused him to exaggerate or whether he really knew no better, Paul seems to denigrate systematically the significance of the Torah for Israel. It would be well to digest this situation before seeking another solution too quickly, and that is the great value of Ruether's presentation. On the other hand, I have lived with the problem long enough that I cannot help but go on. Given the history of Christian bias so well documented by Ruether, perhaps in every case of doubt the positive interpretation should be favoured. This is true with respect to textual criticism,[24] translation,[25] and the many decisions that have to be made on exegetical options.[26] There exist today in Pauline studies the beginnings of such a radical rethinking. This is not done in the spirit of a theological "reparation," as if that were possible, but as a search for a new and better understanding of Paul on the part of those whose eyes have been shocked open. The New Testament may itself contain a foundation for attacking the Christian anti-Judaic myth Ruether so eloquently delineates.

The account of the discussions in Jerusalem, Gal 2:1-10, is crucial for any interpretation of Paul. While he speaks about the conference in terms of its implications for the Galatian situation, I would agree with Schmithals that those who had most at stake in the meeting were the Jerusalem Christians whose own position would be precarious unless it was made clear that Paul was preaching his law-free gospel only to Gentiles and not to Jews.[27] The results of the conference were an agreement on basic theology, an agreement to disagree on the priority of the Gentile mission, and the arrangement of a collection from the Pauline churches to Jerusalem as a sign of their unity. Most important of all was the division of the mission field: "When they recognized that I had been entrusted with the gospel to the uncircumcised, as Cephas [had been entrusted with the gospel] to the circumcised, for he who has been effective for Cephas for the apostolate to the circumcised was effective also for me [for the apostolate] to the Gentiles, and when they came to know the grace given to me, James and Cephas and John, the influential pillars, gave to me and Barnabas the right hand of fellowship, that we should go to the Gentiles and they to the circumcised" (2:7-9). I assume that Paul kept this agreement throughout his career, confining his preaching strictly to Gentile God-fearers and never encouraging Jews to abandon the Torah, so that he was innocent of the accusations which led to his final arrest. This is consonant with his commissioning: "It pleased him who had set me apart from my mother's womb and had called me through his grace to reveal his son in me, that I might preach him among the Gentiles" (1:15f). Without the special revelation of God which said that Paul should preach Christ among the Gentiles, there would be no legitimacy to his gospel, leaving his Gentile converts, who were not proselytes, still strangers and sojourners and not members of the household of God. Although it is not emphasized, it is important to see that Paul was *not* commissioned to preach among Jews, whether about Jesus Christ or the Torah or anything else. It is perhaps not too fanciful to make a comparison to the prophet Jonah, who was commissioned to deliver a specific message to the Gentile Ninevites, but to whom was given no word of the Lord to Israel.

What is the content of Paul's gospel (Rom 2:16, etc.), the "gospel to the uncircumcised" (Gal 2:7), which he "preaches among the Gentiles" (2:2), which says that "God would justify the Gentiles" (3:8)? In answering this question it is important to realize that Paul's letters were written to congregations that were overwhelmingly made up of Gentiles, most of whom were former "God-fearers," with only a few Jewish co-workers. This is true of Thessalonica ("how you turned to God from idols to serve a living and true God," 1 Thess 1:9), Corinth ("you know that when you were Gentiles you were led astray to dumb idols," 1 Cor 12:2), Philippi ("watch out for circumcision . . . and do not trust in the flesh," Phil 3:2f), Galatia ("Formerly when you did not know God, you were in bondage to beings that by nature are no gods," Gal 4:8), Rome ("among all the Gentiles, including yourselves,'' Rom 1:5f, cf. 1:13, 6:19, 11:13, 28, 15:15f), to which one can add the deutero-Pauline letters to Colossae (''you who were dead in your trespasses and the uncircumcision of your flesh,'' Col 2:13, cf. 1:21,27) and Ephesus (''you Gentiles in the flesh, called the uncircumcision . . . alienated from the commonwealth of Israel, and strangers to the covenants of promise, having no hope and without God in the world,'' Eph 2:11f, cf. 2:1-3, 4:17-19). Paul writes to Gentile Christians, dealing with Gentile-Christian problems, foremost among which was the right of Gentiles qua Gentiles, without adopting the Torah of Israel, to full citizenship in the people of God. It is remarkable that in the endless discussion of Paul's understanding of the law, few have asked what a first-century Jew would have thought of the law *as it relates to Gentiles*.[28] W. D. Davies has recently been so bold as to claim that the relationship of Israel to the Gentile world was *the* theological problem of Judaism in the first century.[29] But what was the setting for Paul's proclamation?

In her discussion of the Christian anti-Judaic myth, Ruether points out quite correctly that while the schism of particularism and universalism is a major problem for the church, Judaism has long since found an admirable solution (236ff). Alongside the fundamental postulate, ''All Israel has a share in the world to come'' (*MSanh* 10:1),[30] stands the corollary concerning the ''righteous among the nations of the world who have a share in the world to come'' (*TSanh* 13:2—R. Joshua, end of first century). It is precisely Israel's universalistic perspective, which allows non-Jews to relate to God in their own way, which enables Israel to have her own particularity in relating to God through the Sinai covenant. But in order to be called righteous, one must live in some form of relationship with the Creator, and there can be no relationship with God apart from Torah (understood as revelation),[31] and there can be no Torah apart from commandments.[32] What commandments should ''the righteous among the nations of the world'' live by?

As far as I can determine, the first clear Jewish answer to this specific question was given by Maimonides: ''Everyone who accepts the seven [Noachic] commandments and observes them carefully is one of the righteous of the nations of the world and has a share in the world to come. But he must accept and observe them on the ground that the Holy One, blessed be He, commanded them in the Torah and that He informed us through our teacher Moses that the children of Noah had earlier been given these commandments. But if he practices them on the basis of his own rational considerations, then he is not a *ger toshav* [resident alien] nor one of the righteous of the nations of the world, but one of their sages.''[33] Just as for the Jew commandments are to be done *lishmah* (for their own sake, without ulterior motive) and with *kavvanah* (with intention to do them as commandments of God), so also for the righteous Gentile what counts is not the doing of works per se[34] or the number of commandments, but the acknowledgement of a relationship to God. Whether connected with the Noachic commandments or not, and whether with Maimonides' qualification about believing in revelation or not, the concept of righteous Gentiles has since become general within Judaism. But this was not always the case.

Before Maimonides, the concept of the Noachic commandments[35] really has nothing to do with the point under consideration, for "the righteous among the nations" are never mentioned in connection with them. As they are discussed in the Talmud (*Sanh* 56-60a), the context is of actual (if at that time theoretical) court decisions concerning Gentiles living in an independent land of Israel (resident aliens). There is no reference to a covenant of grace or the possibility of repentance and atonement, and the penalty for violation is (theoretically) death. There is still some debate about the number (up to thirty are mentioned) and content of the commandments, and in fact more than seven stipulations concerning the "stranger who sojourns among you" are to be found in the Pentateuch, such as those in Leviticus 17-18 which are taken up in the apostolic decree of Acts 15, 21. The point is to keep the land from being polluted, and such stipulations have nothing to do with the "righteous among the nations of the world." Of the commandments chosen, one comes from Gen 9:4, and the other six are ingeniously derived from Gen 2:16, "And the Lord God commanded Adam." This is an important verse because it shows that from the beginning God related to his creatures through commandments and that Adam is an appropriate figure to use when thinking about the relationship between God and the Gentile world.

I return to the two statements concerning Israel and the righteous among the nations cited above. How old is the concept that all Israel has a share in the world to come? Recent studies show that "in the entire body of Palestinian Jewish literature between Ben Sirah and the redaction of the Mishnah, with only the exception of 4 Ezra, membership in the covenant is considered salvation."[36] With respect to the concept of the "righteous among the nations of the world," the evidence is mixed. There is one clear parallel in *Test. Naph.* 8:3, which says that in the end times God will appear "to save the nation of Israel and to gather together the righteous from amongst the Gentiles," but it does not say how the righteous are to be defined. In addition to proselytes, there were many in the ancient world who were attracted to Judaism as a kind of religious philosophy and attached themselves to the synagogues, keeping many of the customs (commandments) without in any sense being Jews: the so-called "God-fearers." (The terminology is unclear; the term "God-fearer" often designates Jews or proselytes, but that many Gentiles were interested in Judaism cannot be denied.) Were they considered righteous? It seems that in the conversion of the royal family of Adiabene,[37] Ananias held King Izates to be such without circumcision. While Josephus's attitude to God-fearers is not at all clear, he seems to sound a positive note when he observes (*Ag. Ap* 2.282), "There is not a single Greek or barbarian city, not a single people, to which the custom of Sabbath observance has not spread, or in which the fast days, the kindling of lights, and many of our prohibitions about food are not heeded." If Klein is right,[38] there was an extensive catechism literature produced for God-fearers, reflected in pseudo-Phocylides, the two-ways catechism, and some of the Sibyllines and Derech Eretz literature. However, the God-fearers kept many commandments, not just the Noachic ones, but without circumcision and their status as being "righteous," while probable, is not really clarified.

It is because of this uncertainty that legalism—the doing of certain works in order to win God's favour and be counted righteous—arose as a Gentile problem and not a Jewish problem at all.[39] Salvation and God's grace are for all who are under the covenant and have not cast off the yoke of the Torah, but God-fearers *not* under the covenant must establish their righteousness by the performance of certain works, compounded by uncertainty about what these works should be. M. Barth has shown that the phrase "works of the law," which is not found in any Jewish texts, refers to the adoption of selected Jewish practices on the part of Gentiles and their attempt to impose them upon others as means of self-justification.[40] Such people are called Judaizers, those who want "to live according to the Jewish way of life," at least in part. That there were such Gentile Judaizers in Asia Minor and that their message was a temptation for the church is shown by Rev 2:9 and 3:9, "those who say they are Jews and are not," and two interesting passages in Ignatius: "It is monstrous to talk of Jesus Christ and to Judaize" (*Mag.* 10:3; of course, it is not at all monstrous to believe in Jesus and be a Jew), and "But if anyone interpret Judaism to you do not listen to him; for it is better to hear Christianity from the circumcised [such as Paul] than Judaism from the uncircumcised" (such as the Judaizers, *Phil.* 6:1). Recognition of the existence of such legalistic Gentile Judaizers is an important part of the background for understanding Paul's polemic

In addition to the Jewish concept of righteous Gentiles sketched above, there is another which is just as old. That is the concept that God offered the covenant-Torah to all the nations of the world but that it was accepted only by Israel. Moore says concerning it, "Did it consist with the justice of God that the heathen of all generations should be doomed for not keeping a law which neither they nor their fathers had ever known? Some such reflections, I conceive, gave rise to the persuasion that the law must have been revealed to the Gentiles also; not alone the rudimentary law given to Adam and repeated to Noah, but the law in its Sinaitic completeness."[41] Of the many passages containing this idea, I cite just one concerning God's voice on Sinai, "How did the voice go forth? R. Tanḥuma said: The word of the Lord went forth in two aspects, slaying the heathen who would not accept it, but giving life to Israel who accepted the Torah."[42] How can the one Torah be both a Torah of life [for Israel] and a Torah for death [for Gentiles]? We must look more closely at the understanding of Torah.

In early Judaism the concept of Torah developed in two directions. On the one hand, Torah as the revelation of God came to mean God in his knowability, in his presence, in his electing will, in his covenant. The concept of covenant, so important in the Hebrew Bible, does not disappear in Hellenistic or Rabbinic Judaism, but the terminology changes. In Greek *diathēkai* means decrees or promises,[43] even in the literal sense of testament (will), while in Hebrew *berith* became more and more restricted to circumcision. Hence, with the disappearance of a separate designation, the concept of covenant came to be more and more expressed by the words *torah* or *nomos*. Failure to understand the gracious, covenantal aspect of Torah has been one of the major reasons for Christian misconceptions of "law" within Judaism, but there has been some progress. Rössler has shown that in apocalyptic one's status before God is determined by an attitude to Torah as a document of election and not by the performance of individual commandments.[44] His thesis was given the necessary corrective by Nissen[45] and Sanders,[46] who demonstrate that the same holds also for Rabbinic Judaism. Contrary to earlier assumptions, the Greek word *nomos* in many passages of the Septuagint and pseudepigrapha also maintains the Torah connotations of revelation and covenant rather than mere law.[47] The wide-reaching richness conveyed by the word Torah is exceedingly important for understanding the nature of Judaism, but it *might* also tend to exclude Gentiles from any meaningful relationship to God. Israel's openness to the Gentile world qua Gentiles is as old as Amos, but it was not universal within Judaism, for there was a major strand which says that concern for Gentiles implied their incorporation into Israel. This tendency was reinforced by the development of another aspect in the understanding of Torah.

The concept of Torah was widened in a different direction when it became identified with wisdom, which first occurs clearly in ben Sira (Ecclesiasticus). Wisdom was international, it was incorporated into creation itself, and therefore Torah was seen not as the privilege of Israel but as "the light of the law which was given for to lighten every man" (*Test Levi* 14:4), "the guide of life" (*Sib* 3.195), the *torath ha-Adam* (law of humanity, *Sifra* 86b). What this might mean for Gentiles can be shown by a passage in ben Sira: "The Lord created man out of earth. He filled them with knowledge and understanding, and showed them good and evil. He bestowed knowledge upon them, and alloted to them the law of life. He established with them an eternal covenant, and showed them his judgments. Their eyes saw his glorious majesty, and their ears heard the glory of his voice. And he said to them, 'Beware of all unrighteousness.' And he gave commandment to each of them concerning his neighbor. He appointed a ruler for every nation, but Israel is the Lord's own portion'' (Sir 17:1,7,11-14,17). But although wisdom was offered to the whole creation, it found no abiding place in the Gentile world, and it settled in Israel. ''Then the Creator of all things gave me [wisdom] a commandment, and the one who created me assigned a place for my tent. And he said, 'Make your dwelling in Jacob, and in Israel receive your inheritance.' All this is the book of the covenant of the Most High God, the law which Moses commanded us an inheritance for the congregations of Jacob'' (Sir 24:8, 23). Here we find the earlier counterpart to the Rabbinic midrash on the offering of Torah to all nations and its acceptance only by Israel.[48] As soon as the Torah is identified with *wisdom*, then all nations are under the Torah as they are under the laws of creation,[49] but as soon as wisdom is identified with *Torah*, then the nations must keep all the laws given to Israel without being part of the covenant God made with Israel.

This background can help explain a rather strange phenomenon in many of the apocalyptic writings of the period. In the Hebrew Bible and in Talmud and midrash there are two extreme conceptions concerning the fate of the Gentiles in the end times, complete destruction or salvation by incorporation into Israel. There is also, as noted above, the idea that the ''righteous among the nations of the world'' need come under neither Israel's covenant nor Israel's laws in order to attain salvation at the judgment. In the writings of the Apocrypha and Pseudepigrapha, however, with few exceptions the Gentiles will be condemned at the judgment on the ground that they did not keep the commandments of God given not only to Israel at Sinai but to all humanity through Adam.[50] (It is consistent with this view that that many of these writings emphasize that the Patriarchs, who lived before Moses, nevertheless kept the Sinai commandments.)[51] But apart from the Patriarchs, there is said to be no hope for descendants of Adam who do not have the antidote to sin[52] given at the Sinai covenant. One quotation will have to stand for many:[53] ''Let many perish who are now living, rather than that the law of God which is set before them be disregarded! For God strictly commanded those who came into the world, when they came, what they should do to live, and what they should observe to avoid punishment. Nevertheless they were not obedient, and spoke against him; they devised for themselves vain thoughts, and proposed to themselves wicked frauds; they even declared that the Most High does not exist, and they ignored his ways! They scorned his law, and denied his decrees; they have been unfaithful to his statutes, and have not performed his works'' (4 Ezra 7:20-24). For Gentiles, who do not have the Torah as covenant, Torah as law functions in an exclusively negative way, to condemn. When this is allied with the notion, common in certain circles, that this law is administered by the seventy guardian angels of the nations, who were present at Mt. Sinai and heard the law proclaimed, then we can understand not only Paul's background but also that of later Gnosticism.

Within Pharisaic Judaism, the group that stood closest to this strict application of the law to Gentiles was probably the House of Shammai. I am thinking here not of the personal animosity to Gentiles attributed to Shammai and Eliezer b. Hyrkanos in some stories and sayings but of an attitude which shows that they were less open than some to compromise on matters of the law in relationship to proselytes, their pessimism concerning Gentiles, and in general their greater zeal for the law. Thus as a counterpoint to the leniency of Ananias in the story of the conversion of King Izates, Eleazar later insisted on circumcision and the whole law. Especially significant were the nationalistic Eighteen Measures against Gentiles forced through by the House of Shammai at the beginning of the war of C. E. 66-70.[54] While the word ''Zealot'' did not acquire the technical meaning of a specific party before the war, the concept of being zealous for the law certainly fits the Shammaites better than any other Pharisees. There are many indications that Paul was a Shammaite.[55] He also always uses the word ''zealous'' whenever he refers to his earlier life: ''with respect to zeal persecuting the church'' (Phil 3:6), ''being exceedingly zealous for the traditions of my fathers'' (Gal 1:14), and even Acts, ''being zealous for God . . . I persecuted this Way to the death'' (22:3f). On the basis of Gal 5:11, ''but if I still preach circumcision,'' many have also concluded that Paul had been a missionary to the Gentiles even before his commissioning.[56] As a Shammaite living in the Diaspora, he was in a unique position. On the one hand, he was firmly convinced that since all are to be judged by their works in conformity to the laws of Sinai, there is no hope for the Gentiles except for those who have been ''brought under the wings of the Divine Presence,'' that is, as proselytes who became members of the covenant-Torah. On the other hand, his close proximity to the Gentile world would have given him sympathy for his neighbours and an urgency for his task. His commissioning outside Damascus was therefore most significant not because of what it meant for him personally but because it provided a meaningful answer from God himself to his quandry concerning Gentiles and the law.

To attempt to understand Paul's many statements about the law from the perspective of their significance for Gentiles is such a radically new departure that a full exposition is impossible at the moment, and yet only that could be really convincing. What follows, then, suggests an approach which might be fruitful if carried out in greater detail. By the very nature of the situation, if one concentrates on the predicament of Gentiles under the law, most references will be to Galatians and Romans. Perhaps this is the place to underline the fact that one of the favourite passages for those who interpret Paul in opposition to Judaism, 2 Corinthians 3, is completely beside the point. That text has nothing to do with law or Scripture (''Old Testament'') or Pharisaic Jews; rather it opposes the attempt of certain Hellenistic Jewish-Christian missionaries to develop a ''divine man'' understanding of Moses as a model for their own behaviour.[57] I turn now to letters where the concept of law actually appears.

It has often been observed that Paul seems to have a double concept of *Torah-nomos*, saying sometimes that it is good and has been fulfilled in Christ and sometimes that it is bad and has been abolished in Christ. This causes a great deal of confusion for any interpretation, but the double expansion of the concept within Judaism noted above should be remembered, for Paul used the only word available to him in the vocabulary of his times. It perhaps helps clarify his thought if the different concepts are distinguished by different words. In what follows I shall use the word Torah when it includes the idea of covenant, whether for Jews or Gentile Christians, and restrict the word ''law'' to the situation of the descendants of Adam who are not part of the Sinai covenant.

In particular, the phrase ''under the law'' is found in no Jewish writing to express the relationship to Torah,[58] but it seems to be used by Paul to designate the Gentile situation. That Gentiles were under the law can perhaps best be shown by Gal 3:21 - 4:11, particularly when the passage is read in the light of its end. Paul's Gentile readers, who ''formerly did not know God and were slaves to 'gods' who actually were not such'' (4:8), were subject to ''weak and beggarly elements'' (4:9), and Paul can be referring to nothing else when he says that ''*we* were children serving under the elements of the universe'' (4:3). Paul can so identify with his readers that the first person plural can actually mean ''we Gentiles,'' as in 3:14, ''that in Christ the blessing of Abraham might come upon the *Gentiles*, that *we* might receive the promise of the Spirit through faith.''[59] The nature of the ''elements'' is perhaps made most clear by Colossians, where they (2:8, 20) are also called ''principalities and powers'' (2:10, 15) and ''angels'' (2:18), where they enforce certain regulations (2:20) such as asceticism (2:16, 18, 21, 23) and astrological periods (2:16), and where they have a ''certificate of indebtedness'' which condemns all humanity who do not submit to their regulations (2:14). To return to Galatians, Gentiles who used to be ''*under* the elements'' are also said to have been minors ''*under* guardians and trustees'' (4:2), school children ''*under* the disciplinarian'' (3:24), ''confined *under* the law'' (3:22). Not under the Torah, for it is the Torah as

Scripture which "has declared the whole world to be prisoners confined *under* sin" (3:22) and has said that those who rely on "works of the law" are "*under* a curse" (3:10). For those under "the law of deeds,"[60] the Mosaic covenant is of no avail (3:19-20). Those who have attempted to interpret the pedagogue (3:24) as a teacher in order to find a subordinate positive use for the law are wrong, for subjection to the law = elements is seen only in the negative sense of that from which we are redeemed. Those who interpret the passage as an attack on Torah are wrong; it is not the past of Jews which Paul is describing but the past of Gentiles. Thus in 3:23 "before faith came" has to mean "before faith came to the Gentiles in Christ," unless Paul means to retract the very impressive things he has just said about the faith of Abraham. When the Torah of Israel is spoken of (3:17), it is not as something negative but as something irrelevant, for the Sinai covenant in fact was not the fulfilment of the promise to Abraham that "in you [and in your seed] shall all the Gentiles be blessed" (3:8,16). The climax of the passage is the assertion that "when the time had fully come, God sent forth his Son, born of woman, born under the law, to redeem those under the law, so that we might receive adoption as sons" (4:4f). By adoption, Gentiles, who were not sons before, although they were under the law, become sons and thus heirs of the promise given to Abraham, of equal status with the natural sons of Abraham.

Other passages which speak of those "under the law" can be dealt with more briefly.[61] The Roman Christians are no longer "under the law" but are now "under grace" (Rom 6:14,15), just as the Galatians are no longer "under the law" if they are "led by the Spirit" (Gal 5:18). 1 Cor 9:20-22 must be interpreted of four groups: the Jews, those under the law = Gentiles (which Paul says he is not), the lawless = the Corinthian antinomians (which Paul said he is not), and the weak = those under discussion in chapters 8-10. Significant is Rom 3:19, "We know that whatever the Torah [Scripture] says, it says to those who are in [the sphere of] the law, so that *every mouth* may be stopped and the *whole world* may be liable to judgment by God." Finally, when Paul says, "Tell me, you who desire to be under law, do you not hear the Torah?" (Gal 4:21), introducing a passage they had not considered, one almost detects a note of the superiority of the Pharisee who really knows the Torah replying to amateurs who are only playing with the idea. For Paul the Torah is the great privilege of Israel (Rom 2:17-20; 3:1-2; 9:4-5), which, seen in the context of the promises to the Patriarchs and the Sinai covenant, should lead to obedience as the life of faith and should not be used in an attempt at self-justification outside that context.[62] The Mishnah (*Ber*. 2:2) says that the Israelite "first takes upon himself the yoke of the Kingdom of Heaven and afterwards takes upon himself the yoke of the commandments." Paul's concern is to say that the Gentiles in Christ are under the equivalent of the yoke of the Kingdom but not under the yoke of the commandments (which would make them righteous proselytes, Jews and no longer Gentiles). At the same time, he wants to say that Gentiles in Christ have been redeemed from being under the law, redeemed from the wrath of God which lies on the descendants of Adam for their disobedience, although they still owe obedience to God.

In Romans Paul deals with the Gentiles and the law in connection with the figure of Adam. This is explicit in 5:12-21, where Paul makes the point that Adam's trespass of God's command was the occasion for sin and death to come into the world. The law is not identified with sin and death but came in as the accompanying circumstance, the occasion (5:20). Sin and death were in the world before the Torah came with Moses, and therefore (cf. 4:15!) all humanity in that period was under the law without the remedy of the Torah (5:14) or the grace of God in Jesus Christ (5:16).[63] The situation of the Gentile world described in 1:18-2:16 also has the Adam story as its background.[64] "The law gives knowledge of sin" (3:20), and the Gentiles "know God's commandment that those who do these things deserve to die" (1:32). "The law produces wrath" (4:15), and the wrath of God in 1:18ff functions as does the law elsewhere, to increase sin (cf. 5:20 and 7:5, "sin's sad consequences which are through the law . . . produce . . . death"). Gentiles, "by nature children of wrath" (Eph 2:3), "are for themselves the law" and "do by nature that which belongs to the law (= sin)" (2:14), for they have "the work of the law (= wrath) written on their hearts" (2:15). Chapter 7 deals even more drastically with the law and Adam (7:7-12) and the consequences for Adam's descendants.[65] If in chapter 1 the Gentiles are subject to the wrath of God and in chapter 6 are slaves of sin, in Chapter 7 it is the law which rules over them (7:1, cf. 6:12) and from which they are freed (7:4, cf. 6:2). In 7:13ff the "law" seems closest to the Jewish concept of the "evil impulse," and there are such strong statements as "the law of sin" (7:23, 25) and "the law of sin and death" (8:2). And yet the overriding purpose of this chapter is to show the goodness of the law, which is "holy" (7:12) and "spiritual" (7:14) and "good" (7:16)!

When Paul is most negative about the law, he opposes it to—the law, that is, the Torah! Opposed to "the other law, the law of sin" is "the Torah of God" (7:22f). The condemnation which lay on the children of Adam (5:16, 18) is overcome in Christ (8:1), because opposed to "the law of sin and death" is "the Torah of the Spirit of life in Christ Jesus" (8:2). Opposed to "the law of works" is "the Torah of [God's] faithfulness" (3:27). Paul can even say most paradoxically that "I through the Torah died to the law" (Gal 2:19). For Jewish Christians, and presumably for Paul himself, Christ was seen as the fulfilment of the Sinai covenant, and the word *nomos* in the passages just cited has the connotation of election. For Gentile Christians, however, who are to come not as proselytes but as Gentiles into the people of God, another word would be more appropriate. The Gentile counterpart to living in the covenant community of Torah is being "in Christ." Christ is the fulfilment of the promise concerning the Gentiles given to Abraham. God shows his righteousness, his faithfulness to his promise, in a new act, apart from the Sinai covenant but not contradictory to it (Rom 3:21).[66] Now it is clear why Paul so seldom connects covenant with law, for a new vocabulary is necessary when he speaks of the new relationship of God to Gentiles. He also never speaks of repentance, for that means turning *back* to the God of the covenant, and Paul is interested in Gentiles turning *to* him for the first time. Torah would be meaningless without commandments, and this is true also for Gentiles. Those who walk according to the Spirit fulfil "the commandment of the Torah" (Rom 8:4), and Paul can say that for Gentiles the Torah is "fulfilled" by doing Lev 19:18, loving the neighbour (Rom 13:8-10; Gal 5:14). Paul can speak of doing "the Torah of Christ" (Gal 6:2) and of his being not lawless but "in the Torah of Christ" (1 Cor 9:21). The actual content is vague compared with the richness of the Talmud, but whether Gentile Christians keep one commandment or many ("keeping the commandments of God," 1 Cor 7:19), they exist in a covenant and commandment relationship to God which is different from but parallel to that of Sinai.

If Paul's central theological concern was, as I have claimed, a positive justification of the status of Gentile Christians, why should other Jews have opposed his activities (and why did Paul himself earlier persecute the church)? The idea that Jews would persecute Gentiles who adopt some Jewish ideas along with faith in Jesus is absurd. It is equally absurd to think that Jews would persecute those Jews who taught Gentiles to believe in Jesus apart from the Torah. I also think it is false to assume that Jews persecuted other Jews who kept the commandments through faith in the Messiah Jesus. But if it were even suspected that a Jew was teaching other Jews to abandon their Judaism, that is, to throw off the yoke of the Torah, this would be quite another matter, particularly for the Zealots. The accusation made against Paul is stated quite accurately by Luke as follows: those "zealous for the law" say, "You teach all the Diaspora Jews to forsake Moses, telling them not to circumcise their children nor observe the customs" (Acts 21:21). The slightest suspicion that Paul was doing this would not only get him in trouble but would be exceptionally dangerous to the Jerusalem church, which helps explain much of the tension between Paul and James. That Paul was accused of causing Jews to become apostate by abandoning the Torah is clear, but I believe that he was innocent of the charge.

If Paul's central theological concern was *not* a negative disparagement of the significance of the Torah for Israel, then what did he have against other

Jews? If what I have sketched is correct, Paul says nothing against the Torah and Israel but simply bypasses them as not directly relevant to his gospel. Therefore, the figures of Adam (negatively) and Abraham (positively) are much more important for his understanding of the significance of Jesus than are the figures of Moses and David. For Paul, Jesus is neither a new Moses nor the Messiah, he is not the climax of the history of God's dealing with Israel, but he is the fulfilment of God's promises concerning the Gentiles, and this is what he accused the Jews of not recognizing. Paul never accuses Jews of lacking zeal for Torah, and certainly not of legalism, but rather of disobedience to the new revelation given to him. Thus the reproaches in Rom 2:17-24 have to do with Israel's relative failure to become "a light to the Gentiles." Israel is said to have "stumbled" (Rom 9:32; 11:11) because most other Jews did not join Paul in proclaiming his gospel of the righteousness of God to the Gentiles. "Israel did not understand" (10:19) that the time had come to do this. Though zealous, Jews were "ignorant of the righteousness of God and sought to establish their own" (10:3), which of course does not mean that individual Jews attempted to justify themselves by their own actions in defiance of the God of the covenant, but that Israel as a whole interpreted the righteousness of God as establishing the status of righteousness for Israel alone, excluding the Gentiles from election. Had all Israel followed Paul's example, it may be that we would have had a Gentile church loyal to the righteousness of God expressed in Jesus Christ and his fulfilment of the promises to Abraham, alongside an Israel loyal to the righteousness of God expressed in the Torah. But the delay in the consummation of history which Paul had not anticipated and his own successes made anything more than a "bridge generation"[67] unnecessary. With the passing of that first generation of Jewish Christians (who left no direct records), with the development of a New Testament which forces its readers to choose between Torah and Christ, and with the acknowledgement of the legitimacy of the Christian movement by an important strand of later Judaism, Paul's reproach has long since become obsolete.

As long as Judaism is understood as a kind of Christian heresy to be combatted, there will never be an end to Christian anti-Judaism. Is there room in Pauline thought for such a concept as "two religions, two chosen people?"[68] The one who said in another context, "I wish that all were as I myself am" (1 Cor 7:7), probably hoped that all Jews would come to share his faith. But he does not explicitly say so,[69] and the absence of Jesus from Romans 11 (cf. also 1 Cor 15:28) may give a hint in another direction. Paul also says that in Christ "there is neither Jew nor Greek . . . neither male nor female" (Gal 3:28). That means that in Christ there is both Jew and Greek, both male and female. Just as women do not need to become men nor men women to attain their full humanity, so Jews do not need to become Gentiles nor do Gentiles need to become Jews. Paul is of course concerned to argue for the full right of Gentiles to be equal members of the people of God, and it is to this issue, where Christ-language is important, that all of his words are directed (whereas otherwise God-language, as in Romans 11, would be more appropriate). But now that that battle has been won, and in the light of subsequent history, Pauline interpreters today need to emphasize the other side, the right of Israel to remain Israel, without being defined by someone else's "mystery," as equal but elder recipients of the grace of God. All of the positive things Paul has to say about the righteousness of God effecting salvation for Gentiles in Christ need not at all imply anything negative about Israel and the Torah. Indeed, it may be that Paul, and Paul alone among the New Testament writers, has no left hand. Although it has only been hinted at here, I believe that it is possible to interpret Paul in this manner. That it is necessary to do so is the implication of the agonized concern of many in the post-Auschwitz situation, including Rosemary Ruether in her powerful *Faith and Fratricide*.

2

ANGELS AND GENTILES IN EARLY JUDAISM AND IN PAUL

Paul says in Galatians 3:19 that the law was ordained through angels, by the hand of a mediator, who is today almost universally understood to be Moses.[1] Thereby Paul is referring to the well-known Jewish concept of the role of the angels at the giving of the law. How is it certain that the concept was well known? Because all the commentaries say so, and they copy from one another the relevant proof texts. Blunter than most but typical is a popular commentary like Barclay's:

> The law was not given direct by God. In the old story in Exodus 20 the law was given direct to Moses; but in the days of Paul the Rabbis were so impressed by the utter holiness and the utter distance and remoteness of God that they believed that it was quite impossible for God to deal direct with men; therefore they introduced the idea that the law was given first to angels and then by the angels to Moses (cp. Acts 7:53, Hebrews 2:2). Here Paul is using the Rabbinic thoughts of his time. The law then is at a double remove from God. It was given first to angels; and then to a mediator, and the mediator is Moses. Compared with the *promise*, which was given absolutely directly by God, the *law* is a second-hand thing which came through intermediaries.[2]

Thus Barclay, but even the most recent and scholarly commentary by H. D. Betz[3] is able to call "Jewish traditions" something that contradicts not only the text of scripture but a major concern of the Rabbis, that the Torah was given by God directly as his most personal covenant with the people of Israel. That angels should have been present at Sinai when the Torah was revealed was a rather natural conception, perhaps reflected in the Hebrew Bible (Ps 68:18) and certainly contained in the old translations of Deut 33:2 (LXX, "on his right angels with him"; Targum Onkelos, "and with him multitudes of holy ones"; Targum pseudo-Jonathan, "and with him multitudes of multitudes of holy angels"), but in no sense were they there to mediate a Torah that God could not give directly. On the contrary, where the momentous events of the election of Israel are concerned, the recurring phrase is "Not by means of an angel and not by means of a messenger."[4] Various Midrashim on the presence of the angels at Sinai are conveniently collected and discussed by P. Schäfer,[5] but in all of them the law is given by God himself and not by his accompanying angels. Other passages that are commonly cited will have to be examined more closely.

Barclay refers only to Hebrews and Acts as sources for the supposed Jewish tradition. Heb 2:2, which speaks of a "word spoken through angels" says nothing whatsoever about the giving of the law and does not belong here at all.[6] Acts 7:53, on the other hand, does have Stephen say to the Jews: "you have received the law [given] into the administration of angels and you did not keep it." This, however, is in the context of Stephen's view that after the making of the golden calf, "God turned and gave them over to worship the host of heaven" (7: 42). While this is probably the root of the strange later Christian calumny that the Jews worship angels, it can hardly be cited as evidence for a Jewish concept.[7] I will come back later to a possible background of this connection of stars and angels and the law. In *Jub.* 1:27; 2:1 the angel of the presence writes for Moses not the Torah but the book of *Jubilees* itself,[8] and, in any case, the concept of a single angel giving a revelation through a prophet or seer is quite different from a multitude of angels mediating the law.[9] Occasionally reference is made to a passage in Philo:

> What are called *daimones* by the other philosophers the sacred record is wont to call *angeloi*, employing an apter title, for they both carry the biddings of the Father to his children and report the children's need to their Father. In accordance with this they are represented by the law-giver as ascending and descending: not that God, who is already present in all directions, needs informants, but that it was a boon to us in our sad case to avail ourselves of the services of *logoi*, acting on our behalf as mediators (*mesitai*). (*Somn.* 1.14lf.)

Although Philo goes on to interpret Exod 20:19 as a request to the mediators to speak the law, he also makes it quite clear elsewhere that it was God who spoke to Israel "in his own person."[10]

Finally, there is to the passage that Betz calls the "most important,"[11] Josephus, *Antiquities* 15.136, "we have learned the noblest of our doctrines and the holiest of our laws through angels sent by God." Ginzberg says of this passage that "Josephus could not possibly have attributed the giving of the Law to the angels," since he elsewhere "expressly states that the Law was given directly [by God]." Ginzberg therefore concludes that prophets as messengers from God are meant.[12] However, it is more probable that angels really are meant, albeit not in connection with Sinai. The passage comes from a speech of Herod in which he rouses his forces against the atrocity of the Arabs who have killed the envoys sent to them, an act which is called "contrary to the universal law of mankind."[13] The complete quotation reads: "Those things which are admitted by both Greeks and barbarians to be most lawless, these men have done to our envoys and have cut their throats, although the Greeks have declared heralds to be sacred and inviolable and we have learned the noblest of the degrees and the most holy of the laws through angels from God. For this name brings God to the knowledge of mankind and is sufficient to reconcile enemies one to another."[14] The law in question is international, prohibiting the mistreatment of envoys, and not connected in particular with the Sinai covenant. In this connection it may very well be appropriate to speak of angels.

Upon examination it is apparent that the supposed Jewish tradition of the giving of the law through angels has no foundation. The concept seems to come from a Billerbeck mentality, which, because of a statement in the New Testament, combs the entire mass of pseudepigraphic, Hellenistic, and Rabbinic material looking for so-called parallels read outside their own context. In addition, the concept was consonant with the widespread misconception of the remoteness of the God of Israel which Barclay reflects. When one reads the literature itself, however, one might be tempted to write a book called *The Immanence of God in Rabbinical Literature*, as did Abelson,[15] who shows that the concept of the necessity of mediation precisely at the central event of the revelation on Sinai would be the most absurd misconception of all. That the law was given to Israel by angels must be called exclusively a Pauline concept,[16] if indeed that is what Paul says.

In the context of a letter written by one who says that he was commissioned as an apostle of Christ "in order that I might preach him among the Gentiles" (Gal 1:16), a letter which reflects "the gospel which I preach among the Gentiles" (2:2), "the gospel to the uncircumcised" (2:7), the gospel whose content is "that God would justify the Gentiles from faithfulness" (3:8), a letter addressed to those who "formerly did not know God [but] served gods who essentially are not" (4:8), in such a letter one would expect Paul to be dealing with Gentile problems, using concepts intelligible to Gentiles. With respect to the law being ordained, a close verbal parallel, combining *diatassō* and *nomos*, is found as early as Hesiod, who says in his *Works and Days*: "For the son of Cronos has ordained this law for men, that fishes and beasts and winged fowls should devour one another, for *Dike* is not in them; but to mankind he gave *Dike* which proves far the best." He also says: "For upon the bounteous earth Zeus has thrice ten thousand spirits, watchers [*phulakes*] of mortal men, and these keep watch on judgments and deeds of wrong as they roam, clothed in mist, all over the earth."[17] But rather than trace the Greek concepts of *Moira* or *Dike* or *Nomos*, through whom order is maintained in the cosmos and society,[18] it is better to see how such matters are perceived from the perspective of Judaism.

Israel has found various ways of dealing with the tension between monotheism and election, between affirmation of the covenant with Israel and recognition of God's rule over the whole of creation. According to Deuteronomy, "the sun and the moon and the stars, all the host of heaven" have been "allotted to all the peoples under the whole heaven" (4:19), and "When the Most High gave to the nations their inheritance, when he separated the sons of men, he fixed the bounds of the peoples according to the number of the sons of God. For the LORD's portion is his people; Jacob is his allotted inheritance" (32:8f.). From this developed the concept of the guardian angels of the nations, sometimes but not always specified as seventy (or seventy-two) in number, which is found in ben Sira, Daniel, Jubilees, the Hebrew Testament of Naphtali, perhaps in 1 Enoch and in Philo, in Targum Jonathan, the pseudo-Clementines, the Church Fathers, and is present but not particularly significant in Talmud and Midrash.[19] Caird refers in this connection to "two modes of divine sovereignty":[20] voluntary, direct, and personal over Israel, and unacknowledged, indirect, and impersonal over the nations.

Similar in its effect is another development, in which wisdom becomes a cosmic concept comparable to the Egyptian Ma'at.[21] When, in addition, at least as early as ben Sira, wisdom became identified with Torah, then Torah becomes more than the covenant of God with Israel. Torah is the means, so to speak, of God's ordering his whole creation. Since God is one, therefore his Torah is one: the Torah known by Israel is the same as the Torah which governs the world.

There is one early text which brings together these two concepts of wisdom-Torah in the context of creation and the angels of the nations, ben Sira 17:

1 The Lord created man out of earth,
    and turned him back to it again.
2 He gave to them few days, a limited time,

but granted them authority over the things upon the earth.
3 He endowed them with strength like his own,
and made them in his own image.
7 He filled them with knowledge and understanding,
and showed them good and evil.
11 He bestowed knowledge upon them,
and allotted to them the law of life.
12 He established with them an eternal covenant,
and showed them his judgments.
14 And he said to them, "Beware of all unrighteousness."
And he gave commandment to each of them concerning his neighbor.
17 He appointed a ruler for every nation.
but Israel is the Lord's own portion.[22]

This text comes of course from a time when order in the cosmos was seen to be a good thing, from both the Hellenistic and Jewish perspectives. The regime of the rulers of the nations was presumably a benevolent one. Torah of course also implies commandments, but the text is rather unspecific about the nature of the commandments which are binding on all who come into the world. Even if that is the implication, the text does not directly say that the function of the angels is to teach commandments to the nations they rule and to punish disobedience; nor does any other Jewish text specifically say so.

The pessimistic view in much of apocalyptic concerning the fate of the nations at the judgment derives from such concepts. It is not just that Israel had to experience the consequences of the misrule of the angels of the nations, a concept which may be reflected in Psalm 82. Insofar as the entire world is governed by Torah, it seems also that in certain texts the Gentiles were thought to be obligated to keep all the commandments revealed on Sinai, but apart from the gracious aspects of covenant. One passage reads as follows:

> Let many perish who are now living, rather than that the law of God which is set before them be disregarded! For God strictly commanded those who came into the world, when they came, what they should do to live, and what they should observe to avoid punishment. Nevertheless they were not obedient, and spoke against him; they devised for themselves vain thoughts, and proposed to themselves wicked frauds; they even declared that the Most High does not exist, and they ignored his ways! They scorned his law, and denied his ordinances; they have been unfaithful to his statutes, and have not performed his works (4 Ezra 7:20-24).

There are many parallels to such statements in apocalyptic writings,[23] for the theme of God's judgment over the entire world is central to apocalyptic. The identification of wisdom and Torah has taken a rather fateful turn, in which, to be sure, the justice of God has been upheld, but the tension between universalism and particularism has been violently resolved in a manner which could not ultimately satisfy.

The rabbinic counterpart to the impulses coming from apocalyptic and those coming from wisdom is found in the Agadah that the Torah was offered to all the nations but accepted only by Israel. Thus God offered it first to the Edomites, the Amonites, the Moabites, and the Ishmaelites, each of whom refused for reasons appropriate to what was said of them elsewhere.[24] Or God's voice thundered forth from Sinai in seventy languages at once.[25] Or the nations sent scribes to the altar on Mt. Ebal, where the law was inscribed under the plaster, and transcribed it into the seventy languages.[26] There are two passages which say that the angels of the nations were present at Sinai and that the nations chose their gods from among them,[27] but they do not explicitly refer to the nations or their angels hearing the Torah. This Agadah is early,[28] but contrary to what I had expected, it is not directly helpful. It functions in the service of the concept of the election of Israel, saying that God was not unfair to give such a treasure as the Torah to Israel and not to other peoples. What the nations gave up without knowing it was, of course, the possibility of entering into a covenant relationship with God, and it is covenant not commandments which are of concern. Although the idea of the pre-existence and universality of Torah is expanded in rabbinic Judaism, this has nothing to do with the relation of Gentiles and specific commandments because it was not necessary. A new solution was found to the question of God's universal kingship and the covenant only with Israel, the concept of the righteous among the nations of the world. The rabbinic writings can only be used indirectly as the reflection in transmuted terms of earlier ideas concerning Gentiles, angels, and law.

There are explicit reference to the law administered by the angels of the nations only when that rule is experienced as oppressive. Thus Papias said that God "gave to some of them [namely, the angels who were formerly divine] to rule over the administration of the earth, and he commanded them to rule well."[29] But, he concluded, "it happened that their ordering came to nothing." In early Gnosticism, Simon Magus said, according to Hippolytus, "The angels who created the world made whatever enactments they pleased, thinking by such [legislative] words to enslave those who listened to them,"[30] and, according to Irenaeus, "Through his [Simon's] grace are men saved and not through righteous works. Nor are works just by nature, but by convention, as the angels who made the world ordained, in order to enslave men by such precepts."[31] Basilides speaks specifically of the angels of the nations,[32] Valentinus of the seventy "Logoi which are heavenly angels"[33] and the Nag Hammadi text *On the Origin of the World* of "the 72 gods [who] receive a pattern . . . so that they might rule over the 72 languages of the nations."[34] While the general background of ruling powers is a common Hellenistic conception,[35] the name "angels" and the numbers seventy or seventy-two reflect, as if a photographic negative, the specifically Jewish concepts just discussed. Values are simply reversed in Gnosticism. Philo, for example, emphasizes the agreement between the Torah and the moral order of the universe, and he is describing a good order when he says that God governs the world through *logoi* and powers and angels. Gnosticism arises out of a collapse of confidence in the basic structures of creation and society and human existence, and the anti-Jewish elements in Gnosticism stem not from an attack on Torah and covenant and Israel but from a revolt against God's governance of the world, using Jewish concepts among others. The Gnostic evidence then reflects the continuation of the association found in ben Sira of cosmic Torah and the angels of the nations of the world.[36]

It was Schlier who first made extensive use of Gnostic material to explain the law and the angels of Galatians 3:19.[37] Bo Reicke then published in 1951 a provocative article on "The Law and This World According to Paul."[38] What misled both of these interpreters, however, was the persistence of the idea that there were Jewish traditions of the giving of the law to Israel on Sinai through angels. They did not think of making the important distinction involved in asking how, according to early Judaism, the law was related to God's rule of Gentiles. Particularly in a study of the theology of the Apostle to the Gentiles this is the most appropriate line of inquiry. Before returning to Galatians, however, it is necessary to look briefly at another situation involving Gentiles and angels, that of Colossae.

The Colossian church was exclusively Gentile ("you who were dead in your trespasses and the uncircumcision of your flesh," 2:13), and the letter does not refer to the law of Sinai anywhere. Instead, there are certain regulations (*dogmata*, 2:14, cf. 20) to which the Colossians submitted in humility (2:18, 23). They involved the abstention from certain foods and drinks (2:16, 21), the observation of certain days and periods connected with the cycle of nature and the planets (2:16), and in general ascetic mortification of the body (2:18, 23). It seems that those who submitted to the regulations were promised access to the fullness (*plērōma*) of deity (2:10), while those who did not were threatened by a "certificate of indebtedness" (2:14). These regulations were administered by beings called "elements of the universe" (2:8, 20), or "principalities and powers" (2:10, 15), or "angels" (2:18). It is probable that these powers were seen positively ("worship of angels," 2:18) as representatives of the *plērōma*, rather than negatively in a Gnostic sense ("fear of angels") as hostile powers which block the way to the *plēroma*.

A brief word must be said about the *stoicheia tou kosmou*.[39] They are simply the four elements out of which the world is composed: earth, water, air, fire (or five with the addition of aether). There is however a polemical tradition at least as old as the Wisdom of Solomon (13:1-2) and at least as late as Maimonides which warns against worshipping them.[40] Philo, for example, speaks of "those who revere the elements, earth, water, air, fire, which have received different names from different peoples" (*Cont.* 3).[41] Nikolaus Kehl has collected extensive references from the literature of Hellenistic Judaism and the early Christian fathers warning against the worship of the elements.[42] Here then is a phenomenon of the non-Jewish world in which powers and regulations are connected. In Jewish terminology, one would speak of angels and Gentiles and cosmic law which cannot be unrelated to Torah.

It is not just the common reference to the *stoicheia* which suggests that Galatians ought to be interpreted in the light of Colossians. The Gentile Galatians formerly "served gods who essentially are not" (4:8), that is, "the weak and impotent *stoicheia*" (4:9). That service involved the following of certain regulations, of which only some astrological observances are named (4:10). Reading backward through Paul's imagery reveals that living "under the *stoicheia*" (4:3) is comparable to the situation of minor children, being "under the guardians and trustees" (4:2), school children "under the disciplinarian" (3:25). The *stoicheia* seem to have exercised a certain positive function in the administration of order in creation, but in a world come of age their rule has come to be confining and oppressive. The situation is simply the normal one in the Hellenistic world of this period, and insofar as Paul proclaims liberation from the powers through the knowledge of God (4:9), it is his solution, not the Galatian "heresy" which most anticipates Gnosticism.

The situation would be quite clear if Paul did not also speak of the Galatians having been "under law" (3:23; 4:5). Is it really true as Reicke says, that Paul equates Israel's situation under the Sinai covenant with that of the Galatians under pagan gods? Why should such a strange conception be attributed to him when another is at least conceivable? There is a tradition which identifies Gentile deities with the angels of God, the seventy angels of the nations, and there is at least the strong possibility that their function was to administer the law of God in realms beyond the covenant with Israel. Certainly in Pauline thought there is a parallelism between statements like being confined under law (3:23) and being slaves to *stoicheia* (4:3), the weak law (Rom. 8:3) and the weak *stoicheia* (4:9), dying to the law (2:19), dying to the world (6:14), and dying to the *stoicheia* (Col. 2:20).

Whether the administrators are called elements or powers or angels, they have administered a law from which Gentiles have been redeemed in Christ according to Paul's gospel.

It would have been much simpler for everyone if Paul had used a different word than *nomos* when he wanted to speak of the law outside the context of the covenant, but of course he could not, no more than could ben Sira and 4 Ezra. Because God is one, his law is one, but this law has quite a different effect when it is administered directly by God himself for his people Israel than when it is administered by the angels of the nations.

To come finally to the text of Galatians 3:19f., I would argue that it can be understood as follows.[43] Paul says that the law was "ordained through angels." He does not say that God did not give the law; the passives in verses 19a and 21b imply that he did. He does say that God's law was ordained or administered (as Lightfoot translates) by angels,[44] by which he means the seventy angels of the nations. "Ordained through angels, in the hand of a mediator," or more precisely, "in the hand of each of the seventy mediators," as will emerge from the following. Paul does not say that the mediators are not mediators between God and people, for in a sense they are, but there might be an implication that it would be better to have no mediator at all, as in the case of Israel, who is "the Lord's own portion" (Sir 17:17). "Now the mediator [in question][45] is not one [of a kind]."[46] The definite article shows that this is not a general statement defining the concept of mediator, and *henos* can be translated as a genitive of quality. The problem with the angels of the nations is that there are seventy of them; they are not unique, and they cannot fulfil the promise of God to Abraham and his "one seed" concerning the Gentiles. "But God is one." The confession of God's unity here has the same function as in Rom 3:29-30, namely, to justify the inclusion of the Gentiles: "Or is it of the Jews only that God is God? Not also of the Gentiles? Of course also of the Gentiles, since God is one, who will justify the circumcised out of his faithfulness and the uncircumcised through the same faithfulness." Here in Galatians, because God is one, he has fulfilled his promise in the one seed of Abraham, he has redeemed the Gentiles from the curse of the law and from slavery to the powers, and made all one in Christ Jesus the one seed. One final question which needs to be touched on concerns the time when the law was given in these verses. In terms of the chronology in the previous verses, it is natural to think of Sinai as the occasion, but in terms of the bondage of the Gentiles to the law, creation or Adam would be the appropriate context (as is the case in Romans 5 and probably 1 and 7). It is not possible to answer this question. Paul finds no more of a contradiction than does Judaism when it affirms both the eternity of Torah and the giving of the Torah at Sinai. This naturally happens when Torah and wisdom are identified.

Whether or not the interpretation I have given is plausible, there are at least certain advantages to it. Rather than relying on a non-existent Jewish tradition of the giving of the law to Israel through angels, one can appeal to the documented concept of the angels of the nations. Doing so provides a logic to the sequence of sentences, hard enough to do otherwise, and avoids the problem of a chain of mediators: God, angels, Moses, people.[47] There is no longer need to puzzle over what Schoeps calls Paul's "fundamental misapprehension" concerning the law.[48] It also makes it possible to understand this teaching within the context of the central concern of the Apostle to the Gentiles, namely, the gospel of the righteousness of God now made manifest to Gentiles in Jesus Christ, apart from but in no sense contradictory to the covenant made with Israel and the Torah given to Israel. Paul does not express himself very clearly in this passage, but then, if he had, these verses would not have become the cross of so many interpreters, and there would be no need to suggest still one more possible interpretation.[49]

3

ABRAHAM AND THE RIGHTEOUSNESS OF GOD

A truly Biblical theology would be one which takes the whole Bible with equal seriousness and does not consciously or unconsciously subordinate the first half to the much smaller second half. The obstacles to the recovery of such a Biblical theology are great indeed. The displacement theory, which says that the church has effectively displaced Israel as God's people, goes back to the earliest days of the emerging church and is still the pervasive Christian presupposition for doing theology or Biblical study. Not only does this theory cut off all possibility of theological co-operation between Christians and Jews, but also it introduces an unbridgeable chasm into Scripture itself. Insofar as the so-called New Testament is understood to be the "antithesis" of the so-called Old Testament, then a Biblical theology of continuity is impossible. Now, however, there has arisen the possibility of a renewed listening to the Biblical text on the part of those whose ears have been opened by understanding the Holocaust as a major event *also* in the history of the church and the refounding of the State of Israel *also* as an end to the "fossil" dogma and as an invitation to dialogue with a living Judaism. It is my conviction that the Hebrew Bible can speak with its own voice to the Christian church when the church acknowledges the full legitimacy of Judaism and that when this happens, and only when this happens, does it become possible to understand the New Testament in continuity with the Hebrew Bible and parallel to Judaism rather than in opposition to them.[1]

One of the instances where discontinuity is most clearly evident has to do with the Pauline understanding of Genesis 15:6, in which Abraham functions as a paradigm first for Christian faith and second for justification by that faith. That Paul is thereby deliberately and provocatively contradicting the theology of the synagogue is said by almost all commentators. That he also effectively "desacralizes" and "paganizes" the history of Israel and thus calls into question in the most radical way the canonical status of the document of that history for the church has been asserted most strongly by G. Klein.[2] As Jülicher had said, insofar as Paul teaches a "system which allows for men before Christ no righteousness but only sin and wrath," then indeed he has "himself broken his system" by using Abraham as an example.[3] As Klein put it, "If the possibility of experiencing the righteousness of God has a chronological *terminus ante quem non*, and if this is identical with the historical date of the death of Jesus, then how can the scriptural proof for the righteousness of God be attached to a figure like Abraham, who is a representative of that time in which the righteousness of God could not yet be experienced at all?"[4] If such premises are true, then indeed Paul's own statements about Scripture and the continuity of his gospel with it would have to be seen as inconsistent and needing correction. It may be, however, that it is not Paul but the premises which need correction and that a new look at Genesis 15:6 could aid in that correction.

The matter of continuity in the relationship between the Testaments was not a problem for the church in the past—when it ignored the Biblical understanding of the synagogue and before the rise of the historical critical method—and today the Old Testament is still commonly read through New Testament glasses. Even so great an exegete as G. von Rad was not completely immune from this temptation. It may be true that Gen 15:6 is "a striking and perhaps even revolutionary formulation,"[5] but it is very doubtful whether in the context "everything centres upon the subjective attitude of Abraham to the promise of Yahweh."[6] When faith is defined as a "spiritual self-commitment of the human soul" and the story as "subjective and inward looking, so that the accent is now upon the inward and personal attitude of the worshipper," then it is probably being read through Christian and specifically modern Christian glasses. That Hahn subsequently honours von Rad's reading of the text, saying that "this text approaches the Pauline interpretation to a high degree,"[7] is not particularly surprising. But perhaps there is another way of relating Abraham and Paul.

While an acknowledged or covert "Christological reading of the Old Testament" is customary, what would a "covenantal reading of the New Testament" be like? What would happen if it were assumed that Paul specifically was neither guilty of a "fundamental misapprehension" of the place of Torah in Judaism[8] nor engaged in polemic against Jews when he proclaimed his gospel of the righteousness of God now made manifest to the Gentiles in Jesus Christ? What if Paul did not share the modern Christian "view of Rabbinic religion as one of legalistic works-righteousness?"[9] What if Paul's claims that "his" gospel is already proclaimed in the Old Testament (Gal 3:8; Rom 1:2, etc.) and that he interprets current events through Scripture and not the other way around were taken seriously? To interpret Biblical texts against a major thrust of the entire Christian exegetical tradition is an absolutely impossible task at the beginning. I therefore approach the task in a spirit of playfulness. It is precisely those interpretations which seem possible but most improbable which are most attractive to the playful, and I hope that spirit will be allowed in this experimental run at a most serious question.

To do so, it is necessary to try to read Gen 15:6 not in the light of a Christian concept of justification by faith, but as if encountering it for the first time. I shall for the moment read verses 1 to 6 as a unit, without raising the question of sources. Abraham receives a vision/word from YHWH, promising that his reward will be very great (v 1). The reason for the reward is not stated, and it is doubtful if it should be connected (as the Targumim do) with Abraham's generosity with respect to the spoils of war (14:20-24). The nature of the reward is also not stated, but from the following it is clear that it concerns offspring (cf. earlier, 12:1-3; 13:14-17). Abraham's first reaction is an objection, expressed twice (vv 2, 3), that he has no child as a link to his posterity. This is followed by a double promise from YHWH: that Abraham's own son will be his heir (v 4b) and that his descendants will be as numerous as the stars of heaven (v 5). The story then concludes with "the reaction of Abraham to the promise."[10]

wh'mn byhwh
wyḥšbh lw ṣdqh

This verse could be interpreted completely in terms of Abraham's reaction, that is, also the second clause. Given the phenomenon of Hebrew parallelism, the subject should not be changed unless it is indicated or required. The natural translation would then be:

And he [Abraham] put his trust in YHWH
And he [Abraham] counted it to him [YHWH] righteousness.

From the perspective of Hebrew grammar, there is nothing to make such a translation impossible. Whether or not it is likely depends on a number of other factors. The following considerations would seem to speak against it:

1. No interpreter of the Hebrew Bible has ever understood the sentence in this way.

2. The only other place in the Hebrew Bible where there is a combination of "righteousness" and "to count," Ps 106:31, clearly understands the righteousness to be counted not to God but to Phinehas.

3. Also LXX and Targum Neofiti, which translate the second clause of Gen 15:6 by a passive verb, seem clearly to rule out an understanding which

would attribute the righteousness to God.

4. There is no text earlier than these versions which would indicate that the clause was ever understood as I have suggested.

5. It would be most unusual to find in a text of the Pentateuch an understanding of God's righteousness which otherwise is most characteristic of Deutero-Isaiah and many Psalms.

To deal with the first objection first: there is indeed an interpretation of Gen 15:6 which understands the righteousness to refer to God. Although it is not the majority interpretation in the Jewish tradition, it is nonetheless a significant voice, that of Ramban (Nachmanides, 1194-1270). Although this text is available in almost every university or seminary library in the standard "Rabbinic Bible" (Mikraoth Gedoloth), it is not as well known[11] as it should be, and so I translate it here:

> "And he believed in the LORD and he counted it to him righteousness." Rashi[12] explained that the Holy One, blessed be He, counted to him righteousness and merit because of the faith with which he had believed in him. But I do not understand what that merit is. Why should he not believe in the faithful God [*'lwhy 'mt*], since he is a prophet in himself, "and God is not a man that he should lie?" (Num 23:19). And he who believed to sacrifice his son, his only son, the beloved son, and [endured] the rest of the trials, how should he not believe in the good tidings? What would be correct in my judgment is that it is said [= is to be interpreted as follows:] that he believed in the LORD and thought [*ḥšb*] that in the righteousness of the Holy One, blessed be He, he would give him seed in any case, not in the righteousness of Abram and as his reward, even though he said to him: "Your reward will be very great" (v 1). And from now on he need not fear that sin might prevent [the reward from being given]. And even though at the first prophecy [i.e., Gen 13:14-17] he had thought that it would be conditioned according to the reward for his deeds, yet now he perceived that he [God] had promised him that he need have no fear of sin (v 1) and that he would give him seed (v 5), and he believed that "the word is established by God" (Gen 41:32), "truth he will not depart from it" (Ps 132:11). For it is the righteousness of the LORD and there is no ceasing in it in this matter, as it is written, "By myself have I sworn," says the LORD, "from my mouth has gone forth in righteousness a word, and it shall not return" (Isa 45:23).
>
> Or, it may be said [as an alternative interpretation] that Abram believed that he would have seed as an heir in any case, and the Holy One, blessed be He, counted [*ḥšb*] to him further this promise, that he

promised to him righteousness, for in the righteousness of the LORD it will be done so, as (it is written:) "God thought [*ḥšb*] it for good" (Gen 50:20), and thus "it was counted to him for righteousness" (Ps 106:30), as in the case of Phinehas, in which he [God] counted to him that trust with which he trusted in the LORD when doing this deed "for righteousness for all generations" (Ps 106:31). For forever God will keep his righteousness and steadfast love for him for the sake of it [his trust], in the sense of "I will keep my steadfast love for him forever" (Ps 89:29).

Can the first possibility advocated by Ramban, that the righteousness of Gen 15:6 is God's righteousness in the same sense that this word is used in Isa 45:23 and Deutero-Isaiah in general, be correct? Ramban insists that the promise of God to Abraham in this passage, whether or not it be also designated as his righteousness, should be understood in an unconditional sense. In no sense is Abraham being rewarded for his merit, whether this be understood in terms of faith or anything else. Insofar as Abraham should be understood as a model for the faithful Israelite, it is in terms of the ten trials, and particularly the binding of Isaac, but not Genesis 15.[13] Ramban's initial puzzlement is real. While it may be difficult to continue to trust in a God who commands bad news (Gen 22), there is certainly no merit to believing in a God who promises good news. One reason why the verb *h'myn* appears so often negated in the Hebrew Bible is that faith is the natural and expected thing and it is only the lack of it that calls for comment. Seen in itself, Gen 15:1-6 is clearly about God and his promise and not about Abraham and his faith. The God of the covenant exercises righteousness in relationship to Israel prior to the response of Israel to his covenant grace, whether this response be expressed in terms of Israel's righteousness or Israel's faith.

Ramban, of course, read the text of Gen 15:6 in a kind of timeless dialogue with other Biblical and post-Biblical texts. Modern Westerners seek to read texts within the historical context of their origin, which can be very illuminating as long as that historical context is understood correctly. Attempts to understand Genesis 15 in terms of the classical sources of Pentateuch criticism have not been helpful. Indeed, as was long ago recognized, Genesis 15 cannot be divided between J and E, and once such an attempt has been abandoned, the tendency has been to see the text as late rather than early.[14] Most scholars understand 15:7 to be the beginning of a new unit, perhaps dependent on verses 1-6, and in spite of the obvious difficulties involved, verses 1-6 are read as a single unit. Recently in a very stimulating study, J. van Seters has argued that the unit is dependent on the theology of Deutero-Isaiah.[15] However, this controversial question does not need to be discussed here; it is enough to point out that any objections to my thesis on the basis of dating would be very difficult to substantiate. Van Seters has pointed out the parallelism between many concepts of Deutero-Isaiah and Gen 15:1-6 without, unfortunately, turning his attention to the word "righteousness."

In speaking of the form critical genre to which Gen 15:1-6 might belong, I begin with Kaiser's assertion that it is an oracle of salvation.[16] Kaiser appeals to one of the most fruitful, if most problematic, discoveries in Old Testament form criticism, the "priestly oracle of salvation" identified by Begrich in 1934.[17] Begrich brought together the lament of the individual, found mostly in the Psalter (with a few hints of a pronouncement of salvation), and the oracle of salvation, found mostly in Deutero-Isaiah (with a few hints of a situation of lament). While discussion of and further refinements in the whole concept are still going on and while Gen 15:1-6 contains too many mixed motifs to be a pure form of anything, in general the combination of lament and promise fits so well with Begrich's hypothesis that Kaiser's identification has won wide acceptance. This is not the place to try to give definitive support to it, but there are certain consequences such an identification has for the understanding of Gen 15:6b which, strangely, have never been drawn.

Westermann outlines the structure of Gen 15:1-6 as follows:

1a. Introduction: the word of YHWH comes to Abraham.
1b. Pledge of salvation and prosperity.
2. Reply: statement of grievance.
3. Reply: statement of grievance.
4. God's answer: a. future salvation: a consanguineous heir;
5. b. confirming sign.
6. Conclusion: Abraham believed. . . .[18]

It is really not surprising that verse 6b should be missing completely from the structure, for the current translation of it does not fit at all. There is simply no room in the oracle of salvation for a structure which would look like this: Lament—Promise of Salvation—Reaction of the Lamenter: faith and praise of God—Reaction of God to the Reaction: praise of the lamenter. Westermann can maintain the relationship he sees to the oracle of salvation only by ignoring verse 6b or (a solution which did not occur to him) by translating it as a further expression of the praise of God. In accordance with the postulated form, it would not at all be inappropriate for Abraham to conclude by ascribing righteousness to God.

The form-critical question can be approached from another angle by looking at the correlative of the oracle of salvation, the individual lament. It consists of the following elements: "address, lament, confession of trust or assurance of being heard, petition, vow of praise (or praise of God where the petition has been answered)."[19] In Gen 15:1-6 the address to God has been replaced by an oracle from God, the petition is only implicit in the lament, and two separate promises (an heir, many descendants) have been combined in a brief narrative. Nevertheless, the analogy is clear, and it is quite appropriate for the passage to end with both a "confession of trust" (6a) and a "praise of God" (6b). The elements of praise in psalms of individual lament have frequent references to God's righteousness: typical is Ps 7:17, "I will give to YHWH the thanks due to his righteousness, and I will sing praise to the name of YHWH, the Most High" (cf. also Ps. 5:7-8; 22:30-31; 31:1; 35:28; 36:5-6, 10; 40:11; 51:13-15; 69:27; 71:14-15a, 18b-19, 24; 88:12; 143:1, 11). Once more, in accordance with the postulated form, it would certainly be appropriate for Abraham to ascribe righteousness to God. The major difficulty in this suggestion is that the verb "count" is never otherwise used with God's righteousness as the object. As the verbs that are used vary, however, and "count" is broad enough that it could be used in this sense, I shall so understand it in the absence of arguments to the contrary. This explanation is certainly preferable to the technical sense von Rad posits,[20] when he combines the "liturgy of the gate" (for example, Ezek 18:9) (which never refers to "count") with the pronouncement of a priest in connection with sacrifice (Lev 7:18; 17:4; Num 18:27) (which never refers to "righteousness").[21] Besides, if the word really were being used in a technical sense of a priestly declaration, the Qal would seem to require the preposition *l* or *k* which is lacking in Gen 15:6.[22]

If Gen 15:1-6 is called an oracle of salvation, then it must have something in common with those oracles as they were first identified in Deutero-Isaiah. What is most interesting is not the "fear not" assurance which first suggested the identification, but rather the use of the concept of God's righteousness in the context of oracles of salvation. I shall here examine only those two which also refer to Abraham, 41:8-13 and 51:1-8.[23]

The assurance of salvation in Isa 41:8-13 is expressed in both nominal and verbal form: "Fear not, for I am with you, be not dismayed, for I am your God; I will strengthen you, I will help you, I will uphold you with the right hand of my righteousness" (v 10). This assurance that God's righteousness will intervene on the side of a despondent Israel is an answer to the implied lament "YHWH has cast us off" (v 9, cf. 54:6). In order to reassure an Israel whose very existence as a people has been radically called into question, the introduction is exceptionally long: "But you, Israel, my servant, Jacob, whom I have chosen, the seed of Abraham, my friend; you whom I took from the ends of the earth and called from its farthest corners, saying to you, 'You are my servant, I have chosen you and not cast you off'" (vv 8-9). Here Israel's conviction of its election as God's people is supported by a reference to the call of Abraham, and Israel's return from the exile is paralleled with God's call of Abraham from Haran.[24] The word of salvation is not, however, addressed to Abraham in the past, but the righteousness of God is being exercised now in the present in his reaffirmation of Israel and in the future rescue from enemies (vv 11-12). That Abraham is called God's friend is not in a passive but an active sense ("he who loves me"), and one could ask whether Abraham's past act of love is related to God's present act of righteousness. It is in any case significant that Israel should be reassured both by the proclamation of God's righteousness now and a reference to their descent from Abraham.

The relationship between the righteousness of God as his present saving action for Israel's election in Abraham is even stronger in Isa 51:1-8. Israel, those who "pursue righteousness"[25] and "seek YHWH" (v 1a), are told to look to the rock and quarry, to Abraham and Sarah (v 1b-2a). There they will find the promise of YHWH's righteousness (viz., in Gen 15:6). That YHWH "called" Abraham was that he might continue (imperf.) to "bless"[26] and "multiply" him (v 2b). God's action was not only for the sake of the "one" but also for the many, contemporary Israel, Zion which YHWH is in the process of comforting (v 3). By reference back to Abraham, Israel is urged to take comfort in and rely on the righteousness of God which is now being exercised. Now are being fulfilled the promises contained in Abraham's call and blessing and multiplication, which really refer to Israel's election and blessing and peoplehood. Here (v 1) and in the concluding lines of the poem (vv 7-8) the blessing of Abraham now being fulfilled for Israel is called very impressively the "righteousness of God."

It is significant that the middle strophe (vv 4-6)[27] refers to the Gentiles in this connection.

Listen to me you peoples; you nations, hear me.
For Torah goes out from me; and my justice as a light to the peoples.
I bring near in an instant my righteousness; and my salvation has gone forth.
The islands wait for me; and for my arm they hope.
Lift up to the heavens your eyes; and look at the earth beneath.
For the heavens like smoke vanish; the earth like a garment wears out.
But my salvation will be forever; and my righteousness will not be shaken.

It is not necessary to see here a conscious reference to Gen 15:5 as North does[28] in order to be impressed by the connection of salvation for the Gentiles with the figure of Abraham. That salvation for both Israel and the nations is called the "righteousness of God" may be an interpretation of Gen 15:6 (or Gen 15:6 may draw on this passage), but in any case it provides an association for the later tradition of the understanding of Abraham.

Two late additions[29] to the Pentateuch are of interest because they refer to a promise of God to Abraham concerning Gentiles and are probably dependent on the theology of Isaiah 51. If they also reflect an understanding of Gen 15:6, it is in terms of the concept of the "merits of the fathers," a different understanding which will be discussed below. "By myself I have sworn, says YHWH, *because* you have done this and have not withheld your son, your only son, I will indeed bless you and I will multiply your seed . . . and by your seed shall all the nations of the earth bless themselves, *because* you have obeyed my voice" (Gen 22:16-18). "To you and to your seed I give all these lands, and I will fulfill the oath which I swore to Abraham your father. I will multiply your seed . . . and by your seed all the nations of the earth shall bless themselves, because Abraham obeyed my voice and kept my charge, my commandments, my statutes, and my laws" (Gen 26:3-5). One very interesting text somewhat earlier than Deutero-Isaiah may connect the blessing of the nations with the righteousness of God in connection with the faithfulness not of Abraham but of Israel: "If you swear, 'As YHWH lives, in truth, in justice, and in righteousness,' then nations shall bless themselves in him, and in him shall they glory" (Jer 4:2).[30]

"It is in the period of the exile that we find a radical new importance attached to the figure of Abraham, and to the tradition of the covenant made with him by God."[31] Indeed, Abraham is never mentioned in the pre-exilic prophets, and when he first appears, Ezekiel (30:24) rejects a saying of the people which anticipates Deutero-Isaiah: "Abraham was only one man, yet he got possession of the land; but we are many; the land is surely given us to possess." It is when Israel no longer has its land that the promises to the patriarchs are remembered, and especially when Israel is in danger of dying out as a people that it remembers the number of descendants promised to Abraham. But especially it is the blessing of Abraham that is remembered. To recall Abraham is to recall God's promises of faithfulness and is a way of appealing to the grace of God. Typical is Mic 7:18-20, "Who is a God like thee, pardoning iniquity and passing over transgression? . . . Thou wilt show faithfulness to Jacob and steadfast love to Abraham, as thou hast sworn to our fathers from the days of old." Israel's interest was never in the historical faith or righteousness of Abraham as a model to be imitated but in the righteousness of the God of Abraham who could be appealed to in the present.

Finally, we come to the objection that Gen 15:6 cannot mean that Abraham ascribed righteousness to God because no later text so understands it. The long prayer of confession in Neh 9:6-37 is late enough to have been influenced by Genesis 15 and close enough to its wording as to make such influence probable.[32] The relevant verses are 7 and 8: "Thou art YHWH, the God who didst choose Abram and brought him from Ur of the Chaldeans[33] and gave to him the name Abraham; and thou didst find his heart faithful before thee[34] and didst make with him a covenant[35] to give the land[36] of the Canaanite, the Hittite, the Amorite, the Perizzite, the Jebusite and the Girgashite[37] to his seed;[38] and thou hast fulfilled thy promise, for thou art righteous."[39] Here is a much more significant "thou art righteous" than the one von Rad posits, and it is found in a text with dependence on, or at the very least clear affinity to, Gen 15:6.

Even if I am correct in my understanding of the original meaning of Gen 15:6, the later transmission of the verb "it was counted" in the passive still has to be accounted for.[40] Here I turn to Ramban's alternative explanation for help. Even if God rather than Abraham is the subject of the verb "to count," and he must be the actual subject when the verb is passive, this still does not necessarily give the verb a declarative sense: "thou art righteous, Abraham." Ramban suggests that the righteousness is still God's and that now the sentence is a promise that God will exercise his righteousness in the future for Abraham's benefit. As soon as the story is understood as having happened in the remote past, then the reversal of subject makes good sense. It is not so much that God acted righteously with respect to the historical Abraham as that he promised to continue to act righteously with Abraham's descendants.

Ramban refers to the one other verse where "count" and "righteousness" occur together, Ps 106:30f:

> Then Phinehas stood up and interposed,
> and the plague was stayed.
> And that has been counted to him for [*l*] righteousness
> from generation to generation forever.

It is possible that Phinehas is being praised for his righteous deed and that his reputation for righteousness will be perpetual, but this is not necessarily the case. It is more likely that the reference in verse 31b is to the "covenant of peace; and it shall be to him *and to his descendants* after him the covenant of a perpetual priesthood, because he was jealous for his God" (Num 25:12f; cf. Sir 45:23f). Ramban therefore is not wide of the mark when he interprets the statement as God's promise to keep his steadfast love to Phinehas's descendants. In any case, it is presumably the wording of Ps 106:31a which has influenced the rendering of Gen 15:6b in the LXX. The addition of a preposition (*eis*) in the LXX is just as significant as the change to a passive verb, "was counted." It is now much easier to understand the verb in the commercial sense, which it can have in both Hebrew and Greek.[41] It can almost mean "to deposit in someone's account," although when that account would be drawn upon depends on the context and is not inherent in the word itself.[42] The LXX would then understand Gen 15:6 in terms of the concept that was later to be called the "merit of the fathers."[43] It should not be necessary to add that this has nothing to do with a kind of works righteousness, as many Christian interpreters assume.[44] The emphasis is not on the "merit" that Abraham had but on the free grace of God, the righteousness of God, that is given to the children of Abraham.[45]

Abraham was certainly considered in early Judaism to be the very model of righteousness, and it would be very natural to understand Gen 15:6b, particularly in Greek, as the occasion on which God applied this predicate to him. One of Philo's paraphrases makes this explicit: "Abraham believed God and he was held to be righteous."[46] Nevertheless, if the expression originally referred to the righteousness of God, one would also expect to find this understanding reflected, even in Greek texts. The sense would then be not that God says, "Good for you Abraham; I call that righteousness," but rather: "Good for you Abraham; you have some righteousness coming to you, which I shall exercise on a later occasion." Such an understanding can indeed be found.

Perhaps the clearest example is found in *Mekilta*,[47] in the context of a series of answers to the question: Why did God divide the sea for Israel? Abtalyon has God say, "'The faith with which they believed in Me is deserving that I should divide the sea for them,' for it is said 'And the people believed' (Exod 4:31)." Shemaiah, on the other hand, has God say, " 'The faith with which their father Abraham believed in Me is deserving that I should divide the sea for them,' for it is said, 'And he believed in the LORD' (Gen 15:6),"and (continuing with Marmorstein's paraphrase),[48] "he counted it unto him [i.e. at the sea] for [doing] charity [with his children]." If Marmorstein is correct, and it is hard to follow Shemaiah's logic otherwise, the righteousness is God's, and it is exercised not toward Abraham as such but toward Israel at the Exodus.

James shows a similar understanding: "Abraham our father was justified on the basis of works [presumably his acts of hospitality, Genesis 18][49] when he offered his son Isaac upon the altar" (2:21). Thereby "the scripture *was fulfilled* which says, 'Abraham believed God, and it was counted to him unto righteousness' " (v 23). Righteousness was promised to Abraham when he believed (Genesis 15) and was "counted to" Abraham when God spared Isaac (Genesis 22). To be sure, Abraham deserved that righteousness, according to James, on the basis of his faith and his works, but it is still the righteousness of God which is promised on one occasion and given "as a reward" on a later occasion. The understanding in 1 Macc 2:52 is not so clear: "Was not Abraham found faithful when tested, and righteousness was counted to him?"[50] As often (cf. Sir 44:20; *Jub.* 17:18; 19:8; *Aboth* 5:3; et al.) it is the Akeda, the sacrifice of Isaac, which is the supreme example of Abraham's faithfulness and, it may be, of his righteousness. But is is also possible that the reference is to Abraham's faithfulness being rewarded by God's righteousness in preserving Isaac. There is another interesting paraphrase in Philo on this point. After a long exposition of Gen 15:6a, the faith of Abraham in which Philo is mostly interested (*Abr* 262-272), he comes to verse 6b as follows: "God marvelling at Abraham's faith in Him repaid him with faithfulness [*pistis*] by confirming with an oath the gifts which He had promised" (273). Gen 15:6 is probably reflected in Heb 11:11, "by *faith*, (even though Sarah was barren), he [Abraham] received strength for procreation, even though he was past the age, since he considered him *faithful* who had promised."[51] Luke-Acts views the figure of Abraham in terms of promise, for Israel (Luke 1:55, 73; 13:16; 19:9; et al.) and the Gentiles (Acts 3:25). But the only clear reference to Genesis 15 is to verses 13-14 (Acts 7:6f), with no mention of Abraham's faith.[52]

One final reference to Abraham, and possibly to the theme of God's righteousness, will be cited because of the reference to the blessing of the nations.

> Abraham was the great father of a multitude of nations
> And no one has been found like him in glory.
> He kept the law of the Most High
> And was taken into covenant with him.
> He established the covenant in his flesh,
> And when he was tested he was found *faithful*.
> Therefore the Lord has assured him by an oath
> That the nations would be blessed through his posterity,
> That he would multiply him like the dust of the earth,
> And exalt his posterity like the stars,
> And cause them to inherit from sea to sea
> And from the River to the ends of the earth.
>
> (Sir 44:19-21)

If I have been correct in the exposition above, Abraham received the promise of the righteousness of God on one occasion, but it was "paid out" to him, 1. on the spot (Philo, perhaps 1 Macc 2:52), 2. at the birth of Isaac (Philo, Heb 11:11), 3. when God spared Isaac (James 2:23, perhaps 1 Macc 2:52), 4. at the crossing of the sea (*Mekilta*), 5. whenever God was gracious to Israel (Isa 41, Neh 9; cf. Exod 32:11-13, 2 Kgs 13:23, Deut passim, Ps 105:42, Lk-Acts, etc.), or 6. in the blessing of the nations (Isa 51, Sir 44). I shall examine how it is with Paul.

The question which must now be raised is whether in Paul there is a radically different conception of the importance of Abraham and the significance of Gen 15:6. Most interpreters think so and believe that Paul understands the passage to refer to Abraham being justified by faith apart from works as a model for Christians to do the same. It is assumed that Paul operates with a sharp distinction between believing and doing, between having faith in Christ and doing the works of the law, between faith and law as the way to salvation. Since the Abraham example is not a particularly good one to make this particular point (the most famous example of the one who does God's will being the faithful Abraham, the friend of God), it is further assumed that discussion of this figure has been forced on Paul by his opponents and that therefore he is driven to such a contrived reinterpretation. Apart from all the other difficulties such an assumption causes (such as a complete misinterpretation of early Judaism), it is not often noted how it makes Paul into the supreme legalist. The problem is that in Gen 15:6 the believing comes before the counting of righteousness, and with the emphasis on the faith of Abraham (and the Christian), the second half of the statement becomes only God's reaction to the first half. Only great subtleties of interpretation make it possible to escape the idea that "justification is reckoned as the reward given by God to man's achievement of faith," as Deissmann pointed out.[53] Many interpreters seem to be saying: faith is well pleasing to God; if then one follows the good example of Abraham (difficult enough to do!) and believes, then the believer will be rewarded like Abraham by being called or made righteous and will thereby be justified. Most interpreters are a bit more subtle than Mussner but mean the same: "The promised blessing is not simply freely given by God according to Paul, but the condition which must be fulfilled by the Gentiles in order to receive it is faith."[54] Could it be that Paul has been misunderstood on this point and that in fact he interprets the figure of Abraham not against but with the traditional understanding?[55]

Paul's major theological concern I understand to be not the justification of individuals by their faith but the justification of the legitimacy of his apostleship to and gospel for the Gentiles. He describes his commissioning as a revelation of Christ "in order that I might preach him among the Gentiles" (Gal 1:16), he calls himself apostle to the Gentiles (Rom 1:5; 11:13; 15:16, 18), speaks of "my gospel" (Gal 1:8,11; Rom 2:14; 16:25; 2 Cor 4:3; 11:4; 1 Thes. 1:5), "the gospel which I preach among the Gentiles" (Gal. 1:10; 2:2), "the gospel to the uncircumcised" (Gal 2:7). The content of that gospel is described as the righteousness of God, that is, "the power of God for salvation, for the Jew of course but also for the Greek" (Rom 1:16), or concretely, "that God would justify the Gentiles from faithfulness" (Gal 3:8). If Paul was concerned to find his gospel of salvation for Gentiles prefigured in the Torah, there is no other figure to whom he could turn but

Abraham. If in addition he wanted to find the righteousness of God[56] applied to the salvation of Gentiles, there is no other passage in the Torah to which he could have turned but Gen 15:6.[57]

Paul draws an astonishing conclusion from his citation of Gen 15:6 in Gal 3:7: "Know then: those *ek pisteōs*, these are the children of Abraham."[58] Those who think that Paul is most interested in the statement that "Abraham believed" as a model to be followed by Galatian believers must speak here of an "unexpressed premise"[59] and cannot understand why Paul does not clearly conclude that "Christians, like Abraham, are justified by believing and not by works of law." In what follows, however, Paul speaks not of Abraham's faith (except perhaps in v 9) but of the seed of Abraham (vv 16, 19, 29), the heirs of Abraham (vv 18, 29), the blessing of Abraham (vv 8, 14), the grace of God to Abraham (v 18), and the promise to Abraham (vv 14, 16, 17, 18, 19, 21, 22, 29). Paul's interest is in God's activity in "counting to Abraham for righteousness," and he hears in this passage "the gospel proclaimed beforehand to Abraham," the gospel which says that "God would justify the Gentiles from faithfulness" (v 8). All of this is possible only if Paul writes not against but in conformity with the exegetical tradition I have sketched, particularly as it is mediated through Isaiah 51 and ben Sira 44.

It is perhaps a bit much in an argument for understanding Gen 15:6 as referring to the righteousness of God also to assume that Rom 3:3 "the faithfulness of God" is determinative for many of the uses of the word *pistis* in Paul.[60] That the phrase *pistis Christou* (Rom 3:22, 26; Gal 2:16, 20; 3:22, 26; Phil 3:9; Eph 3:12) is to be translated "the faithfulness of Christ" has been argued by many.[61] G. M. Taylor states further that other instances of *pistis* in Galatians 2-3 are also to be understood as referring to the reliability of Christ as a kind of trustee, the *fidei commissum* of Roman law.[62] The phrase "those *ek pisteōs*" of Gal 3:7 and 9 has its closest parallel in Rom 3:26, which says that God justifies "'the one *ek pisteōs* of Jesus.'"[63] In any case, the word *pistis* here seems to interpret the "righteousness" of verse 6 rather than the "Abraham believed," since the whole argumentation (cf. vv 6, 9, 14, 18, 29 for a skeleton) has to do not with the faith of Abraham but the children of Abraham.

The use of Genesis 15 continues throughout the chapter. The human legal institution (v 15) to which Paul draws an analogy may be the Roman *fidei commissum* or more likely the Jewish *mattanat bari*,[64] but in any case something is promised to Abraham in trust. This trust lies dormant until the coming of the seed (v 19) or the *pistis* (vv 23, 25) or concretely Christ (vv 16, 22, 24), when it is "spent" by the seed for the benefit of the Gentile Christians. *When* was this trust given? Paul says that it was 430 years before the giving of the Torah, that is, according to Rabbinic chronology,[65] at the time of the covenant between the pieces, Genesis 15. *What* was given at that time? Paul frequently uses the word "promise," which never appears in the Abraham stories in the LXX, and the word "blessing," which does not occur in Genesis 15. Genesis 15 does not speak explicitly of God's grace as does Gal 3:18. The phrase "to your seed" appears in 15:18 and elsewhere (12:7; 13:15, 18; 17, 8; 24:7; 26:3; 28:4, 13; 35:12) only in connection with the promise of the land.[66] The promise that Abraham's seed will be as numerous as the stars (Gen 15:5) could hardly be directly appealed to in a context where Paul emphasizes the singularity of the seed, and the same would be true of the heir (Gen 15:4; Gal 3:29). There remains as a locus for what Paul calls promise and blessing and grace in Genesis 15 only the passage he explicitly quotes about the righteousness of God being counted to Abraham.

The contrast throughout this chapter is not between faith and works but between the law and promise, whereby the word "law" is used in at least two senses.[67] On the one hand it refers (in 3:2, 5, 10, 11, 13, 23, 24; 4:4, 5) to law without covenant, the curse from which the Gentiles have been redeemed, the law administered over creation by the "gods who essentially are not [gods]" (4:8), the "elements of the world" (4:3, 9), the guardians and administrators (4:2), the custodians (3:25), the angels of the nations (3:19). On the other hand, the word "law" refers (in 3:17, 18, 21) to the covenant law given to Israel on Sinai, which is not "against the promises" (3:21) but also is not *for* this specific promise to Abraham concerning Gentiles being blessed. It is in this sense that the law cannot make alive and that "righteousness" does not come through law (v 21). Righteousness does not come through law because it is equivalent to "the promise from the faithfulness of Jesus Christ" (v 22). Also Hab 2:4 must be understood in this way.[68] The law is not "from faithfulness" (v 12) because in the law "no one is justified before God" (v 11, citing Ps 143:2). Justification comes not from doing or from believing but from "the faithfulness" or "the righteousness" of God, as in Ps 143:1.[69] That from which the righteous will live is then, according to Paul, the faithfulness of God of Hab 2:4, which is an interpretation of the righteousness of God of Gen 15:6.

A major concern of Paul's theology and of Galatians 3 in particular is the justification of the inclusion of Gentiles in the people of God apart from the covenant and law of Sinai. If the reality of this inclusion is found in Jesus Christ and the gift of the Spirit, the primary scriptural basis for Paul's argument is Gen 15:6 understood through a long tradition. Paul's gospel, "that God would justify the Gentiles from faithfulness," is found in God's promise to Abraham that "in you all the Gentiles will be blessed." "*Therefore*," Paul concludes, "those *ek pisteōs* will be blessed" (v 9). "Those from faithfulness" are identified with the Gentiles of the promise.

The phrase has the same meaning in Paul's earlier conclusion (v 7) directly from Gen 15:6: "know then, those *ek pisteōs*, these are children of Abraham." Paul hears in this verse not a statement about the righteousness of Abraham's faith but a promise for the future, and a promise which has specifically to do with Gentiles. Christ has redeemed us "in order that for the Gentiles the blessing of Abraham might become a reality in Jesus Christ, in order that we might receive the promise, i.e. the Spirit, through *the* faithfulness" (v 13). The interpretation in Galatians is then something like Ramban's first explanation.

The understanding of Gen 15:6 in Romans 4 is similar but much richer. That Paul understands the passage to speak of God's grace toward Christians and not just toward Abraham is stated explicitly at the end of the discussion: "These words 'it was counted to him' were not written for his sake only but also for our sake, to whom it is to be 'counted'" (vv 23-24a).[70] The preceding context also argues strongly in favour of an understanding of the righteousness being God's righteousness now being exercised toward Gentiles.[71] Romans as a whole can be understood to centre on the theme of the faithfulness (*pistis*, *dikaiosynē*, *alētheia*, Rom 3:3, 5, 7) of God, the firmness of which toward Israel is in no sense denied (3:3; 11:1, 29, et al.) when Paul argues for the inclusion now also of Gentiles on the basis of God's faithfulness to his promises concerning them. At the end of the letter we read that "Christ became a servant to the circumcised for the sake of God's truthfulness, in order to confirm the promises given to the fathers and the Gentiles might glorify God for his mercy" (15:8-9a).

That Rom 3:21-31 concerns the inclusion of Gentiles has been argued forcefully by Howard.[72] "Now, however, apart from the Torah (but not against it, cf. Gal 3:21), that righteousness of God has been made manifest to which the Torah and the prophets have testified, the righteousness of God through the faithfulness of Jesus Christ" (3:21f). As in Gal 3:20 one argument for the inclusion of Gentiles is the unity of God;[73] God acts because he is God "also of Gentiles, since 'God is one,' who will justify the circumcised out of [his] faithfulness and the uncircumcised through the [same] faithfulness" (3:29-30). Paul leads into the discussion of Abraham with the assertion that he does not "render the law obsolete through this faithfulness"; on the contrary, he says that he "confirms the law" (3:31). In what way is Paul's gospel a confirmation of the law? Where does the law (the Torah) "testify to the righteousness of God?" It can only be in Gen 15:6!

Romans 4 is not about Christian faith, but differing from Galatians, it does speak of Abraham's faithfulness. Attempts to understand Abraham as a hero of faith to be imitated by Christian believers cause insuperable difficulties, which the commentators gloss over. Thus, one cannot really say that the promise to Abraham came *through* the righteousness of his faith (v

13) or that the inheritance *depends* on faith (v 16). *Pistis* is parallel to "promise" in verse 14 and to "grace" in verse 16 and must refer to God's faithfulness to his promise, as does the phrase "[God's] righteousness, i.e. faithfulness" in verse 13. Abraham's *pistis* appears in a formula "the one *ek pisteōs* of Abraham," which reminds us of "the one *ek pisteōs* of Jesus" in 3:26 and "those *ek pisteōs*" in Gal 3:7 and 9. The chapter is not about faith but about grace, expressed in the constantly recurring phrase that God "counts righteousness" to Abraham's heirs (vv 5, 6, 9, 11, 23, 24) and that "according to grace" (v 4).

The content of the promise, that which Abraham believed, is that "he should be heir of the world" (v 13), again in the tradition of ben Sira 44. The promise of Gen 15:5, "thus will your seed be," is interpreted in the light of 17:5, "I have made you the father of many Gentiles." God is faithful, who gives life to the Gentiles who are dead in their sins and calls into being the church which did not exist (v 17).[74] Abraham's faith must not be interpreted as an existential abstraction,[75] as a quality; it has a specific content, the future justification of Gentiles, and it seems that it has this for Paul also in the statement of Gen 15:6.

Abraham is understood in Romans 4 not primarily as the *type* of the later believers but as the *father* of later believers, Jews and Gentiles. Differing from Galatians, Romans does not present Christ as the fulfilment of the promise for Gentiles until the very end of the chapter. Paul is much more careful here than in Galatians not to negate Abraham's fatherhood for Israel when he emphasizes that it is now also for Gentiles. The promise is sure for *all* the seed, for those of the Torah and also for those of the *pistis* of Abraham (v 16). Abraham was a Gentile when he believed the promise concerning Gentiles, but he also later received "the sign of the circumcision covenant (*berith mila*)" (Gen 17:11) in order that he might become the father of all who believe as uncircumcised and also the father of the circumcised (vv 11-12). Paul's major concern of course is to demonstrate Abraham's paternity for Gentiles, and it is only to this group that *the* righteousness (viz., of Gen 15:6) is explicitly counted.

As in Galatians 3 so also here Paul hears a promise concerning Gentiles specifically in Gen 15:6. That God is the one "who justifies the godless" (Rom 4:5, cf. 5:6) is best interpreted in the light of Gal 3:8, "Scripture, knowing beforehand that God would justify the Gentiles." The "one who does not work" is perhaps a contemporary Gentile,[76] and one may ask whose faith is counted as righteousness, his own or Abraham's. The counting of righteousness is called a blessing (cf. the similar word Gal 3:8, 9, 14) in the light of Ps 32:1f, which also refers to a "counting." The non-counting of sins, in a psalm which does not mention works but also does not mention faith, is an act of pure grace, which interprets the counting of Gen 15:6. Psalm 32, however, was understood to refer only to Israel, the circumcised blessed under the covenant and its cult. Paul then explicitly says it refers to a blessing for the uncircumcised also and cites Gen 15:6 as the reason. That the promise was given to Abraham while he was a Gentile is a secondary argument, not found in Galatians 3. There and here it is in the "counting for righteousness" as such that Paul hears the promise that God would justify the Gentiles.

We have noted that Abraham's act of believing is emphasized more in Romans than in Galatians, and indeed it can even be spoken of as a kind of merit. That is the logic of the "therefore" after the impressive description of Abraham's faith in verses 19-21: "therefore 'it was counted to him unto righteousness'" (v 22). This emphasis recalls Ramban's attempt to explain God's expression of grace in Gen 15:6 alongside the statement of Abraham's great reward in 15:1. The word in the LXX is *misthos*, the same word that Paul says is "counted as a due to the one who works" (v 4). In that sense Abraham was justified on the basis of works and does have grounds for boasting (v 2). But . . . Paul is not interested in Abraham's righteousness or in Abraham's reward but in God's grace toward those of whom Abraham is father, and then Abraham cannot boast. What Abraham "merited" for later generations is pure grace, as in the Rabbinic concept of the merits of the fathers. Paul certainly shared the concept of the merit of the fathers where Israel was concerned ("as regards election they are beloved for the sake of their forefathers" Rom 11:28); why should he not also use this same concept as a basis for speaking of God's gracious action toward the Gentiles? The interpretation in Romans is then something like Ramban's second explanation.[77]

Such a brief survey of the tradition of the understanding of Gen 15:6 down through the time of Paul can do little more than raise the question of the possibility of a fresh interpretation. What I have said about Paul's understanding of the significance of Abraham in Galatians 3 and Romans 4 in particular runs against the grain of the entire Christian exegetical tradition. The search for a new paradigm of understanding was occasioned by what must surely become for modern times a fundamental hermeneutical principle. Every interpretation of Paul that is based on a misrepresentation of Judaism is to be rigorously excluded. Why should "opponents," against whom Paul's words must be understood as "polemic," be assumed where none are indicated? (Paul has enough real problems in making himself understood to his churches without our conjuring up a fabricated *Spätjudentum* to be his enemy.) If it is possible to interpret Paul in continuity with the tradition before him, why not do so? (Paul strives hard enough to understand the relationship of the new revelation of the righteousness of God to the revelation of that righteousness in Scripture without unnecessary obstacles being put in his way.) Why should the understanding of Scripture of later Judaism not be used to cast light on Paul's interpretation rather than as the negative foil which Paul *ex hypothesi* must be opposed to? (Paul might well feel more at home in the world of a Ramban than that of an Augustine or a Luther.) We might then look forward to the day when everyone, Jews and Christians, Paul and Ramban, can join together with the faithful Abraham in praising God for his righteousness.

4

PAUL AND THE LAW IN GALATIANS 2 AND 3

If it is true that there is a long history of anti-Judaism in the Christian church, then the exegetical traditions of the church cannot remain unaffected. What is at issue is not the positive gospel of the Apostle to the Gentiles but the negative shadow side of a Pauline "theology of Judaism." Sandmel described Paul's situation as follows: "The practical issue was Should new converts be compelled to observe the Jewish practices? The theoretical, theological issue was What was the 'true nature' of Judaism, and in the light of that true nature, what place, if any, was there for Jewish observances *in Judaism*?"[1] Instead of raising the whole question of whether or not such a "theology of Judaism" is Pauline or Marcionite and doing so in a discussion of Paul's most polemical letter, I will attempt in experimental fashion to identify the issues which would have to be raised if many of the traditional assumptions concerning Paul's "theology of Judaism" in Galatians 2-3 were to be challenged.

"Has God rejected his people?" (Rom 11:1). "Do we then render obsolete the law through this *pistis*?" (Rom 3:31). Does Paul "teach all the Jews who are among the Gentiles to forsake Moses, telling them not to circumcise their children or observe the customs?" (Acts 21:21). I would understand an affirmative answer to these or similar questions to represent theological anti-Judaism. And yet Barclay only sums up a commonplace of our exegetical tradition in titling his exposition of Gal 2:14-17 "The End of the Law."[2] Also the first question is decisively answered in the affirmative in an influential essay by Klein.[3] His thesis is also a provocative illustration of how this line of interpretation calls into question in the most radical way not only

Judaism but also the scriptural status of what Christians call the Old Testament and the faithfulness of God to his promises and God's righteousness *ante Christum natum*. If the theological implications of the traditional view are immense, the major exegetical problem is that one must assume Paul was guilty of a "fundamental misapprehension"[4] in his teaching about the law. But what would happen to interpretation if one were to start from the premise that Paul knew at least as much about "covenantal nomism" and Jewish "soteriology" as does E. P. Sanders?[5] It would then be impossible to say, as does the latest commentary on Galatians,[6] that Gal 2:16 is a "denial of the orthodox Jewish (Pharisaic) doctrine of salvation." In any case, the premise that Paul did understand the Judaism of his contemporaries will be assumed in the present exegetical experimentation.

The passage on which I will put the premise to the test is one of the most difficult in the Pauline corpus, Galatians 3. Like many other interpreters,[7] I find it impossible to consider Galatians 3 except in the context of 2:15-21 (just as it is impossible to understand Romans 4 except in the context of 3:21-31). Since translations are to a large extent the distillation of longstanding exegetical trends, and since it is precisely these traditions which are being called into question, I begin with an alternative translation of Gal 2:15-21. Some vital issues are therefore discussed only in the notes to the translation. An alternative translation also immediately presupposes an exegesis of all other passages where the word or concept appears. But a beginning has to be made somewhere, and this translation has been made with the knowledge of other passages and the belief that the translation can be consistently justified. Finally, in the light of the initial compact "statement of theses" in Galatians 2, I shall look briefly at some aspects of Paul's discussion of the law in Galatians 3.[8]

> (15) We who are Jews by birth and not sinners from the Gentiles, (16) knowing [therefore][A] that a [Gentile][B] human being is not justified from works of law, but [rather][C] through the faithfulness of Christ Jesus,[D] we too became believers[E] in Christ Jesus, in order that we might be justified from the faithfulness of Christ[D] and not from works of law, because [as it is written:][F] by works of law "all" flesh "is not justified" (Ps 143:2). (17) But, since[G] seeking to be justified in Christ we ourselves too have been found to be [Gentile] sinners,[H] is consequently[I] Christ in the service of sin? Of course not! For[J] since[G] I again build up (18) that which I tore down, I commend myself openly as an "apostate."[K] (19) For[J] through the law I have died to the law, in order that I might live to God. I have been co-crucified with Christ. (20) I live yet [really] no longer I, but [rather] Christ lives in me. What I now live in the flesh, I live in the faithfulness of the son of God,[D] who loved

me and delivered himself for me. (21) I do not set at nought the grace of God; for since[G] through law is [the] righteousness [of God],[L] consequently[I] Christ has died as a free gift.[M]

NOTES ON THE TRANSLATION

A. Omit *de* with p^{46} and Nestle-Aland,[26] or in any case do not translate "but," since the implied contrast between "being Jews" and "knowing" exists only in the mind of the modern interpreter. *Eidotes hoti* "is frequently used to introduce a well known fact that is generally accepted," BAG^2, 556, 1.e.

B. I believe that it can be shown in general that Paul uses Adam or *anthrōpos* to discuss the situation of specifically non-Jewish humanity. In any case, this meaning is suggested here by the contrast found in the *kai hēmeis* and *kai autoi* of verses 16 and 17.

C. *Ean mē* is an ellipsis, for the conjunction should properly introduce a subjunctive verb (BAG^2, 211, 3.b.): if (he or she is) not (justified) through. . . . It is not here exceptive, cf. Burton, *Galatians*, 121.

D. The correctness of this translation, reintroduced in modern times by J. Haussleiter (*Der Glaube Jesu Christi und der christliche Glaube* [Leipzig, 1891]) and advocated most forcefully by K. Barth in his *Romerbrief*, cannot be substantiated here. See E. R. Goodenough, "Paul and the Hellenization of Christianity," *Religions in Antiquity* (ed. J. Neusner; Leiden: Brill, 1967) 35-80; G. M. Taylor, "The Function of *PISTIS CHRISTOU* in Galatians," *JBL* 85 (1966) 58-76; M. Barth, "The Kerygma of Galatians," *Int* 21 (1967) 131-46; G. Howard, "On the Faith of Christ," *HTR* 60 (1967) 459-84; "The 'Faith of Christ,'" *ExpT* 85 (1974) 212-15; J. J. O'Rourke, "Pistis in Romans," *CBQ* 34 (1973) 188-94; H. Ljungman, *Pistis* (Lund: Gleerup, 1964) 38-40.

E. The aorist denotes a specific action in past time as distinguished from the constant "knowing."

F. For *hoti* as an indication of a quotation, cf. 3:11; Rom. 3:20 (*dioti*), etc., and J. Bonsirven, *Exégèse rabbinique et exégèse paulinienne* (Paris: Beauchesne, 1938) 343. That Paul does not use the LXX's *pas zōn* is probably because he uses *zaō* in a theological sense in verse 19-20.

G. There are three (four counting 2:14) conditional sentences in this section, all with *ei* + indicative, *realis* (BDF 372). Paul can write unreal periods (BDF 360, but there they are called "remarkably scarce") as in Gal 1:10; 3:21; 4:15, but then the protasis should be an augmented indicative, and the apodosis should contain *an*. Paul uses the *realis* in Gal. 3:29; 4:7; 5:15; 6:3, although the protases of the *realis* in 3:18; 5:11 clearly represent an unreal case. I will assume here the truth of the protasis unless there should appear to be strong reasons to the contrary, and since the sense "is often closely bordering on casual 'since'" (BDF 372:1), I shall for the moment somewhat provocatively translate *ei* as "since."

H. That the word *hamartōloi* is used here in the sense of Gentiles, those not under the covenant, is shown by the clear usage in verse 15. The word is rare in Paul and can in every case be understood to refer to the situation of Gentiles (Rom 3:7; 5:8, 19; 7:13). Cf. in the NT also Mark 14:41 par; Luke 6:32-33 (par Matt *ethnikoi*); 24:7; and for earlier usage *Pss. Sol.* 2:1; 17 passim; *Jub.* 23:23f; 4 Ezra 4:23; 1 Macc 1:34; Tob 13:6; etc. For the sense, cf. Rom 1:18-32; Eph 2:1-3; 4:17-19.

I. Reading in both cases *ara* with an acute accent. That a question can follow this particle in verse 17 is stated by BDF, 440:2.

J. The *gar* here and in verse 19 is to be given its normal force, in spite of *RSV* and Lambrecht, "Line of Thought," 491-93.

K. It is very misleading to translate *parabainō*, *parabasis*, *parabatēs* as transgress, transgression, transgressor, insofar as these imply the inadvertent or regretted breaking of a commandment. Both Judaism and Christianity (though very seldom in Paul) can speak of the forgiveness of sins, atonement following repentance, but *parabasis* is much more serious. Contrary to what is said by many commentators, neither in Galatians 2 nor elsewhere is *parabatēs* simply equivalent to *hamartōlos*. The LXX speaks frequently of *parabainein tēn diathēkēn*. (Josh 7:11, 15; 23:16; 2 Kgs 18:12; Ezek 16:59, etc; cf. *As. Mos.* 2:7), and the concept means not so much law breaker as covenant breaker. In Rabbinic terminology it is equivalent to "casting off the yoke" or "denying the covenant," a conscious and deliberate denial of the right of God to give commandments and thus a self exclusion from the covenant. Even if true, it is very misleading to say, as does J. Schneider, *TDNT* 5: 741, 739, "In the NT the *parabatēs* is one who transgresses a specific divine commandment" and "Transgression is sin only where there is disregard for the *entolē* of God." It is not only the presence or absence of law (Rom 4:15) but the intention and effect which are important (Rom 5!). The church fathers who used this word when a technical concept of apostasy developed were therefore correct, and even if it involves a certain anachronism, this translation will be used here.

L. A full discussion of this important concept cannot be provided here. Fundamental to the understanding presupposed is the starting point in the usage especially of 2 Isaiah and the Psalms, as advocated by H. Cremer, *Die paulinische Rechtfertigungslehre im Zusammenhang ihrer geschichtlichen Voraussetzungen* (Gütersloh: Bertelsmann, 1900). This understanding has been carried forward by A. Schlatter's commentary on Romans, *Gottes Gerechtigkeit* (Stuttgart: Calwer, 1935) and (with modifications) E. Käsemann, "Gottesgerechtigkeit bei Paulus," *ZThK* 58 (1961) 367-78, and others. I would understand the phrase "righteousness of God," then, to mean something like "the power of God for salvation" (Rom 1:16), through which God's "grace might reign" (Rom 5:21). Some passages in which the word *dikaiosynē* appears without qualification by genitive or adjective also must be understood as speaking of God's righteousness; only a detailed exegesis of the context can decide.

M. *Dōrean* cannot be translated "in vain" for the following reasons:

1. The Greek word in itself always means "gratis, for nothing, without recompense, as a gift," and is so used by Paul (Rom 3:24; 2 Cor 11:7) and in the NT (Matt 10:8; 2 Thess 3:8; Rev 21:6; 22:17).

2. Paul uses other words to express the concept "in vain, to no purpose": *eis kenon* (2 Cor 6:1; Gal 2:2; Phil 2:16 bis; 1 Thess 3:5), the adjective *kenos* (1 Cor 15:10, 14 bis, 58; 1 Thess 2:1), or *eikē* (Rom 13:4; 1 Cor 15:2; Gal 3:4; 4:11).

3. Because the Hebrew *ḥnm* can have the related meaning "gratuitously, undeserved, without cause" *dōrean* too can be used in the LXX in this sense (1 Sam 19:5; 25:31; 1 Kgs 2:31; Job 1:9; Ps 35:7,19 (= John 15:25); 69:4; 109:3; 119:161; Isa 52:5; Lam 3:52; Sir 20:23; 29:6,7) alongside the meaning "gratis, without payment" (Gen 29:15; Exod 21:2,11; Num 11:5; 2 Sam 24:24; 1 Chr 21:24; Mal 1:10 [probably, cf. 2 Sam 24:24]; Isa 52:3; Jer 22:13; 1 Macc 10:33). Prov. 1:17 and Ezek 6:10 (see W. Zimmerli, *Ezechiel* [Neukirchen: Neukirchener Verlag, 1969], 141) do not have *dōrean* in the LXX. I can sum up the discussion to this point by citing Burton (*Galatians*, 140-41): "*dōrean* means not 'without result,' a meaning which it apparently never has . . . but 'without cause,' 'needlessly' as in John 15:25."

4. Ignatius, *Trall.* 10, cited by BAG^2 in the sense of "in vain," can be used as a test case. R. M. Grant, *The Apostolic Fathers: Vol. 4 Ignatius of Antioch* (Camden: Nelson, 1966), translates: [If Jesus' death was not real,] "then I die in vain. Then I lie about the Lord." But Ignatius is not speaking of a purpose he hopes to achieve by his death. On the contrary, he is saying, "I die gratuitously, as a gift, having received nothing, if in fact Christ has not really died for me" or less likely, "I die needlessly, without a cause, if that to which I witness in my death is not true."

5. While the second, LXX meaning is a possibility for Gal 2:21, the most natural sense of "Jesus died without cause" would be that no one had any grounds for killing him. If "without cause" is understood theologically to mean that humanity had no cause to deserve such a death, then the meaning is very close to the first, Greek meaning. Accordingly we translate, as in Rom 3:24, "as a free gift."

The question of the relationship of Gal 2:15-21 to Paul's reply to Cephas in Antioch (2:14) has long been discussed. H. D. Betz, who analyses Galatians according to Greco-Roman rhetorical principles, gives a fairly decisive literary answer by calling the section the *propositio*, a statement of theses which prepares for the following *probatio*, arguments from Scripture.[9] The function of the *propositio*, according to Betz, is also to sum up the preceding *narratio* of facts concerning Paul himself—and (I would add) "the gospel preached by me" (1:11), "the gospel I preach among the Gentiles" (1:16; 2:2), "the gospel to the uncircumcised" (2:7). It is unfortunate that Betz connects the summary primarily with the Antioch affair after all, as if Paul's argument were essentially with Cephas rather than with the Galatian Judaizers and as if Paul were more interested in correcting Cephas' "gospel to the circumcised" than in defending his own "gospel to the uncircumcised" (2:7). I agree that the *propositio* sums up the preceding *narratio*, but it sums up the whole narration, not just the last event recounted, and if anything with special reference to 1:15-16.

The problems caused by understanding this section as primarily addressed to Cephas are insuperable even if seldom recognized. Paul then seems to deny that *Jewish* Christians should keep the commandments, in breach of the agreement just described. The "works of law" are made to refer to a Jewish "doctrine of salvation," against all the evidence. Verse 18 is made to refer to *Cephas*, in spite of the grammar. Further, it is assumed that Cephas was guilty of a serious violation of one or more commandments. In order to make a connection between Paul's "tearing down" of the whole Torah and Cephas' actions in Antioch, assumptions are made which simply are not justified by the sources.[10] Even if the Zealots might have opposed all contact with Gentiles and even if the *ḥaverim* refused to sit at the same table with the *am ha-areṣ*, there is no commandment binding on all Jews anywhere in Bible or Mishnah which prohibits eating with Gentiles.[11] Whatever happened in Antioch, then,[12] it did not provide Paul with an occasion to make a sweeping statement about the abolition of commandments for Jewish Christians or for Jews.

This section begins with sentences in the first person plural (2:15-17) and ends with sentences in the first person singular (2:18-21), including two with an emphatic *egō* (19, 20a). It begins explicitly with "we Jews" and ends impressively with "I, Paul." Is there a transition where "we" means "we Jewish Christians?" Or, in the light of the distinctive apostolates reported in 2:7-9, do some of the "we's" refer specifically to "we who are engaged in the Gentile mission?" Paul speaks about himself (and his co-workers?) and to the Galatians and about himself as a model to be imitated by the Galatians (4:12); unless there are compelling arguments to the contrary, there is no reason to expect a "we" in the sense of "the Jerusalem church and I." Paul is not ascribing his own views to Cephas, and he certainly is not writing a "theology of Judaism" in this section. That this is the case can only be shown by a closer examination of the flow of his *propositio*.

Verses 15-16. The distinction between Jew and Gentile is a fundamental one for Paul,[13] and it is not to be dissolved in favour of a "third race." The closest correlate to the phrase "Jews by nature/birth" is found in the writing which is even more Pauline than Paul, Eph 2:3: "children of wrath by nature/birth." It is to this bleak situation that Paul speaks and in comparison with which the Jews have an advantage. As in Rom 3:1-2, that advantage is here expressed in terms of knowledge based on Scripture. It should not be necessary to cite passages from the Hebrew Bible, Qumran texts, or sayings of the Tannaim to show that the knowledge of verse 16a is specifically Jewish knowledge. Of course, the positive counterpart would state: "but rather through the faithfulness [*'mwnh* = *alētheia* LXX]" and "righteousness of God," as in Ps 143:1. While a stronger case can be made for verse 1 being in Paul's mind when he cites Ps 143:2 in Rom 3:20,[14] it is also a possibility in Gal 2:16.[15] Even without this support, however, one must translate "the faithfulness of Christ," moving now to specifically Christian knowledge.

I find it very doubtful that "when Paul thinks of works of law, he thinks of existence as a Jew."[16] Markus Barth insists that the phrase, which appears in no Jewish writing,[17] must be interpreted from the only context where it does appear, Romans and Galatians, as meaning the adoption by Gentile Judaizers of selected commandments understood as prerequisites for salvation.[18] Even more important is the consideration that the common understanding of the phrase only perpetuates "the view of Rabbinic religion as one of legalistic works-righteousness."[19] The classic study of the phrase is by Ernst Lohmeyer, who begins by stating that the only natural grammatical possibility is a *genitivus auctoris* ("die vom Gesetz gewirkte Werke").[20] He then, however, creates a problem since he presupposes that the phrase *must* mean "Werke, die das Gesetz fordert." In the context of an experiment which questions traditional assumptions, it is necessary to look carefully at the first of Lohmeyer's alternatives. The phrase *erga nomou* occurs three times in this verse and in Rom 3:20 and 28 as the opposite of *pistis Christou* as a means of justification. In Gal 3:2,5 it is the opposite of *akoē pisteōs* as a means of supplying the Spirit, and in 3:10 those "from works of law" are under a curse, contrasted with those "from *pistis*," who are blessed. An important clue is found in the one passage where the singular is used, Rom 2:15.[21] Gentiles have "the work of the law written on their hearts," and from the context (1:18-2:16) it is clear what that work is: "the law works wrath" (4:15). As God's or Christ's faithfulness is expressed in a work done for human blessing, so the law apart from covenant also does works for human cursing. It is then at least possible to understand "the works of the law" in a way that does not refer to Jews keeping commandments but to God punishing Gentiles. I leave the question open for now, pending a more thorough study.[22]

The sentence which began with a distinction between Jews and Gentiles continues in the same way, as is shown by the contrast contained in the *kai hēmeis* (and the *kai autoi* of verse 17). This means that the "human being" of which the sentence speaks is specifically a Gentile human being. This and the purpose clause *hina* have led Barth to speak of Jews who, having come to know that Gentiles are justified by the faithfulness of Christ, therefore also became believers out of a kind of envy (cf. Rom 11:11)![23] But it is not at all clear that Paul means to include Jewish Christians like Cephas in the "we's" of verse 16 and even more doubtful if Cephas or the Jerusalem church would have agreed with the formulation. The language is that of the Gentile mission and not that of "the gospel/mission to the circumcised" (2:7,8). The true parallel to the purpose clause I believe to be 1:16, which speaks of the Son of God being revealed in Paul "in order that I might preach him among the Gentiles." Paul uses the first person in 2:16-17 not to speak about Jews or Jewish Christians but in order to state fundamental theological theses that apply to himself in relation to the Gentile Galatians. It is Paul and not Jewish Christians as such for whom faith in Christ and commissioning to the Gentiles coincide. The content of Paul's revelation is that "God would justify the Gentiles from the faithfulness [of Christ]" (3:8), and therefore he too became a believer. Paul too is justified, not on the basis of the faithfulness of God on Sinai but through the faithfulness of Christ on Golgotha. Paul describes in the purpose clause of verse 16 what happens to Gentile believers as a result of Paul's own commissioning and believing, something which is more than the knowledge of 16a, but he continues to use the first person "we." Does that mean that Paul so identifies with the Gentiles to whom he is sent that he himself in a sense has become a Gentile? Rather than being only the statement of a condensed theological thesis, verse 16 even more recounts Paul's own history (N.B. Paul's, not Cephas's), and therefore the pronoun referring to him (we) shifts in meaning as the story progresses.

Verse 17. This suggestion of a shift in the significance of "we" at least has the advantage of making some sense of the following verses. Verse 17, in which the word "sinner" must have the same meaning as in verse 15, makes clearer what was implied in verse 16 by drawing out a false implication. When "we too" became believers, it meant that "we ourselves too" have been found to be sinners, that is, Gentiles. It does not however follow from this acknowledged fact that Christ is in the service of sin. As often in Paul, such a false conclusion is simply vehemently denied and not argued. It can also be noted that the justification "in Christ" of 17 justifies the translation "the faithfulness of Christ" in verse 16

Verse 18. This famous *crux* is such only for the interpreter who insists that the law must be the object of the verbs and who wants to connect it with Cephas' action in Antioch. In spite of the deliberate shift to the first person singular, most interpreters manage to read the sentence as if it began: "you, Cephas."[24] Many commentators have difficulty with the *gar*'s, but in my view verse 18 follows from verse 17 and leads to verse 19. Paul is referring here to building or tearing down not the law but the *church*. He uses the concept of building (*oikodomeō, oikodomē*) otherwise always of the church,[25] which he (Rom 15:20, 2 Cor 10:8; 12:19; 13:10) or others (1 Thess 5:11; 1 Cor 8:1, 10; 10:23; 14:2, 3, 4, 5, 12, 17, 26) build up. This is occasionally contrasted with tearing down the church: Rom 14:20 (*kataluō*), 2 Cor 10:4, 8; 13:10 (*kathairesis*). In Galatians Paul has twice referred to his earlier persecution of the church, seeking to destroy it (1:13, 23, *portheō*). Verse 18 makes explicit the change in Paul's status from one under the covenant to a Gentile, of which verse 17 spoke. That does not make Christ an agent of sin because concomitant with the shift, Paul began to build up the church he had previously persecuted. In what sense is Paul an apostate? The following verse explains.

Verse 19a. "For *through the law* I have died *to the law.*"[26] This paradoxical formulation raises the question of the different senses in which Paul uses the word *nomos*, comparable to the wide range of meanings of Torah in early Judaism. The parallel passage in Rom 3:21-31 contrasts the "law of works" and the "law of faithfulness" and says that the law testifies to the righteousness of God which has now been made manifest (also) apart from the law.[27] I believe that a thorough discussion would show that Paul uses the word in at least the following senses: 1. the covenant of grace on Mt. Sinai, the election of Israel but only Israel, 2. the administration of order and retribution over the whole creation, through the principalities and powers, 3. as equivalent to Scripture, the revelation of God, whose righteousness and saving power now extends also to the Gentiles in Jesus Christ, and 4. that not only from which Gentiles are redeemed (sense 2) or by which they are redeemed (sense 3) but also that for the fulfilment of which they are redeemed (Gal 5:14; 6:2, 13; Rom 8:4; 13:8-10). In the present sentence Paul states that he is an apostate in that by means of the faithfulness of Christ (sense 3) he has deliberately cast off the yoke of the covenant (sense 1). Amazed at this positive use of *nomos*, Bultmann pointed to Rom 7:4 as the closest parallel:[28] "Therefore, brothers-and-sisters, also you have died to the law *through the body of Christ*, in order that you might become another's, his who has been raised from among the dead, in order that we might bear fruit for God." Paul is an apostate and commends himself openly as such without apology, for his life is subordinate to his calling to proclaim the righteousness of God among the Gentiles.

Verses 19b-20. This is probably the most important single verse for understanding Paul's theology, and it therefore cannot be discussed in all its details here. It its present context it not only sums up Paul's own self-understanding in the *narratio* but is also a statement of the life to which he calls the Galatians in the following: "I beseech you, become as I am, for I also have become as you are" (4:12).

Verse 21. I am embarrassed by the boldness of this radically different translation. I am especially troubled by the sharp contradiction to 3:21,[29] but I am even more troubled by the contradictions to lexicography in the usual translation of *dōrean*. If the translator's work is properly done, then the exegete will simply have to make the best of it. It is not only the word *dōrean* in Rom 3:24 that impresses in terms of parallels between this statement of theses before discussing Abraham and the later, clearer Rom 3:21-31. That section ends: "Do we then render obsolete the law through this faithfulness? Of course not, but we rather confirm the law." Paul's apostasy from the covenant (law in sense 1) could very well be seen as a denial of the grace of God, and these are not the only two passages where he has to defend himself against such a false conclusion. It is surely a better formulation in Romans to say that Christ's death as a free gift is an expression of the righteousness of God to which the law *witnesses* (sense 3), now made manifest *outside* the context of the Sinai covenant (sense 1). Nevertheless, the formulation in Gal 2:21 is also a possible one, particularly in the light of the usage of verse 19, and it does in fact provide a good transition to what will be said in Chapter 3. The verse can be understood this way, and if the translation is correct, it must be so understood.

It is in the light of these fundamental statements (about himself) that Paul goes on to speak of their scriptural basis (for the Galatians). "Righteousness" has been used in the sense of God's righteousness (2:21), which will be the case also in what follows. The word *pistis* (faithfulness) has been used three times with the genitive "of Christ" or "of the Son of God" (2:16 bis, 20) and can now be so understood even when the genitive is not explicit. *Pistis* appears in the context of an act of God which is called "justifying," the opposite of which is "works of law" which do not justify (2:16 ter). Not only "works of law" but also "law" is something to which it is good to have died. On the other hand, "law" can also be the means of dying (to the law) and living to God (2:19), and the "law" contains the gospel of the righteousness of God, expressed in Christ's death as a free gift. The parallels to many of these concepts in Rom. 3:21-31 are evident. As in Romans, so also in Galatians, the initial statements prepare for the discussion of Abraham.

Coming to Galatians 3 with these presuppositions brings a quite different understanding of the text than coming with a different set of presuppositions. It might be helpful to list what some of the traditional assumptions have been. It is usually assumed that Paul is attacking a position of his opponents, who used the figure of Abraham to argue that we are saved through merits, through the doing of commandments specified in the law. Paul then counters by using Abraham as a model of faith to be imitated by the Galatians, who would then for their faith receive a similar reward of being called righteous. Paul is understood to be contrasting two fundamental types of human activity, that of believing (in Christ) and that of doing (God's commandments); one leads to blessing and life, and the other leads to a curse and death. The problem with the law is its unfulfillability, which is the point of the citation of Deut 27:26, pronouncing a curse on everyone who does not do every last commandment. Paul profoundly disagrees with a statement of the Torah (Lev 18:5), which he proceeds to contradict by citing a passage from the prophets (Hab 2:4). The principles involved in the contrast between believing and doing are universally valid, not only for those being addressed but also and even specifically for Jews. According to the usual understanding, Paul then goes on to a brief digression on the history of Israel in 3:15-29, a passage which concerns the Galatians only in the sense of an example to be avoided. The law came to Israel on Sinai long after the time of Abraham, at best given only indirectly by God (3:19-20), at best only a temporary restrainer (3:22-25), but a fulfilment of no promises (3:17-18,21). Now that faith has been revealed, that is, that Christ has come, there should be no more Jews or Greeks and certainly no more law, for the third race has been founded in Christ, in which the principle of faith apart from law reigns supreme.

How might chapter 3 look if it is to be understood not from the presuppositions just listed but in the light of 2:15-21? Paul begins with an appeal to reality: the Galatians have received the Spirit (and that not "from works of law" but "from preaching of faithfulness"); and then he raises the question of possibility: how can this be? what is the Scriptural justification for the gift of the Spirit to Gentiles?

The starting point and the conclusion of Paul's argumentation from Scripture are clear. His gospel, the gospel he preaches among the Gentiles, the gospel to the uncircumcised, is found already in Scripture, in the law.[30] The content of that gospel is that "God would justify the Gentiles from faithfulness," and its form is that of a promise, that "in [Abraham] all the Gentiles will be blessed" (3:8). The fulfilment of that promise and the reality of that gospel do not occur for Paul before or outside of but only in Christ, who died "in order that for the Gentiles the blessing of Abraham might become a reality in Jesus Christ, in order that we might receive the promise, i.e. the Spirit, through the faithfulness'' (3:14). The contrast throughout Galatians 3 is not between legalism and faith but between law (as that from which Gentiles are redeemed) and promise (as God's act of righteousness in Christ). The enclosing verses speak explicitly of Gentiles, and one would expect that the enclosed verses, which speak of the law as curse, would also speak of the situation of Gentiles. Schoeps complains of Paul that he does not see the connection between covenant and commandments;[31] I would say that it is precisely because Paul does see this connection that his description of law outside the context of covenant is so bleak. This is reinforced by the possibility that he was accustomed to viewing the Gentile world through the glasses of Shammai and apocalyptic.[32] In any case, the bracketing verses speak of the blessing of Abraham for the Gentiles, which corresponds to the curse of the quotations from Deut 27:26 and 21:23.[33] Since the ones ''Christ has redeemed from the curse of the law'' are explicitly called Gentiles in verse 14, the curse of verse 10 must also be one which lay upon Gentiles. Paul is able to find this in the LXX (not the MT) of Deut 27:26 which inserts the word *pas* twice: *everyone* is under a curse, including Gentiles, who do not do *all* the commandments, not just those incumbent on God-fearers. One might think that those who do remain in the commandments ''to do them'' would be under a blessing,[34] for to those ''who do them'' is promised life (Lev 18:5). Indeed, in another context Paul does use Lev 18:5 in this positive sense: ''For Moses writes that the human being who does the righteousness which is from Torah will live by it'' (Rom 10:5). A further connection is made by the parallel ''will live'' in Hab 2:4.[35] The contrast here is not between believing and doing but between those whose life is based on works of the law (Gentiles) and those whose life is based on the faithfulness of God (Christians; also Jews?). The latter group will ''do them'' (Cf. 5:14; 6:2; Rom 8:4; 2:13)[36] and as ''righteous'' ones ''will live.'' As the word *alla* shows, verse 12b cannot be understood as a prooftext for 12a. In a paradox comparable to 2:19, the sentence must say: ''The law (sense 2) is not 'from faithfulness' but on the contrary those who do the law (sense 4) will not be under the curse but will live.'' The law apart from covenant is not ''from faithfulness,'' but Lev 18:5 is, for it is to be understood in the light of Hab 2:4. All of this is very compressed and will be expressed more adequately in Romans. In the context of Galatians, Paul wants to speak not of the promise of Torah but of the promise in Torah to Abraham, and therefore the word *nomos* is consistently used here to refer to law outside the covenant, the law which works wrath (Rom 4:15), the curse of the law as it applies to Gentiles.

That Paul is speaking of Gentiles who need to be redeemed from the law is shown most clearly as the argument progresses to speak of ''the elements of the world.''[37] The Gentile Galatians once ''served [as slaves] gods who essentially are not," beings further identified as "the weak and impotent elements, whom you wish to serve [as slaves] anew" (4:9). Paul also says that "we minor children were enslaved under the elements of the world" (4:3). Colossians helps identify these "elements of the world"; there they (2:8, 20) are also called "principalities and powers" (2:10, 15) and "angels" (2:18), who enforce specific regulations (2:20, etc.) and who have a "certificate of indebtedness" which condemns all those who do not submit to their regulations (2:14), a curse of their law, so to speak. In Galatians, slavery to pagan gods (4:9) means being "under the elements of the world" (4:3), "under guardians and administrators" (4:2), "under the custodian" (3:24), "imprisoned under sin" (3:22). It is, however, also said that the same people were "held in custody under the law" (3:23-24), until Christ came "in order that he might redeem those under law" (4:4-5). There is also reference to a law administered by the angels of the nations (3:19), apart from the covenant.[38] This identification of pagan gods with elements and angelic administrators and with the law as such shows the sense in which the word must be understood in much of Galatians 3. This is the law under which Christ became a curse for us, for according to Paul he was crucified by "the rulers of this age" (1 Cor 2:8); this is the law from whose curse (3:10) Christ has redeemed the Gentiles (3:13-14). When Paul speaks of the law in this specific sense of how it relates to Gentiles, he says nothing whatsoever against the Torah of Israel or about the significance of the law for Jews or Jewish Christians.

The law in the sense of the covenant made with Israel (sense 1) was not in fact the fulfilment of the promise and gospel which interests Paul. That law is not "against the promises" (3:21), but neither is it *for* this specific promise. For the Galatians it is simply irrelevant, unless they are to become converts to Judaism, a possibility Paul vehemently opposes. I would understand the word *nomos* to be used in this sense in 3:17, 18, 21 ter, and 5:3. Paul says nothing whatsoever about the significance of *nomos* in this sense for Israel or for Jewish Christians; he speaks only of its irrelevance for the Gentile Galatians.

Finally, Paul can also use the word *nomos* in the positive sense of God's revelation (sense 3), although this never occurs explicitly in Galatians 3. If my translation of 2:21 is correct, then the law contains the gospel of the righteousness of God, which resulted in Christ dying as a free gift, and in 2:19 it is through the law that Paul died to the law. The righteousness of God for Gentiles is for Paul a promise in Scripture before it is reality in Christ, and Paul's whole argument concerning the promise of God made to Abraham presupposes a concept of "the law of faithfulness" (Rom 3:27) or "the law of the Spirit of life" (8:2). As Paul can use the word *nomos* in Gal 4:21 in the sense of Scripture, so the word *graphē* is used in the sense of

Torah in 3:8, 22; 4:30. It is only because of the situation addressed that Paul does not say that "the *law*, knowing beforehand that God would justify the Gentiles from faithfulness, proclaimed the gospel beforehand to Abraham" (3:8).[39] *Nomos* in the sense of what Christians have been liberated to fulfil (sense 4) is also found in 5:14 and 6:2.

Trying to sort out the different senses in Paul's use of the word is a difficult if not impossible task. Räisänen has recently warned that it may not be possible at all and that a number of anomalies will always remain in Pauline thought.[40] E. P. Sanders, however, has made an important advance in urging close attention to the particular questions to which Paul's various statements about *nomos* provide answers.[41] I would like also to urge that the distinction between Jews and Gentiles be taken seriously and that *nomos* might function in relation to one group quite differently than it does in relation to the other.[42] It would, of course, be simpler for all if Paul had used different words for different aspects, particularly if in fact he speaks about law outside the context of covenant, but of course he could not do so. Because God is one, therefore his law is one, and the more the concept of *Torah/nomos* is enriched by wider associations, the more different senses the word will acquire. I hope that the discussion above will at least show the necessity of rethinking the issue of how Paul speaks of the law in Galatians 2 and 3.

I began with the question of the assumptions usually made concerning Paul's theology of Judaism in Galatians. If these assumptions are put to one side, what then are the exegetical possibilities for understanding what is being said in the context of a letter addressed polemically to Gentiles? It may be that a more thorough study would support at least some of those assumptions, but in this experiment I have made an attempt to suggest radically different options.

APPENDIX: PAUL AS APOSTATE

It is perhaps necessary to spell out in more detail the reasons for claiming that Paul was consciously an apostate in the technical sense of one who deliberately throws off the yoke of the covenant. Although few would use the word, for most Paul's apostasy is axiomatic.[43] If Paul was "converted" from the Jewish to the Christian religion, if he really did die to the Sinai covenant (the law, Gal 2:19), then of course he was an apostate. It should be clear that I am speaking of an "Apostat *stricto sensu*,"[44] a technical meaning of the term, a shift from election at Sinai to election in Christ, a move which Christians praise and Jews should not hold against him. Did Paul for his own person deliberately turn away from the Torah as covenant and thus from the obligation to keep the commandments, at the same time that he was not turning away from God but on the contrary being obedient to his revelation? It is not easy to answer this question.

That Paul was accused of apostasy by later Jewish Christians is clear.[45] He was accused by Jews (or perhaps Jewish Christians) at the time of Luke (and perhaps during Paul's lifetime) of something much worse: "[Those] zealous for the law have been told about you that you teach apostasy from Moses to all Jews [who live] among the Gentiles, saying that they should not circumcise their children or walk in the customs" (Acts 21:21). Insofar as Paul was persecuted by Jews and insofar as he himself earlier persecuted the church, it was presumably from zealous motives and on this charge. It would therefore occasion no surprise if he also had to meet a similar accusation in Galatia (2:18). I believe that Paul was completely innocent of this charge since he confined his preaching to Gentiles and did not encourage Jews to abandon the covenant. I used to believe that he did not do so himself and agreed with W. L. Knox, "It is clear that Paul throughout his life continued to practice Judaism, and that he expected Jewish converts to do so. . . . On his principles, if he obeyed the law at all, he was bound to obey it as a Pharisee";[46] W. D. Davies, "Paul observed the law and that in the pharisaic manner, throughout his life";[47] F. C. Grant, "Not only in his attitude toward the law, as the source and record of a divine revelation, but in his allegiance to the great religious affirmations of the early Pharisees, Paul remained a Pharisee to his dying day."[48] There is nothing at all inconsistent about an apostle remaining himself a member of the Sinai community keeping commandments while being entrusted with a gospel for Gentiles, calling them into the community of Christ without commandments.

However, perhaps it is not quite so simple. The issue was raised here in an attempt to make some sense of Gal 2:18. If Paul used to act like a Zealot in seeking to destroy the church (1:13-14), it seems that he could be accused of doing the opposite by now building it up (2:18). It seems that Paul just this once accepts the accusation, but then goes on to interpret it positively as not denying the grace of God (2:19-21). How far does Paul go in identifying himself with the Gentiles to whom his gospel is addressed?[49] Within Galatians itself, there are passages in which "we" must mean "we Gentiles." The parallel purpose clauses in 3:15 are significant: "in order that *for the Gentiles* the blessing of Abraham might become a reality in Jesus Christ, in order that *we* might receive the promise, that is, the Spirit, through the faithfulness." When Paul says that Christ came "in order that he might redeem those under law, that is, in order that *we* might receive adoption [as children]," he can hardly be referring to Jews unless he contradicts himself in Rom. 9:4, "They are Israelites, and to them belong the *huiothesia* . . . . ." I find it incredible to think that Paul could say that "we [Jews] were enslaved under the elements of the world" (4:3) in the light of the same phrase in 4:9, but that could perhaps be debated.[50] Barth has argued that the verb "to live" in 2:14 should be understood in the fullest sense of life, as in 2:19-20.[51] If that is so, then Paul affirms that there are two ways of having "life" in the fullest sense, *ethnikōs* and *Ioudaïkōs*. (It is very doubtful that Cephas would have agreed with this statement about how he lives, but Paul may really be speaking about himself.)[52] Paul refers to something which can only be called apostasy in Phil 3:7-9, although, of course, he is not speaking of works-righteousness. I would argue that verse 9 must be translated: "that I may be found in him, having my righteousness not from the Torah but through the faithfulness of Christ, the righteousness from God which [leads] to the faith of knowing him." Here too Paul does not deny the righteousness (= election) given through the Torah to Israel when he affirms another righteousness given through Christ to Gentiles and also chooses the latter possibility for himself. On a more speculative note, when Paul prays "that I myself be accursed and cut off from Christ for the sake of my brothers-and-sisters, my fellow-citizens according to the flesh" (Rom 9:3), is there an implication that he has been cut off from the covenant for the sake of the Gentiles whose apostle he was called to be?

The reasons for Paul's apostasy presumably have to do with his apostolate. Not to have so identified with those to whom he has been commissioned to preach "his" gospel, that "God would justify the Gentiles from faithfulness," would have caused great difficulties, of which Galatians is a good illustration. The Judaizers thought that there was an advantage to being, like Paul, both a Jew and a Christian, for they did not like being called "Gentile sinners." To make his point, Paul tells how he has for his own person renounced the covenant and become like them a Gentile. What Paul had a right to and freely gave up, the Gentiles should not try to attain, particularly in an amateurish manner. The Galatians might have been in the position of wanting to model themselves on their founder and of accusing him of not preaching what he practises. Paul therefore had to put himself into the same status as that of his converts if his gospel and person were to be followed. Very significant is Gal 4:12, "I beseech you, become as I am, for I also have become as you are."

Paul is not as clear as he might be with respect to his apostasy for two reasons. First, he wanted to continue to express his loyalty to Israel. When challenged, he too could boast of his Jewish credentials (2 Cor 11:22; Phil 3:4-6; Gal 1:14). That Paul five times received the punishment of *Makkot* in the synagogues (2 Cor 11:24) shows that he accepted the jurisdiction of the synagogue and presumably continued to worship there. An apostate who had completely renounced Judaism, like Tiberius Alexander, Philo's nephew, was never beaten in the synagogues. Whether or not Paul continued to keep the commandments is probable but not sure. If P. Richardson is right in his understanding of 1 Cor 9:19-23, perhaps he did not.[53] It may be that Paul wanted to have it both ways, to understand himself as an apostate in relationship to his Gentile converts but as a loyal son of Israel in relationship to Jews.

If Paul was occasionally in his own mind an apostate in the technical sense, much more important for his own self consciousness was the sense of being one of the few faithful Israelites (Rom 11:1). If I had to imagine an appropriate setting for Paul's revelation and commissioning (Gal 1:15-16), it would not be the fireworks of the Lucan accounts but rather Paul all alone late at night pondering the text of the second Servant song (Isa 49:1-6). It is the consciousness of fulfilling Israel's calling to be the light to the Gentiles which was the driving force in Paul's life, and it was the conviction that now was the time in God's *Heilsgeschichte* for the expression of his righteousness toward Gentiles which was the content of Paul's mystery (well summed up in Eph 3:3-6). What he holds against his Jewish contemporaries in such passages as Rom 2:17-24 and 9:30-10:4 is not a lack of zeal (= faith) and certainly not works-righteousness but a lack of understanding of the arrival of the eschatological hour for the Gentiles. This is why the word "apostate" in Gal 2:18 must be put in quotation marks, as an accusation bitterly accepted once for the sake of a larger loyalty not only to his mission but also to Israel. Paul understood himself, then, to be a faithful Israelite in God's *Heilsgeschichte*, who for the sake of his mission relinquished any personal advantages stemming from Sinai to make himself a Gentile sinner.

If Paul was an apostate, did he think that other Jewish Christians should follow his example? In the light of the mutual recognition of two apostolates in Gal 2:7-9, I would assume not.[54] Most interpreters believe that the Jerusalem church continued to keep the commandments and that Paul respected this. There is, however, a significant theological issue which may not have been apparent in the first century. To judge from such formulae as 1 Cor 11:23-25; 15:3-7; and perhaps Rom 3:24f, Jewish Christians understood Christ as a confirmation of the covenant and as expiation for the forgiveness of sins. That is, for Jewish Christians Christ probably replaced the temple as the locus of atonement but not Sinai as the locus of election.[55] For Paul, however, Christ died not so much for our sins as to give life to the dead, and in Paul's "pattern of religion," Christ occupies almost exactly the same place with respect to election as does Sinai within Judaism. The logic of Paul's theology is such as to make Jewish Christianity only a transitional period. In terms of what he does say, however, Paul speaks of apostasy only with respect to himself. He can be understood, at least implicitly, as affirming something like the two-covenant concept of F. Rosenzweig.[56] That is, Paul affirms the new expression of the righteousness of God in Christ for the Gentiles and for himself as Apostle to the Gentiles without in any sense denying the righteousness of God expressed in Torah for Israel.

5

ISRAEL'S ENEMIES IN PAULINE THEOLOGY

On 10 November 1975 the United Nations General Assembly adopted Resolution 3379, which condemned "Zionism" as "a form of racism and racial discrimination." The reaction of some Christian supporters of Israel was to complain of the injustice involved in ascribing "racism" to the people who has suffered most from this phenomenon. But if the UN resolution was unjust in ascribing to Israel the name of Israel's traditional enemies, was not Paul equally unjust to speak of the Israel of his day under the names of Ishmael (Gal 4:22; Rom 9:8) and Esau (Rom 9:13) and even Pharaoh (Rom 9:17)?[1] This would be even more malicious on Paul's part if already at the time of writing Ishmael was understood to represent contemporary Arabs and Esau the Roman Empire. Even if Paul's name-calling was relatively innocent, the effects in the later history of the church were fateful. Rosemary Ruether has pointed out how Paul's use of Sarah and Hagar in Galatians 4 and Jacob and Esau in Romans 9 became the source for the types of the triumphant church and the enslaved synagogue in patristic exegesis, and Paul's use of allegory the excuse for finding these types in many other texts.[2] In the light of the challenge of Ruether and others, it is necessary to look anew at certain Pauline texts and to question long established interpretations.

Even those persuaded by P. Richardson that in general Paul is not the founder of the "displacement theory,"[3] which appropriates such theological concepts as Israel for the church and denies them to the synagogue, there nevertheless remain certain problem texts. I shall consider two of them here, Gal 4:21-31 and Rom 9:6-29. Is it possible to understand them in a way that does not involve Paul ascribing to Israel the names of Israel's traditional enemies?

Before beginning with the text of Gal 4:21-31, it might be helpful to list some basic methodological considerations which differ from the traditional assumptions.

1. The first involves the hermeneutics of experimentation already mentioned. If Ruether and others are right, theological anti-Judaism has pervaded the entire history of the church. Since the historical-critical method means primarily the radical criticism of the assumptions of the interpreter, that means that I begin by assuming that everything I have ever learned about Paul in relationship to Judaism must be false. Since there is little left on which to build, every new approach to a text must partake of the nature of an experiment. Many experiments fail, but one can never know without trying.

2. It is usually assumed that the argument of Galatians is directed against Judaism, generalizing from the persons of James or Cephas or the troublemakers in Galatia. But Paul's letter is written not to Jerusalem or Antioch, and there is no indication whatsoever that those troublemakers were urging conversion to Judaism; on the contrary, Paul says that they were "perverting the gospel of Christ" (1:7) by urging the Galatians to add circumcision to that gospel (5:2; 6:12-13). Besides, it is important to remember that the letter is not addressed to the troublemakers at all but to the Gentile Galatians.

3. It is assumed that Paul's theology must stand in direct antithesis to that of Judaism. Whatever Paul says, Jews or Jewish-Christian opponents must have said the opposite. The task of the interpreter, then, is to reconstruct what they must have said in order to understand Paul's reply. The procedure runs a great risk of being circular. Clearly, the situation addressed must be understood as well as possible, but nothing should be read into it which is based more on presuppositions than on explicit references in the text. In the present case, it seems that the troublemakers who try to get the Galatians to Judaize are themselves Gentile Judaizers (the *peritemnomenoi*, and most important, those who do not keep the law, 6:13), so that Judaism is not an issue at all.[4]

4. To avoid a Marcionite reading of Paul, it might be best to assume that he stands in continuity with the traditions of Judaism rather than in opposition to them, if this is at all possible. He himself says that "his" gospel, "that God would justify the Gentiles from faithfulness" (3:8) is contained in Torah. This must be taken very seriously.

5. If in fact Paul's gospel was directed against Judaism, then one must finally conclude with Schoeps that he was guilty of a "fundamental misapprehension" in his teaching about the law.[5] But why not assume that

Paul knew at least as much about "convenantal nomism" as does E. P. Sanders and that he did not share the modern Christian "view of Rabbinic religion as one of legalistic works-righteousness?"[6] If Paul really does know about covenant as the context of commandments for Judaism, it may be that when he speaks of "the curse of the law" apart from covenant he is not speaking of Judaism at all.

6. In the context of a letter written by one who says that he was commissioned as an Apostle of Christ "in order that I might preach him among the Gentiles" (1:16), a letter which reflects "the gospel which I preach among the Gentiles" (2:2), "the gospel to the uncircumcised" (2:7), the gospel whose content is "that God would justify the Gentiles from faithfulness" (3:8) and that "Christ has redeemed us from the curse of the law . . . in order that for the Gentiles the blessing of Abraham might become a reality in Jesus Christ" (3:13-14), in a letter addressed to those who "formerly did not know God [but] served [as slaves] gods who essentially are not" (4:8), in such a letter one would expect Paul to be dealing with Gentile problems and Gentile redemption. I take this to be true also when Paul uses the word *nomos*. I have argued elsewhere that the one law of God (how could there be more than one since God is one?) has quite a different effect whether it is experienced within the context of the covenant of grace or not.[7] As R. Tanḥuma said concerning God's voice on Sinai: "How did the voice go forth? The word of the Lord went forth in two aspects, slaying the heathen who would not accept it, but giving life to Israel who accepted the Torah."[8] In any case I will try to read Galatians not as a polemic against Judaism or Jewish Christians or troublemakers but as the gospel of the liberation of Gentile Christians, against the dark background of their previous servitude and with the warning not to fall back into that servitude. I turn now specifically to the text of Gal 4:21-31 and some the common assumption that are made about its interpretation.[9]

Even though the details differ, there are some aspects common to all interpretations. The most fundamental contrast is between the present Jerusalem and the Jerusalem above, and all would agree with the thrust if not the textual emendation of Marcion,[10] who actually reads for the former *tēn synagōgēn tōn Ioudaion* and for the latter *hagian ekklēsian*. It is usually assumed that the fundamental contrast is between Judaism and Christianity[11] and that Paul appropriates the figure of Sarah for Christianity, while Hagar and the Jews are utterly rejected.[12] Another way of expressing this contrast is to speak of faith versus the law, although the former appears not at all and the latter only paradoxically in the introductory verse. It is very common to introduce into the passage a contrast between an old covenant and a new covenant,[13] although there is nothing to indicate that the "covenants" here stand in a temporal relationship. According to the way Paul is usually understood, he should be contrasting children of Sarah (or Jerusalem or Israel) *kata sarka* and *kata pneuma*,[14] and the introduction of Hagar presents a problem. Finally, the statement that "Jerusalem is in slavery with her children" is taken by most to be axiomatic, which can be used to explain Hagar = Sinai, whereas the statement is not demonstrated in any but the most arbitrary allegorical sense. Altogether, this passage would not be missed if it were removed from Galatians, for it is an embarrassment for most interpreters.[15]

If the text really does contrast two entitles called Judaism and Christianity, then indeed it is an anachronism, and at least verses 24b-27, 30 must be omitted as a later gloss, as O'Neill argues.[16] If that solution be too radical and easy, one could perhaps excuse Paul by saying that the subject matter was thrust on him by his opponents, as C. K. Barrett has claimed.[17] Doing so acknowledges that the correct understanding of the Sarah-Hagar tradition really is on the side of the opponents and that Paul was forced to wrest the text violently from them by "a wilful distortion in sheer Hellenistic midrash speculation."[18] But quite apart from the fact that Paul can use the same tradition in Romans 9 and the questionable methodology involved in appealing to statements of opponents which are never explicitly mentioned, one hesitates to postulate a Paul arguing desperately in a losing cause. It may be that rather than finding excuses for Paul, the basic assumptions of Pauline interpretation should be questioned.

Although Paul uses the word allegory, those who discuss his hermeneutics usually speak in terms of typology[19]—and then after all give an allegorical interpretation of this passage. I would like to suggest rather that Paul is engaging in *heilsgeschichtliche* midrash, making some use thereby of the Pythagorean tables of contraries. C. H. Dodd said, "In the one place where Paul expressly speaks of 'allegory' . . . his use of the term *systoichein* in itself betrays that he is following the well-accepted rule of the game, to arrange two series of terms in parallel *stoichoi* or columns, in such a way that they correspond in pairs (*systoichousin*), the terms in the left-hand column being figurative, and the terms in the right-hand column indicating the significance attached to them. . . . This is allegory proper, conforming to the rules."[20] It is indeed allegory proper, and one could make up a series of pairs from, for example, Matt 13:37-39, but it has nothing whatsoever to do with the verb *systoichein*. Also Burton makes use of this term to justify a series of allegorical equivalents: Hagar = Sinai covenant = present Jerusalem; Ishmael = Jews; Sarah = new covenant = Jerusalem above; Isaac = Christians.[21] While this is certainly allegorical in the sense of being arbitrary, one would have to appeal to *allēgorein* and not to *systoichein*. No one really knows what the verb means,[22] and the only place where it occurs in ancient literature throws little light on Gal 4:25.[23] Following Chrysostom, the ancient church thought it meant "borders on (geographically),"[24] which makes little sense here. Modern understanding ranges from the precise (but false) "has the same alphabetical value as"[25] to the too contextual "to answer to . . . of a type in the OT which answers to the antitype in the New"[26] to the generally accepted (but vague) "to correspond to." Considerations of the use of the noun *systoichia* by the Pythagoreans as reported by Aristotle perhaps allows some progress.[27]

Other members of this same school say there are ten principles, which they arrange in two columns of cognates (*kata systoichian*):

limit	and	unlimited
odd	and	even
one	and	plurality
right	and	left
male	and	female
resting	and	moving
straight	and	curved
light	and	darkness
good	and	bad
square	and	oblong

These pairs are called "definite contrarities," but other references make it clear that the term *systoichia* refers not to the pairs of opposites but to the vertical column or row (*stoichos*) which can be placed next to another (*syn-stoichia*).[28] One passage makes this quite clear: "the opposites are divided up into two columns, so that each is classed with that which is akin to it (*hekaston pros tēn syggenē systoichian*), e.g., right is in the opposite column to left and hot to cold."[29] Although the verb *systoichein* does not appear in this connection, how might it have been used? To take the Pythagorean table, would one say that "odd" *systoichei* with "limit" or "even"? The answer is not clear, but it may be that Dodd was correct in saying that "they correspond in pairs (*systoichousin*)," or better: *systoichein* = to correspond to the opposite member of the pair in the other column (*stoichos*). In any case, it is clear that Paul is not indulging in allegory but drawing up two columns of opposites, beginning with real people and continuing with the history of their descendants, which can be called the Hagar column and the Sarah column.

Hagar	*Sarah*
Son (Ishmael)	Son Isaac
from the slave	from the free

born according to flesh	born through the promise
covenant from Sinai	—
giving birth into slavery	our mother is free
those born according to flesh persecute	children of promise persecuted
to be cast out	to inherit

I argued above that it is important to understand Galatians within the context of Paul's justification of his gospel for the Gentiles, dealing with specifically Gentile problems. I also said that it is best methodologically to try to understand Paul in continuity with the traditions of Judaism unless there are explicit grounds to the contrary. Is there anything in those traditions which might throw light on Paul's use of his Hagar and Sarah columns? That individuals in the stories of Genesis also incorporate their later descendants does not need to be demonstrated. Insofar as Genesis 17 is in Paul's mind, there is no chapter in the whole of Genesis in which the word *bryt* appears so frequently, and the association of the covenant with Sarah is natural, although there is nothing there to connect it with Hagar. There are, however, three later traditions of interpretation concerning Ishmael I would like to cite.

One is the old midrash on Deut 33:2 concerning the offering of Torah to the nations. I cite the version in *Mekilta*, Baḥodesh 5:

> And it was for the following reason that the nations of the world were asked to accept the Torah: In order that they should have no excuse of saying: Had we been asked we would have accepted it. For, behold, they were asked and they refused to accept it, for it is said: "And he said: 'The Lord came from Sinai,'" etc. (Deut 33:2). He appeared to the children of Esau the wicked and said to them: Will you accept the Torah? They said to Him: What is written in it? He said to them: "Thou shalt not murder" (ibid. 5:17). They then said to Him: The very heritage which our father left us was: "And by thy sword shalt thou live" (Gen 27:40). He then appeared to the children of Amon and Moab. He said to them: Will you accept the Torah? They said to Him: What is written in it? He said to them: "Thou shalt not commit adultery" (Deut 5:17). They, however, said to Him that they were all of them children of adulterers, as it is said: "Thus were both the daughters of Lot with child by their father" (Gen 19:36). Then He appeared to the children of Ishmael. He said to them: Will you accept the Torah? They said to Him: What is written in it? He said to them: "Thou shalt not steal" (Deut 5:17). They then said to Him: The very blessing that had been pronounced upon our fathers was: "And he shall be as a wild ass of a man: his hand shall be upon everything" (Gen 16:12). And it is written:

> "For, indeed, I was stolen away out of the land of the Hebrews" (ibid. 40:15). But when He came to the Israelites and: "At His right hand was a fiery law unto them" (Deut 33:2), they all opened their mouths and said: "All that the Lord hath spoken will we do and obey" (Exod 24:7).[30]

Because God is said to have come from Mount Paran, the midrash concludes that he was offering his Torah to the Ishmaelites. Here the geographical locations of Sinai, Paran, and Seir as mountains in Arabia provide the Biblical basis for the widespread and early Agadah that God offered the Torah to all the nations but it was accepted only by Israel.[31] This Agadah functions to alleviate the tension between the concepts of the election of Israel and God's rule over creation, saying that God was not unfair to give such a treasure as the Torah only to Israel and not to other peoples. What the Ishmaelites and others refused was the covenant of election, but that does not mean that they are excused from the obligation of obedience to God. I have argued elsewhere that as a consequence of the identification of the law and wisdom (ben Sira), the whole of creation was seen by some early Jews (for example, 4 Ezra) to be under the law of God, but law without covenant, law which enslaves, law which works wrath.[32] The point of citing the Agadah here is to show that Ishmael (and others) could very well be used to indicate the situation of contemporary Gentiles living outside the covenant God made with Israel. That contemporary nations (Arabs in general, including Nabateans) were in fact understood in Paul's time to be descendants of Hagar and Ishmael can be shown not only by Biblical passages but also by more contemporary texts.[33]

The second text is from that part of the book of Jubilees which is parallel to Genesis 17, where after the account of the circumcision of Abraham and his household we read:

> And do thou command the children of Israel and let them observe the sign of this covenant for their generations as an eternal ordinance, and they will not be rooted out of the land. For the command is ordained for a covenant, that they should observe it for ever among all the children of Israel. For Ishmael and his sons and his brothers and Esau, the Lord did not cause to approach Him, and he did not choose them [although] they are the children of Abraham, for He knew them, but He chose Israel to be His people. And He sanctified it, and gathered it from amongst all the children of men; for there are many nations and many peoples, and all are His, and over all hath He placed spirits in authority to lead them astray from him. But over Israel he did not appoint any angel or spirit, for He alone is their ruler, and He will preserve them and require them

at the hand of His angels and His spirits, and at the hand of all His powers in order that He may preserve them and bless them, and that they may be His and He may be theirs from henceforth for ever. (15:28-32)

Once more the figures of Ishmael (and Esau) provide the occasion for reflection about God's relationship to Israel and the nations. Here the distinction is in terms of the motif of the guardian angels of the nations, a concept which began with Deut 32:8-9 and had become widespread by the time of Paul. Caird speaks in this connection of the two modes of God's sovereignty: direct, personal, and liberating in the case of Israel, and indirect, mediated through angels, unacknowledged, and enslaving in the case of the nations.[34]

The third text is practically forced upon the commentator by Paul's reference to Ishmael "persecuting" Isaac, a detail which can be explained only on the basis of a post-Biblical tradition of interpretation.[35] The full implications of Targum pseudo-Jonathan at Gen 22:1 have not yet been noted:

And it came to pass after these things, that Isaac and Ishmael were disputing. Ishmael said: "It is right for me to be the heir of my father, since I am his first-born son." But Isaac said: "It is right for me to be the heir of my father, since I am the son of Sarah his wife, but you are the son of Hagar, the handmaid of my mother." Ishmael answered and said: "I am more righteous than you because I was circumcised when 13 years old; and if it had been my wish to refuse I would not have handed myself over to be circumcised." Isaac answered and said: "Am I not now 37 years old? If the Holy One, blessed be He, demanded all my members I would not hesitate." Immediately, these words were heard before the Lord of the universe, and immediately, the word of the Lord *tested Abraham, and said unto him "Abraham" and he said "Here I am."*[36]

Isaac was circumcised and Ishmael was circumcised, but the promise was through Isaac and Ishmael was a Gentile. At the time of Paul only the Arabs among the Gentiles still practised circumcision,[37] so that if one wanted to consider the difference between Israel and Gentiles from this perspective, only the figure of Ishmael would serve. Ishmael, however, was circumcised as a young adult,[38] and this provided the basis for his boasting of his righteousness. If the troublemakers in Galatia were not only boastful but specifically were boasting of being circumcised as adults (Gal 6:12-13), then Paul must have immediately thought about Ishmael when he heard of them.

After an appeal to the experience of the Galatians (3:1-5), Paul gave the Scriptural basis (Gen 15:6) for his gospel that "God would justify the Gentiles from faithfulness" (3:6-29) and described the past of the Gentile Galatians as slavery to the elements of the world (4:1-11). Now after another appeal to experience (4:12-20), Paul again returns to a Scriptural argument concerning Abraham. What was called "promise" in the earlier section becomes "freedom" in the paraenetic section, and 4:21-31 provides such a transition. Paul has referred to the troublemakers who "want to shut [the Galatians] out" (4:17) without advising what to do (4:20). More important, something is missing from the earlier Abraham discussion, namely Sarah, who must be included to support the injunction to "stand fast" and not to let themselves "be subjected again to a yoke of slavery" (5:1).

Verse 21. Paul uses the word *nomos* in two senses in a paradox worthy of 2:19. On the one hand, it refers to the former situation of the Galatians "under law" and their present desire "again to serve as slaves anew the elements" (4:9). On the other hand, *nomos* as Scripture (as 3:8, 22; 4:30), which they should hear and obey, proclaims their redemption from such slavery.

Verses 22-23. Abraham indeed had (at least) two sons, Ishmael and Isaac. Both sons were circumcised (Ishmael, Gen 17:24; Isaac, 21:4), both had the promise of descendants (Ishmael, 16:10; 17:20; 21:13; Isaac, 17:16; 21:12). But the covenant (17:19, 21) and the inheritance (21:10) were to be only through the son of Sarah. If in Romans 4 Paul will find it sufficient to appeal to the promise to Abraham (Gen 17:5), here he must appeal to the promise concerning Sarah: "She shall be for the Gentiles; kings of peoples shall come from her" (17:16).[39] In 4:28 Gentiles are children of promise; the promise has to do with the gospel for the Gentiles and their inclusion in the people of God, and thus so does Sarah and the covenant and the line of those born from the free woman. As the texts cited earlier show, it is not unreasonable to see in Hagar and Ishmael and their unfree Gentile descendants an opposite column.

Verses 24-26. There are problems in these verses which go beyond the sense in which they are called allegory. It is not unnatural to say that Hagar and Sarah have to do with different covenants for their descendants, but there is no later *de* to match the initial *mia men*. The subject of *douleuei* (25c) is not clear; as the feminine *autēs* shows, it cannot be Sinai or *to Hagar*. It is difficult to think of Jerusalem, for if the goal of Paul's daring allegory is to assert the slavery of Jerusalem, he would have had to write *systoichei de autō* (scil. *tō Sina*) *hē nyn Ierousalēm, douleuei gar*. . . . The subject of *systoichei* (25b), on the other hand, must be Sinai, for otherwise 25a is left dangling. The very word order *Sina oros*, differing from the more common *oros Sina* in verse 24, seems to suggest that reference to another mountain, quite a different mountain, is anticipated. It is also necessary to make some sense of the three *gar*'s. Insofar as there are two *systoichiai*, one of them is not complete. One would have expected that verse 26 would have read something like: *deutera de apo orous Siōn, eis eleutherian gennōsa, hētis estin Sarra.*[40] One would indeed expect a "Zion" in the Sarah column over against Sinai (as in, for example, Heb 12:18, 22), but the "Jerusalem above" cannot fill that role if it is already taken to be opposite the "present Jerusalem." If it is strange to use the word "present Jerusalem" for "the political and religious institutions of Judaism,"[41] it is even stranger that Paul should use the word Jerusalem at all in such a bad sense, particularly in the context of a letter where he wants the Galatians to contribute to the collection for Jerusalem.[42] *Nyn* and *anō* are not really opposites, and the entire Jewish tradition which speaks of a heavenly Jerusalem does so in the sense of a promise to the present Jerusalem.[43] Also Paul's logic seems to make sense only if the two references to Jerusalem are somehow related, the one explaining the other, like the two references to Sinai in verses 24 and 25. It is the position of "the present Jerusalem" in the Hagar column which causes the exegetical problems. In considering in addition the necessity of finding a subject for verse 25c, I shall for the moment bracket verse 25ab, so that the text reads: "For these [women] are two covenants: the one, on the one hand, from Mount Sinai, giving birth into slavery; she is Hagar, for she serves [as a slave] with her children. The Jerusalem above, on the other hand, is free—she is our mother."

Verse 24. Betz is probably correct in defining the word *diathēkē* here as "a world order decreed by divine institution."[44] He is surely incorrect, however, in reading into the passage a contrast between an old and a new covenant. The two "covenants" are clearly simultaneous and not successive.[45] The lines of descent with promise and without promise have continued from the time of Sarah and Hagar down to present Israel and Gentiles. Paul has already spoken of slavery to the non-gods (4:8), to the elements of the world (4:3, 9), to specifically Gentile slavery, even when the situation is called being under law (3:23, 25; 4:5). It may be that the slavery of the Gentiles under a law administered by angels is referred to in the obscure 3:19.[46] In any case, the Gentile Hagar is here associated with both slavery and Sinai, with very little explanation. Insofar as Paul meant to communicate and not confuse, this presupposes a prior knowledge by the Galatians of the traditions connecting Gentiles with Sinai and the angels of the nations (cf. *Mekilta* and *Jubilees* above). But then, nearly every interpretation of this passage presupposes some prior knowledge on the part of the readers.

Verses 26-28. The line of promise is through Sarah, and it is for the children of Zion. It is therefore very appropriate for Paul to cite Isa 54:1, a word of comfort spoken to the present Jerusalem because of the promise of the new Jerusalem (vv 11-17). In the light of Isa 51:2 (the only place where Sarah appears in the Bible outside Genesis), it may be that already the original text had in mind the earlier *'qrh* Sarah when it renewed the promise of descendants to contemporary Jerusalem.[47] The citation does not serve to show that Sarah/Zion is free (that was the starting point in verse 22), but that she is our mother. It is especially in Deutero-Isaiah that the children of Zion (and Sarah, cf. 51:4-6) are also joined by the Gentiles.

As a later reader who best understood Paul put it, the Gentiles are no longer "alienated from the *politeia* of Israel and strangers to the covenants of promise . . . no longer strangers and sojourners but fellow citizens with the saints" (Eph 2:12, 17). This surely is Paul's point in Galatians, to claim for the Gentile Galatians the promises of the line of Sarah/Zion, the Jerusalem above, and not to deny them to the Jews or the present Jerusalem. The letter concludes after all with the benediction: "whoever follow this criterion, peace be on them and mercy, and also [peace and mercy be] on God's [people] Israel" (6:16).[48] If in the words of Deutero-Isaiah Sarah has more children than Hagar, it is because with the fulfilment of the promise Gentiles are being called from the Hagar column into the Sarah column. This is the column in which the Galatians stand, for they are "children of promise according to Isaac."

Verses 29-30. Paul's positive point is that the Galatians have been called to be Isaac people: children of promise. The negative warning is that they should not become again Ishmael people: children of slavery. Mussner is quite right in his insistence that Paul uses Gen 21:10 not in order to pronounce the rejection of Israel but to urge the expulsion of the troublemakers, those people on whom Paul had pronounced a solemn curse (1:9).[49] They were engaged in "persecuting"[50] the Galatians in that they tried "to shut them out" (4:17), as they "persecuted" Paul by trying to destroy his work (5:11). As it is necessary to draw on post-Biblical tradition to understand Ishmael's persecution of Isaac, so it may be that that same tradition can explain who the Ishmael people in Galatia are: they are those who undergo voluntary circumcision as adults (6:13) and urge it on others (5:2; 6:12) as an achievement and a boast. Paul's argument is not against circumcision (or Judaism) as such, but for adult Gentiles to circumcise themselves would mean seeking to earn something and thus deny God's grace. Such Ishmael people are not heirs of the promise, for even if they are in a sense children of Abraham, they are not children of Sarah.

Verses 4:31 and 5:1. Paul returns to his major point, that the Galatians are not only heirs of the promise (cf. 3:14, 29) but as children of Sarah are also free. To follow the urging of the Ishmael people would mean "to be subjected *again* to a yoke of slavery." That means that they were also in the Hagar column before, a column which can in no sense represent Judaism but must refer to Gentiles, under the law but apart from the covenant of grace. The slavery from which the Galatians, as heirs of the promise to Sarah, have been liberated is slavery to the non-gods, "the weak and impotent elements, whom *again* they wish to serve as slaves anew" (4:9). Gal 4:21-31 can then be understood not as a digression directed against Jews but as part of Paul's proclamation of his gospel "that for the Gentiles the blessing of Abraham might become a reality in Jesus Christ" (3:14). That gospel is greatly enriched by the statement that the Gentiles also inherit from Sarah and thus like her are free.

Verse 25ab. It is time to remove the brackets around verse 25ab. Purely on text-critical grounds the reading *to gar Sina* (without *Hagar*) is to be preferred.[51] It also avoids the rather bizarre concept that Paul is using a pun on an Arabic word to convince the Galatians that Hagar ought to be connected with Sinai.[52] To be sure, the statement "for Sinai is a mountain in Arabia" is meant to provide a basis for that association, but I would argue that it is on the basis of the midrash on Deut 33:2 which says that Torah was offered in the dessert to the surrounding nations before it was accepted by Israel. It is clear that Paul understands the word Sinai in a very unusual sense when he associates it with Hagar and Gentiles and slaves rather than with the election of Israel. That election, into which the Galatians have now been called, is spoken of in terms of Sarah and Mount Zion, the heavenly Jerusalem, from which the present Jerusalem really cannot be detached. The only thing which stands in the way of verse 25ab fitting into the context of the exegesis of 21-31 given above is the difficult word *systoichein*. But a possible solution is at hand. Translating according to the considerations outlined above would produce: "It [Sinai] is in the opposite column from the present Jerusalem, for she [Hagar] serves [as a slave] with her children." Thereby the problems caused by the current understanding of the present Jerusalem are avoided. It is also only now possible to account for the logic of the supporting sentences: the slavery Sinai covenant is Hagar, *for* Sinai is in Arabia; that is the opposite of Jerusalem, *for* Hagar is in slavery; Jerusalem is free and our mother, *for* Isaiah 54 says so. Sentences which previously were very obscure now fall into place, if only it is possible to find a new way of understanding a very rare verb, *systoichein*. It is not certain whether the proposed solution is philologically correct, but it is at least preferable in having recourse to the hypothesis of a gloss.[53]

It is doubtful that I have completely demonstrated that Paul does not use the figure of Hagar to designate contemporary Israel, but at least I have made the traditional interpretation problematic. If it is true that "wirklich verständlich ist [Rom 9] v 8 überhaupt nur für den, welcher Gal 4:21-31 im Kopfe hat," as Lietzmann writes,[54] then a problematic passage can no longer dominate a clearer one. I now turn to a brief look at Romans 9.

Almost all interpreters bring to Romans 9 the same presuppositions that have affected the understanding of Galatians 4. That is, it is assumed that Paul's basic argument is with Jewish opponents and that it is directed against Judaism as such. His understanding of Biblical passages must therefore be diametrically opposed to that of his predecessors and contemporaries in Judaism. It is further assumed that Paul does not understand "the truth of the election which includes all Israelites, both righteous and sinners"[55] and that he is ignorant of the fact that "in the entire body of Palestinian Jewish literature between Ben Sirah and the redaction of the Mishnah, with only the exception of 4 Ezra, membership in the covenant is considered salvation."[56]

The most astonishing presupposition has to do with the major thesis of Romans 9. While it is almost universally held by exegetes, I will cite only three examples. "The basic fact which, *although it is never actually mentioned*, lies behind every verse in the opening paragraph, and sets in motion the whole long argument for chs. ix-xi, is that, notwithstanding her privileges, and his apostolic labour, Israel has rejected the Gospel Paul preached."[57] "Ihr [der Trauer] Grund wird *nicht ausdrücklich genannt*, ist aber aus V 3 zu erschliessen: der Unglaube der Juden gegenüber dem Evangelium."[58] "The Apostle . . . *has never definitely stated* [his theme] but it can be inferred: . . . in spite of these privileges Israel is rejected. . . . He naturally shrinks from mentioning too definitely a fact which is to him so full of sadness."[59] How is it that people can say that chapter 9 deals with the unbelief of Israel when it is never mentioned, and all human activity, whether doing or believing, whether Jewish or Gentile, is expressly excluded from consideration? How can people say that Paul teaches the divine rejection of Israel in chapter 9 when he later expressly says the opposite (11:1)?[60] How can people say that the purpose of 9:6-13 is to declare that Israel is not defined by physical descent from the patriarchs when Paul later says that "as regards election they [= all Israel] are beloved for the sake of the patriarchs" (11:28)? How has Romans 9 been turned into an anti-Jewish polemic?

Part of the answer has to do with what Stendahl called "the introspective conscience of the West."[61] At least since Augustine Westerners have been preoccupied with the importance of individual belief or unbelief and the question of human freedom over against God's election. As a result, the concept of Israel's unbelief has come to the forefront as a negative example for Christians, and a tension has entered the structure of these chapters. Chapter 9 must deal with Israel's unbelief from the perspective of God's electing and rejecting will; chapter 10 with the same question from the perspective of human responsibility and guilt; and chapter 11 provides a future resolution in dialectical fashion so that contradictions between 9 and

11 are not only to be expected but also provide the key to the interpretation. Although I will deal here only with 9:6-29, it will be necessary to indicate at the end something of my undialectical understanding also of chapter 10.

Ever since the time of Irenaeus,[62] it has become customary to see Esau as a type of the synagogue and Jacob as a type of the church. That means to read Romans 9 semi-allegorically, which might have been justified by an appeal to Galatians 4:24. If that support falls, however, there is certainly no reason to call Ishmael "die fleischliche Art des Judentums";[63] or to say that Esau "represents the physical Israel";[64] or to make the equation of "the Pharaoh of the Exodus . . . as the prefiguration of that disobedient Israel which is now opposed to the gospel";[65] or to find that "the chapter ends by seeing in Sodom and Gomorrah types of the present state of Israel as a whole."[66] The people mentioned here have to be themselves first, and Paul must be allowed make his own application to the present.

Because Paul's argument must *ex hypothesi* be directed against Judaism, it is not uncommon to hear especially in verse 14 the voice of "der jüdische Gegner,"[67] "a definite opponent, a typical Jew,"[68] or even "his Pharisaic opponents."[69] And yet this is said in the context of a section (cf. 11:13, 28) and letter (1:5-6, 13; 15:15-16) which is explicitly addressed to Gentile Christians and which, differing from other letters, makes no reference to opponents at all (cf. 1:12; 15:14).[70] Unless there develop strong reasons to the contrary, it should be assumed that Paul says what he says because he thinks those addressed, and not some third party, need to hear it. Assuming in addition that Paul understands himself in continuity with Biblical and post-Biblical Jewish traditions,[71] I turn now to the text.

Verse 6a. "Now it is not that the word of God has lapsed." If this needs to be stated, it is presumably to the same people who ask, "Has God rejected his people?" (11:1) and who need to be warned not to boast with respect to the Jews (11:18, 20, 25). Eichholz took a big step forward when he said that Romans 9 should be understood "nicht als primär israelkritisch sondern als primär kirchenkritisch."[72] Paul writes to the Roman Gentile Christians, but he writes about Israel's past and the "standing" of the word of God. It is a further step forward when Barth and Cranfield read these chapters under the general heading of God's mercy and faithfulness.[73] The word of God which has not lapsed refers to the foregoing impressive list of the "privileges" of Israelites, Paul's kinsmen according to the flesh (3-5). What Israelites are has nothing to do with what Israelites do, good or bad, "in order that God's purpose of election might stand—[based] not on works but on the one who calls" (11); it has to do not with human "willing or running but with God being merciful"(16). If what is said of Israelites is true, it is because of God's grace and God's promise, and this is the word of God which has not lapsed.

Verses 6b-7a. "For not all who are from Israel are Israel, nor are all the children [of Abraham] Abraham's seed."[74] Michel sees very clearly that the traditional interpretation would require this sentence to begin with an *alla* rather than a *gar*, but he nevertheless persists with the old interpretation.[75] The point is that verses 6b-7a is not at all the "Leitthese"[76] for the chapter but the *ground* for the thesis of 6a and thus 4-5. God's grace toward Israel, Abraham's seed, stands, even if election also involves those not chosen: Abraham's other children, those *ex Israēl.*[77] I shall return later to the non-chosen.

Verses 7b-9. Isaac was chosen because his birth was in accordance with a word of promise; all "the children of [God's] promise are counted as 'seed.' " Once more, as in Galatians 4, it is necessary to name Sarah specifically, and not just Abraham, as the one about whom the promise was given.

Verses 10-13. Jacob was chosen and Esau was not. They had the same mother, the same father, came from the same drop of semen (*koitē*), and had not done anything at all, good or bad, when Jacob became the recipient of God's gracious election. That reference is made both to Ishmael and to Esau may add some support to our thesis that Paul knew something like the midrash in *Mekilta* cited above. In any case it is clear, both from Genesis and from Paul's use of it, that Ishmael and Esau are Gentiles and not chosen and, conversely, that Isaac and Jacob and their decendants were chosen and so the word of God has not fallen and the designations of Israelites still hold. While the supposition is not necessary for my exegesis, great poignancy would be added to the Malachi citation if the identification of Esau with Rome were old enough to be known by Paul and even more if it were known by his Roman readers.[78]

I conclude that Paul does not dispute but emphatically affirms in these verses the common Jewish concept of the election and that by grace alone. The word of God has not lapsed, and Israel's election remains. Even if there might be problems for Gentiles (or even for individual Jews who become apostate, *ex Israēl*), it is clear that the Jews of Paul's time are seen to be descendants of Abraham and Isaac and Jacob and not of Ishmael and Esau. I could close the discussion here if there did not remain too many unanswered questions.

Verse 14. I now return to those not chosen in verses 9-13. "Is there injustice with God?" It certainly must seem so to Ishmael and Esau and their descendants and to all the Gentiles who do not share the "privileges" of Israel (4-5). If one speaks of election, which "is not a matter of human willing or running" (16), it makes no sense to blame the non-elect, and they might very well find God to be unfair. I believe that the same objection is raised in the close parallel to Romans 9 in 3:1-9. There God's faithfulness and righteousness and truth are not nullified by the unfaithfulness of Israel. God in his mercy has granted to Israel the possibility of repentance and forgiveness (Ps 51!), concepts glaringly lacking in Paul's gospel to the uncircumcised. The objection in 3:5-8 is then specifically a Gentile objection, which Paul does not immediately answer, but he refers rather to the accountability of the whole *world* (3:6, 19);[79] only then comes the resolution of the difficulty (not justification of the complaint!) in the new manifestation of the righteousness of God (3:21-31).

Verses 15-16. God is not unfair to the non-chosen because it is his very nature to be merciful. Thus Paul declares in the words of the definition of God's name in Exod 33:19. Here in this most central of all Torah texts is expressed the way Israel understands God and therefore the way Israel understands itself. It is a perfect summary of what was said about the way God has had mercy in verses 6-13, but it is not at all clear how this statement is the reason (*gar*) for the rejection of the objection in verse 14. It is precisely because of God's great mercy shown to Isaac and Jacob that the Ishmaels and Esaus raised the question of fairness in the first place. It is not at all a matter of human activity or worth but of "God being merciful." A further explanation is necessary.

Verses 17-18. A further reason is found in God's statement to Pharaoh. Here it is not a matter only of Ishmael or Esau, who also had their promises, not just a matter of those who "had not yet done anything good or bad," but of Israel's greatest enemy, the Pharaoh of the Exodus (and all his oppressive successors?). This Pharaoh is not even interesting in himself but was brought into existence ("raised up") only to provide an occasion for God to demonstrate his power for salvation (cf. 1:16)[80] for his people Israel, and in order that his saving activity in the Exodus might be proclaimed in all the earth (Exod 9:16). The only hint of any divine patience toward Pharaoh is found in the uncited previous verse, where God says that he could have killed Pharaoh and all the Egyptians with pestilence but refrained. But even that is not said by Paul. If Pharaoh is allowed to live, it is not for his own sake but only so that he can serve as an instrument for God's act of mercy to Israel. God has mercy, yes, but there are also those he hardens, that is, makes stubborn, strengthens to fulfil his purposes. Israel's great enemy was such a one, but he existed only that God could exercise his mercy toward Israel.

Verses 19-23. These difficult verses can be dealt with only in summary fashion. In making a general statement now for the first time, Paul builds on his history of God's mercy to Israel in the past but introduces new concepts. The complaint with which the section begins is still very much a Gentile complaint, as the close parallel in Wisdom 12:12 shows.[81] Also Wisdom, particularly in chapters 11-19, wrestles with the question of Israel and the nations, and a comparison with Paul is instructive. Seen from the perspective of God's mercy toward Israel, the Egyptians (11:15-12:2) and Canaanites (12:3-11) are less favoured because they are the enemies of Israel (12:20),[82] and so the author turns back the complaint of the Canaanites: "Who will say, 'What hast thou done?' Or who will resist thy judgment? Who will accuse thee for the destruction of nations which thou didst make?" The solution is that God was gracious toward the Egyptians and Canaanites in that he did not destroy them at once but overlooked their sin (11:23), in order by his longsuffering and limited punishment to allow them time to come to repentance (12:2, 10, 15, 20). This concept of God's longsuffering with respect to Gentiles is something of a commonplace within Hellenistic Judaism.[83] It is found in the New Testament in Acts 14:16; 17:30; 2 Peter 3:9; and once in Paul, Rom 2:4, although repentance is otherwise not part of his preaching. When Paul says in 9:22 that "God endured instruments of wrath with great longsuffering," it is of course against this general background, but there are significant differences. The statement is clearly related to the citation concerning Pharaoh in verse 17a, but there Pharaoh would have to be called rather an instrument of mercy. The reference to wrath is new here. When Paul says in verses 22b-33 that God's endurance with great longsuffering was "because[84] he wanted to make known his power [for salvation] and [moreover did so] in order to make known the wealth of his glory" on Israel (cf. 9:4), that too is in accordance with what is said of Pharaoh in verse 17b, with the exception of the addition of "to show forth his wrath." I shall return to the new concepts added in this section.

To this point, then, Paul has spoken only of God's mercy toward Israel. Since consideration of any human activity has been rigorously excluded, it is completely undeserved and rests completely in the grace of God. Israel has no cause whatsoever for boasting in its election, but since that is not a particular characteristic of Judaism nor is Paul writing to Jews, this emphasis may well be for the benefit of someone else. The Gentiles have so far came into focus only as those not chosen (Ishmael, Esau) or as those God uses, not for their own sakes but solely as instruments of his grace toward Israel (Pharaoh).

Verses 24-26. I come now to the climax of Paul's discussion of the mercy of God. The Gentiles are also included, they are also "called." Paul differs from Wisdom in his understanding of God's longsuffering toward Gentiles, because what Gentiles need is more than repentance and what they receive is more than a second-class mercy. "After the ignoring of previous sins in the clemency of God it was to demonstrate his righteousness in the present time in that he is righteous and thus justifies a human being out of the faithfulness of Jesus" (Rom 3:25b-26). What the Gentiles need is not repentance but life from the dead, not a turning back (*tšwbh*) but a "turning to (*epistrephein*) God from idols" (1 Thess 1:9). What they receive is complete incorporation into the elect people of God. The importance of not relativizing the "privileges" of Israel is seen in the many parallels between Romans 8 and Romans 9,[85] between the church and Israel: *huiothesia* (8:15; 9:4), children of God (8:16-17, 21; 9:8), glory (8:18, 21; 9:4, 23), God's election (8:28; 9:11) and calling (8:28, 30; 9:7, 12). Roman Gentiles must understand that Israel's election depends solely on God's mercy because their own election depends on that same mercy. This has been the point of the whole chapter.

Verses 27-29. I would understand Paul's use of the two citations from Isaiah in a positive sense.[86] "Seed" (cf. vv 7-8) will be left to Israel; God will never abandon his people. God's election of course never promised a rose garden, but just as Israel survived the Assyrians in Isaiah's time, so they will survive (the Romans?) in Paul's time. The concept of "remnant" has nothing at all to do with Jewish Christians as such. Rom 9:1-29 deals exclusively with the theme of the mercy of God.

I have now completed my task. Because the chapter deals with the mercy of God, with the faithfulness of God to his own word, completely apart from any human activity (11b-12a, 16), therefore there has been no reference to the unbelief or faith of Israel or anyone else, just as (except for verse 5) the person of Christ never appeared. In such a context it is absolutely impossible that such figures as Isaac, Jacob, Moses should have to do with anything but Israel, or Ishmael, Esau, Pharaoh with anything but non-Israel, the non-elect, the Gentiles. If my reading of this chapter is to have any hope of being convincing, however, certain other questions will have to be tentatively addressed.

1. Predestination. Paul introduced new categories into verses 19-23, in particular the concept of God's wrath. It may be that the *skeuē orgēs* refer to the objects of God's wrath and the *skeuē eleous* to the objects of his mercy, thus introducing the concept of predestination. If so, the section simply goes beyond verses 6-18 but should not be used to interpret those verses, for there is absolutely no reference to God's wrath in the earlier section, not even with respect to Esau and Pharaoh. If Paul speaks of predestination here, it must be understood within the context of what he says about God's mercy. If Gentiles are "by nature children of wrath," Paul's gospel proclaims that God in his mercy has given them life (Eph 2:3-5); if in Gal 4:21-31 there was a slave and a free column, God's new act in Christ was to change Gentiles from the first to the second; if in Romans 9 there are objects of wrath and objects of mercy, Romans 11 says that God changes the first into the second. It is however also possible to translate *skeuos* as "instrument," which would make a better connection with what is said about Pharaoh in verse 17.

2. The instruments of mercy. It is conceivable that "we who were called, not only from the Jews but also from the Gentiles" as "instruments of mercy which he prepared beforehand" were prepared for the glorification of others, that is, that the reference is to those who carry out the mission to the Gentiles. (Verse 27 refers to a saved remnant; when the concept next appears in chapter 11, it seems to refer to a saving remnant, for the only example given of that remnant is the Apostle to the Gentiles himself.) If so, then the concept would refer forward and not backward, for there is nothing to prepare for it in 9:1-18. The concept would help explain the strange parable of the olive branches. God would have preferred to use as his instruments of mercy the good olive branches, but since they would not he had to make do with wild olive branches, Gentiles, as his missionaries. Israel is an unwitting instrument of mercy in 11:11-12, and in 11:30-31 Jews and Gentiles are instruments of mercy each to the other. But such considerations are highly speculative.[87]

3. The instruments of wrath. This translation is much easier to establish, for it appears already in the LXX (Isa 13:5; Jer 27:25). The prime example of an instrument of wrath is Assyria, the rod of God's anger from the same chapter in Isaiah (10) which Paul cites. The concept of wrath is very important in Romans, and it makes sense to say that God needs people (or powers) through whom his wrath can be executed. The difficulty is to see how it fits into these chapters. It does not appear in 9:1-18, for Pharaoh is neither an object of God's wrath (Pharaoh is not blamed in verse 17 — God raised him up for his own purposes, apart from whether he had done "anything good or bad") nor an instrument of God's wrath (he was rather an instrument of God's mercy). It is significant that Munck, who champions this interpretation but strangely thinks of Jews as the instruments of wrath, is forced to resort to Acts for instances of Jews persecuting Christians.[88] But Jews persecuted Gentile Christians neither in historical fact nor in the view of Paul, and one looks in vain for anyone or anything in Romans 10 and 11 which could be called an instrument of wrath.

4. Does Pharaoh have a counterpart in Paul's present? The answer to this question depends on the degree to which Romans, particularly 13:1-7, can be read in the context of the political situation.[89] If Pharaoh is seen as the example of the oppressor of Israel and if Paul were interested in hinting at the political situation, then Pharaoh's counterpart could be seen in the Roman emperor. Esau, whom God "hated," might already have been a name for the empire in the first century. In the *Mekilta* the descendants of Esau said that "the very heritage which our father left us was: 'And by thy sword shalt thou live.' " It is conceivable that all of this is reflected in Romans 13:4, where the "one in authority . . . bears the sword" and is "the servant of God to execute his wrath." This would bear investigation,

but it has nothing whatsoever to do with Romans 9-11 except to account for the anticipatory "instruments of wrath" in 9:22.

5. The place of Romans 10. Insofar as Romans 9 and 10 have been thought to reflect two sides of the same reality, namely God's rejection of Israel, a word must be said here. I would understand Romans 9 to speak primarily of God's election of Israel and Romans 10 to refer to the new expression of his righteousness which calls Gentiles into the people of God. The chapters then are not to be seen dialectically but successively. Rom 9:30; 10:3b-18, 19b-20 deal with the theme of the inclusion of the Gentiles.[90] Interpreters have been misled by the fact that formally Paul presents his gospel of Gentile inclusion as the content of what Israel did not understand (9:31-10:3a, 19a).

6. Paul's complaint about Jews. Romans 9 is not about the unbelief of Israel nor the rejection of Israel. Paul does refer elsewhere to Israel's lack of understanding (10:3, 19), to Israel's disobedience (10:21; 11:11-12, 31) and to Israel's lack of faithfulness (3:3; 11:20), all with respect to the Gentile mission. In Rom 2:17-24 Paul refers bitterly to Israel's task of being a light to the Gentiles, a task in which they have failed in his opinion. But he really does not, in Romans 9-11 or elsewhere, charge Israel with a lack of faith or a concept of works-righteousness.

7. Congruence with the conclusion. Just before his final great doxology, Paul sums up what he has said in these chapters in 11:28-32. "In the spreading of the Gospel" (NEB) Jews are enemies (6 above), but "as regards election they are beloved for the sake of the patriarchs" (cf. 9:1-18). "For irrevocable are the *charismata* (the "privileges" of 9:4-5) and the *klēsis* (the *kalein* of 9:7,12) of God." Everything is "not a matter of human willing or running but of God being merciful" (9:16), and ultimately all "instruments" turn out to be instruments of mercy, even though all disobeyed. "For God has imprisoned all to disobedience, in order that he might have mercy on all."

6

WORKS OF LAW AS A SUBJECTIVE GENITIVE

Torah has a richness of meaning in ancient Jewish texts which may be paralleled by *nomos* in other texts,[1] but which is greatly distorted by the translation "law." That is because "law" is used in a special theological sense in Christian, and especially Protestant, systems of thought that is quite inappropriate for the ancient texts themselves. Such deep-seated theological presuppositions about what a word or phrase must mean thus take precedence even over normal rules of lexicography and grammar. Here I will look at the work of one scholar who attempted to break through such presuppositions, and whose work therefore is still worth reading, but who ultimately succumbed to them and who therefore stands as a warning example. I shall look at a very specific phrase and examine one very specific question of grammar to see if it might open new possibilities of seeing what *nomos* might mean in a first-century context.

Legalism has been a perennial Christian problem, one which became very explicit at the time of the Reformation.[2] Insofar as the concept of "faith versus works" becomes a central theological issue, the meaning of the phrase "works of law" seems obvious. It is usually not discussed as such,[3] but the explicit statement of Burton may be taken as typical: "By *erga nomou* Paul means deeds of obedience to formal statutes done in the legalistic spirit, with the expectation of thereby meriting and securing divine approval and award."[4] I will put aside for the moment the question of how such a concept might function within Judaism and whether or not Paul's denial of it is "the denial of the orthodox Jewish (Pharisaic) doctrine of salvation."[5] I shall also put aside the question of the usefulness of such a concept in a system of Christian religion and the appropriateness of opposing it to a concept of "faith." The question is whether the phrase *erga nomou* grammatically *can* mean what the theologians say it *must* mean.

"The famous Pauline phrase *erga nomou* appears so easy in its literal sense and so understandable in itself that the question of its meaning and the nature of its grammatical connection seems superfluous." That is the first sentence of one of the few and certainly the most thorough discussion of the phrase in an essay by Ernst Lohmeyer published in 1929.[6] Although he says that the only natural grammatical possibility is a *genetivus auctoris*, "the works worked by the law," he nevertheless asserts that it obviously must mean "works which the law prescribes." He is then faced with the problem of how the phrase can mean what obviously it must mean. A number of possibilities are tried and rejected: *genetivus auctoris*, *genetivus objectivus*, *genetivus qualitativus*. In the light of Deissmann's *genetivus mysticus*, Lohmeyer even briefly considers a *genetivus nomisticus* before rejecting such a conclusion as silly. Some forty pages later, he is still unable to answer his own question,[7] but the intervening journey is very interesting.

It is important at first to note a number of observations Lohmeyer makes while establishing the problem, before looking at his own solution. He is interested almost exclusively in the concept of "works." He says that the word "works" is never used absolutely in the New Testament except for Paul and James 2. It is usually qualified, by an adjective (for example, "good") or by a genitive. He claims that this is otherwise always a *genetivus auctoris*, whether it speaks of works of men, of God, of Christ, of the devil, of darkness, or the like. He finds no parallel to the Pauline phrase *erga nomou*,[8] except for the title of a late midrash, *Ma'ase Torah*,[9] which speaks of the good things Torah has done and does and is therefore irrelevant. He notes that the phrase is never connected with a genitive of the person, "the Judaizers' works of law" or the like. Similarly, no one is ever said to do works of law, although Paul can speak of doing (*poiein*, *prassein*)[10] or keeping (*phylassein*)[11] or fulfilling (*telein*, *plēroun*)[12] the law. The phrase always follows the preposition *ek* (once *chōris*) to indicate the source of something. The phrase applies to Gentiles as well as to Jews.[13] Finally, the phrase seems to be related to another undefinable genitive, *pistis Christou*.[14]

The bulk of Lohmeyer's essay is devoted to a discussion of the concept of works, particularly as found in *Pss. Sol.* and 4 Ezra. Like the LXX, these writings speak of the works of God and the works of men, whereby the latter by themselves are usually seen to be bad. The works of God and human works come together in the commandments, which mean both God's demand *and* God's reward, works done by people *and* works done by God. Thus, especially in 4 Ezra, works and grace, law and grace, belong together. Although Lohmeyer tried and in my opinion failed to establish the usage in the Hebrew Bible,[15] the writings he analyses have many parallels to the Pauline exhortation "to work the work of the Lord."[16] Whether any human work is in fact the work of the Lord will not be known until revealed at the judgment, but in the meantime it is the past, present, and future service of God, done with trust in the grace of God. Lohmeyer finds a close parallel between Akiba's saying, "All is foreseen, but freedom of choice is given; and the world is judged by grace,"[17] and Paul's saying, "Work out your own salvation with fear and trembling; for God is at work in you, both to will and to work for his good pleasure."[18] In connection with 4 Ezra 9:31, "For behold, I sow my law in you, and it shall bring forth fruit in you," Lohmeyer even speaks of the good work of the law, of works of law as the opposite of "our own works," but he does not follow this up.[19] Works, he says, are "the form of religious existence of the pious Jew,"[20] and he assumes (though he never really states) that Paul is arguing for quite a different form of religious existence. That is, he discusses the phrase "works of law" but never explicitly the Pauline sentence "by works of law no one is justified."[21] All of his explicit discussion serves to throw important light on the many passages where Paul speaks of "works" or "work" in a good sense. It remains to be seen whether it helps in understanding the specific phrase *erga nomou* and the way it is used.

Lohmeyer does not live up to his own best insights. He says clearly that Paul's language about justification speaks about God's will and not human ability and that it is therefore not suitable to answer Luther's famous quest for a gracious God, but he does not follow this up. Most readers of Paul bring to the text the religious question: What must I do to be saved? and therefore hear in the text answers having to do with human activity: the right kind, believing, or the wrong kind, doing works, or even worse, doing works which are on a list, "doing what the law demands," as the NEB rather plumply translates our phrase. While there are Pauline texts well suited to the question "What ought we to do?" this should not automatically be assumed with every text. If a text speaks of works, they may not be human works; if it speaks of faith, it may not be human faith; if it speaks of righteousness, it may not be human righteousness. If it is never said of anyone that that person does "works of law," it could also never be said that anyone "works (*ergazesthai*)" the law. Could it be said of the law that it works anything?

There are two other debated genitives about which I will not speak here. Is *dikaiosunē theou* to be understood as a kind of objective genitive: that righteousness (a person's own) which counts before God? Or should one take it as a genitive of origin: that righteousness (a person's) which comes from God? I shall here follow the interpretation of Cremer, Schlatter, Käsemann, and Williams[22] which refers to a quality or, better, activity of

God: it is a simple subjective genitive, and the righteousness is God's own. There is even less agreement about the genitive *pistis Christou*. Is it a kind of objective genitive meaning "faith in Christ"? I shall here follow the interpretation of Barth, Howard,[23] and others, which would understand it as the faith or, better, faithfulness of Christ. It is a simple subjective genitive, and the faithfulness is Christ's own. (Indeed if we follow the important but neglected essay by G. M. Taylor,[24] *pistis* can mean this in Galatians even without the accompanying genitive.) What now is to be done with a phrase which appears in close conjunction with such subjective genitives?

The phrase *erga nomou* appears eight times in Romans and Galatians. The passages are listed in the accompanying table for convenience of reference. Five times the phrase has to do with what is *not* the source of justification, which I take to be an action of God, as opposed to what *is* that source, twice called "the faithfulness of Christ" and once called simply "by faithfulness." The other two, which are citations from Psalm 143, have no positive counterpart, but it might be possible to understand: not by works of law but by God's truth and righteousness, from verse one of the same psalm.[25] Twice there are references to other actions of God: "Whence did you receive the Spirit?" (Gal 3:2) and "Whence did the one [God] who supplies the Spirit to you and works wonders among you [do it]?" (Gal 3:5). The answer to both questions is "not from works of law but from preaching of faithfulness," if I may so translate it. In all of these instances God's activity is said to have come from one source as contrasted to another source. What is this other source?

	Action	*Not*	*But by*
Gal 2:16	one is justified	*ex ergōn nomou*	the *pistis* of Christ
2:16	we might be justified	*ex ergōn nomou*	the *pistis* of Christ
2:16 }	all flesh shall be	*ex ergōn nomou*	(God's truth and
Rom 3:20 }	justified		righteousness, Ps 143:1)
Rom 3:28	one is justified	*chōris ergōn nomou*	*pistis*
Gal 3:2	you received the Spirit	*ex ergōn nomou*	*ex akoēs pisteōs*
3:5	[God] supplies . . . works	*ex ergōn nomou*	*ex akoēs pisteōs*
3:10	under curse	are those *ex ergōn nomou*	but not those *ek pisteōs*
(3:11)	no one is justified	*en nomo*	God justifies the Gentiles *ek pisteōs* (3:8)

Early Judaism and early Christianity agree that salvation or justification or the like comes from God's activity and not from our own, and this includes, of course, Paul as well. Thus, if all the negative genitives in the centre column of the table were changed to *ex ergōn hēmōn* the result would be quite consistent with Pauline theology. Although the exact phrase does not appear, there are passages which refer to "works" absolutely in a negative way, and it is clear that they refer to human activity: Rom 4:2, 6; 9:11, 32; 11:6. There are also passages from the Pauline school which do use *hēmōn*: Eph 2:8, "you have been saved . . . not *ex humōn* and not *ex ergōn* . . . but by grace"; 2 Tim 1:9, "God saved us . . . not *kata ta erga hēmōn* . . . but by his purpose and grace"; Tit 3:5, "God saved us . . . not *ex ergōn* . . . *ha epoiēsamen hēmeis* . . . but by his mercy." If Paul had also written that way, everything said by Lohmeyer about works would clearly apply, without the necessity of dealing with a troublesome genitive.

The last reference, Gal 3:10, is somewhat different, and it is not at all sure that we could simply substitute "our works" for the Pauline phrase. "Works of law" here are not just part of a negative "not by A but by B" statement, but they seem to do something active: they put people under a curse, a curse so serious that it requires the act of God in Christ to redeem them from it. I will not repeat what I have said elsewhere about the logic of this passage[26] except to note that Paul is speaking explicitly about the situation of Gentiles in the enveloping verses 8 and 14. Most important for present purposes is the fact that in verse 11 a statement parallel to our familiar one states that "in the law no one is justified before God." Similarly, when in 5:4 people would be justified by law (*en nomō*), Paul states in 3:21 that righteousness is not from law (*ek nomou*). It seems that law is after all the determining factor and that the phrase *erga nomou* does not want to say something rather commonplace about works but something peculiarly Pauline and therefore complex about the law.

Galatians is the letter which comes closest to what some have called a Qumran type of two-spirit determinism.[27] When chapter five refers to certain "fruits of the Spirit," it is quite clear that Paul is speaking of effects actively produced by a power called the Spirit. The parallel series, "the works of the flesh," also refers to effects actively produced by a power called the flesh. It is this phrase, *ta erga tēs sarkos*, that I would like to understand as the direct parallel to *erga nomou*. Also the law is active: it acts as a *paidagōgos*, however that is to be understood, and it puts people under a curse. If one were allowed to see the *stoicheia* and the administrators and the pagan gods as something similar, it does much more. It should be emphasized that I am speaking of law apart from covenant, law as it applies to Gentiles, but that is the topic of another chapter.[28] The thesis here is that *erga nomou* in Galatians refers not just to a negative foil to language about God's grace but to a positive power which works disastrous consequences. It is doubtful if an analysis based on Galatians alone can be persuasive.

In Romans there is much more said about the activity of the law. The law closes every mouth and makes the whole world stand guilty (3:19); it brings knowledge of sin (3:20); it charges sin (5:13); it increases Adam's fault (5:20); it has authority over a human being (7:1); it provides an occasion for sin (7:8,9); it deceives (7:11); it causes death (7:10); it kills (7:11). There is one sentence in particular which ties together important themes in Romans. In that the phrase *erga nomou* is under investigation here, it is very important since it is the only sentence which brings together the word "law" and a verb from the stem *erg-*. With this sentence I am almost prepared to rest my case. It is Romans 4:15, "the law works (*katergazetai*) wrath." No wonder the works of law are not a source of justification. No wonder that they can be said to put people under a curse. No wonder that they are opposed to the "faithfulness of Christ" as God's act of redemption.

There is one final passage that can be used to put this thesis to the test, one often neglected in this context because "work" is singular and not plural, Romans 2:14-16.[29] Here once more the religious question of what people ought to do to be saved gets very much in the way of a proper understanding. Who are the ones in this passage who get all the credit for obeying God? Are they good pagan Gentiles or specifically Christians? Do they know God's commandments because their conscience makes known to them the natural law or because Jeremiah's promise of a law written on the hearts has been fulfilled? I submit that such natural religious questions obscure the context of this passage in a part of Romans which contains anything but conciliation or good news. God is impartial in his judgment, judging Greeks as well as Jews. All have sinned, Greeks as well as Jews. But how can Gentiles have sinned when they were not given the law? Answer: because they did have the effect of the law. Without having the law Gentiles do *ta tou nomou*. What Gentiles *do* has been rather impressively described in 1:18ff. What they do is sin, and that is what is here called *ta tou nomou*. What they do not do is keep the commandments, and if Paul had meant this he could have used a phrase similar to 2:13, 25 or 27 in this very same chapter. What chapter one describes as the process of the wrath of God, this passage calls doing the things of the law. Why? Because, as Paul will later say, "the law works wrath" (4:15). What Gentiles do is not by God's will and not really by free choice, but "by nature," just as Gentiles are described in Eph 2:3 as "by nature children of wrath." This has nothing whatsoever to do with Jeremiah's Torah or the Stoic combination of *physis* and *nomos*, and the NEB completely misses the point when it translates "carry out the precepts of the law by the light of nature." As if the only thing the law did was to give precepts! As if Gentiles were not really the sinners portrayed earlier! As if alongside Torah there were another law, an unwritten law, only a similar law, a law not identical to the one Torah of the one God! What such Gentiles do when they sin is to become law for themselves, to become a parody of Torah, to put themselves idolatrously where only God's Torah belongs. That is why the things of the law have such bad effects. By idolatrous sinning they show that the work of the law is written in their hearts, not the law itself, but the work of the law, that is, wrath and sin. Along with that goes a kind of knowledge, the Gentile conscience and thoughts, just as in 1:32 Gentiles "have known God's decree (*dikaiōma*) that those who do these things are deserving of death" and do them nevertheless. Is there any doubt what will be the result of God's judgment of the secrets of human beings through Jesus Christ, according to Paul's gospel (2:16)?

I began with a theological axiom and a grammatical anomaly. The axiom was that justification is on the basis of God's activity and not human activity. The anomaly was the problem of making "works of law" refer to human activity. If the problem can be solved, then the axiom can be shown to be true also for Paul, as Lohmeyer very effectively shows, and he may be right. Lohmeyer does not operate with another theological axiom characteristic of some interpreters, which would contrast two types of human activity and say that justification is by the good kind, believing, rather than from the bad kind, doing, which would definitely not be true of Paul. Lohmeyer's analysis is a profound one and causes some difficulty only for two passages, Galatians 3:10 and Romans 2:15. If, on the other hand, these two passages are taken as guides, the grammatical anomaly is easily solved—"works of law" is a normal subjective genitive—but the theology turns out to be different. This theology is not a Jewish commonplace but one peculiar to Paul, in which the law actively works in the Gentile world to create a situation from which people need redemption. Here, outside the context of covenant, law exercises retribution for human sinfulness in a process called "wrath." The temptation is to make the decision on the basis of the resultant theologies. I would submit that it is incumbent on all those who follow the traditional understanding of "works of law" to learn from Lohmeyer how to speak more appropriately about it and to address themselves consciously to Lohmeyer's grammatical anomaly, which he did not resolve, and to do it better.[30] Otherwise I believe they are bound by the rule which says that grammar must take precedence over theological presuppositions.

7

PAUL AND JERUSALEM

"There is nothing whatever to indicate that the primitive church in Jerusalem, or any elements in it, differed from St. Paul either in the matter of Christology or in sacramental practices and ideas." So wrote Professor F. W. Beare at the beginning of the supplementary note to his eloquent radio broadcast on "Jesus and Paul."[1] The attempt to separate Jerusalem and Paul stems from nineteenth-century liberalism, as he correctly points out. Sometimes it took the form of a dislike of Paul's "high" Christology and ecclesiology coupled with a romantic longing for the simple piety and practice of the primitive church; sometimes it took the form of a dislike of the "Jewish legalism" of James coupled with a romantic admiration for Paul as the perfect hero of faith. It is also important to avoid a romanticism of the earliest church as a pure virgin, relegating all differences and "heresies" to the post-apostolic period. I will certainly try to avoid these extremes when expanding on and testing Beare's initial statement.

First, it is important to adhere to the language which says that this comparison is to be between Paul and the Jerusalem church[2] and not something called "Jewish Christianity." The latter term has been used in so many different senses as to make communication almost impossible.[3] An influential book by Daniélou uses it in a sense so broad as to be almost meaningless.[4] He refers to the influence of Jewish ideas, particularly apocalyptic, on the entire Christian movement down to the middle of the second century. Another important book, by H. J. Schoeps, studies only the pseudo-Clementines and other second- and third-century literature without making any explicit connection with the pre-70 C.E. period.[5] To use specific Christian ideas such as an Ebionite Christology[6] or anti-Paulinism[7] and the exaltation of James[8] as criteria raises the question of the meaning of the adjective "Jewish." Any attempt to try to understand a first-century phenomenon on the basis of second- or third-century sources completely begs the question of continuity.[9] Malina, who advocates the term Christian Judaism, gives a conceptual definition but without any discussion of the sources.[10] A minimal definition in his view should include at least circumcision[11] and enough relation to Torah as covenant and commandments to justify the noun and enough relation to Jesus to justify the adjective. I will try here to avoid confusion by not using the term "Jewish Christianity" at all and by limiting my inquiry geographically to Jerusalem and temporally to Paul's lifetime.[12]

What are the sources that can be used to recover something of the theology of the Jerusalem church? To use material later than the first century raises the issue of continuity without any control, and therefore it must be completely put aside for the moment. If at one time the early chapters of Acts and particularly the mission speeches could be used for this purpose,[13] current scholarship on Luke no longer allows it.[14] If at one time it was thought that the Synoptic Gospels could be used for this purpose, there is today a growing consensus that all three are not only addressed to Gentile Christians but were also written by Gentile Christians.[15] The Synoptic Gospels must surely contain earlier traditions,[16] but contemporary study of the gospels with its concern for redaction criticism would need to develop criteria for distinguishing Jerusalem traditions from other traditions. I believe that in fact the synoptic traditions and traditions in Acts and even to a degree later Christian Judaism can be used to corroborate and fill out a picture drawn from other sources, but they certainly can no longer serve as a self-evident starting point. Paul then remains the only witness.[17]

The study of "Jewish Christianity" will always be associated with the name of F. C. Baur, who made extensive use of the Pauline epistles. He created a synthesis brilliant in its simplicity when he declared all of the opponents mentioned in Paul's letters to be identical and then connected them via Galatians 2 and Acts 15 with Jerusalem.[18] This thesis can no longer be a presupposition, and a very cautious methodology must be developed. In the first place, the argument should be confined to opponents who are explicitly mentioned, and they should not be confused with the congregation actually addressed. In the second place, the kind of mirror reading which assumes that whatever Paul affirms or denies, his opponents must have said the opposite must be excluded.[19]

The opponents are most clearly identified in 2 Corinthians. They are clearly Christian Jews in Malina's sense (11:22-23a), but Judaizing or the law are not issues at all. This is true also of 2 Corinthians 3, where not Moses as law giver but Moses as a *theios anēr* model for ministry is the point of the discussion.[20] The Galatians were in danger of Judaizing according to Paul, and the relation between the Galatians and the law is a major theme of the letter, but the identity of the troublemakers (1:6-9; 4:17, 30; 5:10-12; 6:12-13) is not at all clear. Paul says that they "do not keep the law," that is, are not Jews in his opinion.[21] It is now clear that the opponents in Colossians are in no sense Jews nor is the Jewish Torah in any sense an issue.[22] There is nothing to distinguish opponents referred to vaguely in Philippians 3 and Romans 16 from those in 2 Corinthians 10-13. In Romans 1-15, 1 Corinthians, 1 Thessalonians, and Philemon there is no reference to opponents at all. In any case, Paul never connects any of his opponents with Jerusalem, and therefore they cannot be the starting point in the inquiry.

Paul always speaks of the Jerusalem church in positive terms.[23] He refers to two visits to that church (Gal 1:18; 2:1) and a planned third visit (Rom 15:25). The church was in existence then at least between the years 37 and 56. He mentions "the churches of Judea" (Gal 1:22 [1 Thess 2:14]), but the language of Rom 15:31 may suggest that by that he means only the church of Jerusalem; there is no hint of the possible existence of Christian communities in Galilee. Paul calls the Jerusalem Christians "the saints" (Rom 15:25-26, 31; 1 Cor 16:1; 2 Cor 8:4; 9:1, 12), but one cannot be sure that this was their own self-designation.[24] He mentions leaders of the Jerusalem church as "apostles" (1 Cor 9:4; 15:7; Gal 1:19; 2:8) and "brothers of the Lord" (1 Cor 9:4), and he mentions by name James (1 Cor 15:7; Gal 1:19; 2:9, 12) and John (Gal 2:9) and Cephas (1 Cor 1:12; 3:22; 9:5; 15:5; Gal 1:18; 2:7 v.l., 8 v.l., 9, 11, 14). Since Cephas is not a proper name but an Aramaic nickname ("Rock"),[25] presumably the church spoke (also?) Aramaic. When in addition one recalls that three leaders are called "pillars" (Gal 2:9) and that the Jerusalem Christians may be referred to as "members of the house of faithfulness" (Gal 6:10), the implications for their self understanding as God's temple are great.[26] If 1 Thess 2:14 is not Pauline, as I believe, nothing is known of a persecution of the church, for Paul's own persecutions were not in Judea (Gal 1:22-23). There is, however, mention of the possibility of persecution (presumably by Zealots) if "the saints" associate themselves too openly with Paul, who was suspected of causing Jews to become apostate (Rom 15:31).[27] Exceedingly important to Paul was the collection from his churches for the Jerusalem church (Gal 2:10; 6:6-10;[28] 1 Cor 16:1-4; 2 Cor 8-9; Rom 15:25-33).[29] One of the motivations he gives for it is gratitude to Jerusalem for the "spiritual blessings" (Rom 15:27) they have given to the Gentiles. When to all this is added Paul's statement of complete agreement with the gospel of Jerusalem—"whether it was I or they, so we preach and so you believed" (1

Cor 15:11)—I could simply express complete agreement with the statement with which this paper began and stop. Almost.

The account of the Jerusalem conference in Gal 2:1-10 has been read for so long in the light of a theory about Paul's "Jewish-Christian" opponents that it is difficult to confine oneself to what is actually said there. My proposal, however, is to learn as much as possible about the Jerusalem church from Paul alone as a control over any such theory. Paul says that when he outlined "his" gospel—the gospel which he "preaches among the Gentiles" (2:2; 1:16), "the gospel to the uncircumcised" (2:7)—for certain influential pillars, James and Cephas and John, they recognized that he had been entrusted with that gospel (by God) and acknowledged the grace (thereby) given to him. Paul also says that God "has been effective for Cephas for the apostolate to the circumcised" (2:8), so that the recognition was mutual. He claims that Titus, since he is a Greek, was not compelled to be circumcised (2:3), but he does not say that the "interloping false brethren" were members of the Jerusalem church at all (2:4). According to Paul, the idea of the collection from his Gentile churches for the Jerusalem church came about by mutual agreement (2:10). It may be that the tangled syntax in verses 4-6 indicates that perhaps things did not go as smoothly as Paul says, but I will remain with what is actually stated.

In the midst of all this mutual recognition, there are astonishingly great theological differences between Paul and Jerusalem. Evidently they agreed on two gospels, one to the circumcised and one to the uncircumcised, and on two apostolates, one to the circumcised and one to the uncircumcised. One can further infer an agreement that the circumcised would continue to obey the commandments of the Torah (cf. 5:3; 1 Cor 7:18), while the uncircumcised would be responsible for none of them. Presumably this is what is meant by "nothing being imposed" and by "preserving our freedom" and "not submitting to the subjection" (2:5). The Jerusalem church is characterized by circumcision, by Torah, and by a mission restricted to Israel.[30] These are considerable differences indeed from Paul's own emphases. Since the incident at Antioch[31] did not occur in Jerusalem, I will not need to deal with it except to point out that while Paul has harsh words for Cephas and Barnabas and the behaviour of certain Jews in Antioch, nothing whatsoever is said against James or the Jerusalem church. Nevertheless, must not differences in such vital areas as circumcision and Torah and mission have other theological consequences, even if they were not recognized by Paul?

I will go now beyond specific references to Jerusalem to see if anything further can be gleaned about the theology of that church. There is considerable agreement today that it is possible to isolate certain formulae cited by Paul.[32] Often these are identified as being "Jewish Christian" in origin, although the criteria for this designation are seldom spelled out and rarely clear. I shall look briefly at a number of them without going into the complex issues of just how they are to be isolated,[33] beginning with those which most clearly can be identified with Jerusalem and using a kind of "criterion of coherence" to help in other cases.

Most would say that 1 Cor 15:3-7 contains a traditional formulation stemming from the Jerusalem church.[34] Not only does Paul specifically introduce it as tradition ("delivered . . . received," 15:3), but also he says in effect that this is the gospel preached by the people named, Cephas and James ("whether then it was I or they, so we preach," 15:11). There is also a fair amount of consensus on the extent of the formula:[35]

died, for our sins, according to the Scriptures
was buried,
was raised, on the third day, according to the Scriptures
appeared to Cephas, then to the Twelve
to James, then to all the apostles.

Specific aspects of the theology of the Jerusalem church here include the following. They had a concept of apostle which, especially if it is understood to be parallel to the Twelve, differed from that of Paul.[36] That the number twelve was chosen shows a claim of the group on all of Israel but also only on Israel. Jesus' death and resurrection were seen to be "according to the Scriptures," that is, as the climax and culmination of the whole history of Israel which is the subject of the Hebrew Bible. Insofar as these were understood as eschatological events, one can assume an apocalyptic background to the entire conception. Finally, Jesus' death was seen to have expiatory significance: it was "for (*hyper*) our sins."

Paul speaks of a tradition being received or delivered also in the liturgical formula in 1 Cor 11:23b-25, and the connection with the Jerusalem church is indicated by the close parallel in Mark 14. If a covenant theology was merely implicit in 1 Corinthians 15, here it is explicit: the cup is called "the new covenant." Jesus' death is referred to as his "blood," which may well have sacrificial or even specifically covenantal connotations (Exod 24:8). The reference to a new covenant (Jer 31:31) is thus not one of contrast but of culmination and fulfilment. Some have seen in *paradidomi*, in connection with Jesus' death, traces of a "*Dahingabeformel*," which may go back to the Jerusalem church (cf. Rom 4:25; Gal 1:4).[37] Jesus' death is said to be "for you" (11:24), and it is probable that Matthew has correctly captured the sense of this statement in the Jerusalem church when he adds more precisely "for the forgiveness of sins" (26:28).

Kramer identifies a pre-Pauline tradition in what he calls a *pistis* formula, which is to be distinguished from a *homologia.*[38] Thus Rom 10:9b would reflect a formula such as, "We believe that God raised Jesus from the dead," a formula that goes back to the earliest church. If it is true that this formula is older than the more complex one in 1 Cor 15:3-5, then there may have been a stage in the Jerusalem church during which the fundamental significance of Jesus was seen in his resurrection as a revelation that his preaching of the Kingdom of God was indeed true because the church was now living in the end time.

In its present form the formula in 1 Thess 1:9-10 cannot come from the Jerusalem church because that church did not engage in Gentile mission.[39] Nevertheless, it is often referred to as "Jewish Christian,"[40] and the last three lines could represent Jerusalem theology.

> (How you turned to God from idols to serve a living and true God)
> and await his Son from heaven,
> whom he raised from the dead,
> Jesus who delivers us from the coming wrath.

This is a *pistis* formula, a strong expectation of the parousia, and an expectation of judgment. The way in which Jesus delivers from the wrath is not stated, but it is presumably through the forgiveness of sin.

Gal 1:4a has been identified as a pre-Pauline formula,[41] and it fits in well with Jerusalem theology:

> who gave himself for our sins
> in order that he might liberate us from the present evil age.

Here again the *Dahingabeformel* expresses expiatory self-sacrifice for sins. Bovon argues that the verb *exaireisthai* is to be connected in particular with the Exodus tradition. Liberation in Christ is seen as the new exodus through the forgiveness of sins.

The formula in Rom 4:25 contains language which by now should be very familiar:

> who was delivered up for the sake of our faults
> and raised up for the sake of our justification.

Once more the *Dahingabeformel* and the statement that Jesus' death atones for our sins appear. In the light of the usage in the Qumran scrolls it is not surprising to find that justification is a concept of the Jerusalem church and not unique to Paul.[42] Whether justification functions in the same way in the two theologies remains to be seen.

There are complicating considerations with respect to the formula in Rom 1:3-4. While the wording is easy to isolate from its Pauline embedding, there are Pauline additions within the formula itself. It seems clear that the words "in power," should be omitted, but whether the contrast "according to the flesh—according to the Spirit of holiness" was part of the original formula is disputed.[43] I use the shortest formula here for the sake of simplicity:

who was born of the seed of David . . .
who was appointed Son of God . . . since resurrection of the dead.

The Jerusalem church called Jesus "Messiah" and that in two senses. On the one hand, he was the Messiah as son of David, but then later he became the Messiah as Son of God. The Christology is adoptionist. I have until now avoided any discussion of Christological titles which may have been associated with the formulae. Much work has been done on them by Kramer and Hahn,[44] but confidence in their solutions is not shared by all. To see that this particular formula is clearly messianic, whatever name or title be the antecedent of the relative pronouns, is enough here.

The formula most useful for the present task, Rom 3:24-26a, also presents the most difficulties and therefore has been kept to the last. First, Bultmann and Käsemann were confident they could identify the text in 3:24-26a simply by omitting as Pauline additions "as a free gift by his grace" in 3:24 and "through faith" in 3:25.[45] However, it has become increasingly difficult to show why 3:24 is not Pauline, with the possible exception of the word *apolytrōsis*, and it is hard to make sense of the supposed insertion in 3:25.[46] Second, the translation of 3:25b-26a is exceedingly difficult, and yet the sense of the whole formula depends on how these phrases are understood. I shall tentatively reconstruct and translate as follows:

whom God set forth as a means of expiation,
through [Jesus'] faithfulness at the cost of his blood,[47]
in order to demonstrate his righteousness,
because the prosecution of sins committed in the past was dropped in the forbearance of God.[48]

In his classic study of the formula Käsemann speaks of the righteousness of God as his "*Festhalten am Bunde*";[49] it has to do with "the patience of God which demonstrates his covenant faithfulness and which effects forgiveness."[50] This is in the tradition of Exod 34:6-7, "The LORD, the LORD, a God merciful and gracious, slow to anger, and abounding in covenant loyalty and faithfulness, keeping [LXX adds 'righteousness and'] covenant loyalty for thousands, forgiving iniquity and transgression and sin."[51] Jesus' death is seen in cultic terms, and whether or not one is to think specifically of the "mercy seat," it is clear that it replaces what would otherwise have been the function of the temple and its sacrifices. The righteousness of God is a concept also of Jerusalem theology, and it expresses itself in the forgiveness of sins. This formula is said by many to have its *Sitz im Leben* in the Eucharist.[52]

To summarize what has so far been learned about the theology of the Jerusalem church: Jesus' resurrection was seen as the confirmation of his proclamation of the nearness of the Kingdom of God, as the revelation by God that Israel was living in the end time. In Bultmann's apt phrase, the church understood itself as the eschatological congregation.[53] The significance of this was expressed in terms of covenantal theology. What happened in Christ was God's act of eschatological righteousness in his faithfulness to the covenant made with Israel by providing a final means of atonement for the forgiveness of Israel's sins. Jesus' death signifies then the renewal of the covenant, the re-affirmation of the covenant and the commandments, the establishment of Torah. On the other hand, his death means the supersession and replacement of the temple and its sacrifices as a means of expiation. This atonement was celebrated in the Eucharist, now by the church but soon by all Israel. Then would come the final pilgrimage of the Gentiles to Mt. Zion. This is clear "pattern of religion," to use the words of E. P. Sanders,[54] and it is clearly a different pattern from that of Paul.

The Jerusalem church said that Jesus' death was "for our sins" (1 Cor 15:3; Gal 1:4a; Rom 4:25; 3:25), but Paul speaks always of Sin in the singular as a power and never of sins in the plural as guilt.[55] Paul also says that Jesus died (Rom 5:6,8; 14:5; 1 Thess 5:10), was given up (Rom 8:32; Gal 2:20; Eph 5:2,25), was crucified (1 Cor 1:13), was made sin (2 Cor 5:21), was made a curse (Gal 3:13) *for* (*hyper*)—but it is always for us, for you, for persons, and never for our sins. Rom 8:3 says significantly that Jesus was sent for (*peri*) sin, not sins. Not only that, but Paul never speaks of forgiveness[56] and hardly ever of repentance.[57] The word atonement, for Paul, means not a way of dealing with sins but a one-time act of incorporating Gentiles into the body of Christ, the people of God, the giving of life to the dead. For Paul this takes place at baptism, when one participates in the death and resurrection of Christ. Little is known about the significance of baptism for the Jerusalem church; it may even have involved repeated lustrations.[58] Though the Jerusalem church spoke in terms of the covenant and renewed covenant, Paul never uses this concept.[59] Though for Jerusalem the righteousness of God effects forgiveness of sins, for Paul it refers to the incorporation of Gentiles into the people of God. Though the Jerusalem church spoke of Jesus as the Messiah, Paul never does.[60] For Paul, Jesus relates neither to David nor to Moses but to Adam and to Abraham. Jesus is neither the climax of the history of Israel nor the fulfilment of the covenant but the one who overcomes the powers which enslave the creation by fulfilling the promises of God concerning Gentiles.[61] Paul's basic confession is "Jesus is Lord," and Jesus is infinitely more important to his theology than he ever could have been for Jerusalem. For Paul, Jesus is not only the revelation of God's eschatological activity but of God himself, and therefore the doctrine of the Trinity is a legitimate development from Pauline theology.

The theology of Paul and the theology of Jerusalem are completely different, and yet Paul can say they are the same (1 Cor 15:11) and that each acknowledged the position of the other (Gal 2:1-10). What makes them different is, of course, the fact that one gospel is addressed to Gentiles and one to Israel. Yet there was such a common core of conviction that many of the differences outlined may not have been seen by the first-century participants. There is a real sense in which Professor Beare's statement with which I began is true. Perhaps one should speak of transmutations rather than differences. Paul pays tribute to the gospel of the Jerusalem church and is grateful to it for "spiritual blessings" which flow to the Gentiles (Rom 15:27). At the same time, the common kerygma spoken in a different situation takes on a greatly transformed significance. The theology of the Jerusalem church had, of course, no future and certainly cannot be revived today, while the theology of Paul triumphed to such an extent that it is only with difficulty that the theology of Jerusalem can be recovered. Nevertheless, I expect that in the Kingdom of God Paul and James will still be friends. If Paul can have such a different "pattern of religion" from that of the Jerusalem church, how much more different would his "pattern" be from the teaching of Jesus. And yet Paul was firmly and happily convinced that the gospel he preached among the Gentiles was given to him by a revelation of God in Christ (Gal 1:15-16) and that he had the full approval of his Lord. Who is to say that he was wrong?

8

FOR *ALL* THE BELIEVERS

The Inclusion of Gentiles as the Ultimate Goal of Torah in Romans

One might say that the key word for understanding Romans is *pas*, "all" or "every."[1] But this must not be interpreted in a disinterested, even-handed, universalizing theological manner. I would understand it rather to function as a kind of "inclusive language"; it is used by Paul to include the formerly excluded, namely, the Gentiles.[2] It might be possible to argue something similar with respect to Paul's use of "Adam," not only explicitly as in 5:12-21 but also implicitly in 1:18-32 and 7:7-13, and one should at least ask the question whenever *anthrōpos* appears.[3] In any case the theme of Romans could be characterized as something like the universality of sin and salvation, but seen, I believe, from the perspective of the inclusion of the previously excluded.

Even Romans is not written by Paul the systematic theologian. As in his other letters, he is writing to Gentile Christians (1:5, 13-15; 11:13; 15:15-21), dealing presumably with a Gentile-Christian situation. The specific occasion of his writing Romans is clear: he wants to establish a partnership with Greek Christians to begin to carry the gospel to barbarians —specifically, he wants Roman moral and financial backing for his forthcoming mission to Spain (15:22-29). Because of the surprising omission of the word "church," it has been suggested that Paul needs to found a unified church in Rome for this purpose as a self-assurred community alongside the synagogue.[4] He writes not to convert them or to correct a false gospel (15:14) but to encourage them and to remind them of their equal status in the people of God with Israel (and not with Jewish Christians as such). The election of the church does not mean the rejection of Israel

(9-11); it does mean the inclusion of *all* Gentiles, Spaniards as well as Romans. Thus the theoretical theme of the epistle, that God's righteousness is his power for salvation for the Jew of course but *also* for the Greek (1:16-17), is stated in support of the practical thrust that this gospel is for the Greek of course but *also* for the barbarian (1:14-15).

After all that has been said on the topic of the "righteousness of God" (*dikaiosynē tou theou*), it is not necessary to add to the discussion. It is perhaps enough to say that I understand the significant essay by S. K. Williams to culminate the earlier discussion and to be my starting point.[5] There is, however, one additional consideration. There are places (Phil 3:9 is the classic one) where *dikaiosynē* refers to a characterization of human beings, although this is not the place to discuss whether such righteousness is imputed or imparted or "earned." But what about the cases where *dikaiosynē* is not qualified by a genitive or possessive? In what follows, I will always ask the question, "Whose righteousness is meant?" and not rule out the possibility that also here one ought to think in terms of the righteousness of God.

The word *pistis* poses special problems. It is a modern position to think that faith is both difficult and meritorious and that one ought to strive for ever greater degrees of it. For Paul, however, it is the normal, expected response to the gospel. The participle *hoi pisteuontes* refers to Christians as such, with no particular reference to how they became such nor to how they ought to behave now that they are "believers."[6] A non-believing Christian would be a contradiction in terms, but Paul does not lay any particular weight on believing as a virtue, and the term is missing from his discussion of the Christian life in Romans 5-8. The word "unbeliever," on the other hand, does not refer so much to one who has no faith as it does to one who is not a Christian. In order then to counter the post-Luther tendency to separate works and faith, doing and believing, with an emphasis on the latter, I will regularly translate *pistis* in accordance with normal Hellenistic Jewish usage as "faithfulness." An additional proposal will be more controversial. It is to be hoped that the recent study of R. B. Hays will finally convince Pauline scholarship to understand the phrase *pistis Christou* as the "faithfulness *of* Christ."[7] In the light of the occurrence of "faithfulness of God" in Rom 3:3, I would like to go further. As with *dikaiosynē* so also with *pistis*, when it occurs without a qualifying genitive or possessive I will ask whose faithfulness is meant. Is it that of the believer, or is it rather God's or Christ's?

Two other preliminary remarks must be made. One concerns a very important discovery that has been strangely neglected in New Testament studies. G. Howard points out that in none of the now considerable LXX texts from the first century is *kyrios* used for the tetragrammaton, which is written in Hebrew letters.[8] He concludes that the use of *kyrios* was begun by Christian scribes in the second century, who applied it also to New Testament texts. This means that Old Testament citations in New Testament manuscripts originally contained the tetragrammaton. It will be seen that this makes a considerable difference in the interpretation of many texts. The second is a plea by N. Dahl and others to recognize that Paul has a *theo*logy and not just a Christology.[9] Nowhere is this more important than in the interpretation of Romans.

On the basis of these preliminary considerations then, I will examine the theme of the inclusion of Gentiles in Romans. The participle "believer" is found with *pas* in Rom 1:16; 3:22; 4:11; 10:4, 11, and "Gentiles" together with *pas* in 1:5 and 15:11. These are the passages I will discuss in their several contexts.

Insofar as Rom 1:16-17 are taken to be thematic, a proper exegesis depends on how one understands the rest of the letter. The present discussion therefore cannot demonstrate a case but hopes to set a tone. Paul defines the gospel as "the power of God leading to salvation for every believer." This is the gospel which he said was already contained in the prophets in the Holy Scriptures (1:2) and to which he had been set apart as apostle, "for [bringing about] obedience to [God's] faithfulness[10] for the sake of his name among all the Gentiles" (1:5). It is then possible to put the accent on the word "every," which functions to include the Gentiles. In any case, it would be a mistake to put it on the word "believer," which would make God's power dependent on human faith as a necessary precondition. It is then possible to take full account of the *te* and *prōton* and translate, somewhat provocatively, "for the Jew of course, but *also* for the Greek." This can be supported by the "not only . . . but also" pattern later in the epistle. God is God not only of Jews but also of Gentiles (3:29). The blessings of Psalm 32 are not only for Jews but also for Gentiles (4:9). Abraham is the father not only of Jews but also of those Gentiles who follow in his footsteps (4:12b, 16b). Gen 15:6 applies not only to Abraham but also to all believers (4:23-24). God has called instruments of mercy not only from the Jews but also from the Gentiles (9:24). God's power leads to salvation for Israel especially, of course (11:26), but also for Gentiles (11:25). The last instance shows why *prōton* is to be understood not temporally[11] but of degree. But if the Jews are "in the first place,"[12] it is clear that Paul's interest is almost exclusively with those in second place, with those now being included, with the Gentiles.

If 1:16 is to mean something like the above, then verse 17, which supports it, must be consonant with this interpretation. "For God's righteousness is revealed in it, from [his] faithfulness to [our] faithfulness, as it is written: 'The righteous shall live by faithfulness' (Hab 2:4)." How to construe the

Habbakuk citation has been greatly debated. I am convinced both grammatically[13] and theologically[14] that Paul understands the statement not to answer the question "How is one made or declared righteous?" but rather the question "How is the righteous one (= the 'believer' of verse 16) to live, that is, to come to salvation?" The direct answer is: by God's righteousness, or, as it is expressed in the citation: by his faithfulness.[15] Although they are not identical, there is a close relationship among God's righteousness, his faithfulness, his power leading to salvation, and the gospel. While it could mean many things, the rhetorical phrase "from *pistis* to *pistis*" fits in very well with this reading. It is then possible to see in the statement of the theme in Romans an expression of God's righteousness now active to include the Gentiles.

If Gentiles are included as recipients of the promise of salvation through God's righteousness, they are also included in the threat of judgment. That Rom 1:18-32 is to be understood under this perspective is well known. Differing from the kerygma within a Jewish context that can immediately speak of the solution, the kerygma to the Gentiles must also speak explicitly of the problem (cf. Acts 17:31). However, since I believe that this aspect of the theme of the inclusion of Gentiles continues throughout the whole of 1:18-3:20, I will survey the rest of the section briefly from this perspective. It is widely recognized that this section contains more pre-Pauline traditions than usual, and two recent studies have claimed that these traditions and thus many statements here are utterly incompatible with Paul's theology otherwise.[16] But perhaps at least part of the problem lies once more in the assumptions one is accustomed to bringing to the text.

"The most crucial structural problem is the meaning of 2:1."[17] The shift to direct address and to the present tense does not of course in itself mean a shift from Gentiles to Jews, and it has been so interpreted only because of the mistaken idea that Paul wants to be evenhanded in condemning Jews equally with Gentiles (and perhaps an unexamined assumption that Jews tend to be more judgmental than other people, an assumption that needs only to be stated for its emptiness to become apparent). Indeed, many interpreters go much further and say, "The argumentative point of Rom 1:18-3:20 is not an equal and separate indictment of Gentile and Jew. . . [Paul's] specific aim is directed against Jewish superiority and pride."[18]

It is not only the *dio* (therefore) which prohibits a separation of 2:1-3 from the foregoing. As J. Bassler has shown, there are too many connections: *anapologētos* in 1:20 and 2:1, *pas* with *anthrōpos* in 1:18 and 2:1, "doing" three times in 1:32 repeated in 2:1-3, judging (2:1) because they know God's command (1:32), the virtual repetition of 1:32a in 2:2.[19] In addition, there is a Hellenistic Jewish pattern underlying this section, which is not complete unless 1:18-2:11 is taken as a unit. Nauck lists the following elements of the pattern: creation (1:20, 25), providence (2:4?), worship of God (1:23, 25), knowledge of God (1:19f), ignorance (missing!), repentance (2:4), judgment (2:5f, 8f), and salvation (2:7, 10).[20] Breaking the section at 2:1 obscures the pattern and encourages the thought that 1:18-32 contradicts 3:25f, "the passing over of former sins in the clemency of God." But the pattern is "that they [the Egyptians] might learn that one is punished by the very things by which he sins. . . . But thou dost overlook men's sins, that they may repent" (Wis 11:16, 23). Rom 1:18-2:16 must then be read as a unit, dealing exclusively with the situation of the Gentile world.

That world is characterized by idolatry (falsehood, 1:25; cf. 18), godlessness and injustice (1:18) and could fairly be said to be under sin (3:9). That world is definitely under wrath, which at first refers to a karma-like process in history, from Adam to the present,[21] but which is also stored up for the day of judgment. It is not generally recognized that that world can also be said to be under law. In the first place, "the law works wrath" (4:15). In the second place, differing from the expected ignorance motif, Paul says that they "know God's decree" (1:32) and are therefore "without excuse" (2:1; cf. 1:20). That law and the threefold "God delivered them" (1:24, 26, 28) are a kind of providence, God's governance of the world. The reason he has not destroyed the idolators is that his kindness is meant to lead to repentance. But on the day of judgment God "will render to *everyone* according to his works, including Gentiles, who are to be held to the same standards as Jews. I have discussed elsewhere my understanding of 2:12-16 and Paul's warning that all Gentiles, without exception, would be condemned at the judgment.[22] Insofar as there are paraenetic aspects to 2:1ff they also point to Gentiles, whether in their attitudes to such barbarians as Spaniards or even such oriental barbarians as Jews.[23]

In the light of the excellent study by J. Bassler,[24] a word must be said about the theme of Divine impartiality, which must not be confused with evenhandedness. The phrase "there is no partiality with God" is used Biblically (for example, Deut 10:17 and 18) to show that there precisely *is* partiality, namely, toward the disadvantaged, in order to include them so God can be impartial to *all*. Bassler has shown how the theme of impartiality took on more national tones in ben Sira and Wisdom: that there is no partiality with God means that Israel will be vindicated through the judgment of her more powerful oppressors. If Paul uses the pattern of speaking of Gentiles seen especially in Wisdom 11-15, could it not be that he does so because he basically agrees with it? The statements in 2:7-10 are commonplace with respect to Israel, but not everyone would have agreed on including the Gentiles in this manner. What Paul says is that the coming day of judgment is for *every* human being (*pas* with *anthrōpos*), for the Jew, of course, but *also* for the Greek.

Against the background of the hopeless situation of the world Paul sketched in 1:18-2:16,[25] his Gentile reader must have been aghast to hear him answer his question: What is the advantage of being a Jew? and What is the benefit of circumcision? with: "Much in every respect." The *logia* of God with which Jews have been entrusted I understand with most to be God's promises, both with respect to Israel (cf. 9:4-5) and the Gentiles (3:21-4:25). I agree with recent studies which would more or less equate God's faithfulness (3:3), his truth (3:4, 7), and his righteousness (3:5) and point out how important this is for understanding the end of the chapter.[26] I further agree with Käsemann and others that Paul understands Psalm 51 in terms of the covenant lawsuit to say that God is victorious and expresses his righteousness by forgiving sin.[27] I would however like to pay much more attention to the pronouns than is usually done. Paul speaks about the Jews in the third person only in 3:1-3. Verse 4 combines *pas* and *anthrōpos* in a way that is characteristic of his inclusion theme. It also asserts that every human being is a *liar*, a word previously used for idolatry (1:25; cf. 1:18; 2:2, 8). The contrast between our idolatry and God's truth is important enough for Paul to repeat it in verse 7. The shift from third person to "every human being" to first person is then not insignificant, and the shift from "some" in verse 3 to "every" in verse 4 is not "a blatant non sequitur."[28] The point is that different groups are involved, Jews and Gentiles, and the objections Paul counters are specific Gentile objections. The problem with God's covenant loyalty is that it applies only to Israel, and just as in 9:14ff, the Gentile complains about God's unfairness. It is the Gentiles who have been characterized by injustice (1:18, 29; 2:8), who have been under wrath (1:18; 2:5, 8), and Paul says that God will judge the *world* (3:6).

The connection with the following verses has been obscured by the text and strange renderings of verse 9a, which should be translated "What then do we put up as a defence?"[29] Paul continues to reply to the slanderers. "We have already charged that Jews of course but *also* Greeks are *all* under sin." Indeed he has, and even if God has been faithful to his promises to Israel, the Greeks have no right to complain about the wrath they deserve so well. Whatever its origins, most of the quotations in the catena 3:10-18 "do not speak of the universality of sin but sketch its character."[30] All of the Psalms included in the catena speak of the wicked in contrast with the righteous. Psalm 14, for example, mentions "all the evildoers who eat up my people as they eat bread, and do not call upon the LORD" and contrasts "the fools," "the children of men," and "the evildoers" with "my people," "the generation of the righteous," "the poor whose refuge is the LORD," "deliverance for Israel," and "his people." The oppressors in Psalm 9 (LXX) are referred to seven times as "*ta ethnē*" (vv 5, 11, 15, 17, 19, 20, 37). The catena is not evenhanded but excoriates Gentile sinners.

"Scripture [*nomos*] speaks to those who are in the law [*nomos*], in order that *every* mouth may be closed and the *whole world* [*pas ho kosmos*] stand guilty before God, because by works of law '*all* flesh [*pasa sarx*] shall not be justified before him,' for through the law comes knowledge of sin." It is because of the wording of the conclusion 3:19-20 that I have departed from the usual interpretation and have understood all of 1:18-3:20 (with the exception of 2:17-29) as an indictment of the Gentile world. (Even the exception has to do indirectly with Gentiles, as must be shown in another context.)[31] Gentiles are guilty and without excuse because they know God's commandment (1:32). One consequence of the reading indicated above is that Gentiles too are under law, but law not in the context of covenant, law which functions in a negative way. There are indications elsewhere that this is Paul's view.[32] The main advantage of this reading is that it does not understand Romans as an abstract philosophical treatise but as a passionate address to people otherwise clearly identified as Gentiles. If it is harsh, that is because Paul thinks "backwards," as E.P. Sanders says,[33] and 1:18-3:20 was composed in the light of 3:21-31. What about the Jews? Unlike Sanders, Paul did not preface his pattern of soteriology for Gentiles with a long exposition of Israel's pattern of soteriology for Jews. I assume he would have agreed with most of what Sanders says. The Bible clearly says that Jews are sinful and provides means (covenant, repentance, and so forth) for dealing with that fact. The case Paul wants to argue, however, is not stated so clearly in Scripture. Whatever is true for Israel is true now *also* for Gentiles, including sin and responsibility and judgment. Here too Gentiles are included. The positive aspect of their inclusion comes in the next section.

Romans 3:21-31 is clearly about the inclusion of the Gentiles,[34] so the discussion can be brief. "Now, however, apart from the law [in the sense of covenant], that righteousness of God has been made manifest to which the law [in the sense of Scripture] and the prophets have testified, the righteousness of God through the faithfulness of Jesus Christ. It is for *all* the believers, for there is no [longer any] distinction." S. K. Williams has a thorough discussion of how God's "holding back" and "restraint" with respect to previously committed sins (25b-26a) refer specifically to the situation of Gentile idolators.[35] Israel has always had cultic means of expiation, but now God has presented Christ Jesus as such a means for the Gentiles, apart from or alongside his covenant with Israel.[36] The boasting which is now excluded is of course not "as to righteousness in the law blameless" (Phil 3:6) but rather the prayer, "Thou didst choose the seed of Abraham to the exclusion of (*para*) all the nations" (*Pss. Sol.* 9:9). The "human being" who is justified in verse 28 must mean primarily the Gentile if the connection with the following verse is to be understood: "Or is it of

Jews only that God is God? Not also of the Gentiles?'' Then comes one of those extraordinary statements to be found only in Romans which indicate that Paul is moving close to the two-covenant theology of F. Rosenzweig. ''If indeed God, who will justify the circumcised out of [his] faithfulness, is one, [he will justify] *also* the uncircumcised through the same [*tēs*] faithfulness.''[37] Inclusion of Gentiles does not mean exclusion of Jews.

I have argued elsewhere that Romans 4 is not about Christian faith nor about justification by that faith.[38] Paul understands Gen 15:6 to refer to the inclusion of Gentiles, by having the righteousness of God counted to them, because God is faithful to the promises he made to Abraham. In a manner unparalleled even in Romans 11, Paul explicitly affirms the continuing standing of Israel before God when he says that Gentiles are also included. The ''not only . . . but also'' pattern appears four times in the chapter. I shall look at the occurrences beginning with the clearest, which means beginning at the end and working backwards.

Abraham trusted God's promises of descendants, and ''therefore 'it was counted to him as righteousness.' But these words 'it was counted to him' were written *not only* for his sake *but also* for our sake. It will be counted to us [Christian] believers'' (4:22-24a). Here in the conclusion is the key to Paul's understanding of Gen 15:6—the promise that righteousness is counted not only to Abraham but also to us Christians; it is then the righteousness of God of 3:21.

In that light one sees something of the idea ''not only to Abraham but to his offspring'' in verse 13, even if it is not so expressed. Before giving a translation, I recall what was said at the beginning about *pistis*, the virtual identification of God's faithfulness, truth, and righteousness in 3:3-5, and the consideration that the chapter is about how Gentiles benefit from God's promise to Abraham.

> For the promise to Abraham, or his offspring, that they should be heirs of the world, did not [come] through law but through [God's] righteousness, i.e. faithfulness. For if [only][39] those of the law [covenant] were heirs, then [his] faithfulness would be empty and [his] promise void. . . . Therefore [the inheritance is] from [God's] faithfulness, in order that it might be according to grace, so that the promise may be certain of fulfillment for *all* the offspring:
>
> *not only* for the one of the law
> *but also* for the one of the faithfulness of Abraham
> who is the father of us *all*.

Paul then supplements his basic text which mentions only offspring (Gen

15:5) with Gen 17:5 which speaks explicitly of Gentiles. They have been included because God promised Abraham he would do so. Given the subject matter here, it is probable that the ascription of God as the one "who gives life to the dead and calls into being what does not exist" (4:17) refers to the creation of the Gentile church (cf. 1 Cor 1:28; *2 Clem.* 1:8; Eph 2:5).

Rom 4:12 is unfortunately not so clear. The article *tois* before *stoichousin* has always caused problems for commentators because they have been so sure that Paul could not possibly be speaking of two groups here. When it is not simply ignored in translation, commentators follow Beza in a conjecture emending the text or dismiss it as a "simple mistake," whether by Paul or Tertius.[40] If preconceptions about what Paul must be saying about Jews and Gentiles are abandoned, there is a clear chiastic structure. Abraham has been made:

> the father of all who believe in a state of uncircumcision, in order that the righteousness may be counted *also* to them,
> and the father of the circumcised;
> [father] not only to those of the circumcision,
> but *also* to those who follow in the footsteps of the trust our father Abraham had in a state of uncircumcision.

Abraham is then said to be the father of Gentiles, Jews, Jews, Gentiles, whereby the first and fourth lines referring to Gentiles are understandably much more full, given the purpose of Romans.[41] The major problem with this reading is the exceedingly awkward placement of the first article in the phrase *tois ouk ek peritomēs monon alla kai tois stoichousin*. . . . The sentence would have been much clearer if Paul had written *ou tois*. But word order in Hellenistic Greek does not always conform to what one would expect.[42] Perhaps the aberrant order was caused by the shift from a genitive to a dative construction. But this difficulty is surely minor in comparison with the violence done to the text by those who completely ignore the second *tois*. And speaking strongly in favour of the translation proposed here is the very close parallel in the unambiguous verse 16.

I turn now to another translation problem in 4:1. The textual and grammatical convolutions of the traditional interpretation are caused by the assumption that the subject matter of Romans 4 is what Abraham found, namely justification apart from works. That is, many interpreters translate as if Paul had written *ti oun heuren Abraam*? But the most natural translation of the text as it exists is that of Zahn and Hays: "What then shall we say? Have we found Abraham to be our forefather according to the flesh?"[43] This preserves the Pauline formula *ti oun eroumen*, makes the "we" of the previous verb the subject of the infinitive,[44] allows the infinitive to have its expected object and a predicate noun, and accounts for the perfect infinitive rather than the aorist. I refer to Zahn and Hays for detailed discussion and note only that I do not follow them in assuming that "we" = we Jews. Perhaps one should even translate "Have we obtained Abraham as our forefather according to the flesh?" The question has to do, I take it, with how Abraham has become the ancestor (*propatōr* instead of the usual *patēr* is significant) of the Roman Gentile Christians. The implied answer I would understand to be something like: *ouch, alla kat' epangelian*.

Everyone knows that justification is by faith and not by works, that Abraham is the supreme example of this principle, and that Rom 4:2-8 is the passage where it is stated most clearly. But in the light of the rest of Romans 4 perhaps one should say that justification is not by human activity, whether believing or doing, and that Abraham is the ancestor of Jews and Christians because of whose faithfulness God promised to count righteousness also to them. Gen 15:6 is important to Paul not because of what it says about Abraham but because of what it promises to Abraham's seed. The emphasis is accordingly on the second half of the verse: *logizesthai* appears eleven times in Romans 4.[45] The God in whom Abraham believes is the one "who justifies the godless," that is, the Gentiles (cf. 1:18; 5:6). Paul's "interpretation in 4:6 stresses that God now gives forgiveness for sins (regarded as a sign of the people of God) even to those who are outside the Jewish covenant."[46]

Paul explicates his understanding of Gen 15:6b, probably as a *Gezera Shawa*,[47] through the *logizesthai* of Ps 32:2. The man whose sin is not counted is of course not Abraham[48] but rather a contemporary Gentile. Does Paul understand Ps 32:1 to refer to Gentiles because it uses the word *anomia*?[49] Does he do so because of the word "man" in verse 2 rather than "Israelite"?[50] Such suggestions would seem fantastic except that Paul in fact goes on to argue along such lines. "Is this blessing then *only* [not in the best text but the proper sense] for the circumcised or *also* for the uncircumcised?" Once more one encounters the "not only . . . but also" pattern, explicitly as an interpretation of Psalm 32. Not only that, but when Paul rounds off the section with an *inclusio*, "[For the latter also,] since we say, trust 'was counted to Abraham as righteousness,'" he indicates that he also understands Gen 15:6b with reference to righteousness being counted to Gentiles.

It is often said that Genesis 15 was attractive to Paul because it speaks of Abraham's faith and not his works, but that is not quite true. Gen 15:1 says his "reward" (*misthos*) will be great, and Targum Neofiti has a long discussion of Abraham's works which receive a reward and their relationship to the following unconditional promise. Paul has seen the same problem. I would understand verse 2 in this fashion: Abraham was justified on the basis of works (cf. 2:13) and receives a reward, but that cannot be counted as grace for future generations.[51] Verses 4 and 5 would then describe the same person (Abraham) under two different aspects, as the one who works and receives the reward and as the one who does not work and receives the promise for the future.

If Genesis 17 had appeared in the text before Genesis 15, I believe Paul would still have argued his case for the inclusion of Gentiles from Gen 15:6. But as the text of Genesis in fact stands, he can strengthen his argument that the promises made to Abraham concerning his descendants refer to Gentiles as well as Jews.[52] *How*, that is, under what circumstances, was righteousness counted to Abraham, when he was circumcised or while he was still a Gentile? Abraham put his trust in God's promise while he was still a Gentile, in order that the righteousness may be counted also to them, and he later received the sign of the circumcision-covenant[53] as a seal of the righteousness counted to his trust as a Gentile. Therefore Abraham is the father *not only* of the Jews (the circumcised) *but also* of the Gentiles.

It may surprise some to find Romans 9:30-10:21 included in a discussion of the inclusion of Gentiles. This chapter after all has almost universally been entitled something like "the fall and responsibility of Israel."[54] What caused Israel to fall was Christ, the stone God placed in Zion, and their guilt is their obstinate refusal to believe in Christ (Gentiles on the other hand earned the right to be called righteous by their meritorious act of faith, but that is said only parenthetically). Faith and law, Moses and Christ, are understood as opposites, as are the two righteousnesses each derived from one or the other. Because Jews (all Jews, without exception, as it seems, in this chapter) sought to become righteous by zealously keeping the law, therefore they did not believe in the law's antithesis, Christ, and thus they are guilty and responsible for their own rejection. But such a view not only causes great tension with what is said in the surrounding chapters 9 and 11, it also finds no support in the text, as I hope to show.

"What then shall we say?," namely about the Gentiles, who were so surprisingly called God's "people" and "beloved" and "children of the living God" at the end of a chapter speaking of God's gracious election of Israel. They are now being included, but how? Paul speaks about a race that is even stranger than the Caucus-race in *Alice in Wonderland*.[55] The finish line is called "righteousness of God" or "the Torah of righteousness." One runner, Israel, pursues this goal with great zeal but stumbles over a rock on the race track and so does not yet arrive.[56] Other runners, Gentiles, do not race at all and yet surprisingly, dramatically, suddenly arrive at the goal they had not pursued. What is the source of this strange picture?

There are many reasons for thinking that Isa 51:1-8 lies behind this section of Romans, in spite of the fact that it is not explicitly cited.[57] The concept of pursuing the righteousness of God[58] is found only here,[59] also in a context which speaks of righteousness for Gentiles. This is the passage which seems to lie behind Paul's discussion of Abraham and Gentiles in Romans 4.[60] *Nomos* and *dikaiosynē* are parallel concepts in Isa 51:7 (cf. Rom 9:31), where the law is in the heart (cf. Rom 10:6-10). The relevance of this text is then evident:

> Hear me, you who pursue righteousness; you who seek YHWH.
> Look to the rock from which you were hewn; and to the quarry from which you were dug.
> Look to Abraham your father; and to Sarah who gave you birth.
> For I called him as a single one; and I blessed him and multiplied him.
> For YHWH will comfort Zion; he will comfort all her ruins,
> And he will make her wilderness like Eden; and her desert like the garden of YHWH.
> Gladness and rejoicing will be found in her; praise and the voice of singing.
> Listen to me, you peoples; you nations, hear me.
> For Torah goes out from me; and my justice as a light to the peoples.
>
> I bring near in an instant my righteousness; and my salvation has gone forth.
> The islands wait for me; and for my arm they hope.
> Lift up to the heavens your eyes; and look at the earth beneath.
> For the heavens like smoke vanish; the earth like a garment wears out.
> But my salvation will be forever; and my righteousness will not be shaken.
>
> Hear me, you who know righteousness; you people in whose heart is my Torah.
> Fear not human reproach; be not dismayed by their insults.
> For like a garment the moth eats them; and like wool the moth-worm eats them.
> But my righteousness will be forever; and my salvation for generations.

Israel is *the* nation who pursues righteousness, that is, who seeks YHWH. Israel is *the* nation who knows righteousness, in whose heart is God's Torah. Gentiles by definition do not pursue righteousness; indeed, they "suppress the truth by injustice" according to Paul (1:18). Nevertheless, in Isaiah 51, Gentiles who do not pursue but at the most wait and hope find that God unexpectedly brings his righteousness near, that his Torah and justice and salvation goes out to them. God's righteousness, in the sense of his "power for salvation'' is then for both, Israel and Gentiles, as the parallel statements in Isa 51:6c and 8b show. But what was clear to Isaiah and clear to Paul was not to Israel, who stumbled on the rock and did not reach the goal. Many details in Paul's exposition become clear when seen from this perspective.

Verse 30. Righteousness means God's righteousness and therefore his power for salvation, as the parallels not only in Isa 51:6, 8 but also Rom 10:10 show. As it did not come by any human effort, even the effort to believe, it is probable that *ek pisteōs* refers not to a human means (that would require *dia*) but a divine source, that is, God's own faithfulness. ''The Gentiles who do not 'pursue righteousness' have obtained righteousness, the righteousness [of God] which is from [his] faithfulness.''

Verse 31. It has long puzzled exegetes why Israel's goal is differently described as ''the Torah of righteousness'' or simply ''the Torah.'' The virtual equivalence of the two terms in Isa 51:7 can help explain this usage. Perhaps I can go further and read the phrase as a normal subjective genitive: righteousness has a Torah through which it speaks to Israel, but it also is operative ''apart from Torah'' for Gentiles (Rom 3:21). But it must be remembered that this new expression of the righteousness of God is witnessed to by Torah, is contained in it, and is its ultimate goal. In any case, this verse contains no criticism of Torah nor of Israel for pursuing it. Nothing whatsoever is said about the unfulfillability of commandments or the inappropriateness of seeking righteousness in the Torah. In terms of Isaiah 51, Paul's only complaint is that Israel did not take seriously enough the middle stanza. ''Israel, on the other hand, in pursuing the Torah of righteousness [for Israel alone] did not attain to [the goal of] the Torah.''

Verse 32. It is not sure whether this verse contains two sentences, the first without a verb, or only one, but because Israel's fault lay not in pursuing but in stumbling, it seems best to understand it as one sentence. ''Why? Because they stumbled on the stone of stumbling, not from faithfulness but as it were from works.'' Here, as often, Paul gives his own understanding of a text before he cites it. This is important to note, because otherwise scholars have given too much importance to Isaiah 28, particularly as it is cited in 1 Peter 2, in interpreting the stone. Once he hit upon the idea of a stone (from Isa 51:1b?), everything that is necessary to make Paul's point is found in the LXX of Isa 8:14, ''And if you put your trust [*pepoithōs ēs*] in him (viz., YHWH), he will be for you as a sanctuary, and you will not encounter him like a stumbling-stone or like a tripping-rock.'' Israel did not reach the goal of the race because it stumbled on the rock, and it stumbled because of lack of trust or faithfulness, because it was distracted, as it were, by works. Not that Paul has anything against works, but in themselves they do not lead to the goal.[61] To be faithful to the goal of the law means to acknowledge that the righteousness of God is there also for Gentiles.

Verse 33. This is not the place to rehearse the complex history of the understanding of Isa 28:16 and 8:14 and the relationship between them.[62] I can only note that there is no evidence of a pre-Pauline understanding of either text and that the rich associations of Isaiah 28 with the community as a temple are not at all in Paul's mind. It is not the case that Isaiah 8 is inserted into the main citation of Isaiah 28,[63] but only that the inscription from Isaiah 28 is cited to interpret the Isaiah 8 passage. "As it is written: Behold I establish in Zion a stone of stumbling and a rock of offence (Isa 8:14), and the one who trusts in it will not be put to shame (Isa 28:16)." What is the stone which, on the one hand, has been the occasion for Israel's stumbling and, on the other hand, is an object of trust? Until very recently a Christological interpretation was assumed by almost everyone, but surely that must be abandoned.[64] Barrett, Toews and Meyer have given good reasons for concluding that the stone must be the Torah itself.[65] Dinter has argued that the stone is the gospel, specifically the "word of faith" of 10:8.[66] There are elements of truth in both positions, although I believe the first to be too general and the second to be too specific. To state the conclusion at the beginning, I would understand the stone to be the gospel contained in Torah, the gospel of the inclusion of Gentiles. Concretely, what Israel did not acknowledge was the middle stanza of Isa 51:1-8, the first stanza of which speaks of Abraham as the source of election in calling him a rock. Of course one cannot say that the rock simply is Abraham, because for Paul Abraham is the father of both Jews and Gentiles. It is the gospel announced to Abraham, the gospel contained in Torah, which is at issue, the gospel "that God would justify the Gentiles from faithfulness" (Gal 3:8). Of this gospel it is true to say, according to Paul, both that Israel stumbled over it and that it is good news for Gentiles.

Romans 10:1-3. These verses deal briefly with the stumbling motif, which is then dropped until it is taken up in chapter 11 and needs to be discussed in that context.[67] I will note, however, what they do not say. They do not contrast faith and action, they do not contrast self-righteousness and righteousness given by God, and they do not refer to individuals. Israel has great faith in pursuing righteousness (what else does "zeal" mean!), but they thought of it as being a righteousness for Israel alone and did not subordinate (*hypotassō*) that to the wider purpose of God's righteousness. Since Israel did not acknowledge the truth of Isa 51:4-6, therefore verse 7 is reversed and they do not know God's righteousness.

Verse 4. Now comes the positive statement of what Israel did not understand, introduced by "for." This famous sentence has problems: "For the *telos* of the law Christ *eis* righteousness to every believer." What is the subject of the sentence? Where should one supply a verb? What is the meaning of *eis*? What is the meaning of the dative? What is the meaning of *telos*? If the sentence is read in connection with what went before, then one must agree with J. C. O'Neill that it is the word "Christ" that is the grammatical (and theological?) intrusion.[68] *Eis* cannot mean "as a way to" (NEB margin), and it is doubtful if it can be governed by a proper name. *Telos eis* . . . however makes good grammatical sense (cf. Heb 6:8), and after the racing imagery earlier one would expect to hear of the goal.[69] "The goal of the law is righteousness for everyone." That is the best reason for the statement in verse 3, and indeed for everything going back to the reference to Isaiah 51 in 9:30, but I do not of course think that is what Paul wrote. He wants to go on to the positive statement of how Christ is the means whereby God's righteousness becomes a reality for Gentiles, and so there is here a transition from purely *theo*logical, Israel-language to Christological Christian language. I would translate: "For the goal of the law, Christ, is righteousness [of God] for *every* believer.[70] Again I note the use of "every believer" as a kind of code name for Gentiles, and I have underlined *pas*, Paul's word to indicate inclusion. The dative tells who the righteousness is for, not the condition whereby it is acquired. The function of Rom 10:4 is then to include Gentiles,[71] not to exclude Jews, and it says that this is the real intention of Torah.

Verse 5. Where does the Torah say that its goal is the expression of the righteousness of God for Gentiles? Verses 5 to 8, beginning with "for" explain, even if asking the question in this way result in an interpretation different from the standard one. Most interpreters see a contrast between verses 5 and 6, between self-righteousness and God-given righteousness, between Moses and Christ,[72] and most bring in presuppositions concerning Paul's so-called critique of the law, such as the letter-spirit contrast or the notion of the unfulfillability of the commandments.[73] All that has not been without influence on the textual history of the passage,[74] and I translate according to the *lectio difficilior* in earlier editions of Nestle. "For Moses writes that 'the human being who does' the righteousness which is from Torah 'will live by it'" (Lev 18:5). The gracious purpose of the Torah is to give life, and Paul cites the classic text which Judaism always understood in that sense.[75] For Paul, of course, the "human being" now includes also the Gentile human being.[76] Because of the righteousness of God, that human being will live.

Verses 6-8. The second passage in which Paul hears an expression of the righteousness of God may well have been suggested by Isa 51:7, where those who "know righteousness" are also those "in whose heart is my Torah." Because it is clearly God who speaks and not human virtue, one should begin: "And the righteousness from faithfulness speaks thus" . . . . I will not here discuss possible sources of this pesher-midrash[77] but only indicate that the point lies in the positive statement in verse 8 that "the word is near to you." That word is the word of faithfulness, the Torah of faithfulness (3:27), the word which in the new manifestation of God's righteousness according to the gospel Paul proclaims is addressed directly to his Roman readers.

The content of that word can be stated in terms of a homologia "Jesus is Lord,"[78] or of a pistis-formula "God raised him from the dead."[79] Both say the same thing in different words. It is important to emphasize that although the sentence has the form of a conditional statement, it is not really one. It is addressed to those who already confess and believe, to those to whom this word is near, in their mouths and hearts, and its purpose is to proclaim to them salvation. To underscore the point that the focus is not on the believer and confessor but rather on the near word, verse 10 repeats verse 9 but in the passive, and the goal is named not only salvation but also righteousness. This is what God has done, as he promised in the Torah.

Verses 11 to 13 are the heart of Paul's gospel of inclusion. The word *pas* appears four times in three verses, along with the characteristic phrase "also the Greek." Isa 28:16 is cited again, but with the significant addition of "everyone," which is the point. *Pas ho pisteuōn* is Paul's phrase to include the Gentiles (cf. 1:16; 3:22; 4:11; 10:4). "Everyone who believes in him," that is, in God, the nearest antecedent. Inclusion means that Gentiles may now worship the living God (Christ being the means); cf. 3:29, "Is it of Jews only that God is God? Not also of the Gentiles?" However, the main reason for understanding *theo*logical language here is the discovery by Howard that first century LXX texts retained the Tetragrammaton,[80] which would include the Joel citation of verse 13. There is no distinction, the Greek is also included, for YHWH is Lord of all, of Gentiles as well as Jews, and he is generous (9:23; 11:12, 33 [cf. Eph 2:4, 7]) toward all. These traditional Divine epithets are now very appropriate in their context. The way in which God is Lord is by his grace and generosity, and that now includes also Gentiles, because "*everyone* [not just Israel] who will call upon the name of YHWH will be saved."

The chain of four questions in verse 14-15a reads like Paul's autobiography.[81] He was sent as apostle, he proclaimed, Gentiles heard, they believed, they called upon the name of YHWH, and therefore they have now been included. The citations in 15b and 16 recall the source of Paul's self-understanding as Apostle to the Gentiles. It is to fulfil the task of the Isaianic servant that he is sent.[82] First he cites Isa 52:7, "How beautiful are the feet of those who proclaim good tidings of good!" and then he cites Isa 53:1, "YHWH, who has believed our message?"[83] The latter is the Scriptural warrant for the statement that not all have become obedient, but since the message in Isaiah is addressed to "nations" and "kings," so also Paul must be speaking of Gentiles, not Jews, who did not heed the gospel.

Lest it be objected that Paul does not actually cite Isa 52:15 here, I should point out that he does cite the second half of that verse in Rom 15:21, "They shall see to whom it was not announced about him, and those who have not heard shall understand," in a context which refers explicitly to the Gentile mission. Finally there is the passage quoted to the effect that they have indeed heard, Ps 19:5, "Their voice has gone out to all the earth and their words to the ends of the inhabited world."[84] Paul would hardly speak that way about the apostolate of Peter! Indeed, even applied to his own apostolate, it would be an intolerable exaggeration without Rom 15:19. From Paul's perspective, as soon as he gets to Spain, the "ends of the inhabited world" would have heard the word of his gospel. There is, by the way, an interesting parallel in the *Kerygma Petrou*,[85] which may reflect early knowledge of this passage: "And after twelve years go ye out into the world that no one may say, 'We have not heard'" (frag 3); "[preach] to the end that those who hear and believe may be saved, and that those who believe not may testify that they have heard it and not be able to excuse themselves saying, 'We have not heard'" (frag 4). Everything in the paragraph Rom 10:14-18 points to the Gentile mission, and no one would ever have thought of bringing in Jews were it not for a misreading of 9:30-10:4.

Only in verse 19 is Israel introduced, in a way that makes clear that Paul is turning to a new topic, or better, returning to the question of Israel's understanding from 10:3. The sense of 19a, "But I say, did Israel not know?" is then "Should Israel not have known?" Israel stumbled on the stone and did not understand the goal of the Torah, the new act of the righteousness of God Paul has been expounding in 10:4-18. But they ought to have known about the non-people whom God would call "beloved" and "children of the living God" (9:25-26), because Moses had already spoken about them. Israel ought to have understood (but did not), and Israel will understand, because God promises to make them jealous. But the jealousy motif points forward to chapter 11 and needs to be discussed in that context.[86]

At the end, Paul returns to his starting point, concerning the Gentiles who did not seek but who nevertheless found (9:30). Because of the use of the word *ethnos*, Paul applies Isa 65:1 to the Gentiles, and because of the word *laos*, he applies verse 2 to Israel.[87] In that Israel is characterized as disobedient and rebellious, there is a reference back to 10:3-4, but in that God continues to stretch out his hands to them, there is a reference forward to chapter 11. I take it that the latter is what Paul wants to say about Israel. As for what he wants to say to Gentiles, the *inclusio* of 9:30 and 10:20 makes it clear. Those who did not seek God or his righteousness nevertheless have found them. Their inclusion in the people of God is by pure grace. If Romans 10 is not about the "responsibility" of Israel (and it is not), it is certainly not about the "responsibility" of Gentiles. It is about the righteousness of God, proclaimed in Isaiah 51 and the goal of the Torah, which has now been made effective also for Gentiles. They are included.

I conclude with a brief look at 15:7-13, which restates at the end the theme of Romans stated in 1:16-17.[88] Commentators underestimate this passage when they see it only as the conclusion to 14:1-15:6, a function which it does not even fulfil very well.[89] Much more important are the links back to 3-4 and 9-11, God's truth (3:5-6; 9:6) and promises (4:13, 14, 16, 20) and mercy (11:31).[90] The theme of this section is the inclusion of the Gentiles.[91]

The grammatical construction of the sentence in 8-9a is not clear. The debate is usually along the following lines. Many commentators think of two parallel clauses dependent on *legō*: "For I tell you a) Christ has become a servant to the circumcised to show God's truthfulness, in order to confirm the promises given to the patriarchs, and b) the Gentiles glorify God for his mercy."[92] Others make the two parallel clauses dependent on *eis to*: "For I tell you Christ has become a servant to the circumcised to show God's truthfulness, a) in order to confirm the promises given to the patriarchs and b) [in order that] the Gentiles might glorify God for his mercy."[93] The real problem in my view lies in thinking of parallel clauses at all. In the first place it is hard to see how *b* relates to *a* in either construction, and it does not do to assist Paul by adding to *b* words like "and also a servant to the uncircumcised" as an unexpressed but essential thought.[94] In the second place, interpreters are tempted to see the parallel clauses as contrasts,[95] so that the Jews are recipients only (!) of God's truth and promises, but the Gentiles receive his mercy.

S. K. Williams has put forth a new solution based on a translation of *diakonos peritomēs*, not as "servant to the circumcision" but as a genitive of origin, "servant from the circumcision."[96] I believe that he is basically right, and in addition to his excellent arguments I would like to add one more. Christ is called *diakonos* by Paul in one other passage, Gal 2:18, "is Christ a servant of sin?" F. F. Bruce is not alone in interpreting that as "agent of sin."[97] The risen Christ of Paul's preaching (and he never speaks of the "historical" Jesus) is the source and cause of the Gentile mission, and he is Israel's agent in this task. He is the Jew who is "a guide of the blind, a light for those in darkness, an instructor of the foolish, a teacher of the immature" (2:19-20). As soon as one gets rid of the idea that once more Paul wants to be evenhanded and to speak of the significance of Christ for the Jew, on the one hand, and the Gentile, on the other hand, then the problems of the sentence disappear. Following Williams, then, I translate accordingly: "For I tell you that Christ has become a servant from the circumcised for the sake of God's truthfulness, in order to confirm the promises to the fathers and [consequently] the Gentiles might glorify God for his mercy.'' The sentence now gives support to verse 7, ''Christ has accepted you [Roman Gentile Christians],'' and leads to the four quotations concerning Gentiles in verses 9b-12. This section deals solely with the theme of Gentile inclusion.

Exploring a major theme of Romans is not the same as writing a complete theology of Paul. I hope, however, to have shown that at least in this letter the good news of Paul's gospel for Gentiles is not part of a polemic against Torah or Israel. Without at all excluding Jews, he is able to argue very effectively and very passionately that the inclusion of Gentiles was always the goal of the Torah, which has now been realized through the righteousness of God manifested in the faithfulness of Jesus Christ.

9

ISRAEL'S MISSTEP IN THE EYES OF PAUL

Christian theologians have often in the past developed a theology of Judaism on the basis of the Pauline epistles. Judaism was whatever Paul opposed or even the opposite of everything Paul said positively. Only in recent times have the scholarly maxim *ad fontes* and the religious injunction not to bear false witness been combined in the ideal of writing about Judaism solely from Jewish sources, read from the perspective of those sources. After the work especially of E. P. Sanders,[1] it will never be possible to return to old habits. Whatever positions Paul was opposing, none of them could be called Judaism as such. Nevertheless, he does have something against his fellow Jews, and I will discuss those passages where he speaks about them. First, however, I want to look briefly at some passages which ought not to be included in such a discussion.

Since every one of Paul's letters is addressed explicitly to Gentile Christians, it is not known what he would have said to Jews. That he would have had occasion to do so is clear from 2 Cor 11:24, where he says that he was punished in synagogues five times. Since that could only happen if he voluntarily put himself under their jurisdiction, it means that Paul went to synagogues, presumably to worship. If Acts is put rigorously to one side, as methodologically must be done, there is no evidence from Paul's own hand that he ever preached to Jews, in synagogues or anywhere else.[2] From the account of the Jerusalem council in Galatians 2, it would appear that Paul was at one time in favour of Peter's preaching to Jews and that he acknowledged Peter's gospel and apostolate. In Romans, on the other hand, there is not a hint even of this.

Can statements about Paul's own past prove anything about what he thought of other Jews or even of Judaism? Did his prophetic commissioning as Apostle to the Gentiles also mean for him personally an advantage, a liberation from law perhaps, or a new hope for salvation? He does not say so. There is no indication that "making progress more than many contemporaries in my people, being to a greater degree zealous for the [oral] traditions of my fathers" (Gal 1:14) was a bad thing to do. To be "circumcised on the eighth day, from the people of Israel, of the tribe of Benjamin, a Hebrew of the Hebrews, with respect to the law a Pharisee . . . with respect to righteousness in the law blameless" (Phil 3:5-6) is said by Paul to be an advantage (*kerdos* 3:7) and to give that up a distinct loss (*zēmia* 3:7, 8). What he regrets about his past is not his "Judaism" but his persecution of the church (3:6; Gal 1:13; 1 Cor 15:9). But apart from that his advantages were real advantages, which he deliberately gave up. "Indeed, I count all things as loss for the superiority of the knowledge of Christ Jesus my Lord, for whose sake I have lost all things and count them as excrement, in order that I might gain Christ and be found in him, having my righteousness not from the law but through the faithfulness of Christ, the righteousness from God which [leads] to the faith of knowing him" (Phil 3:8-10). It seems that it is possible to have a status of righteousness from either of two sources, from the law (in the sense of covenant) or from the faithfulness of Christ. Paul once had the former (cf. v 6) and has shifted to the latter. He does not say that he wishes other Jews to do the same. Knowing Jesus Christ as Lord he says is superior (*hyperechon*, v 8), but he does not deny at all the validity of life in Torah. Since Romans 7 is not autobiographical,[3] it seems that no critique of Judaism can be drawn from Paul's statements about himself.[4]

Galatians ought not to be included in this summary. Whoever the troublemakers are who are causing the Galatians to Judaize, and I am convinced that they are Gentile Christians, what Paul opposes is not what they have to say about *Judaism*. Even if the troublemakers should be Jews, they are Jewish Christians,[5] and the debate concerns what *Gentiles* ought to do to be faithful Christians (circumcision or not).[6] I have dealt in other chapters with some problem texts in Galatians,[7] and their conclusions do not need to be repeated here.

2 Corinthians ought not to be included in this survey. Paul's rivals are here clearly to be identified as Jewish Christians, and their views can be more clearly established than is the case in Galatians. Judaizing appears not to be not an issue at all, and the word "law" is found nowhere in the whole epistle. If Georgi is even partly right in his characterization of the opponents,[8] had Paul the Pharisee encountered them before Damascus, his rejection of them would have been just as sharp. 2 Corinthians 3, however, is

a different matter and deserves a separate discussion.[9]

Philippians also ought not to be included. The opponents in the fragment in chapter 3 seem so much like those of 2 Corinthians 10-13 that nothing more need be said about them.[10] It has been suggested that here Paul is referring not to Jewish Christians but to local Jews,[11] but even so, it is doubtful if one could infer very much from such intemperate language about his attitude to Jews in general, to say nothing of Judaism as such. His vicious invectives in Phil 3:2 and Gal 5:12 are hardly to be regarded as serious responses to the question "what is the value of circumcision?" (Rom 3:1)!

1 Thess 2:13-16 ought to be included in the survey and discussed at some length, but it will not be. In the first place, I am firmly convinced that at least the relevant parts are an interpolation and would have difficulty imagining them to be otherwise. In the second place, they have been much discussed lately, and I have nothing to add to the arguments already adduced against Pauline authorship.[12] Nevertheless, something can be said. The best discussion of the tradition of the killing of the prophets lying behind these verses is by O. H. Steck,[13] and he points out the one phrase least derivable from the tradition: "hindering us from speaking to the Gentiles that they might be saved" (v 16a). The interpolator may have included this phrase as a memory of the Pauline situation.

In sum: Paul had real opponents who caused real difficulties for his apostolate to the Gentiles. Many of them were Jewish Christians, and some may have been non-Christian Jews. Paul's sometimes violent disagreements with them, however, were not about the importance of Torah in the life of a Jew but about how Gentiles ought to relate to the law (Galatians) or about how Jewish apostles ought to relate to Gentiles (2 Corinthians). There presumably was also Jewish opposition to Paul not reflected in these inner Christian discussions. There is the charge in Acts 21:21 that some Jews (or Jewish Christians) said that Paul "teaches all the Jews who are among the Gentiles to forsake Moses, telling them not to circumcise their children or observe the customs." If the charge were true, then Paul really would have a fundamental quarrel with Jews in general and Judaism as such. I believe the charge to be false, but if even some believed it, it could have been a hindrance to Paul in carrying out his apostolic task for the Gentiles.[14] One could imagine an inner Jewish debate between Paul and Gamaliel,[15] even though I seriously doubt if either had in fact even heard of the other. Such a debate would not have been about the central concerns of Judaism but about the somewhat peripheral "Jewish theology of Gentiles," if I may use a very non-Jewish expression. It would have been about how Gentiles relate to Torah and election and the timing of their entry into God's people. But if that is true, those same issues might very well be on the agenda of a debate between Paul and James. What is at issue between Paul and Judaism is not the Torah of Israel but Paul as Apostle to the Gentiles.

I turn now to one of the two passages where Paul expresses himself at greater length. Rom 2:17-29 is a section which is in many ways puzzling. Even if its function were to show that Jews are as bad or even worse than Gentiles, which I doubt, it is difficult to understand it as a universal indictment of all Jews. The emphasis on doing as a prerequisite for salvation, with no reference to covenant or grace, would seem to make Paul into the supreme legalist. The identity of the uncircumcised is the despair of commentators. And there are many other problems. Perhaps one should cease to assume that what Paul ought to be saying can be derived from 3:9 and 19 and first look at the section apart from its context.

Three recent interpreters have done so and come to conclusions surprising for traditional law-gospel exegesis. J. C. O'Neill says, "This is a fine appeal to a Jew from a fellow Jew to keep the law which they both profess."[16] H. Räisänen says that the conclusion of Paul's argument is "that circumcision is of no avail to a Jew who is guilty of serious transgressions of the law, and that a true Jew is one who behaves like one (whether circumcised or not)."[17] E. P. Sanders describes the intent of the passage this way: "What one should do is to examine one's motives to make sure they are pure, to be sure that observance of the law is not merely external, and to act in such a way as not to bring disgrace on the synagogue; in short to repent and to mend one's ways."[18] These seem to me to be rather sensible readings of the text, but they are achieved only at a cost. For O'Neill the section is a later interpolation into the letter, for Sanders it is part of a virtually unchanged synagogue sermon incorporated by Paul, and for Räisänen it is an example of Paul's complete inconsistency in dealing with the question whether the law can be fulfilled. But keeping their conclusions that Paul is here urging Jews (not Gentiles) to keep the law better, it is possible to make more sense of why he would want to say that.

In Rom 9:4-5 Paul gives a list of what characterizes Israelites, a list with which Jews could agree. His list here, however, is quite different: "You bear the name of Jew and trust in the Torah and boast in God and know his will and discern what is excellent, being instructed from the Torah, and are confident of being a guide of the blind, a light for those in darkness, an instructor of the foolish, a teacher of the immature, having in the Torah the embodiment of knowledge and truth." That is not a description of a Jew as such but specifically of a Jewish missionary to Gentiles.[19] The section is then not about Jews as such nor about the law as such, and it is certainly not about soteriology; it centres on the accusation that "because of you the name of God is blasphemed among the Gentiles" (2:24). The description of the ideal is one in which such missionaries could recognize themselves, and it is not at all meant ironically. What then is the meaning of the three accusations of theft, adultery, and robbing temples? The strange last case is the most absurd if one is thinking of a universal indictment; as Sanders says,[20] "Did they all rob temples?" No, but four did, and it may be that Paul even has that specific case in mind.[21] The scandal of swindling the proselyte Fulvia of gifts she was sending to the Jerusalem temple in C.E. 19 was great enough to have at least four thousand Jews expelled from Rome, something serious enough to be long remembered. It was also a great setback to the missionary enterprise.[22] Even occasional scandals like that are enough to warrant the statement that "the name of God because of you is blasphemed among the Gentiles."

That, after all, is the point. Paul is accusing not all Jews but Jewish missionaries, and he is accusing not all missionaries but only some (cf. 3:3) of flagrant violations of Torah. But most important he does so not to speak of Jewish "theology" but of the bad effect such activity has for attracting proselytes. Even Josephus's "complete scoundrel," if he repented and restored the money, if he circumcised his heart, would be justified at the judgment, but the harm will still have been done. What follows in verses 25-29 is not directed against Torah and circumcision, even if some of the rhetoric about the latter is quite strong and will be corrected in 3:1. On the contrary, it is in favour of doing Torah and circumcision of the heart. But why does Paul go on after having made his point? Is it true, as some have maintained, that he himself had been such a missionary before Damascus and that therefore he got carried away? Does he hope that other Jews, in faithfulness to Torah, will help him, at least passively, in his new Gentile mission?

I now return to the question of why this rhetorical aside is placed where it is in the midst of Paul's indictment of the Gentile world 1:18-3:20. Its function in that context may be to say that one possible solution to the Gentile problem, that they become proselytes, has not worked well in the past (and is not necessary in the present, after 3:21). In any case, it is an aside and not part of an evenhanded invective against Jews as well as Gentiles. The larger context speaks of all Gentiles in relation to God, but the aside speaks of some Jews in relation to Gentiles. What then is the significance of the language of "the Jew and also the Greek"? That needs to be discussed in another context.[23]

I will now state a kind of preliminary summary, which needs to be tested in Romans 11. The oft-quoted conclusion of one of the most important books on Paul in this generation is this: "That is what Paul finds wrong with Judaism: it is not Christianity."[24] That is, of course, provocatively overstated, and its author also rightly says that Paul hardly ever speaks of Judaism.[25] But taking it as it stands, in the same spirit I will formulate my alternative thesis: "This is what Paul finds wrong with other Jews: that they did not share his revelation in Damascus."

Romans 11 is not a good chapter on which to base a Christian theology of Israel, if only because of the many tensions it contains.[26] There is something in the chapter which makes interpreters answer Paul's question, "Has God repudiated his people" by saying, "Well, yes, he did repudiate almost all of them, but only (!) for the period between Paul and Parousia," which is hardly the same as Paul's vehement *mē genoito*. The word "election" in verse 7 is a very small number contrasted with "the rest," while in verse 28 it refers to "all Israel." Although they tripped, Israel did not fall in verse 11, and yet they do seem to be fallen in verse 22. The chapter emphasizes God's action: it is God who blinds (vv 7, 25), trips (v 11), stupefies (v 8), imprisons in disobedience (v 32), and yet Jews are said to be broken off because of *their* unbelief (v 20). Paul speaks of God's mercy and grace (vv 5, 32), a grace not from works (v 6), and yet in verses 22-23 everything seems to be conditional on the human work of believing. In 10:19 and 11:11 God makes Israel jealous, and at the end the Redeemer will save all of them, while in 11:14 Paul makes Israel jealous, to save some of them. Most of the problems seem to centre on the olive tree section, verses 13-24, and I shall put it to one side on the first glance through the chapter.

If my reading of Romans 9 is correct,[27] Paul says nothing there whatsoever which is critical of Israel. On the contrary, these chapters must be understood "nicht als primär israelkritisch—sondern als primär kirchenkritisch."[28] It is important that the Roman Christians understand that God's election of Israel, which is not based on works or faith, still stands, and that Gentiles who were not chosen in the past had no valid ground for complaint. It is however also important that they understand that God, in a new act of righteousness, has now called also a new people, the Gentiles (9:25-26), who share the same advantages of election (8:28-39). I would now be even more positive about the election of Israel. Dinter has shown how later generations (for example, LXX) understood such remnant language as Isa 10:20-23 as an act of salvation for all Israel who survived the Assyrian crisis.[29] There is no "only" in the Isaiah text,[30] and it seems that what was a threat in the original situation was later understood as a promise. The "remnant" which is to be saved in 9:27 is the same as the "all Israel" which is to be saved in 11:26, even "though the number of the children of Israel be as the sand of the sea." YHWH Sabaoth *has* left Israel "seed," and Israel did *not* become like Sodom and Gomorrah. Romans 9 ends like Romans 11 with the proclamation of God's mercy on both Gentiles and Israel.

There is another clue to interpretation from the end of the discussion when it becomes clear what specifically Jews have been hostile to (11:28): it is the gospel, Paul's gospel, the gospel that God would justify the Gentiles by faithfulness (Gal 3:8). I would also now like to be less tentative about "the instruments of mercy . . . whom God called, even us, not only from the Jews but also from the Gentiles." They are quite specifically those whom God has called to the mission to the Gentiles, Paul and some Jews and some Gentiles. There is then both continuity and discontinuity between the end of Romans 9 and the beginning of Romans 11, continuity in concept and discontinuity in language. But before taking up the continuation of this thread, there are passages in 9:30-10:20 which also bear on an interpretation of Romans 11.

In another context I looked at the race toward the goal from the perspective of what Gentiles obtained.[31] Now what Paul says there about Israel and what he does not say must be noted. First of all, he speaks about Israel as a whole and not only about some Jews. Paul, of course, knows that some Jews responded to "the gospel to the circumcised" (Galatians 2), but faith in Christ is not an issue in Rom 9:30-10:4; it is rather openness to Gentiles. Paul would have said, for example, that the Jew who transmitted the saying of Jesus "Go nowhere among the Gentiles and enter no town of the Samaritans, but go rather to the lost sheep of the house of Israel" (Matt 10:5-6) had stumbled just as much on the stone as did the non-Christian Jew. Israel was right to pursue the Torah of righteousness and was wrong only in not realizing that the goal of that Torah, in which God's righteousness would be extended also to the Gentiles, was now at hand. Being distracted by works (which of course should be done), Israel was faithful to Torah as it relates to Israel, but with respect to the goal of that Torah as it relates to Gentiles, they stumbled and were unfaithful. But even so it is doubtful if one should speak of the "guilt and responsibility of Israel," since they stumbled on a stone which was providentially put there by God precisely to make them stumble. Paul praises Israel's zeal but not Israel's knowledge (10:2). They did not subordinate themselves to the righteousness of God because they were ignorant of it (10:3). Nevertheless, Paul prays for their salvation, knowing that it stands firm in the purpose of God (that is, from a literary perspective the function of 10:1 is to prepare for 11:26f).

In spite of its popularity, I believe it is simply wrongheaded to try to read these verses as a definition of "justification by faith." It is also not legitimate to appeal to Phil 3:9, about which F. W. Beare comments, "If we did not possess Romans and Galatians, we would find his words [here] all but incomprehensible."[32] Besides, as I have shown, it is possible to understand Phil 3:9 in a way that does not deny the righteousness of God given to Israel through Torah when it affirms that righteousness now given to Gentiles (and Paul!) through Christ. Rom 10:3 is not about an individual righteousness or self-righteousness but about Israel's righteousness which, while it comes from God, is not enough, according to Paul. The righteousness of God for Gentiles, which is the goal of the Torah, has now been manifested, and it is the failure of Israel to acknowledge this which is what Paul holds against them.

Paul has a very strong opinion on how to answer the question, "Has God repudiated his people" (11:1).[33] Not only does he indignantly reject the question but he also states positively, "God has not repudiated his people, whom he previously chose."[34] Paul's first witness to this fact is astounding: since he himself is an Israelite and God has not repudiated him, therefore God has not repudiated Israel. As if Israel's rejection is not total but only 99.99999 per cent, since God has spared one out of ten million! If Paul were tempted to say with Elijah, "I alone am left," then he would deserve the same rebuke. In any case, the second witness is not Elijah but what the divine revelation says to him. "I have left for myself seven thousand men who have not bowed the knee to Baal." Because of the seven thousand all Israel was spared. Paul, who pleads to God not against Israel but for Israel (9:1-3; 10:1), hears in these words the answer to his prayer, the answer expressed most clearly in 11:26. How is this so?

"So then also in the present time there has been a remnant according to the election of grace. . . . What then? What Israel seeks, that it did not obtain. But the election obtained it, while the rest were blinded" (11:5, 7). The identity of the remnant, the election, has seemed so obvious to most as to not need discussion; it must be Jewish Christians in general, those Jews who responded favourably to Cephas's "apostolate to the circumcised" (Gal 2:7). I believe that cannot be the case for the following reasons: If that is what Paul had meant, it would have been so easy for him to refer in verse 1 to "the saints in Jerusalem" (15:26). Instead, he refers only to himself, surely not as an example of a Jewish Christian but as the Apostle to the Gentiles. Had he gone on to name others, they would have included such fellow Jews from chapter 16 as Andronicus and Junia, Herodion, and Lucius and Jason and Sosipater, but not Jewish Christians as such. When he speaks of Israel seeking but not obtaining, there is a clear reference back to 9:31, where as I have argued the goal of the Torah is the inclusion of Gentiles.[35] The election, the remnant, refers to those Jews who like Paul are engaged in the Gentile mission. They are the "instruments of mercy" (9:23) whom God called in order to express his righteousness now for Gentiles.[36]

The remnant is "according to the election of grace. But if by grace then not from works, since [in that case] grace would not be grace" (11:5-6). Just as in chapter 9, Paul must emphasize that he is speaking of God's action in accomplishing his own purposes and that it is not a matter of any human achievement whatsoever, whether believing or doing. If the remnant were a remnant of achievers, then the vast majority could be blamed, but that is not the case. The vast majority were blinded[37] but blinded by God,[38] to fulfil his purposes, both for Israel and for Gentiles. The rest are not repudiated, and their blinding is not a punishment but part of God's action for salvation. It has been a longstanding assumption that Paul uses the remnant concept in order to disinherit Israel. That is not the case.[39]

Paul returns to his original question and comes to a preliminary conclusion. "I ask then, have they stumbled so as to fall? By no means! But by their misstep salvation [will come] to the Gentiles, in order to make them jealous. But if their misstep [means] riches for the world and their deficit riches for the Gentiles, how much more [will mean] their fullness?" (11:11-12). Israel has stumbled over the rock God put in Zion (9:32f), but Israel has not fallen, and there is the prospect of their "fullness." For reasons that are not spelled out, this stumbling means salvation and riches for Gentiles, riches from God (10:12; 11:33). There is brief reference to the jealousy motif, which must refer to Israel, as in 10:19. That too seems to be a promise, parallel to the fullness, so that somehow Israel's deficit and misstep will be overcome. The language is rhetorically artful but tantalizingly vague.

I pass over for now a certain digression and pick up the argument again in verse 25b, beginning with a recapitulation of 11-12: "a partial blindness has come on Israel until the fullness of the Gentiles comes in." Since Israel stumbled but did not fall, and since there were only some things that Israel did not understand, it seems best to understand *apo merous* to refer to a partial blindness[40] rather than to a division between the majority and the minority. It also follows better the first half of the sentence, where the Gentiles understand many things but perhaps not the "mystery." Since the fullness of Israel in verse 12 seems to be the same as all Israel in verse 26, the fullness of the Gentiles should probably be understood in the same way, but it must be remembered that Paul is speaking of groups and not individuals. As many have noted, the "coming in" refers to the eschatological pilgrimage of the Gentiles.

I come now to the mystery proper, found I believe not in the recapitulation but in the new statement only hinted at earlier: "and thus all Israel will be saved, as it is written: There will come from Zion the Redeemer; he will turn impieties from Jacob; and this is my covenant with them, when I take away their sins" (Isa 59:20-21a; 27:9).[41] This means to understand the disputed *kai houtōs* with the following,[42] for the mystery is contained in the Scripture cited.[43] Stendahl has recently advanced the idea that the Redeemer is God as in Isa 59:20 rather than the returning Christ as in 1 Thess 1:10,[44] and in terms of the discussion up to now he is surely right.[45] The key word is "covenant," a concept that applies only to Israel for Paul,[46] and the covenant is, of course, the Sinai covenant,[47] according to which God in his covenant loyalty forgives Israel's sins. The reason for Paul's change of "to Zion" (MT) or "on account of Zion" (LXX) to "from Zion" is not clear. It probably would be too subtle to refer back to the stone "in Zion" which God is about to remove by the entry of the Gentiles, and for Paul, writing before 70 C.E., God now dwells *in* Zion. It is more likely that the concept of the eschatological pilgrimage of the Gentiles "coming in" (v 25) has influenced the wording here, perhaps even specifically by the "from Zion" of Isa 2:3.[48] The general contours of Paul's mystery are I think clear. They and the rest of the whole discussion in Romans 9-11 are summed up in the conclusion.

Like most of what precedes, the summary deals with two global entities, Israel and Gentiles, seen from the perspective of God's purposes and not their own responses.[49] As Stendahl has emphasized, Paul is dealing in these chapters not with theological anthropology but with Jews and Gentiles. "With respect to the gospel, to be sure, they are hostile for your sake, but with respect to the election they are beloved for the sake of the fathers" (11:28). Israel, all Israel in the context of these statements, is hostile[50] to the gospel, Paul's gospel to the Gentiles, and at the same time beloved as the elect Israel. Both of these statements are important for the Roman Christians to ponder. Without the first, the gospel would not have been preached to them, and without the second, their own election (8:28-39) would be doubtful. "For irrevocable are the gracious gifts and calling of God" (11:29). Here is a clear restatement of what was said concerning Israel's "advantages" and election in chapter 9 and support for 11:28b. Verses 30-31 comprise a beautiful chiastic construction, which conceals the fact that the two halves do not really balance. It goes without saying that not only the mercy but also the disobedience are seen from the perspective of their source in God.[51] "For as you were once disobedient to God but now have received mercy because of their disobedience, so they also now have become disobedient with respect to the mercy [shown] to you, in order that they too may now receive mercy" (30-31). For the disobedience of Gentiles and the mercy shown to them I could refer back to Romans 1-3, but the relationship between Gentile mercy and Israelite disobedience, referred to also in 11:11, is not at all clear and must be reserved for a further discussion below. The dative in verse 31 is different from that in verse 30 and must mean something like "with respect to," which shows the real disproportion in the two statements. Differing from that of the Gentiles, Israel's disobedience is only partial, it is caused by God, and it has two good outcomes, both in order that the Gentiles might receive mercy *and* in order that Israel too may now receive mercy. It is doubtful whether Paul noted this discrepency, as the evenhanded conclusion in verse 33 shows. The final doxology is not a cry of despair that only God and not Paul can understand such things, but on the contrary a prayer of deep thanksgiving that Paul *has* been given understanding and that his prayers of intercession in 9:1-3 and 10:1 have been answered. I return now to material skipped over before.

It has been important for Paul throughout Romans 9-11 to make the point to his Roman readers that God has chosen Israel by grace alone and will save Israel by grace alone. The Roman Christians must understand themselves as being in no worse but also in no better a position than that. Beginning in Rom 11:1, he speaks *to* Gentiles *about* Jews. There is then a significant shift in 11:13-24, where Paul turns to the Gentiles with explicitly paraenetic intentions. This new address begins with a personal note and rather than Biblical material as in the surrounding sections uses an analogy, a mode of rhetoric not the most successful in Paul's hands.[52] The paraenetic point is especially clear: "do not boast over the branches" (17); "it is not you who support the root but the root [supports] you" (18); "do not think haughty thoughts but fear [God]" (20); "consider then the goodness and severity of God" (22a); "you too might be cut off" (22b); "if you have been cut off from [your] native wild olive tree and against all nature grafted onto the cultivated olive tree" (24); and finally in the solemn transition to the next paragraph "I do not want you to be ignorant, brothers, of this mystery, lest you be wise for yourselves [in your own eyes]" (25). W. D. Davies has made the very interesting suggestion that the image of the olive tree was chosen because for Greek Gentiles "the olive tree could serve as a symbol as powerful as was the vine among the Jews." The Roman Christians are then provocatively told that they are only wild olive trees, that they "had nothing to contribute. To be fruitful they had to be grafted on to the cultivated olive tree which had [not Athena but] Abraham, the father of Israel, as its root."[53] In retrospect it is even possible to wonder if the jealousy motif was chosen not so much because of Israel but because it makes Gentiles recognize that without Christ they are "not a nation" and "a foolish nation" (10:19). It seems that the statement "branches were broken off so that I might be grafted in" is not only hypothetical. Roman Christians were boasting triumphantly that God preferred them to Jews, and Paul's explicit rebukes here are consonant with the implicit ones throughout Romans 9-11. All this is clear enough, but the problems come with the details.

"Now I speak to you, the Gentiles. Inasmuch as I am Apostle to the Gentiles, I glorify my ministry in the hope that I may make my flesh jealous and I will save some of them" (11:13-14). Already there is a subtle rebuke. Important as Paul's commissioning is to him otherwise (15:16), here it is only a means to an end. Gentile Christians, far from feeling superior, should understand that what is happening with them is in the service of the salvation of Israel. That here Paul makes Israel jealous can probably be understood as his participation in God's act of doing so (10:19), but it is not at all clear why he thereby saves "some." Is it really only "diplomatic caution which does not yet lay the cards on the table,"[54] whereby Paul really expects that God will save all when he brings the collection? Or is the expression merely a careless one because Paul's attention is now directed toward the Gentiles? This is not the only problematic statement in this section.

Verse 15 is in many ways a restatement of verse 12. Israel, or more precisely the vast majority, the "rest," have rejected Paul's gospel, or better the missionary task (presumably that is what is meant and not the rejection of Israel by God),[55] and that opens the way for the reconcilation of the world (cf. 2 Cor 5:18f). Because Israel did not accept the task of being "the light for the Gentiles" that has opened the way for Christ to be that light. Their acceptance (of the task? of the fear of the Lord?[56] their acknowledgment of the truth of the reconciliation?) means then the comsummation of all things, life from the dead. It is again rather vague, but suggestive of promise, and it makes the Gentiles understand themselves in relation to Israel.

Are the two metaphors in verse 16 to be understood in the same way, so that both first fruit and root refer back to the remnant (11:5) or forward to the patriarchs (11:28)? While that would be the most natural way of interpreting them, there are good reasons for dividing them.[57] "If the first fruit is holy, so also the lump." Because the Jewish-Christian missionaries to the Gentiles, like the seven thousand in Elijah's time, have been faithful to God's calling, therefore all Israel is holy and will be spared. "If the root is holy, so also the branches." Because of election, or in the Jewish way of putting it, on account of the fathers (*bzkwt 'bwt*), all Israel is beloved and will be spared. Both metaphors encourage the Roman Christians to look on Israel as holy.

The second metaphor is then expanded into the confused and confusing figure of the olive tree. It does not seem possible to sustain the idea of missionaries, so that the branches broken off might represent people like the false "super apostles" in Corinth. Indeed, it does not seem possible to read the figure allegorically in any consistent way. The branches broken off, for example, are not burned or the like but continue to live; and what about the tree trunk? Paul's entire interest is with the branches grafted in, who must be warned that they are only wild olive branches, that the root supports them, and that they must not boast over the branches broken off. Paul's concern is not at all with the broken-off branches as such, and the statement that "God is able to graft them in again" (23) is not a prediction about Jews as much as it is a warning to Gentiles, comparable to John the Baptist's statement that "God is able from these stones to raise up children to Abraham."[58] Even the more explicit "how much more shall those who naturally [belong to it] be grafted onto their own olive tree'' (24) functions primarily to underline the unnatural and miraculous grafting of the wild olive branches. Paul also shows no interest at all in the cultivated branches not broken off;[59] it is not Jewish Christians but Roman Gentile Christians and their relationship to Israel which is his concern. It is only because the Roman Christians stand by faith and not by boasting that the branches are said to be broken off ''by unbelief'' (20, 23). It is only because of the injunction to remain in God's goodness that being cut off becomes a threat of punishment (22) or of being ''not spared'' (21). The olive tree, and particularly the branches broken off, are then not to be interpreted allegorically, and it is the paraenetic nature of this direct address which makes this section 11:13-24 (+25a) inconsistent with the rest of the chapter.[60]

C. Plag has noticed tensions in Romans 11, tensions so great that he felt forced to treat 11:25-27 as an interpolation taken from another letter from Paul.[61] While one can agree with him concerning the tension, I believe that he has isolated the wrong section and that it is verses 13 to 24 which are most out of line.[62] Not that I think it an interpolation nor that I think all the difficulties are confined to that section. Part of the problem with Romans 11 is that Paul gives too many answers to his own questions. I will review the chapter one more time, now from the perspective of what it says about Israel and to Gentiles.

Taking up the question of 9:6, whether ''the word of God has lapsed,'' Paul asks, ''Has God repudiated his people'' (11:1) and responds very firmly: No, because ''all Israel will be saved'' (11:26). This is quite clear and surely the most important thing Paul wants to say on the subject. It is only when he goes on to ask the secondary question ''Why?'' that there are a number of answers, any one of which would suffice, but which are not completely consistent in their plurality.

Why will all Israel be saved? The first answer is that God is faithful to his covenant and forgives (26). Or, to say the same thing in slightly different words, ''irrevocable are the gracious gifts and calling of God'' (29; cf. 9:6). Another way to put the very same thing is to say that Israel is ''beloved for the sake of the fathers'' (28).[63] All of these variants were known to Paul from the Biblical tradition, and they would continue in the later Jewish tradition, to support what E.P. Sanders calls the very centre of the Rabbinic ''pattern of religion,'' *Sanh.* 10:1, ''All Israel has a part in the age to come.''[64]

Why will all Israel be saved? The second answer is that ''there will come from Zion the Redeemer.'' I believe this to be only a variant of the first answer, but it deserves special treatment because most interpreters have seen here a reference to the parousia of Christ. It could be asked whether Paul could ever think of God apart from Christ,[65] but this question can be answered if at all only in connection with an exegesis of 1 Cor 15:28. It may be that Christ was in Paul's mind, but even so it would be completely wrong to speak of an end-time conversion.[66] If Christ is meant, then it is Christ in a different role, Christ as the agent of the "Sonderweg"[67] of Israel's salvation. Some Jews have thought that eschatologically Gentiles would be absorbed into Israel, and most Christians have thought that eschatologically Jews would be absorbed into the church, but Paul's conviction is God's righteousness for salvation for both, without changing one into the other.

Why will all Israel be saved? Because a remnant of Jews, Paul and his Jewish co-workers, responded to the missionary task, therefore God will act graciously toward all Israel. That is how the concept of the representative righteous has functioned from Genesis 18 down to the later Jewish concept of the *Lamedvovniks* (thirty-six righteous).[68] This third answer, with which the chapter begins, is not mentioned again after verse 16a at the latest. While it is consonant with the first answer, it is not really the same, and so it is quietly dropped to be subsumed under the first.

Why will all Israel be saved? Because God will make them jealous of the salvation that has come to Gentiles. It is not said that God will provoke them to faith in Christ, although this is usually assumed without discussion. Paul certainly does not share Luke's concept of the jealousy of Jews (Acts 5:17; 13:45; 17:5), although it shows that "conversion" is not the most natural way to think about it. It has happened again and again in genuine Jewish-Christian dialogue that a nominal Jew became jealous of a faithful Christian and so became a more faithful Jew[69] or that a nominal Christian became jealous of a faithful Jew and so became a more faithful Christian. While Paul does not have individuals as such in mind, surely a good way to understand the jealousy motif (as in Deut 32:21) is that Israel would become more faithful to Torah. Of course, for Paul that means also acknowledging the goal of Torah, the expression of the righteousness of God for Gentiles, but it does not mean abandoning the Torah by making themselves Gentiles. That Paul himself hopes to make some Jews jealous (11:14) need not mean anything very different, if we understand it in terms of the collection and the eschaton.[70] Here is then a fourth answer.

Why will all Israel be saved? *Not* by individual Jews converting to faith in Christ. The one place where this was happening in Paul's time, in the preaching of the gospel to the circumcised by the Jerusalem church, is completely ignored in this chapter. This observation is, I believe, fatal to any attempt to understand Paul as blaming Jews for refusing to believe in Christ and hoping for Jews that they will come to such a belief in the future. Nowhere in these chapters does Paul refer to Jewish Christians as such.[71] When a distinction is made within Israel, it is between those few like Paul engaged in the Gentile mission and the "rest" who do not acknowledge it. Usually, however, he speaks about Israel as a whole in an undifferentiated manner. All Israel stumbled on the stone and all Israel will be saved.

Why will the fullness of the Gentiles come in? Here there are two answers, whose relationship one to the other is not at all clear. One answer is that it is by the preaching of Paul and his associates (10:14-18), by the activity of "the remnant according to the election of grace" (11:5). One could apply here Eckardt's concept of the "bridge generation," which he defines as a "vocational remnant of Jews serving as instruments for the salvation of the world within a relatively faithful Israel."[72] It is for this reason that Gentile Christians owe a debt of love, not just to the Jerusalem "saints" but to all Israel: "for if the Gentiles have shared in their spiritual things, they are obliged to serve them in material things" (15:27). Here is the Pauline version of "salvation is from the Jews" (John 4:22), and it seems to be his normal way of thinking about the matter.

Why will the fullness of the Gentiles come in? The second answer is found only in Romans 9-11 and is harder to understand. It is because Israel has stumbled on the stone, not to fall, but nevertheless stumbled, that salvation will come to the Gentiles (9:30-33; 11:11-12, 15). It appears that to make this point Paul needs to say "all Israel," without differentiation. This line of thought makes no use of the idea of the remnant and certainly not of "Jewish Christianity." Here again Gentile salvation is from the Jews, but now not just a few Jews but all Jews, who as a whole have stumbled. Why this is so is not at all clear, but also from this perspective Gentile Christians owe a debt of love to all Israel. It would be a mistake to read into Paul the Lukan concept that Gentile mission presupposes the failure of Jewish mission. It would be an even greater mistake to suppose that the Lukan portrait represents Paul's actual practice. From his own account, Paul never tried to convert Jews, and apostolate to the Gentiles was never for him a second best. It must also be emphasized that Paul does not speak of stumbling in order to attach any blame to Israel at all. The emphasis is always on God, who blinds and trips Israel in order to save Gentiles. The starting point is, of course, the rock placed in Zion with its double function: stumbling for Israel, inclusion for Gentiles, but why did Paul choose Isa 8:14 as a starting point? Why did Paul think God had to trip Israel in order to make manifest his new act of righteousness for Gentiles? Since Paul does not give an answer one can only speculate. Perhaps it goes back to the parallel apostolates described in Gal 2:7-8 and Paul's reflection that if Peter succeeded then Paul would be unnecessary.[73] If Peter was right then in the normal pattern of centripetal mission of the eschatology not only of the prophets but also of Jesus, the Gentiles would join Israel in the end times. Paul, on the other hand, wanted a Gentile church now as an equal co-partner alongside Israel. That would account for the silence of these chapters on the Jerusalem church and Jewish Christianity as such. Of course, if something like this is what Paul thought, the "blindness" was necessary only for a generation or so until the Gentile church became established. But he does not reflect on this.

What do Gentiles need to learn from what Paul says about Israel? First of all, that God is faithful to his promises to Israel, that the word of God has not lapsed, that all Israel will be saved, and that all this has to do not with human doing or believing but with the grace and mercy of God.[74] They should know this because they have been called into the people of God on exactly the same basis. That is what Paul has to say *about* Israel (and Gentiles). What he has to say *to* Gentiles is related to this but expressed in the quite different mode of paraenesis (11:13-25a). There Gentiles are told that they ought not to think that they have supplanted Jews in God's favour or that the election of Israel, on which their own depends, has in any way been abrogated. That is an important consequence to be drawn from what is said overall in these chapters, but there is a difference between speaking of Israel in God's eyes and speaking of Israel in Gentile eyes, between mystery and exhortation. Failure to recognize this difference and failure to recognize the different mode of address in the olive tree digression has led, I believe, to a distorted understanding of the main point of what Paul was endeavouring to express in Romans 9-11.

10

PAUL AND THE TORAH IN 2 CORINTHIANS 3

The influence of 2 Corinthians 3 has had great consequences in the history of the church. It is this chapter that has produced the fateful designation of the two parts of Scripture: the (obsolete) Old Testament and the (superseding) New Testament. The figure of the blindfolded synagogue, contrasted with the triumphant church, as they appear on the cathedral in Strasbourg, comes from this chapter and may be taken to represent how the church has almost always thought of the synagogue. That "the letter (literal interpretation) kills but the Spirit (allegorical interpretation) gives life" (3:6) was constantly cited by Origen to justify his exegetical method.[1] Paul is understood to compare himself to Moses, to the great discredit of the latter. But he does so by so "massively and deliberately distorting the statements of the Old Testament,"[2] that if the church earlier concluded thereby that Jews are incapable of understanding Scripture, modern scholars have had to admit that Paul is even more incapable. They also assert that Paul misuses Scripture in order to establish "the present Either-Or of Law versus Christ"[3] or to say that "Christ and Moses are just as exclusively contrasted with one another as Christ and Adam in Rom. 5.12ff."[4] And yet it seems incredible that such a contrast would be appropriate here, that Paul would set his gospel in opposition to Scripture, or that he would take just this occasion to ascribe to himself glory. The chapter is clearly a barrier to those who wish to understand the relationship between the Apostle to the Gentiles and the Torah of Israel in a positive sense.

Very influential in contemporary discussion of the passage has been the identification by H. Windisch of 3:7-18 as "midrash."[5] As such it was held to be a digression, with little relevance for its surrounding context. The thesis was carried further by Schultz[6] and Georgi,[7] who thought that the midrash was specifically that of the opponents, which Paul quoted and commented on. Whether or not the word "midrash" is appropriate, it is clear that Exodus 34 is under discussion in much of the passage. It is however also clear that there are too many links between 3:7-18 and the preceding and following contexts to speak of a digression, to say nothing of a non-Pauline insertion. Yet it is only by calling this section a "literarische Einlage" that Windisch could say that its theme is the opposition between "Christentum und Judentum" rather than the contrast between a Pauline and non-Pauline understanding of ministry which otherwise characterizes the whole letter.[8]

Most interpreters throughout the ages have come to 2 Corinthians 3 with well formed concepts of Paul and the Law, Paul and the Old Testament, Paul and Israel, which they have derived largely from a reading of Galatians and Romans and then rediscover in this chapter (but only in this chapter!) of 2 Corinthians. To guard against this tendency, I propose to pay careful attention to the context. This means first of all the unified defence of Paul's apostolic ministry in 2:14-6:13, 7:2-4, even if this is not to be seen as a separate letter.[9] It means also the Corinthian situation in general, as seen perhaps in 1 Corinthians but especially in the light of the missionaries most clearly described in 2 Corinthians 10-13. But it means primarily paying attention to the full literary unit, which I understand to be 2:14 to 4:6. While I will in no sense give in what follows an exegesis of the entire passage and will discuss only those verses which might have a bearing on the topic of Paul and the Torah, the intention is always to do so with an eye on the unit as a whole.

Also very influential in contemporary discussion of this section has been the proposal to see Paul's "opponents" as the key to understanding it. The most impressive discussion of these opponents is by D. Georgi,[10] with which I am in basic agreement. Briefly, they are itinerant Jewish-Christian missionaries who claim the authority of apostles and ministers of Christ in a much more impressive manner than Paul's. Their authority was based on heavenly visions, on esoteric knowledge and a charismatic eloquence, on ancient ancestry and tradition, on letters of recommendation, probably on miracles, and on the fact that they were willing to accept money in recognition of their authority. Whether or not they are to be called "divine men" (*theioi andres*), as Georgi claims, depends on what one thinks of the appropriateness of that term in general. In any case, it seems that they appealed to Moses not in connection with the Torah as such but as a model to be imitated. Whether they themselves said that Paul was deficient in all the attributes that made up their glory or whether it was certain Corinthians who made the invidious comparison is not sure. After all, Paul writes not to the missionaries but to the Corinthians, and it is they who could perhaps more truly be said to be Paul's opponents. While I think all these things are in general true, I doubt very much that one can use 2 Corinthians 3 to reconstruct a supposed midrash of the opponents or even a clear statement of their theology.[11] The text is a Pauline composition, but one which makes very close reference to the concerns and even words of others.[12] I would indeed like to speculate about the opponents' view of Torah as contrasted with Paul's, but I will refrain from doing so until the end.

Like all of Paul's letters, 2 Corinthians is a "conversation in context," to use the subtitle of a widely known book.[13] It must be assumed that the Corinthians understood what Paul wrote to them even when it is now confusing for they knew things about the situation which are now lost. That seems to be true especially of the present passage, which will never be understood completely. Without making too many assumptions, I shall have to make reference to the context in certain cases where it is demanded. When a word is introduced which is unusual and untypical of Paul, it is likely that it comes from the other side of the conversation. When a line of thought takes a surprising turn, so that some commentators can even speak of a non sequitur, there was probably something unspoken about the situation that caused the shift. I shall also of course pay close attention to statements of Paul which are clearly polemical. But otherwise I will not make the opponents nearly as much of a key to interpretation as do some others. Finally, in an attempt to try to overcome longstanding assumptions, I shall approach the text with what I have called earlier a hermeneutic of experimentation.

> (14) Now thanks be to God, who always in Christ leads us as prisoners in his triumphal procession and who makes manifest through us the odour of the knowledge of himself everywhere; (15) for I am the sweet savour of Christ pleasing to God, among those who are being saved and those who are perishing, (16) to the ones a stench of death leading to death, to the others a fragrance of life leading to life. And who could be competent for this [ministry]? (17) For we are not, like the many, adulterators of the word of God. It is rather out of sincerity, claiming to be from God but also responsible before God that we speak in Christ. (1) Are we beginning again to commend ourselves? Or do we need, like some, letters of recommendation to you or from you? (2) You are the content of our letter, which is written on our hearts, known and read by all people. (3) You show clearly that you are a letter written by Christ, of which we are [only] the courier, written not with ink but with the Spirit

of the living God; [written] not on tablets which are [hearts] of stone but on tablets which are hearts of flesh.

This beginning states the theme for everything which will follow in Paul's defence of his apostolic ministry, 2:14-7:4, and specifically for the first major section, 2:14-4:6. After the opening thanksgiving with its glorious complex metaphor describing Paul's ministry,[14] comes the key question: "Who could be competent [*hikanos*] for this [ministry]?"[15] The question is posed in the context of a contrast in the minds of certain Corinthians, who said of some rival apostles that they were competent "ministers of Christ" (11:23), "apostles of Christ" (11:13), and "ministers of righteousness" (11:15), whereas Paul was not (11:6). As I will show, this is the question which dominates the next section, 3:4-6 and thus the whole "midrash." "Who could be competent?" implies a negative answer, "No one of themselves," as the sequence shows: "*for* we are not, like the many, adulterators of the word of God." On the contrary, says Paul, "It is rather out of sincerity, claiming to be from God but also responsible before God that we speak in Christ." The issue is thus drawn: there are two competing concepts of ministry, one which claims competency and one which claims sincerity, claiming to be from God.

Paul does not want to commend himself nor does he "need, like some, letters of recommendation," written by or to the Corinthians.[16] He does not need a letter written with ink because he carries in his heart another letter, which consists of the Corinthians themselves. The author of this letter is Christ, and it is written with the Spirit of the living God. Paul is only the courier of the letter, which he shows not just to the initiate but to *everyone*, whenever he opens his heart (6:11; 7:3) to proclaim his love for the Corinthians and his admiration of their faithfulness. Paul is hurt that the Corinthians would even consider the letters of recommendation brought by the rival missionaries, which after all are written only with ink and on papyrus. How much better is a letter with a divine author written on the heart! The thought of the Spirit writing on the heart calls to Paul's mind the phrase of Ezekiel in which God promises: "I will give them a new heart and put a new spirit within them; I will take the stony heart out of their flesh and give them a heart of flesh" (11:19; 36:26). How much better is a heart of flesh than a heart of stone! The metaphor is becoming a bit mixed, perhaps, but still quite tolerable.[17] The real problem comes with the introduction of the tablets, to which I shall return.

First, however, I want to emphasize not only the polemical apologetic character of this passage but also its many connections with 4:1-6 so that these two sections bracket what is in between and are the key to the interpretation of the whole.[18] When Paul says that he is not "an adulterator of the word of God'' (2:17) and that he has ''rejected shameful mystifications'' and ''does not operate with guileful deception and does not falsify the word of God'' (4:2), he is clearly contrasting himself to people he thinks do just that. When he says that he ''preaches not himself but Jesus Christ as Lord'' (4:5) and that he ''speaks in Christ out of sincerity, claiming to be from God but also responsible before God'' (2:17), Paul speaks against other people whom he accuses of doing the opposite. What is at issue are two opposite concepts of Christian ministry, and that must be true also of the intervening material.

I now return to the strange introduction of the tablets, which, if the text is not to be amended,[19] results in a rather grotesque image. Who introduced them into the conversation?[20] To refer to Moses in verse 7 is only to postpone the question, for who introduced him into the conversation? The obvious tablets which come to mind are the two tablets of the decalogue which Moses brought down from Mt. Sinai, but why does Paul mention the tablets first? There must be some connection between the tablets and those others who came to Corinth bringing letters of recommendation. As one could surmise, those others did not come proclaiming Moses but seeking to imitate him. Now if letters of recommendation serve as an accreditation and legitimation, how much more would heavenly tablets do so? It is not at all necessary to think of the decalogue when the tablets are referred to, for Moses was not the only one to ascend the mountain (or to heaven, as it was later understood) to receive tablets containing a divine revelation. Beginning with *Jubilees* the motif is not uncommon,[21] but I shall refer to only two instances here. Ezra is told to take five men with him to a certain place where over the course of forty days they will receive revelation from God and to ''prepare for yourself many writing tablets.'' He did so, ''and the Most High gave understanding to the five men, and by turns they wrote what was dictated, in characters [letters, Syr. *'twt'*] which they did not know'' (4 Ezra 14:24, 42). The second reference is not to tablets as such but to a book which a heavenly lady wanted to impart to Hermas. ''I took it and went away to a certain place in the country, and copied it all, letter by letter [*pros gramma*]. . . . It was suddenly taken out of my hand. . . . After fifteen days, when I had fasted and prayed greatly to the Lord, the knowledge of the writing was revealed to me'' (Herm., *Vis.* 2.1.4-2.1). It is quite likely that the rival missionaries boasted of visions and even heavenly ascents (cf. 2 Cor 12:1-10). It is more speculative to suppose that they claimed specifically to have seen heavenly tablets of stone, but if that were the case, it would account for the otherwise unexplained sudden introduction of the tablets of stone at the very end of this section.

(4) Such confidence we have before God through Christ; (5) not that we

> ourselves are competent so that [we could] claim something as coming from ourselves, but our competency comes from God, (6) who has truly made us competent ministers of a new covenant, not of the letter but of the Spirit. For the letter kills but the Spirit makes alive.

The verb "to have" is an indicator of the structure of much of the following, and it is interesting to see what Paul claims to have: "such confidence" (3:4), "such a hope" (3:12), "this ministry" (4:1), "this treasure in vessels of clay" (4:7), "the spirit of trust" (4:13). Nevertheless, I shall consider this little section separately from verses 7-11. Once more the competence question is stated even more strongly. Paul is not, like those others, "competent to claim something as coming from himself." No, his "competency comes from God, who had truly made him a competent minister." Two different ministries are being contrasted, one which claims self-competence and one whose competency comes from God. That contrast extends also to the designation of the ministry. Paul clearly claims to be a "minister of a new covenant of the Spirit," but that is hardly language which is usual for him. The concept of covenant is characteristic not of Paul's gospel to the Gentiles but of Jewish Christianity,[22] and talk of a "new" covenant is found most frequently in Qumran.[23] To be sure it was known at Corinth, in terms of the Eucharistic tradition Paul passed on to them (1 Cor 11:25), but it was also apt to be very congenial to the rival missionaries.[24] When Paul speaks of being a "minister of a new covenant of the Spirit," is that in conscious opposition to *their* language of a "ministry of a new covenant of the letter"? I shall argue that that is so.[25]

The contrast between the letter and the spirit is such a familiar one that one is apt to forget the strangeness of the expression in Paul (in addition to 2 Cor 3:6 also in Rom 2:29 and 7:6). There have been two major ways of understanding the contrast in the history of interpretation, which Schneider calls the formalistic and the realistic,[26] but neither proves very satisfactory.

The most prevalent interpretation in the modern period has been the realistic,[27] which understands *gramma* as synonomous with *nomos*, giving a contrast of Law and Spirit. While this is consonant with much of modern theology, there are major exegetical problems. First, no other instance can be cited where *gramma* is used in this sense, and in the context of the other two passages in Paul, *gramma* is clearly distinguished from Law: some without the *gramma* keep the Law (Rom 2:27, cf. 29), and the Law is "holy, just, good . . . and spiritual" (Rom 7:12, 14, cf.6). Second, the word *nomos* appears nowhere in 2 Corinthians, and there is no evidence whatsoever that the super apostles are urging the Corinthians to "Judaize." Third, if the Law were the topic here rather than two contrasting ministries, then it would certainly be a digression unrelated to its context.

The formalistic interpretation was often taken in the ancient church and is somewhat related to the popular usage of today which distinguishes between the "literal" meaning of a text and the deeper meaning of its real intention. Stated in that general form, this interpretation cannot possibly be correct. It is not that such a distinction was unknown in antiquity but different words were used to designate it (*rēton* vs. *dianoia*).[28] In addition, the word *pneuma* clearly refers to the Holy Spirit and not the deep sense of some text. Accordingly, supporters of this position usually treat *gramma* as if it were synonymous with Scripture or the Torah as a written text. Scripture, however, about which Paul always speaks positively, is called by him *hē graphē* and by others also called *ta hiera grammata*. The word *gramma* is so unusual in this sense that those who support the identification are led to suppose that Paul coined it on this occasion to match the singular *pneuma*.[29] Besides, Spirit and Scripture belong together, and even if one could refer to the latter as *mere* text which requires spiritual interpretation, that would still never account for the radical antithesis between the two found here. If by *gramma* Paul meant anything like Scripture, it is hard to see how he could introduce a reference to the Psalms just a few verses later with "having the *same spirit* of faith, according to what has been written" (4:13).

"For the *gramma* kills but the Spirit makes alive." That has so much the form of a gnomic saying, introduced here without explanation to support Paul's statement about his ministry, that some interpreters believe that Paul is citing a well-known maxim (that is, well-known to the Corinthians, not to us).[30] The advantage of this view is that it shows how Paul can later again refer to the expression twice in Romans; the disadvantage is that it still does not explain adequately its significance in the present passage. The Spirit is a power which gives life, and so *gramma* must be equally a power, but one which kills. It is then comparable to Sin[31] and Flesh[32] as powers that kill. In the present context the power that kills is a certain type of ministry: the ministry of death (3:7), the ministry of condemnation (3:9), the ministry of Satan (11:15), service of the god of this age (4:4). *Gramma* can refer neither to the Law nor to Scripture but specifically here to the ministry of the rival missionaries. Did they introduce it into the conversation?

D. Georgi describes very impressively the use of written texts to enhance the glory of the *theios anēr* in the world of Hellenistic Judaism.[33] He also claims that it was the opponents who introduced the word *gramma* into the discussion by calling their ministry a ministry of the *gramma*. He is however not concrete enough to convince, and so I shall try a new hypothesis. One basic meaning of *gramma* is a "letter of the alphabet," which becomes a matter worth mentioning particularly when the alphabet is a *different* one. The Letter of Aristeas, 20, for example, speaks of "the book of the Law of the Jews . . . written in Hebrew characters and in the Hebrew tongue" (*tou nomou tōn Ioudaiōn biblia . . . Hebraikois grammasi kai phōnē legomena*), and other instances could be cited.[34] The texts chosen above concerning heavenly writings were not selected at random. Both of them have to do with heavenly revelation which cannot be understood as long as the characters of the alphabet are unknown. The rival missionaries may have come to Corinth with such "heavenly" texts, or they may have come only with some scrolls of Hebrew Scripture, but in any case they were writings written in an alphabet the Corinthians were not able to read. This provided the Jewish-Christian preachers with an ideal situation in which to use the "letters" for their own purposes, to engage in what Paul calls deception and mystification and falsification (4:2) and adulteration (2:17) of the word of God. After all that has been said about the letter and the spirit, it may well be that the distinction has its origin in Paul's very practical suggestion to the Corinthians that they need not be intimidated by Hebrew characters, for the Septuagint read in the Spirit was perfectly adequate for them.

> (7) But if the ministry of death, in letters and engraved on stones, originated in glory, such that the Israelites were not able to gaze on the face of Moses because of the transitory "glory of his face" (Exod 34:30), (8) how much more will the ministry of the Spirit be [in future] in glory! (9) For if the ministry of condemnation is glory, how much more does the ministry of righteousness abound in glory! (10) Indeed, the thing glorified in this latter case has not been [now] glorified, for the sake of the [future] overwhelming glory. (11) Again, if the transitory [comes] with glory, how much more [will] the enduring [be] in glory!

Commentators are agreed on the structure of this passage: there are three "how-much-more" statements which contrast the amount of glory which attaches to two different ministries. On the one hand, there is "the ministry of death," "the ministry of condemnation," and "the transitory"; and on the other hand, there is "the ministry of the Spirit," "the ministry of righteousness," and "the enduring." This ministry (*diakonia*) is of course directly related to the ministers (*diakonoi*) of verse 6, which contrasts "ministers of the letter" and "ministers of the Spirit." The first "how-much-more" statement stretches the pattern insofar as it contains linkage to what precedes ("in letters" to v 6; "engraved on stones" to v 3)[35] and insofar as it contains a paraphrase of Exod 34:30, which speaks of glory on the face of Moses.

There has also been a traditional interpretation about how the contrast has been understood: it is between the ministry of Moses and the ministry of Paul, or between law and gospel, or between the old dispensation and the new dispensation. Only such considerations could have led to the very strange (and lexicographically completely unwarranted) proposal of RSV to translate *diakonia* as "dispensation." One major problem with such an interpretation is that it puts Paul into the role of an Annie Oakley, saying in effect to Moses, "Anything you can do I can do better." Does Paul really want to say that Moses had so much glory that it blinded people but that he, Paul, has much, much more? If so, then if Moses had to protect people by wearing a veil, as will be said later, then Paul must have had to wear ten veils![36] And yet, in light of the overall thrust of the Corinthian correspondence, it is hard to see why Paul would want to speak of glory at all. Who introduced it into the conversation? Again, if the earlier mentions of the tablets might explain the introduction of Moses here, why would Paul choose this particular episode from Exodus 34? Who introduced this passage into the conversation?

In the light of what other chapters have shown about the way Paul uses Scripture and its post-Biblical interpretation, the text of Exod 34:29-32 should be cited:

> When Moses came down from Mount Sinai, with the two tables of the testimony in his hand as he came down from the mountain, Moses did not know that the skin of his face shone [LXX *dedoxastai*] because he had been talking with God. And when Aaron and all the people of Israel saw Moses, behold, the skin of his face shone [LXX *ēn dedoxasmenē*], and they were afraid to come near him. But Moses called to them; and Aaron and all the leaders of the congregation returned to him, and Moses talked with them. And afterward all the people of Israel came near, and he gave them in commandment all that the Lord had spoken with him in Mount Sinai.

A priori such a text would probably appeal more to Paul's opponents than to him.[37] The text does not really speak of the glorification of Moses, although the Septuagint is moving in that direction. Very illuminating, however, is the only pre-Pauline writer who is known to have used this text, Philo. He says that Moses on the mountain "grew in grace, first of mind, then of body also through the soul, and in both so advanced in strength and well-being that those who saw him afterwards could not believe their eyes. . . . He descended with a countenance far more beautiful than when he ascended, so that those who saw him were filled with awe and amazement; nor even could their eyes continue to stand the dazzling brightness that flowed from him like the rays of the sun."[38] Not only that, but he was also a model for others to imitate: "He beheld what is hidden from the sight of mortal nature, and, in himself and his life displayed for all to see, he has set before us, like some well-wrought picture, a piece of work beautiful and godlike, a model for those who are willing to copy it."[39] Again, "he enters into the darkness, the invisible region, abiding there while he learns [*teloumenos*] the secrets of the most holy mysteries [*teletas*]. There he becomes not only one of the congregation of the initiated, but also the hierophant and teacher of divine rites, which he will impart to those whose ears are purified."[40] This fits very well not only with the Corinthian predilection for mystagogues (1 Cor 1:12) but also specifically with the self-understanding of the super-apostles.

Two ministries are being compared here, one of which, the one based on Moses' example, claims to have glory, which Paul in no way denies. Although it is not necessary to assume so, it may even be that the rival ministers in their ecstatic speech had real glowing faces, auras.[41] In any case, the question of the face is a matter to which Paul returns several times. "We are not commending ourselves to you again but giving you cause to be proud of us, so you will be able to answer those who boast of the face and not of the heart. For if we are in ecstasy, it is [only] for God; if we are reasonable, it is for you" (5:12-13). Paul concedes that that other ministry has ecstasy and glory and possibly literally shining faces.[42] The question is whether or not he here claims even greater glory for his own ministry.

One can think of no situation in which it would be less appropriate for Paul to boast of his glory than that reflected otherwise in the Corinthian correspondence. As Schütz puts it in general terms, "Paul's response elsewhere to hyperpneumatics is to stress the radically other nature of a future they ignore and emphasize the present reality of a contingency, a weakness and death, which they abhor."[43] In every other instance in the corpus Paulinum,[44] Christian participation in *doxa* is reserved for the parousia and the consummation of all things; why should it be any different here? Of the three "how-much-more" comparisons with respect to glory, one has the final verb in the future tense (v 8), one has no verb at all (v 11), and one is in the present tense (v 9). This last instance is, however, immediately corrected by the statement that "the thing glorified [the ministry of righteousness] has *not* been glorified, for the sake of the overwhelming glory" (v 10).[45] What is being contrasted is the present glory of Christian ministry, which exists in the case of the opponents and perhaps even of Paul,[46] with the future glory of God which puts all other glory to shame. Or, to put it more polemically, what is contrasted is a ministry which has its glory only in present ecstasy and a ministry which points beyond itself to an overwhelming glory. When Paul summarizes this section at the beginning of the next, it is not by saying "having such a glorious ministry," but rather by "having such a hope" (v 12). As he will say just a little later, "the present slight tribulation produces for us in great abundance a weight of glory in the age to come, for us who do not look at the visible things but the invisible. For the visible things are temporary [*proskaira*], while the invisible things are of the age to come'' (4:17-18).

It is a Pauline addition both to the Exodus text and to what was said in Corinth to call the glory of Moses' face ''transitory'' (*katargoumenēn*). This participle[47] appears in verses 7, 11, and 13 and the corresponding verb *katargeō*, ''to do away with,'' is found in verse 14. These passages may be considered all together. Exegetes have rather consistently tried to explain the word in terms of the historical Moses. The conception seems to be that Moses' face shone with a kind of phosphorescence which rapidly faded until it could be recharged by renewed exposure to the light source.[48] Not only is there nothing in the Exodus text to suggest such a strange conception,[49] but what little exegetical tradition there is directly contradicts it.[50] Such an idea also causes grave difficulties when combined with Moses' motivation for covering his face, as the next section shows. To be sure, Paul did not think that the glory on Moses' face was eternal, but the whole point here has to do with the glory on the face of Moses' imitators or, more generally, with any glory of any Christian ministry. The parallel to what Paul said earlier about Corinthian charismatics has not often been noted,[51] but it holds, I believe, the key to the interpretation here. 1 Corinthians 13 says of prophecy (v 8), knowledge (v 8), the imperfect (v 10), and the things of a child (v 11) that they all pass away (*katargeō*). As Paul concludes, in another significant parallel, ''now we see in a mirror dimly, but then face to face . . . [only] faith, hope, love abide'' (*menō*, vv 12-13 cf. 2 Cor 3:11, 18). Charismatic gifts, whether to Moses or early Christians, have their relative glory, but they are as nothing when compared with the glory of God Paul hopes to share in the future.

Finally, I return to the two opposing concepts of ministry described here. Is it not a bit strong for Paul to call the ministry of his opponents the ''ministry of death'' or the ''ministry of condemnation''? While the latter designation might only refer to the fact that they condemn the non-charismatics, the former shows that it is much more serious than that. It really is a ministry of condemnation and death when Paul later refers to the opponents as ministers of Satan (11:15) and to the Corinthians as those whose thoughts may be corrupted as the serpent deceived Eve (11:3). The opponents masquerade as ministers of righteousness, that is, as those who serve the cause of the righteousness of God (11:15),[52] but they are just the opposite. On the other hand, for Paul to call his own apostolate the ministry of righteousness and the ministry of the Spirit is consonant with what he says in the rest of 2 Corinthians and elsewhere. What he does not say, in 2 Corinthians or anywhere else, is that his apostolate is a ministry of glory.

(12) Having such a hope, therefore, we speak very freely and openly;
(13) and not like [they say:] ''Moses used to put a veil on his face''

> (Exod 34:33) in order that the Israelites might not gaze on the goal of the transitory. (14) But their thoughts have been dulled. For up to this day that same veil remains during [their] reading of the ancient covenant, and it has not been revealed to them that in Christ it is done away with. (15) But until today whenever Moses is read [by them], the veil lies on their heart. (16) "But whenever one turns to YHWH the veil is lifted" (Exod 34:34). (17) Now "YHWH", that signifies the Spirit; and wherever the Spirit of YHWH is, there is freedom. (18) And all of us, with unveiled face, contemplating as in a mirror the glory of YHWH, are being transformed into the same image, by glory and toward glory, as by the Spirit of YHWH.

The transition from verse 12 to verse 13 involves what M. Hooker calls a non sequitur,[53] and indeed interpreters have gone to extremes in trying to explain it. She finds a second non sequitur in the "but" which begins verse 14, a very real problem not seen by all interpreters.[54] A verb is missing at the beginning of verse 13 and has to be supplied. The motif of the veil comes from the Exodus passage under discussion, but its strange transfer to the hearts of the Israelites is completely without precedent. One can either conclude that this is "one of the most unusual exegetical arguments ever contrived"[55] and despair of following its logic or try a completely new tack.

There are a number of verbal parallels between this section and the next, 4:1-6. Corresponding to the noun "veil" (3:13, 14, 15, 16) and a derivative of the verb (3:14, 18) is the verb "veiled" (4:3 bis). "Their thoughts have been dulled" (3:14) corresponds to "their thoughts have been blinded" (4:4). "That they might not gaze on" (3:13) is echoed in "that they might not see" (4:4). It is also clear that the earlier use of the word "glory" finds its climax in 4:4, 6, and one could also refer to the polemical *inclusio* of "those who are perishing" of 2:15 and 4:3, the self-recommendation of 3:1 and 4:2, and especially the reference to "those who adulterate/falsify the word of God" in 2:17 and 4:2. It is from this perspective that I shall seek to understand the difficult section 3:12-18.

Because Paul has such a hope of future glory, therefore, he says, he speaks with great *parrēsia*, translated as "freely and openly."[56] Since elsewhere in the letter Paul has to defend himself against the charge of lack of frankness (6:11-12; 7:4; cf. 1:12, 17), it seems that here also his claim is polemical defence. The question is what that has to do with Moses' veil. The Exodus text continues as follows:

> And when Moses had finished speaking with them, he put a veil on his face; but whenever Moses went in before the LORD to speak with him, he took the veil off, until he came out; and when he came out and told

> the people of Israel what he was commanded, the people of Israel saw the face of Moses, that the skin of Moses' face shone; and Moses would put the veil upon his face again, until he went in to speak with him (Exod 34:33-35).

It is possible to supply a verb in Paul's reference to the text in verse 13 something like "and not like [Moses did when he]" or "and not like [Scripture says:]," but it is hard to see how that results in a statement which is the opposite of "speaking freely and openly." One explanation is that Moses was deceitfully concealing from the Israelites the fact that his glory faded so rapidly or was at least exercising "pastoral tact" in this regard.[57] But it is difficult to see why Paul would want to attribute such a strange motivation to Moses or how it would be relevant to the present context. It also makes incomprehensible the "but" which follows. *Whose* thoughts have been hardened, and in what sense does this statement stand in opposition to verse 13?

The following paragraph sheds a great deal of light on such questions. There Paul's speaking "freely and openly" is called "the open statement of the truth" (4:2). There is mention of certain unfaithful ones who are perishing, "whose thoughts have been blinded by the god of this age" (4:3). They also charge that Paul's gospel is "veiled" (4:3). Against this much clearer statement of the situation, the connections between 3:12 and 13 and 3:13 and 14 all fall into place. Paul speaks with *parrēsia* and not with a veiled gospel, as they accuse him of doing, following the example of the veiled Moses. They say that, *but* their thoughts have been dulled. Paul says in effect: "I speak freely and openly, not putting a veil over my gospel. Those who say that I do have dulled thoughts." If there are two pictures of Moses involved, they really refer to two concepts of ministry: the Moses who speaks ecstatically after his vision on the mount with glory on his face is the ideal of the rival missionaries; the Moses who says nothing because his face and his message are veiled represents the charge made against Paul. Paul not only dismisses the charge but also goes on to point out how it is a misreading of the Exodus text.

But there are still some exegetical details that need attention. The echo of verse 7 in verse 13, "in order that the Israelites might not gaze on," is so close that it must be deliberate. If it is true, as surmised above, that verse 7 reflects the perspective of the rival missionaries, who emphasized not only the glory on Moses' face but also that on their own after their visions, then verse 13 would be Paul's ironic reprise of the language.[58] This time, however, there is no mention of glory but only of "the goal of the transitory." What is called transitory here in a neuter participle cannot be *doxa* or *diathēkē* or *diakonia*, all feminine nouns; it must refer back to the more general statement of all charismatic phenomena as transitory in verse 11. Ironically, the opponents, "those who are perishing" (4:3), are now seen not as imitators of Moses but as representatives of the Israelites, who cannot see through the veil to learn that the present transitory phenomena of the Christian ministry have a *telos*, a goal.[59] It is perhaps significant that *ta noēmata*, thoughts, is always used polemically in 2 Corinthians,[60] of thoughts which "have been blinded by the god of this age" (4:4), of the thoughts of Satan (2:11) or those seduced by him (11:3), thoughts which Paul must "take prisoner into obedience to Christ" (10:5). That Paul should refer to his opponents under the vague "their" (*autōn*) is consonant with the way he refers to them earlier as "many" (*polloi*, 2:17) and "some" (*tines*, 3:1). It is clear that the passage is polemical.

It is important to emphasize that Paul is not speaking of contemporary Israelites nor even of the Israelites at Sinai, now that they have been ironically identified with the opponents. It is not past history or Jews which are under discussion but the present and the Corinthian Christians. They are the ones whose thoughts have been dulled and over whose hearts lies a veil. The phrase *palaia diathēkē* is strange, with neither Jewish nor early Christian counterpart,[61] and it certainly must stem from the rival missionaries.[62] The propaganda value of representing ancient traditions was powerful, and they refer to themselves with such archaic terms as Hebrews, Israelites, and the seed of Abraham (11:22). Because "the ancient covenant" is something read,[63] it is probable that it refers to their understanding of Scripture, but this is not sure.[64] Because of the veil it has not been "revealed" (the pun is deliberate) that "in Christ it is done away with." What is? Surely not the ancient covenant,[65] and to think of the veil as the subject of the sentence also causes problems. I propose to understand the subject vaguely with Collange as "all that"[66] and to connect it with the earlier participles, "the transitory." In Christ there is no need for ecstasy and shining faces and glory — all that is done away with. It is I believe too early in the argument to speak of the removal of the veil. Verse 15 repeats 14 and prepares for 16. Again, "Moses" being read may refer to Scripture as a whole, or it may refer specifically to the passage under discussion and to how the *person* of Moses is understood as a model. Because of the "but" which begins verse 16, I prefer the latter. The super apostles appealed to the example of Moses in Exod 34:30; they accused Paul of being like the Moses of 34:33; Paul then argues that they have not read far enough in the text. The example to be followed is the Moses of 34:34; Paul deliberately generalizes the language to make it apply to all: "whenever one turns to YHWH the veil is lifted."[67] The tables are turned, and it is Paul with a better use of Scripture who can claim Moses as a model for his concept of ministry.

It should not be asked of this essay to solve all the problems of the notoriously difficult verses 17-18. If the "Lord" of these verses is not YHWH, as I believe,[68] but rather Christ, that would not really affect the overall understanding of this section. Only two points need to be noted here. First, the emphatic "all of us" in verse 18 is to be understood polemically in opposition to a concept of ministry which would restrict the vision of the glory of God only to the charismatic elite. Second, the metamorphosis motif[69] does not after all ascribe glory to Paul and other Christians. When he says just a bit later in the letter that "our inner humanity is being renewed day by day" and that we hope for "a weight of glory in the age to come," that does not mean that we are not living in a "present tribulation" or that it is not true that "our outward humanity is decaying" (4:16-17). Now Paul has confidence (3:4), hope (3:12), this ministry (4:1), a treasure in vessels of clay (4:7); but what he does not claim is glory. Frankness (3:12) and freedom (3:17) yes, but glory not yet.

> (4:1) That is why, having this ministry according to the mercy we have received, we do not lose heart, (2) but having rejected shameful mystifications, we do not operate with guileful deception and do not falsify the word of God, but by the open manifestation of the truth we commend ourselves to every human conscience in the sight of God. (3) And even if our gospel should be veiled, it is for those who are perishing that it is veiled, (4) for those unfaithful ones whose thoughts the god of this age has blinded, in order that they might not see clearly the illumination of the gospel of the glory of Christ, who is the image of God. (5) For we do not preach ourselves but Jesus Christ as Lord, and ourselves as your servants for Jesus' sake. (6) For it is the God who said "out of darkness light will shine" (Isa 9:1) who has shone within our hearts for illumination with the knowledge of the glory of God on the face of Christ.

In a kind of ring composition, Paul returns to the language of the opening section, 2:14-3:3, and he also picks up the major themes of the intervening material so that it can serve as a kind of summary. He had just said that "all of us contemplate as in a mirror the glory of YHWH" (3:18), which is now repeated in "seeing clearly the illumination of the gospel of the glory of Christ" (4:4) and in the "illumination with the knowledge of the glory of God in the face of Christ" (4:6). I shall bypass the interesting Christology and the strangely Gnostic terminology of this paragraph in order to concentrate on its relevance to the foregoing discussion of the two ministries.

Paul accuses certain unnamed ministers of "shameful mystification," "guileful deception," and the "falsification of the word of God" (4:2). It is hard to see what is meant by "word of God" if it is not Scripture, which is being improperly interpreted and proclaimed from Paul's perspective. The language becomes even harsher when those people are said to be "perishing" (4:3) and "those unfaithful ones whose thoughts the god of this age has blinded" (4:4). Paul also seems to imply that they preach themselves rather than Jesus Christ as Lord (4:5) and that they claim that the glory of God is to be seen on their own faces rather than on the face of Christ (4:6). This is the clearest statement yet of the concept of ministry which Paul rejects.

The ministry which Paul defends also seems to reflect certain charges brought against him. He was said to have no charisma like those who imitate Moses and his glory. But Moses himself shows that that is a false view of ministry, as Paul said earlier. Here it is God who gives legitimacy to Paul's ministry. He has it according to the mercy he has received (4:1), he commends himself to everyone in the sight of God (4:2), and it is God who has shone within Paul's heart (and not on his face!) for illumination (4:6). In the phrase "out of darkness light will shine," the light comes from God, and Paul is only the darkness; the treasure is in vessels of clay (4:7), which have as such no glory whatsoever. If certain others were skilled in charismatic oratory, Paul was not (10:10; 11:6); instead he commends himself only by the clear statement of the plain truth, and that in a way understandable to *everyone* with no mystification (4:2). Finally, Paul must protest that his gospel is *not* veiled, regardless of the charge made against him (4:3). I shall return in the conclusion to the question of what this gospel might be and how it could be said to be veiled.

Finally, the implications of the word of God cited in 4:6 must be considered. In spite of the great popularity of this view, it seems most unlikely that Gen 1:3, "Let there be light," is being referred to.[70] Much closer in wording is Isa 9:1, where it is the Gentiles who have walked in darkness and on whom light will shine. It is not often noticed that there are two objects of Paul's preaching: first, Jesus Christ as Lord and second, himself as the servant to the Corinthians, the servant of the Lord of Isaiah, the Apostle to the Gentiles, the bringer of light to the nations (Isa 49:6, etc.). Since 3:18 the Corinthians, as the recipients of Paul's ministry, have come more and more into view. The "god of this age" sounds very much like the principalities and powers, under whose bondage particularly the Gentile world lay in Paul's view.[71] Is it also possible to connect the veil with "the covering that is cast over all peoples, the veil that is spread over all Gentiles" (Isa 25:7)?[72] In any case I now move beyond the contrast between the two ministries and the implication this might have for Paul's understanding of Scripture.

I hope to have demonstated that 2 Corinthians 3 is a complex part of a discussion concerning two different concepts of apostolic ministry: Paul's, on the one hand, and that of many Corinthians, on the other, perhaps supported by the rival missionaries so admired. If the demonstration is not complete, I hope that it is at least sufficient enough to make everyone uneasy who might want to continue the traditional reading as a key to understanding Paul's view of Moses or Judaism or the Law or the "Old Testament." I think that all can now agree with Ulonska when he says, "It is not Israel that Paul attacks but his opponents in Corinth."[73] The question is whether one should also agree with him when he says that the chapter has no relevance whatsoever for "the problem of Old Testament hermeneutics."[74]

It is sometimes useful at the end of a task to take off the academic garb and to try over a cup of tea to imagine what could not be demonstrated. I suspect that the rival missionaries in Corinth began by preaching with the kind of rhetoric characteristic of the popular philosophical schools but soon advanced to a rank allegorical interpretation of the type that even Philo, that master of the art, would have to reprove. At least for certain initiates they proclaimed deep mysteries which could be "unveiled" for those who were worthy and by those who were "competent." That the sacred writing should be said to be veiled is a necessary presupposition for those who seek to penetrate to the deeper allegorical meaning. If it is written in a language and even in an alphabet ("letters") the Corinthians could not understand, the veil is all the more opaque and the ability to penetrate it is all the more impressive.

At least in the eyes of certain Corinthians, if not the rival preachers themselves, Paul's preaching could not compare with such charismatic gifts. When Paul speaks of the charge that his gospel is veiled, the reference may well be to the gospel he finds in Scripture. In contrast to certain others, Paul is not able to lift the veil which lies over Scripture. In contrast to those others, Paul has no "face" to show.

If the situation were something like what I have just imagined, then it would indeed have relevance for a contemporary hermeneutic.[75] To interpret Scripture allegorically, says Paul, would be to "adulterate" (2:17) and "falsify" (4:2) the word of God. Paul rejects "shameful mystifications" and "guileful deception" in favour of "the open manifestation of the truth" (4:2), spoken "freely and openly" (3:12) and with "sincerity" (2:17). Already earlier Paul had to speak against allegorical interpretation in Corinth, with the phrase "Not beyond that which is written" (1 Cor 4:6), if that is the correct way to read a difficult text.[76] Of course, one person's freedom in the Spirit (3:17) may be another's allegory, but Paul claims the former for himself and at least in principle rejects the latter. One should try to understand his use of Scripture in proclaiming his gospel accordingly. In his rejection of allegory and in his reading of Scripture in continuity with its post-canonical Jewish interpretation, one can perhaps learn much from the relationship between Paul and the Torah of Israel.

TRANSLATIONS

ROMANS

1 [1]Paul, a servant of Christ Jesus, called as apostle, set apart for [proclaiming] the
gospel of God, [2]which he promised earlier through his prophets in the Holy
Scriptures, [3]concerning his Son, who was born of the seed of David according to the
flesh, [4]who was appointed Son of God in power according to the Spirit of holiness
since resurrection of the dead, Jesus Christ our Lord, [5]through whom we have
received grace, i.e. apostleship, for [bringing about] obedience to [God's]
faithfulness for the sake of his name among all the Gentiles, [6]among whom also are
ye, called of Jesus Christ;

[7]To all who are in Rome, beloved by God, called to be holy;

Grace to you and peace from God our Father and the Lord Jesus Christ.

[8]First, I thank my God through Jesus Christ for all of you, because your
faithfulness is spoken about in all the world. [9]For my witness is God, whom I
cultically serve in the Spirit [given to me] in [proclaiming] the gospel of his Son, that
I constantly make mention of you, [10]always in my prayers asking whether now at last
I might succeed, if it be God's will, in coming to you. [11]For I yearn to see you, in
order that I might impart to you some spiritual gift, so that ye might be
strengthened, [12]that is, that [we] may be encouraged together in your midst through
[our] mutual faithfulness, yours and mine.

[13]I do not want you to be ignorant, brothers-and-sisters, that I have often intended
to come to you—though until now I have been prevented—in order that I might also
have some fruit among you as among the other Gentiles. [14]To Greeks *and* to
barbarians, to wise *and* to foolish I have an obligation; [15]therefore my eagerness to
preach the gospel also to you in Rome. [16]For I am not ashamed of the gospel, since it
is the power of God for salvation for *every* believer, for the Jew of course, but *also* for
the Greek.

[17]For God's righteousness is revealed in it, from [his] faithfulness to [our]
faithfulness, as it is written: "The righteous shall live by [God's] faithfulness" (Hab
2:4).

[18]For God's wrath is revealed from heaven against all godlessness and injustice of
human beings, who suppress the truth by this injustice; [19]since what is known of God
is evident among them, for God had made it evident to them. [20]For his invisibilities
are clearly seen since the creation of the world, being perceived in [his] deeds, namely
his eternal power and divinity, in order that they might be without excuse. [21][This is
so,] because, having known God, they did not glorify him as God or give thanks, but
they became futile in their thoughts and their ununderstanding heart was darkened.

[22]Claiming to be wise, they became fools [23]and exchanged the glory of the
immortal God "for the likeness" (Gen 1:27) of the image of a mortal "human
being" and "birds" and "animals" and "reptiles" (Gen 1:20-26). [24]Therefore God
delivered them over in the desires of their hearts to the impurity of dishonouring
their bodies among themselves.

[25]They are those who exchanged the truth of God for falsehood [idolatry] and
worshipped and served the creature rather than the creator, blessed be he forever.
Amen. [26]Therefore God delivered them over to passions of dishonour, for their
females exchanged natural intercourse for an unnatural one, [27]and likewise their
males forsook natural intercourse with females and burned in their lust for one
another, males with males working shamelessness and receiving in their own persons
the recompense which was the due of their error.

[28]And as they did not see fit to acknowledge God, God delivered them over to an
unfit mind, to do unseemly things, [29]filled with every injustice, evil, greed, badness,
full of envy, murder, strife, deceit, malice; being gossipers, [30]slanderers, God-haters,
insolent, arrogant, braggarts, inventors of evils, disobedient to parents, [31]foolish,
treacherous, loveless, merciless.

[32]They are those who, having known God's decree that those who do these things
are deserving of death, not only do them but even approve [others] who do them.
2 [1]Therefore, O human being, thou art without excuse, everyone who acts as judge, for
by that in which thou judgest another thou condemnest thyself, since thou the judge
doest the same things. [2]We know that God's condemnation is justly pronounced on
those who do such things.

[3]Dost thou then think, O human being, that thou shalt escape God's
condemnation, thou who judgest those who do such things and dost them thyself?
[4]Or dost thou despise the richness of his kindness, his clemency, and his patience?
Dost thou not know that God's kindness is meant to lead thee to repentance? [5]But
according to thy stubbornness and unrepentant heart thou art storing up wrath for
thyself on the day of wrath and the revelation of the righteous judgment of God,
[6]who "will render to *everyone* according to his works" (Ps 62:13), [7]the life of the age
to come to those who with perseverance in the good work seek glory and honour and
immortality, [8]and wrath and anger to those who are selfish and disobey the truth but
obey injustice. [9]There will be tribulation and distress for every human person who
works evil, for the Jew of course but *also* for the Greek, [10]and there will be glory and
honour and peace for everyone who works good, for the Jew of course but *also* for
the Greek. [11]For there is no partiality with God.

[12]For those who have sinned lawlessly will also perish like outlaws, and those who have sinned against Torah will be judged by Torah—[13]for it is not the hearers of the Torah who are righteous before God, but the doers of the Torah will be adjudged righteous. [14]For when Gentiles, who do not have the Torah, do by nature that which belongs to the law, those who do not have the Torah are a law unto themselves. [15]They show that the work of the law is written on their hearts, their consciousness and their thoughts which accuse or else defend one another witnessing to it, [16]on that day when, according to my gospel, God will judge the secrets of human beings through Jesus Christ.

[17]On the other hand, if thou bear the name of Jew and trust in the Torah and boast in God [18]and know [his] will and discern what is excellent, being instructed from the Torah, [19]and art confident of being a guide of the blind, a light for those in darkness, [20]an instructor of the foolish, a teacher of the immature, having in the Torah the embodiment of knowledge and truth — [21]thou then who teachest another, dost thou not teach thyself? Thou who preachest not to steal, dost thou steal? [22]Thou who sayest not to commit adultery, dost thou commit adultery? Thou who abhorest idols, dost thou rob temples? [23]Thou, who boastest in the Torah, dishonourest God through rebellion against the Torah. [24]For "the name of God because of you is blasphemed among the Gentiles," as the Scripture says (Isa 52:5). [25]For circumcision is indeed of value if thou doest the Torah, but if thou art a rebel against Torah, thy circumcision has become uncircumcision. [26]If then an uncircumcised person were to keep the decrees of the Torah, would not his uncircumcision be counted as circumcision? [27]And would not one who is by birth an uncircumcised Gentile but fulfils the Torah judge thee if despite Scripture and circumcision thou art a rebel against Torah? [28]For it is not in outward appearance that a person is a Jew, nor in outward appearance in the flesh is circumcision circumcision, [29]but inwardly is a person a Jew, and circumcision of the heart, spiritual and not only literal, [is what counts]. [Such a person is a Jew] whose praise comes not from human beings but from God.

3 [1]What then is the advantage of being a Jew, or what is the benefit of circumcision? [2]Much in every respect. First and foremost, that they have been entrusted with the revelation of God. [3]So what if *some* have been unfaithful? Will their unfaithfulness make ineffective the faithfulness of God? [4]Of course not! God must be true even if "*every* human being be perfidious" (Ps 116:11). As Scripture says, "so that thou might be shown righteous in thy words and be victorious in thy trial" (Ps 51:6).

[5]But if our unrighteousness thus serves to bring out the righteousness of God, what shall we say? That God is unrighteous in that he inflicts his Wrath? (I speak in a human way.) [6]Of course not! Otherwise how could God judge the world? [7][Thou sayest,] 'If by my falsehood [idolatry] the truth of God has increased to his glory, why am also I still judged as a sinner? [8]And why should we not do evil in order that good may come?' That is how we are slandered and what certain people say that we say, and their condemnation is just. [9]What, then, do we put up as a defence?

[10]We have already charged that Jews of course but also Greeks are all under sin, as it is written:

"There is none righteous, no, not one;
[11]There is none who understands,
None who seeks for God" (Ps 14-3,2b).
[12]"All have fallen away, all become worthless;
There is none who does good,
There is not even one" (Ps 14:3).
[13]"An open grave is their throat,
With their tongues they deceive" (Ps 5:9).
"Poison of asps is under their lips" (Ps 140:3b).
[14]"Their mouth is filled with cursing and bitterness" (Ps 10:7a).
[15]"Swift are their feet to shed blood,
[16]Destruction and misery are in their paths,
[17]The way of peace they have not known" (Isa 59:7-8a).
[18]"There is not fear of God before their eyes" (Ps 36:1b).

[19]We know that whatever the Torah says, it speaks to those who are in [the sphere of] the law, in order that every mouth may be closed and the whole world stand guilty before God, [20]because by works of the law "all flesh shall not be justified before him" (Ps 143:2). For through the law comes knowledge of sin.

[21]Now, however, apart from the Torah, that righteousness of God has been made manifest to which the Torah and the prophets have testified, [22]the righteousness of God through the faithfulness of Jesus Christ. It is for all the believers, for there is no distinction. [23]For all have sinned and lack the glory of God, [24]and are [thus] justified as a free gift by his grace through the redemption which is in Christ Jesus, [25]whom God presented as a means of expiation, through [Jesus'] faithfulness at the cost of his blood, in order to demonstrate his [God's] righteousness, because the prosecution of previous sins was dropped [26]in the clemency of God, in order to demonstrate his righteousness in the present time, in that he is righteous and thus justifies the one [who lives] out of the faithfulness of Jesus. [27]What room is there then for arrogance? It is excluded. Why? Through the law of works? No, but through the Torah of [God's] faithfulness. [28]We maintain that a human being [a Gentile] is justified by means of [God's] faithfulness apart from works of the law. [29]Or is it of Jews only that God is God? Not also of the Gentiles? [30]Of course also of Gentiles; if indeed God, who will justify the circumcised out of [his] faithfulness, is one, [he will justify] also the uncircumcised through the same faithfulness. [31]Do we then render obsolete the Torah through this faithfulness? Of course not, but we rather confirm the Torah.

4 [1]What then shall we say? Have we found Abraham to be our forefather according to the flesh? [2]For if it is on the basis of works that Abraham was justified, he has grounds for boasting, but not before God. [3]For what does Scripture say? "Abraham trusted God ['s promise] and it was counted to him unto righteousness" (Gen 15:6). [4]For the one who works wages are counted as a due, not according to grace, [5]but for the one who rather than working trusts in him [God] who justifies the godless, his trust is counted unto righteousness, [6]even as David also announces [God's] blessing on the human being to whom God counts righteousness apart from works:

[7]"Blessed are those whose iniquities have been forgiven and whose sins have been covered;

[8]Blessed is the man whose sin YHWH will not count to him" (Ps 32:1f).

[9]Is this blessing then [only] for the circumcision or also for the uncircumcision? [For the latter also,] since we say, "trust was counted to Abraham unto righteousness." [10]Now, how was it counted, in a state of circumcision or of uncircumcision? Not in circumcision but in uncircumcision [11]and he [later] received "the sign of the circumcision-covenant" (Gen 17:10f) as a seal of the righteousness of [his] trust in uncircumcision. This was in order that he might become: the father of all who believe in a state of uncircumcision, in order that the righteousness may be counted *also* to them, [12]and the father of the circumcision; [father] not only to those of the circumcision but *also* to those who follow in the footsteps of the trust our father Abraham had in a state of uncircumcision.

[13]For the promise to Abraham, or his offspring, that they should be heirs of the world, did not [come] through law but through [God's] righteousness, i.e. faithfulness. [14]For if [only] those of the Torah were heirs, then [his] faithfulness would be empty and [his] promise void. [15]For the law works wrath, since where there is no law there is also no rebellion. [16]Therefore [the inheritance is] from [God's] faithfulness, in order that it might be according to grace, so that the promise may be certain of fulfilment for *all* the offspring, not only for those of the Torah, but also for those of the faithfulness of Abraham, who is the father of us *all*, [17]as it is written: "I have made thee the father of many Gentiles" (Gen 17:5). [Abraham is the father also of Gentiles] in the sight of the God whom he trusted, who gives life to the dead and calls into being what does not exist. [18]Beyond hope he trusted hopefully that he would become "the father of many Gentiles," according to the statement: "Thus will thy offspring be" (Gen 15:5). [19]Without weakening in his trust, he considered his own deadened body (for he was about one hundred years old) and the deadness of Sarah's womb. [20]He did not contradict the promise of God with lack of trust, but with trust he became potent [again], and gave God the glory, [21]and a conception resulted, because what [God] had promised, that he was able to do. [22]Therefore "it was counted to him unto righteousness." [23]But these words "it was counted to him" were not written for his sake only [24]but also for our sake. It will be "counted" to us, who are believers in him who raised up from the dead Jesus our Lord, [25]who was delivered up for the sake of our faults and raised up for the sake of our justification.

5 [1]Since, then, we have been justified out of [his] faithfulness, we have peace with God through our Lord Jesus Christ, [2]through whom also we have obtained access to that grace in which we stand, and we boast in the hope of the glory of God. [3]Not only that, but we also boast in tribulations, knowing that tribulation produces endurance, [4]and endurance tested character, and tested character hope. [5]This hope does not put us to shame, because God's love [for us] has been poured out in our hearts through the Holy Spirit which has been given to us. [6]For while we were still weak, Christ died already then for the godless. [7]For scarcely will anyone die for a righteous person; for on behalf of a good person perhaps someone might dare to die. [8]God demonstrates his love for us in that while we were still sinners Christ died for us. [9]Since, then, we have now been justified by his blood, how much more shall we be saved by him from

the Wrath. [10]For if, being hostile, we were reconciled to God through the death of his
Son, how much more, being reconciled, shall we be saved by his life. [11]Not only that,
but also boasting in God through our Lord Jesus Christ, through whom we have now
received reconciliation.

[12]Now then, as through one human being Sin came into the world, and Death
through Sin, and so Death spread to all human beings—from which it follows that all
sinned. [13]For Sin was in the world before the Torah [of Moses] came. But, sin is not
charged when there is no law, is it? [14]Yes, but Death reigned from Adam to Moses
[and therefore there was law], also over those who did not sin in the form of the
rebellion of Adam.

He [Adam] is a type of the one to come, [15]but it is not a matter of: like the fault so
also the work of grace. For if through the fault of the one [Adam] the many died,
how much more did the grace of God, i.e. the gift of grace of the one human being
Jesus Christ, abound for the many. [16]And it is not a matter of: through the one who
sinned [came] the gift. For the judgment in the context of one [fault] [led] to
condemnation, but the work of grace in the context of many faults [leads] to [God's]
decree. [17]For if in the one fault Death began to reign through the one [Adam], how
much more shall those who receive the abundance of [God's] grace and
righteousness reign in life, through the one [human being] Jesus Christ. [18]Therefore,
as through one fault [there resulted] condemnation for all human beings, so also
through one decree [there resulted] justification of life for all human beings. [19]For as
through the disobedience of the one human being the many were appointed sinners,
so also through the obedience of the one the many will be appointed righteous. [20]Law
came into the picture in order that [Adam's] fault might abound. But where Sin
abounded grace superabounded, [21]in order that, as Sin reigned in death, thus also
grace might reign through [God's] righteousness, leading to the life of the age to
come through Jesus Christ our Lord.

6 [1]What shall we say then? Should we remain in sin in order that grace might
abound? [2]Of course not! We who have died to sin, how should we still live in it? [3]Or
do ye not know that we who were baptized into Christ Jesus were baptized into his
death? [4]We were buried with him, then, through baptism into [his] death, so that as
Christ was raised from among the dead through the glory of the Father, so also we
might walk in newness of life. [5]For if we have been united to the form of his death, we
shall certainly also be [united to the form] of [his] resurrection. [6]We know that our
old human being [Adam] has been crucified with him, in order that corporate sin
might be abolished, so that we might no longer be slaves of Sin—[7]for one who has
died has been justified from Sin. [8]If we have died with Christ, we believe that we shall
also live with him. [9]We know that Christ, who has been raised from among the dead,
will die no more—Death no longer exercises lordship over him. [10]For the death he
died he died to Sin once for all, but the life he lives he lives to God. [11]So ye
also—consider yourselves to be dead to Sin but alive to God in Christ Jesus. [12]Let Sin
not reign in your mortal society to obey it, [13]and do not ever offer your members to
Sin as weapons of injustice but offer yourselves to God as being alive from among
the dead and [offer] your members to God as weapons of righteousness. [14]For Sin

shall not exercise lordship over you, since ye are not [no longer] under law but under
grace.
15What then? Shall we sin because we are not under law but under grace? 16Of
course not! Do ye not know that when ye offer yourselves to someone as slaves, to
obey, then ye are slaves of the one ye obey? [This is true] whether [ye are slaves] of
Sin, in the service of Death, or of obedience, in the service of righteousness. 17But
thanks be to God, that ye who were slaves of Sin have given whole-hearted obedience
to that pattern of teaching to which ye have been handed over. 18Ye were liberated
from Sin and have been made slaves of righteousness. 19(I use this human analogy
because of the weakness of your understanding.) Just as in the past ye offered your
members as slaves to uncleanness and lawlessness—and that led to more lawlessness,
so now [I urge you to] offer your members as slaves of righteousness—which leads to
the sanctification [of God's name]. 20When ye were slaves of Sin, ye were not subject
to righteousness. 21What fruit did ye gain then by it all? Nothing but things of which
ye are now ashamed, for their end is death. 22But now that ye have been liberated
from Sin, now that ye have become slaves of God, ye gain your fruit toward the
sanctification [of God's name], and the end of that is the life of the age to come.
23For the wages of Sin is death, but the free gift of God is the life of the age to come
in Christ Jesus our Lord.

7 1Or do ye not know, brothers-and-sisters,—for I speak to those who know the
Torah—that the law has authority over a human being [only] for as long as one lives?
2[For example,] a married woman is bound by the law to her husband as long as he is
alive. But if the husband dies, she is released from the law concerning the husband.
3So, then, if while her husband is living she becomes another man's, she will be
called an adulteress, but if the husband dies, she is free from the law [concerning the
husband] so that she is not an adulteress if she becomes another man's. 4Therefore,
brothers-and-sisters, also ye have been put to death to the law through the
community of Christ, in order that ye might become another's, his who has been
raised from among the dead, in order that we might bear fruit for God. 5For when we
were [living] in the flesh, Sin's sad consequences which are through the law were
active in our members to bear fruit for death. 6But now we have been released from
the law of Death by which we have been held captive, so that we might serve in the
new way of the Spirit and not in the old way of the letter.

7What then shall we say? Is the law sin? Of course not! But I [Adam] would not
have come to experience Sin except through the law. For I would not have known
desire if the law did not say: "Thou shalt not desire." 8But Sin found an occasion
through the commandment and produced in me all [my] desire —for apart from the
law Sin is dead. 9I was once alive apart from the law, but when the commandment
came Sin sprang to life, 10and I died; and the commandment which was [intended]
for life proved for me [to result in] death. 11For Sin, having found an occasion,
'deceived me' through the commandment and through it killed me. 12So then, the law
is holy, and the commandment is holy and just and good. 13Did then that which is
good become death for me? Of course not! Rather, Sin, in order that it might be
shown to be sin, [was] working death for me through that which is good, in order

that Sin might through the commandment become an exceedingly great sinner.
[14]For we know that the Torah is spiritual. But I am of flesh, sold under Sin. [15]For I
do not understand the works that I do, since it is not what I will that I do, but rather
what I hate, that is what I do. [16]If then I do that which I do not will, I agree with the
Torah that it is good. [17]Now in that case, it is not I who do the works but Sin which
dwells in me. [18]For I know that good does not dwell in me, that is, in my flesh. For to
will [the good] lies near at hand, but not to accomplish the good. [19]For it is not the
good that I will that I do, but the evil which I do not will, that is what I do. [20]But if I
do that which I do not will, then it is not *I* who do the work but Sin which dwells in
me. [21]So then I find the Torah (Gen 4:7) that evil lies near at hand to me who wills to
do the good. [22]For in my inner self I rejoice in the Torah of God, [23]but I see [that]
other law in my members which wages war with the Torah my mind acknowledges
and takes me prisoner by the law of Sin which dwells in my members. [24]Wretched
human being that I am! Who will rescue me from the corporate Death? [25]Thanks be
to God through Jesus Christ our Lord! So then I myself serve with the mind God's
8 Torah, but with the flesh Sin's law. [2]For the Torah of the Spirit, of life, liberates in
Christ Jesus from the law of Sin and Death. [1]There is then no condemnation for
those in Christ Jesus. [3]The inability of the law, in that it was weakened by the
flesh—God, having sent his own Son in [our] sinful, fleshy form and for the sake of
sin, condemned sin in the flesh [of Jesus], [4]so that the decree of the Torah might be
fulfilled in us, who walk not according to the flesh but according to the Spirit.
[5]Now, those who are on the side of the flesh are intent on the things of the flesh,
and those who are on the side of the Spirit are intent on the things of the Spirit. [6]For
the mind-set of the flesh is death, but the mind-set of the Spirit is life and peace.
[7]That is because the mind-set of the flesh is hostile toward God, for it does not obey
the Torah of God and indeed cannot do so, [8]and those who follow the flesh cannot
please God. [9]But ye are not in [the sphere of] the flesh but in [that of] the Spirit,
since indeed the Spirit of God dwells in you. If someone does not have the Spirit of
Christ, he is not his [Christ's]. [10]But since Christ is in you, on the one hand the body
is dead because of Sin and on the other the Spirit is life because of [God's]
righteousness. [11]If the Spirit of him who raised Jesus from among the dead dwells
among you, he who raised from among the dead Christ Jesus will also give life to
your mortal bodies, through his Spirit who dwells in you. [12]Therefore, brothers-and-
sisters, we are under obligation, [but] not to the flesh to live according to the flesh.
[13]For if ye live according to the flesh, ye will certainly die, but if by the Spirit ye put
to death the practices of the body, ye shall live.
[14]Now, those who are led by the Spirit of God are sons-of-God. [15]For the Spirit
which ye received is not one of slavery [to lead you] back into anxiety, but ye have
received the Spirit of adoption, in whom we cry: Abba! Father! [16]The very Spirit
assures our spirit that we are children of God, [17]and if children then also heirs, heirs
of God and fellow heirs with Christ, since indeed we suffer with him in order that we
might also be glorified with him. [18]For I consider that the sufferings of the present
time are not comparable with the glory that is to be revealed to us. [19]For the eager
longing of creation is awaiting the revelation of the sons-of-God. [20]For creation was
subjected to futility, not willingly but all because of him who subjected [it], in hope
[21]that also creation itself will be set free from bondage to corruption into the freedom
of the glory of the children of God. [22]For we know that the whole creation groans

together and suffers pangs together until now. 23Not only that, but also we ourselves,
who have the Spirit as the firstfruits, also we ourselves groan among ourselves,
waiting for adoption, that is, the redemption of our body. 24For it is in hope that we
are saved. [The object of] hope which is seen is not [really] hope, for why should
someone [need to] hope for what one sees? 25But since we hope for what we do not
see, we wait for it with patient endurance. 26Similarly, also the Spirit helps our
weakness, for we do not know what to pray for as we ought, but the very Spirit
intercedes with unspoken groans. 27For he who searches the hearts knows what is the
intention of the Spirit, that [the Spirit] makes petition in accordance with God['s
will] on behalf of the saints. 28We know that he [God] works together in all things for
the good with those who love God, with those who are called according to purpose.
29For those whom he chose beforehand he also designated beforehand to be of the
same form as the image of his Son, so that he might be the firstborn among many
brothers-and-sisters; 30and those whom he designated he also called, and those whom
he called he also justified, and those whom he justified he also glorified.

31What then shall we say with respect to these things? If God is for us, who is
against us? 32If it is true that he "did not spare his own son" (Gen 22:16) but
delivered him up for us *all,* how will he not also with him give to us [as inheritance]
all things? 33Who could bring a charge against the elect of God? [Since] God
"justifies, 34who could condemn" (Isa 50:8)? [It is] Christ Jesus who died, or better,
was raised, who is at the right hand of God, who also intercedes for us. 35Who will
separate us from the love of Christ? Tribulation or distress or persecution or famine
or nakedness or danger or sword? 36As it is written: "For thy sake we are being killed
the whole day, we have been reckoned as the sheep of slaughter" (Ps 44:22). 37But in
all these things we are super victors through him who loved us. 38For I am convinced
that [*nothing*], death nor life, angels nor principalities, present things nor future
things, nor powers, 39height nor depth, nor any other created thing, will be able to
separate us from the love of God which is in Christ Jesus our Lord.

9 1I speak the truth in Christ, I do not lie—my conscience bearing me witness in the
Holy Spirit—2[when I say] that I have great sorrow and constant anguish in my heart.
3For I would pray that I myself be accursed, [separated] from Christ for the sake of
my brothers-and-sisters, my fellow-citizens according to the flesh, 4who are Israelites,
whose are the adoption and the Glory and the assurances
and the lawgiving and the worship and the promises,
5whose are the fathers and from whom is Christ according to the flesh,
whose is God, who is over all, blessed [be He] forever. Amen.
6Now it is not that the word of God has lapsed. For not all who are from Israel are
Israel, 7nor are all the children [of Abraham] Abraham's seed, but "In Isaac shall
thy seed be called" (Gen 21:12). 8That is, it is not the children of [Abraham's] flesh
who are the children of God, but the children of [God's] promise are counted as
"seed". 9For this word is [a word] of promise: "At that time I shall come and Sarah
will have a son" (Gen 18:10). 10Not only that but also: Rebecca receiving semen from
one man, Isaac our father—11for while [the twins] were not yet born and had not yet
done anything good or bad, in order that God's purpose of election might
stand—12[based] not on [human] works but on the one who calls—it was said to her:

"The greater shall serve the less" (Gen 25:23). [13]As it is written: "Jacob I loved but Esau I hated" (Mal 1:2-3).

[14]What then shall we say? Is there injustice with God? Of course not! [15]For to Moses he says: "I will have mercy on whom I have mercy and I will have compassion on whom I have compassion" (Exod 33:19). [16]So, then, [it is] not [a matter] of [human] willing or running but of God being merciful. [17]For Scripture says to Pharaoh: "For this very purpose I raised thee up, in order that I might demonstrate in thee my power [for salvation] and in order that my name might be proclaimed in all the earth" (Exod 9:16). [18]So then he has mercy on whom he wills, and whom he wills he "hardens" (Exod 4:21, etc.). [19]Thou wilt say to me then, 'Why does he [God] still blame [us]? For who has [ever] resisted his will?' [20]O human being, on the contrary, who art thou to be answering back to God? Will the thing molded say to the molder: why didst thou make me like this? [21]Has not the potter authority over the clay to make from the same lump the one an instrument for honourable [use], the other an instrument for dishonourable [use]? [22]But what if, on the other hand, God endured instruments of wrath, prepared for destructive [purposes], with great longsuffering, because he wanted to show forth his wrath and to make known his power, [23]and [moreover did so] in order to make known the wealth of his glory on the instruments of mercy, which he prepared beforehand for glory, [24]whom he also called, even us, not only from the Jews but also from the Gentiles? [25]As he [God] says in Hosea: "I will call Not-my-people My-people and Not-beloved Beloved. [26]And instead of it being said to them [by God]: 'Ye are not my people,' then they shall be called sons of the living God" (Hos 2:23; 1:10). [27]But Isaiah cries out for the sake of Israel: "Though the number of the Israelites be as the sand of the sea, the remnant will be saved; [28]for YHWH will accomplish [his] word on the earth completely and decisively" (Isa 10:22-23). [29]And as Isaiah said earlier: "If YHWH Sabaoth had not left us seed, we would have become like Sodom and we would have been made like Gomorrah" (Isa 1:9).

[30]What then shall we say? That Gentiles who do not "pursue righteousness" (Isa
51:1) have obtained righteousness, the righteousness [of God] which is from [his]
faithfulness. [31]Israel, on the other hand, in pursuing the Torah of righteousness [for
Israel alone] did not attain to [the goal of] the Torah. [32]Why? Because they stumbled
on the stone of stumbling, not from faithfulness but as it were from works. [33]As it is
written: Behold I establish in Zion "a stone of stumbling and a rock of offence" (Isa
8:14), "and the one who trusts in it will not be put to shame" (Isa 28:16).
10 [1]Brothers-and-sisters, the desire of my heart and [my] prayer to God on their behalf
[is] for salvation. [2]For I bear witness to them that they have zeal for God, but not
according to knowledge. [3]For being ignorant of the righteousness of God, and
seeking to establish their particular [righteousness, viz. for Israel alone] they did not
submit to the righteousness of God. [4]For the goal of the law, Christ, is righteousness
[of God] for *every* believer. [5]For Moses writes that "the human being who does" the
righteousness which is from Torah "will live by it" (Lev 18:5). [6]And the
righteousness from faithfulness speaks thus: "Do not say in thy heart" (Deut 9:4;
8:17 ?), "Who will ascend into heaven" (that is, to bring Christ down)? [7]or: "who
will descend into the abyss" (that is, to bring Christ up from the dead)? [8]But what

does it say? "The word is near to thee, in thy mouth and in thy heart" (that is, the
word of faithfulness which we proclaim) (Deut 30:12-14), [9][namely] that if thou
confess with thy mouth Jesus as Lord and believe in thy heart that God raised him
from the dead, thou shalt be saved. [10]For with the heart it is believed unto
righteousness and with the mouth it is confessed unto salvation. [11]For the Scripture
says: *everyone* "who believes in him will not be put to shame" (Isa 2816). [12]For there
is no distinction between the Jew and also the Greek, for the same one is YHWH of
all, being generous to *all* who call upon him. [13]For "*everyone* who will call upon the
name of YHWH will be saved" (Joel 2:32).

[14]Now how could they call upon one in whom they had not believed? And how
could they believe one whom they had not heard? And how could they hear without
a proclaimer? [15]And how could [proclaimers] proclaim unless they were sent? As it is
written: "How beautiful are the feet of those who proclaim good tidings of good!"
(Isa 52:7). [16]But not all have become obedient to the good tidings, for Isaiah says:
"YHWH, who has believed our message?" (Isa 53:1). [17]Therefore faithfulness
[comes] from the message and the message [comes] through the word of God. [18]But I
say: Have they not heard? Indeed they did; "Their voice has gone out to all the earth
and their words to the ends of the inhabited world" (Ps 19:4).

[19]But I say, did Israel not know? First Moses says: "I will make you jealous of that
which is not a nation; by a foolish nation I will make you angry" (Deut 32:21). [20]And
Isaiah makes bold to say: "I was found by those who did not seek me; I was
manifested to those who did not enquire for me," [21]and to Israel he says: "All day
long I stretched out my hands to a disobedient and rebellious people" (Isa 65:1-2).

11 [1]I ask, therefore, has God repudiated his people? Of course not! For I myself am
an Israelite, of the seed of Abraham, of the tribe of Benjamin. [2]God has not
repudiated his people, whom he previously chose. Or do ye not know what the
Scripture says in [the passage on] Elijah, how he pleads to God against Israel:
[3]"YHWH, they have slain thy prophets, they have thrown down thine altars, and I
alone am left, and they seek my life" (1 Kgs 19:10)? [4]But what does the [divine]
revelation say to him? "I have left" for myself "7000 men who have not bowed the
knee to Baal" (1 Kgs 19:18). [5]So then also in the present time there has been a
remnant according to the election of grace. [6]But if by grace then not from works,
since [in that case] grace would not be grace. [7]What then? What Israel seeks, that it
did not obtain. But the election obtained it, while the rest were blinded, [8]as it is
written: "God gave them a spirit of stupor, eyes not to see and ears not to hear, until
the day of today" (Deut 29:4; Isa 29:10). [9]And David says: "May their table become
a snare and a net and a trap and a retribution to them. [10]Let their eyes be darkened so
as not to see; and bow down their back forever" (Ps 69:22-23). [11]I ask, then, have
they stumbled so as to fall? Of course not! But by their misstep salvation [will come]
to the Gentiles, in order to make them jealous. [12]But if their misstep [means] riches
for the world and their deficit riches for the Gentiles, how much more [will mean]
their fullness?

[13]Now I speak to you, the Gentiles. Inasmuch as I am Apostle to the Gentiles, I
glorify my ministry [14]in the hope that I may make my flesh jealous and I will save
some of them. [15]For if their rejection [means] reconciliation of the world, what [is]

their acceptance if not life from the dead? [16]If the first fruit is holy, so also the lump;
and if the root is holy, so also the branches. [17]But if some of the branches were
broken off, and thou, a wild olive tree, hast been grafted in among them and hast
become a co-participant in the root, i.e. fatness, of the olive tree, do not boast
triumphantly over the branches. [18]If thou dost boast triumphantly [it is still true
that] it is not thou who supportest the root but the root [supports] thee. [19]Thou
mayest say: 'Branches were broken off so that I might be grafted in.' [20]True enough.
By unbelief they were broken off and by faith thou standest. Do not think haughty
thoughts but fear [God]. [21]For if God has not spared the natural branches, he will
not spare thee. [22]Consider then the goodness and severity of God: severity to those
who have fallen and goodness of God to thee, if thou remainest in his goodness, for
otherwise thou too wilt be cut off. [23]And they too, if they do not remain in unbelief,
will be grafted in, for God is able to graft them in again. [24]For if thou hast been cut
off from [thy] native wild olive tree and against all nature grafted onto the cultivated
olive tree, how much more shall those who naturally [belong to it] be grafted onto
their own olive tree?

[25]For I do not want you to be ignorant, brothers-and-sisters, of this mystery, lest ye
be wise for yourselves [= in your own eyes]: [the mystery that] a partial blindness has
come on Israel until the fullness of the Gentiles comes in. [26]And thus all Israel will be
saved, as it is written: "There will come from Zion the Redeemer; he will turn
impieties from Jacob; [27]and this is my covenant with them, when I take away their
sins" (Isa 59:20-21a; 27:9). [28]With respect to the gospel, to be sure, they are hostile
for your sake, but with respect to the election they are beloved for the sake of the
fathers. [29]For irrevocable are the gracious gifts and calling of God. [30]For as ye were
once disobedient to God but now have received mercy because of their disobedience,
[31]so they also now have become disobedient with respect to the mercy [shown] to
you, in order that they too may now receive mercy. [32]For God has imprisoned all
[human beings] into disobedience in order that he might have mercy on all [human
beings]. [33]Oh the depth of God's riches and wisdom and knowledge! How
unsearched his judgments and how untraced his ways! [34]"For who has known the
mind of YHWH? Or who has been his counsellor? [35]Or who has given to him first
that it should be repaid to him?" (Isa 40:13; Job 41:11). [36]For from him and through
him and to him are all things. To him be the glory forever. Amen.

12 [1]I urge you, therefore, brothers-and-sisters, by means of the compassion of God,
to offer yourselves as a sacrifice, living, holy, acceptable to God, [which is] your
rational act of worship. [2]And do not be conformed to this age but be transformed by
the renewal of the mind, that ye may test what is the will of God, [that is,] what is
good and acceptable and perfect.

[3]For through the grace given to me, I say to every single one of you not to think
beyond what one ought to think but to think with the intention of soberness, as God
has allotted to each one a standard of faithfulness. [4]For just as in one body we have
many members, but all the members do not have the same function, [5]so we the many
are one body in Christ and individually members one of another. [6]Having gifts of
grace differing according to the grace given to us, if [it is] prophecy, [then] in
agreement with the faithfulness [of Christ]; [7]if [it is] ministry, [then] in service; if

[one] teaches, [then] in teaching; 8if [one] exhorts, [then] in encouragement; the
distributor [to the needy] in simplicity; the presider with dedication; the doer of
merciful deeds with cheerfulness. 9[Let] love [be] real.

Abhor the evil; cling to the good. 10Love one another with familial love; with
respect to honour, esteem one another higher [than oneself]. 11With respect to
dedication do not be lazy; with respect to the Spirit be boiling. Serve the Lord;
12rejoice in hope. Endure in tribulation; persevere in prayer. 13Contribute to the needs
of the saints; pursue hospitality. 14Bless persecutors, bless and do not curse. 15Rejoice
with those who rejoice, weep with those who weep. 16Be of the same mind with one
another. Do not think haughty thoughts but associate with the poor. "Do not be
wise in your own eyes" (Prov 3:7). 17Repay to no one evil for evil. "Be concerned
about what is good before all humans" (Prov 3:4). 18If it be possible, insofar as it
depends on you, be at peace with all humans. 19Do not avenge yourselves, beloved,
but make room for the Wrath; for it is written: "Vengeance is mine, I will repay,"
says YHWH (Deut 32:35). 20Rather, "if thine enemy is hungry, feed him; if he is
thirsty, give him to drink; for by doing this thou shalt heap coals of fire on his head"
(Prov 25:21-22a). 21Do not be conquered by the evil but conquer the evil with the
good.

13 1Let every person be subject to the powerful authorities. For no authority exists
except from God, and those which are are appointed by God. 2Thus one who resists
the authority has taken a stance against God's ordinance, and those who have taken
[such] a stance will bring judgment on themselves. 3For rulers are not a [cause for]
fear to the good work but to the evil. Dost thou wish not to fear the authority? Do the
good and thou wilt receive praise from it. 4For it is a deputy of God for thee [to do]
the good. But if thou do evil, fear! It does not bear the sword in vain. For it is a
deputy of God, an agent of punishment for Wrath to one who does evil. 5Therefore it
is necessary to be subject, not only on account of the Wrath but also on account of
the conscience. 6For precisely because of this, pay taxes too. For there are officers of
God devoting themselves to this very thing. 7Pay [thy] debts to all, tax to the one [to
whom thou owest] tax, customs to the one [to whom thou owest] customs, fear to the
one [to whom thou owest] fear, honour to the one [to whom thou owest] honour.

8Owe no one anything except to love one another. For one who loves the other has
fulfilled the law. 9For "thou shalt not commit adultery, thou shalt not kill, thou shalt
not steal, thou shalt not covet" (Deut 5:17-21), and whatever other commandment
are summed up in this word: "thou shalt love thy neighbour as thyself" (Lev 19:18).
10Love works no wrong to the neighbour; therefore the fullness of the law is love.

11And this [ye must do], knowing the time, that it is already the hour for you to
wake from sleep. For now salvation is nearer to us than when we became believers.
12The night has advanced, the day has come near. Let us then put off the works of
darkness and let us put on the weapons of light. 13Let us walk with propriety as in the
day, not in drunken revelries, not in licentious sex, not in jealous strife. 14But put on
the Lord Jesus Christ and do not do the intention of the flesh for [its] desires.

1Accept one who is weak in faith, [but] not for decisions on opinions. 2The one
14 believes to eat everything, the other who is weak eats [only] vegetables. 3Let the eater
not despise the non-eater, and let the non-eater not judge the eater, for God has

accepted him. [4]Who art thou to judge the servant of another? One stands or falls
[according] to his own lord; and one shall stand, for the Lord is able to make him
stand. [5]The one esteems one day above another, the other esteems every day [as equal
to every other]. Let each one be fully convinced in his own mind. [6]One who observes
the day observes it to the Lord. One who eats, eats to the Lord, for one gives thanks
to God; and one who does not eat, to the Lord one does not eat, and one gives
thanks to God. [7]For none of us lives to himself, and none dies to himself. [8]For if we
live we live to the Lord and if we die we die to the Lord. Whether we live then or
whether we die we are the Lord's. [9]For Christ died and lived [again] for this purpose,
in order that he might reign over both the dead and the living. [10]Thou! Why dost
thou pass judgment on thy brother-or-sister? Or thou! Why dost thou despise thy
brother-or-sister? For we shall all stand before the judgment seat of God. [11]For it is
written: "As I live, says YHWH, every knee shall bow to me and every tongue shall
give praise to God" (Isa 45:23). [12]So each of us will give account of himself.

[13]Let us then no longer judge one another but rather adjudge this, not to put a
stumbling block or an obstacle before the brother-or-sister. [14]I know and am
convinced in the Lord Jesus that nothing is intrinsically profane; except that for one
who counts something profane, for that one it is profane. [15]For if on account of food
thy brother-or-sister is grieved, thou no longer walkest according to love. Do not by
thy food destroy one for whom Christ died. [16]Do not then let thy good thing be
reviled. [17]For the Kingdom of God is not eating and drinking but righteousness and
peace and joy in the Holy Spirit. [18]For one who serves Christ in this way is pleasing to
God and approved by humans. [19]So then we pursue the things of peace and mutual
edification. [20]Do not destroy the work of God because of food. All things are pure,
to be sure, but [eating] is bad for the human who eats in a situation [where eating] is
a stumbling block. [21]It is good not to eat meat nor to drink wine nor [do] anything
[else] on which thy brother-or-sister might stumble. [22]The faith which thou hast keep
to thyself before God. Happy is the one who does not judge himself by what he
approves, [23]but the one with doubts is condemned if he eats, because it is not done
15 out of conviction; and everything which is not [done] out of conviction is sin. [1]But
we who are strong have an obligation to bear the infirmities of the powerless and not
to please ourselves. [2]Let each of us please the neighbour for good, for edification.
[3]For also Christ did not please himself but, as it is written: "The reproaches of those
who reproached thee fell on me" (Ps 69:9). [4]Now whatever was written beforehand
was written for our instruction, in order that through endurance and through the
comfort of the Scriptures we might have hope. [5]May the God of endurance and
comfort grant you to agree among yourselves according to [the will of] Christ Jesus,
[6]so that united with one voice ye may glorify God the Father of our Lord Jesus
Christ.

[7]Therefore, accept one another, since also Christ has accepted you, to the glory of
God. [8]For I tell you that Christ has become a servant from the circumcised for the
sake of God's truthfulness, in order to confirm the promises to the fathers [9]and
[consequently] the Gentiles might glorify God for his mercy. As it is written: "For
this reason I will praise thee among the Gentiles and sing praise to thy name" (Ps
18:49). [10]And further it says: "Rejoice, ye Gentiles, together with his people" (Deut

32:43). 11And further: "Praise YHWH, all ye Gentiles, and let all the peoples give him praise" (Ps 117:1). 12And further Isaiah says: "There shall be the shoot of Jesse and the one who rises to rule the Gentiles; in him shall the Gentiles hope" (Isa 11:10). 13May the God of hope fill you with all joy and peace, so that ye may abound in hope in the power of the Holy Spirit.

14As for myself, I too am convinced, my brothers-and-sisters, concerning you, that ye yourselves are full of goodness, filled with all knowledge, and able to admonish one another. 15But I have written to you in part rather boldly, as one who would remind you, because of the grace given to me by God 16to be a [priestly] minister of Christ Jesus to the Gentiles, acting as priest for the gospel of God, in order that the sacrifice consisting of Gentiles might be acceptable [to God], sanctified by the Holy Spirit. 17I have then this boast in Christ Jesus with respect to things pertaining to God; 18for I will not dare to say anything of the things which Christ has not accomplished through me to bring about the obedience of the Gentiles, in word and deed, 19in the power of signs and wonders, in the power of the Spirit, so that from Jerusalem in a circle up to Illyricum I have completed the gospel of Christ, 20being thus ambitious to preach the gospel not where Christ had [already] been named, lest I build on someone else's foundation. 21Instead, as it is written: "They shall see to whom it was not announced about him, and those who have not heard shall understand" (Isa 52:15).

22That is why I have been hindered so many times from coming to you. 23But now, no longer having room in these regions and having for considerable years had the desire to come to you, 24whenever I should go to Spain. . . . For I hope to see you in passing through and to be helped further [on my journey] there by you, if I may first in part be satisfied by you. 25But now I go to Jerusalem to minister to the saints. 26For Macedonia and Achaia have decided to make a certain solidarity [offering] for the poor among the saints in Jerusalem. 27For they have decided and indeed owe it to them; for if the Gentiles have shared in their spiritual things, they are obliged to serve them in material things. 28When I have completed this and sealed this fruit to them, I shall go on by way of you to Spain. 29And I know that when I come to you I will come with the fullness of the blessing of Christ.

30I exhort you through our Lord Jesus Christ and through the love of the Spirit to struggle with me in [your] prayers to God on my behalf, 31in order that I might be delivered from the unbelievers in Judea and [thus] my service might be acceptable to the saints, 32[so] that by the will of God I might come to you with joy. 33The God of peace be with you all. Amen.

16 1I commend to you Phoebe our sister, who is also minister of the church in Cenchreae, 2that ye may welcome her in the Lord, in a manner worthy of the saints, and that ye may stand by her in any matter in which she may have need of you; for she also has been a protectress of many, including myself. 3Greet Prisca and Aquila, my fellow-workers in Christ Jesus, 4who risked their necks [to save] my life, to whom not only I am grateful but all the churches of the Gentiles. 5And [greet] the church in their house. Greet Epaenetus my beloved, who is the first-fruit of Asia unto Christ. 6Greet Mary, who worked very hard for you. 7Greet Andronicus and Junia, my

kinsfolk and fellow-prisoners, who are prominent among the Apostles and who were
in Christ before me. [8]Greet Ampliatus, my beloved in the Lord. [9]Greet Urbanus, our
fellow-worker in Christ, and Stachys my beloved. [10]Greet Apelles, who is [tested and]
approved in Christ. Greet those of the household of Aristobulus. [11]Greet Herodion
my kinsman. Greet those of the household of Narcissus who are in the Lord. [12]Greet
Tryphaena and Tryphosa, who work hard in the Lord. Greet Persis the beloved, who
has worked very hard in the Lord. [13]Greet Rufus, the elect in the Lord, and his
mother—and mine. [14]Greet Asyncritus, Phlegon, Hermes, Patrobas, Hermas, and
the brothers-and-sisters who are with them. [15]Greet Philologus and Julia, Nereus and
his sister, and Olympas, and all the saints who are with them. [16]Greet one another
with a holy kiss. [21]Timothy, my fellow-worker, greets you and [so do] Lucius and
Jason and Sosipater, my kinsmen. [22](I, Tertius, who have written the letter in the
Lord, greet you.) [23]Gaius, my host and [the host] of the whole church, greets you.
Erastus, the city treasurer, and Quartus the brother greet you. [24]The grace of our
Lord Jesus Christ be with you.

GALATIANS

1 [1]Paul Apostle, not from human beings and not through an individual but through
Jesus Christ and God the Father who raised him from among the dead, [2]and all the
brothers-and-sisters who are with me,
To the congregations of Galatia,
[3]Grace to you and peace from God our Father and the Lord Jesus Christ, [4]who
gave himself for our sins, in order that he might deliver us out of the present wicked
eon according to the will of our God and Father, [5]to whom be glory forever and ever.
Amen.

[6]I am astonished that so quickly ye are falling away from the one who called you in
grace [and going over] to another gospel—[7]which does not really exist—except that
there are certain people who are unsettling you and who want to pervert the gospel of
Christ. [8]But even if we or an angel from heaven were to preach a gospel in opposition
to what we have proclaimed to you—may there be a curse [on that one]. [9]As we said
earlier and now I say again, if anyone preach the gospel to ye in opposition to what ye
have received—may there be a curse [on that one]. [10]Now then, am I swaying people
or [even] God? Or am I trying to please people? Yet, if I were pleasing people I would
not be a servant of Christ.
[11]I declare to you, brothers-and-sisters, that the gospel which is preached by me is
not a human message; [12]for I too did not receive it from a human being, nor was I
taught it, but [I received it] through a revelation of Jesus Christ.
[13]For ye have heard of my lifestyle then in Judaism: that I was persecuting the
church of God exceedingly and trying to destroy it, [14]and that I was making progress
in Judaism more than many contemporaries in my people, being to a greater degree
zealous for the [oral] traditions of the sages [of my people]. [15]But when it pleased
him who had set me apart from my mother's womb and who had called [me] through
his grace [16]to reveal his son through me in order that I might preach him among the
Gentiles, I did not consult with flesh and blood, [17]nor did I go up to Jerusalem to
those who were apostles before me, but at once I went away to Arabia, and came
back again to Damascus. [18]Then after three years I went up to Jerusalem to enquire
of Cephas, and I remained with him a fortnight. [19]I did not see another of the
apostles, except for James, the Lord's brother.—[20]That which I write to you, behold
before God I do not lie.—[21]Then I went into the regions of Syria and of Cilicia. [22]I
remained unknown in person to the churches of Judea which are in Christ. [23]They
were only hearing that "the one who once persecuted us is now proclaiming the
faithfulness which he once tried to destroy," [24]and they glorified God with respect to
me.
2 [1]Then after fourteen years I once more went up to Jerusalem, with Barnabas,
taking along also Titus. [2]I went up, however, with respect to [my] revelation. And I
submitted to them [for their consideration] the gospel which I preach among the
Gentiles, i.e. privately to the influential people, [for fear] lest somehow I be running
or have run in vain. [3]But [the following happened:] Titus, who was with me was not
compelled to be circumcised, since he is a Greek. [4]Because of the interloping false
brothers-and-sisters, namely, who had sneaked in to investigate our freedom which

we have in Christ Jesus in order that they might enslave us . . . —[5]And to whom not for a moment did we yield in submission, in order that the truth of the gospel might remain for you. [6]But [on the other hand], from the influential people who were something—what they once were makes no difference to me; God is not partial with persons . . . —For on me the influential people did not impose anything, [7]but on the contrary, recognizing that I had been entrusted with the gospel to the Gentiles, as Cephas [had been entrusted with the gospel] to the Jews—[8]for he who has been effective for Cephas for the apostolate to the Jews was effective also for me [for the apostolate] to the Gentiles—[9]acknowledging [as I said] the grace given to me, James and Cephas and John, the influential pillars, gave to me and Barnabas the right hand of common participation, that we [should continue to go] to the Gentiles, and they to the Jews. [10]Only [we agreed] that we should remember the poor, which very thing I was eager to do.

[11]Now when Cephas came to Antioch, I stood up against him to his face, because he was condemned. [12][I did this] because before certain people came from James, he used to eat with the Gentiles; but when they came, he began to shrink back and to separate himself, fearing the Jews; [13]and also the other Jews acted inconsistently along with him, so that even Barnabas was swept with them through the inconsistency. [14]But when [I came and] saw that they were not walking on a straight path toward the truth of the gospel, I said to Cephas in front of everyone, 'Since thou being a Jew livest in the Gentile and not the Jewish manner, how [canst] thou force the Gentiles to Judaize?'

[15]We who are Jews by nature and not sinners from the Gentiles, [16]knowing [therefore] that a human being is not justified from works of law, but [rather] through the faithfulness of Christ Jesus, we too became believers in Christ Jesus, in order that we might be justified from the faithfulness of Christ and not from works of law, because [as it is written:] by works of law "all" flesh "is not justified" (Ps 143:2). [17]But, since seeking to be justified in Christ we ourselves too have been found to be [Gentile] sinners, is consequently Christ in the service of Sin? Of course not! [18]For since I again build up that which I tore down, I commend myself openly as an "apostate." [19]For through the law I have died to the law, in order that I might live to God. I have been co-crucified with Christ. [20]I live yet [really] no longer I, but [rather] Christ lives in me. What I now live in the flesh, I live in the faithfulness of the Son of God, who loved me and delivered himself for me. [21]I do not set at nought the grace of God; for since through law is [the] righteousness [of God], consequently Christ has died as a free gift.

3 [1]O ye ignorant Galatians, what [demonic power] has possessed you, before whose eyes Jesus Christ was set forth in public proclamation as crucified? [2][The answer to] this [question] only I want to learn from you: from works of law did ye receive the Spirit or [rather] from preaching of faithfulness? [3]Are ye so ignorant [that] having begun [a beginning characterized by] Spirit ye are now ending [an ending characterized by] flesh? [4]Did ye experience such great things in vain?—if it really was in vain (I certainly hope not!). [5]Therefore [God] who supplies the Spirit to you and works wonders among you, [does he do it] from works of law or from preaching of faithfulness?

6Because [as it is written:] Abraham "believed God, and it was counted to him unto righteousness" (Gen 15:6). 7Know then: those from faithfulness, these are 'sons' of Abraham. 8Now Scripture, knowing beforehand that God would justify the Gentiles from faithfulness, proclaimed the gospel beforehand to Abraham [saying] that "in thee all the Gentiles will be blessed" (Gen 12:3). 9Therefore those of faithfulness are blessed together with the faithful Abraham. 10For all who are from works of law are under a curse; for it is written that "Cursed is everyone who does not remain in all the things written in the book of the law to do them" (Deut 27:26). 11That in the law "no one is justified before God" (Ps 143:2) is clear, because: "The righteous one will live from faithfulness" (Hab 2:4). 12But the law is not "from faithfulness," but "The one who does them will live in them" (Lev 18:5). 13Christ has redeemed us from the curse of the law, having become a curse for us, because it is written, "Cursed is everyone who hangs on a tree" (Deut 21:23), 14in order that for the Gentiles the blessing of Abraham might become a reality in Jesus Christ, in order that we might receive the promise, [i.e.] the Spirit, through the faithfulness.

15Brothers-and-sisters, I speak in terms of a human [institution:] no one annuls or adds a codicil to a legally validated testament even of a human being. 16Now to Abraham were said the promises [in question] "and to" his "seed" (Gen 17:8). It does not say: "and to his seeds," as if it were a case of many, but as if a case of one, "and to thy seed," which is Christ. 17Now I maintain the following: a testament previously legally validated [not by a human being but] by God—the Torah which came into being 430 years later does not make it void, in order to destroy the promise. 18For if the inheritance were from Torah, then no longer from promise. But God has been gracious to Abraham through promise. 19Why then the law of deeds? It was established until the seed should come to whom [the promise] was promised; ordained through angels, in the hand of a mediator. 20Now the mediator [in question] is not one [of a kind]; but God is one. 21Then is the law against the promises? Of course not! For if a law had been given which is capable of making alive, then indeed righteousness would be from law. 22But [on the contrary] Scripture has imprisoned everything under Sin, in order that the promise might be given to the believers from the faithfulness of Jesus Christ. 23Now before that faithfulness came we were held in custody under the law, being imprisoned until the faithfulness that was to be revealed. 24Therefore the law has been [only] our custodian until [the time of] Christ, in order that we might be justified from faithfulness. 25But when faithfulness came, we are no longer under a custodian. 26For ye are all sons-of-God in Christ Jesus through the faithfulness. 27For whoever of you have been baptized into Christ have put on Christ. 28There is neither Jew nor Greek, there is neither slave nor free, there is no "male and female" (Gen 1:27); for ye are all one in Christ Jesus. 29Now since ye are of Christ, therefore ye are the seed of Abraham, heirs according to promise.

4 1Now I say: for as long as the heir is a minor child, [the child] does not differ in the slightest from a slave, although [the child] is the [legal] owner of everything, 2but [the child] is under the [legal] guardians and administrators [of the trust] until the stipulated date [set by] the father. 3Thus also [was the case with] us: when we were minor children, we were under the elements of the world enslaved. 4But when the fulness of time arrived, God sent out his Son, born from woman, placed under [the

curse of the] law, [5]in order that he might redeem those under law, [that is,] in order that we might receive adoption [as children]. [6]Now because ye are 'sons,' God has sent out the Spirit of his Son into our hearts, crying: Abba! Father! [7]Therefore thou art no longer a slave but a 'son'; and if a 'son,' then also an heir through God.

[8]But formerly, since ye did not know God, ye served [as slaves] gods who essentially are not [gods]. [9]Now, however, since ye have come to know God, or better: since ye are known by God, how do ye convert again to the weak and impotent elements, whom ye wish to serve [as slaves] anew? [10]Days ye observe, and months, and times, and years! [11]I am afraid with respect to you lest somehow I have laboured for you in vain.

[12]Become like me, for I also have become as ye [are], brothers-and-sisters, I beseech you. In no way did ye do me wrong; [13]ye know rather that it was because of a weakness of the flesh that I preached the gospel to you the first time, [14]and ye did not despise or spit at your temptation in my flesh, but ye received me like an angel of God, like Christ Jesus [himself]. [15]Where then [now] is your blessing [which ye had for me]? For I testify to you that if possible ye would have plucked out your eyes and given them to me. [16]Have I therefore become your enemy by telling you the truth? [17]They court you zealously not in a good way; rather they want to shut you out, that ye might court them zealously. [18]Now, it is good always to be courted zealously in a good way, and not only when I am [personally] present with you—[19]my children, to whom I am again giving birth with labour pains, until Christ takes form among you—[20]but I could wish to be present with you now and to exchange my voice [for this letter], for I am at a loss [to know what to do] about you.

[21]Tell me, ye who want to be under law, do ye not listen to the Torah [and understand it]? [22]For it is written (in Gen 16, 17, 21) that Abraham had two sons, one from the slave woman and one from the free woman. [23]But the one from the slave woman was born according to the flesh, while the one from the free woman [was born] through the promise. [24]These things are to be interpreted allegorically. For these [women] are two covenants: the one, on the one hand, from Mount Sinai, giving birth into slavery. [25]She is Hagar, for Sinai is a mountain in Arabia. She stands in a row with the present Jerusalem, for she serves [as a slave] with her children. [26]But the Jerusalem above is free—and she is our mother. [27]For it is written (Isa 54:1):

"Rejoice, O barren one, who dost not bear,
Break forth into singing and cry out, thou who art not in travail,
For many are the children of the desolate one
more than the one who has a husband."

[28]Now ye, brothers-and-sisters, are children of promise according to Isaac. [29]But just as then the one born according to the flesh persecuted the one [born] according to the Spirit, so also now. [30]But what does Scripture say? "Cast out the slave woman and her son, for the son of the slave woman shall not inherit with the son" of the free woman (Gen 21:10). [31]In conclusion, brothers-and-sisters, we are not children of the slave woman but of the free woman.

5 [1]For freedom Christ has liberated us; stand fast therefore and do not let yourselves

be subjected again to a yoke of slavery. [2]Behold, I Paul tell you that in case ye [now]
become circumcised, Christ will be of no benefit to you. [3]And I testify again to every
human being who gets circumcised that one is obligated to do the whole law. [4]Ye have
been released from a relationship with Christ, ye who are [= seek to be] justified by
law; ye have fallen out of [the state of] grace. [5]For we, by the Spirit, in faithfulness,
are awaiting the hoped-for righteousness [of God]. [6]For in Christ Jesus neither
circumcision has power nor uncircumcision, but faithfulness activated through love.
[7]Ye were running well; who got in your way [to make you stumble, so that ye would]
not obey the truth? [8]The persuasion [to that does] not [come] from the one who calls
you. [9]"A little leaven leavens the whole dough." [10]In the Lord, I have confidence in
you that ye will not think differently [than I]. But the one who is unsettling you will
bear the judgment, whoever that one is. [11]But if I, brothers-and-sisters, if I still
preach circumcision, why am I still persecuted? Then the scandal of the cross has
been abolished. [12]I wish that those who agitate you would further castrate
themselves!

[13]For ye, brothers-and-sisters, were called to freedom; only not to this freedom as
an occasion for the Flesh, but rather through love serve [as slaves] one another. [14]For
the whole Torah is fulfilled in one word, in the "Thou shalt love thy neighbour as
thyself" (Lev 19:18). [15]But since ye bite one another and eat one another up, take
care lest ye be consumed by one another. [16]But I say: walk by the Spirit and ye
[definitely] will not carry out [the] desire of the Flesh. [17]For the Flesh desires against
[the desires of] the Spirit, and the Spirit against [the desires of] the Flesh, for these
[forces] are opposites of one another, so that whatever ye will that ye do not do.
[18]But since ye are led by the Spirit, ye are not [any longer] under law. [19][It is] evident
[what] are the works of the Flesh: they are illicit sexual activities, moral impurity,
sensual debauchery, [20]idolatry, magic, enmities, strife, rivalries, outbursts of rage,
quarrels, dissentions, factions, [21]jealousies, drunkennesses, piggish banquets, and
things like that, with respect to which I warn you, as I have warned [in the past], that
"those who do such things will not inherit the Kingdom of God." [22]But [on the
contrary] the fruit of the Spirit is love, joy, peace, forebearance, kindness, goodness,
faithfulness, [23]humility, self-control. The law does not condemn such things. [24]But
those who [belong to] Christ Jesus have crucified the Flesh with [its] sufferings and
desires. [25]If we live by the Spirit [as we do], following the Spirit let us also march.

[26]Let us not become self-glorifying, challenging one another, envying one
6 another, [1]brothers-and-sisters. In case it should ever happen that a human being is
entrapped by some trespass, ye the 'spiritual ones' restore such a one in a spirit of
humility, examining thyself critically, lest thou too be tempted. [2]Bear one another's
burdens, and thus ye will fulfil the Torah of Christ. [3]For if someone thinks to be
something, while being nothing, one deceives oneself. [4]But let each one test his own
work, and then he will have his own boast with respect to himself only and not with
respect to the other. [5]For everyone will bear [his] own load.

[6]Let the one who is instructed in the word share in all good things with the one
who instructs. [7]Do not be deceived; God is not [to be] mocked. For whatever a
human being sows, that one will also reap: [8]the one who sows unto his flesh, from

the flesh will reap destruction; but the one who sows unto the Spirit, from the Spirit will reap the life of the age to come. [9]In doing good let us not weary; for in its appropriate season we shall reap if we do not become weak. [10]Therefore, then, as long as we have time, let us work the good for all, but especially for the members of the house of faithfulness.

[11]See with what large letters I am writing to you in my hand [-writing]. [12]Those who want to be esteemed in the flesh are the ones who [try to] force you to get circumcised—only [they do it] in order that they might not be persecuted in the cross of Christ. [13]For even those who are getting circumcised do not themselves keep the law, but [rather] they want you to get circumcised, in order that they may boast in your flesh. [14]But far be it from me to boast except in the cross of our Lord Jesus Christ, through whom the world has been crucified to me and I to the world. [15]For neither is circumcision anything, nor uncircumcision, but new creation. [16]And whoever follow this criterion, peace be on them and mercy, and also [peace and mercy be] on God's [people] Israel. [17]From now on let no one cause me troubles; for I bear the marks of Jesus on my body.

[18]The grace of our Lord Jesus Christ [be] with your spirit, brothers-and-sisters. Amen.

NOTES

NOTES TO THE INTRODUCTION

1. An impressive statement of the contours of such a theology is I. Greenberg, "Cloud of Smoke, Pillar of Fire: Judaism, Christianity, and Modernity after the Holocaust," *Auschwitz: Beginning of a New Era? Reflexions on the Holocaust* (ed. E. Fleischner; New York: KTAV, 1977) 7-55.
2. J. Isaac, *The Teaching of Contempt: Christian Roots of Anti-Semitism* (New York: Holt, Rinehart and Winston, 1964). His influential *Jesus and Israel* (New York: Holt, Rinehart and Winston, 1971) first appeared in France in 1948.
3. See my "The Messiah of Israel as Teacher of the Gentiles; The Setting of Matthew's Christology," *Int* 29 (1975) 24-40; and "Anti-Judaism and the Passion Narratives in Luke and Acts," *Anti-Judaism in Early Christianity: Vol 1, Paul and the Gospels* (ed. P. Richardson with D. Granskou; Waterloo: Wilfrid Laurier University Press, 1986) 127-53.
4. See especially his monumental four-volume *A Theology of the Jewish-Christian Reality*, of which two have been published: P. van Buren, *Discerning the Way* (New York: Seabury, 1980) and *A Christian Theology of the People Israel* (New York: Seabury, 1983).
5. See G. F. Moore, "Christian Writers on Judaism," *HTR* 14 (1921) 197-254; C. Klein, *Anti-Judaism in Christian Theology* (Philadelphia: Fortress, 1978); E. P. Sanders, *Paul and Palestinian Judaism: A Comparison of Patterns of Religion* (Philadelphia: Fortress, 1977), and *Jesus and Judaism* (Philadelphia: Fortress, 1985).
6. See J. G. Gager, *The Origins of Anti-Semitism* (Oxford: Oxford University Press, 1983), a work which is exceedingly important for demolishing the myth of pagan antisemitism.
7. E. Käsemann, "Paul and Israel," *New Testament Questions of Today* (Philadelphia: Fortress, 1969) 184.
8. The classic statement of such a case is F. C. Baur, *Paul the Apostle of Jesus Christ* (London: Williams and Norgate, 1875).
9. For a thorough and convincing refutation of Baur's thesis, from two different perspectives, see J. Munck, *Paul and the Salvation of Mankind* (London: SCM, 1959), and W. Schmithals, *Paul and James* (London: SCM, 1965).

10. See Chapter 10.
11. H. J. Schoeps, *Paul: The Theology of the Apostle in the Light of Jewish Religious History* (Philadelphia: Westminster, 1961) 213-18.
12. H. Räisänen, *Paul and the Law* (Tübingen: Mohr, 1983).
13. See Sanders, *Paul.* A pioneer is W. D. Davies, *Paul and Rabbinic Judaism* (London: SPCK, 1948).
14. The discussion of the law in E. P. Sanders, *Paul, the Law, and the Jewish People* (Philadelphia: Fortress, 1983), is under the heading "Different Questions, Different Answers."
15. Sanders's statement in *Law*, 19, "The argument of Galatians 3 is against Christian missionaries, not against Judaism," is much more helpful than some of his more sweeping generalizations about Paul's critique of Judaism.
16. See my "Legicide and the Problem of the Christian Old Testament: A Plea for a New Hermeneutic of the Apostolic Writings," *Transformations in Judaism and Christianity after the Holocaust* (ed. I. Greenberg, et al.; Bloomington: Indiana University Press, forthcoming)
17. See e.g. P. Vielhauer, "Paulus und das Alte Testament," *Oikodome* (Munich: Kaiser, 1979) 196-228.
18. See J. A. Sanders, *Canon and Community: A Guide to Canonical Criticism* (Philadelphia: Fortress, 1984), and the works cited there.
19. This principle was stated most forcefully by J. Knox, *Chapters in a Life of Paul* (New York: Abingdon, 1950), and it is followed in two recent studies of Paul's life: R. Jewett, *A Chronology of Paul's Life* (Philadelphia: Fortress, 1979), and G. Lüdemann, *Paul, Apostle to the Gentiles: Studies in Chronology* (Philadelphia: Fortress, 1984).
20. See among many others N. A. Dahl, "The Missionary Theology in the Epistle to the Romans," *Studies in Paul* (Minneapolis: Augsburg, 1977) 70-94.
21. This was pointed out long ago by W. Wrede, *Paul* (Boston: American Unitarian Association, 1908), and A. Schweitzer, *The Mysticism of Paul the Apostle* (New York: Holt, 1931). The former calls justification a "polemical doctrine" (123) and the latter a "subsidiary crater" (225).
22. It is one of the advantages of J. C. Beker, *Paul the Apostle: The Triumph of God in Life and Thought* (Philadelphia: Fortress, 1980), to emphasize this.
23. See especially K. Stendahl, "The Apostle Paul and the Introspective Conscience of the West," *HTR* 56 (1963) 199-215, reprinted along with other essays in his *Paul among Jews and Gentiles* (Philadelphia: Fortress, 1976).
24. See J. Jeremias, *Jesus' Promise to the Nations* (London: SCM, 1958).
25. See Munck, *Paul*, and Stendahl, *Paul.* S. Kim, *The Origin of Paul's Gospel* (Tübingen: Mohr, 1981), is moving, I believe, in a retrograde direction.
26. P. Richardson, *Israel in the Apostolic Church* (Cambridge: Cambridge University Press, 1969).
27. N. A. Dahl, "The Messiahship of Jesus in Paul," *The Crucified Messiah and other Essays* (Minneapolis: Augsburg, 1974) 37-47; W. R. Kramer, *Christ, Lord, Son of God* (London: SCM, 1966). See also M. de Jonge, "The Earliest Christian Use of *Christos*: Some Suggestions," *NTS* 32 (1986) 321-43.

28. See A. T. Kraabel, "The Disappearance of the 'God-fearers,'" *Numen* 28 (1981) 113-26.
29. See F. Siegert, "Gottesfürchtige und Sympathisanten," *JSJ* 4 (1973) 109-64; and Gager, *Origins*.
30. Sanders, *Law*, 179-90.
31. Tertullian, *Adv. Marc.* 5.2.1.
32. See my "Judaism of the Uncircumcised in Ignatius and Related Writers," *Anti-Judaism in Early Christianity: Vol. 2, Separation and Polemic* (ed. S. Wilson; Waterloo: Wilfrid Laurier University Press, 1986) 33-44.
33. Beker, *Paul*. Because he does not take seriously enough the considerations concerning Gentile addressees outlined above, he understands Paul's theology as being directed primarily against Judaism.
34. W. Wink, *Naming the Powers* (Philadelphia: Fortress, 1984). Especially helpful is his discussion of the "angels of the nations" (26-35). I believe he is completely misguided in his understanding of the "elements of the universe" (67-77, and "The 'Elements of the Universe' in Biblical and Scientific Perspective," *Zygon* 13 [1978] 225-48).
35. See G. Aulén, *Christus Victor* (London: SPCK, 1953).
36. Sanders, *Paul*, 463-72, under the heading "transfer terminology."
37. The classic treatment, which needs updating, is A. T. Hanson, *The Wrath of the Lamb* (London: SPCK, 1957).
38. See Räisänen, *Paul*. I am not convinced that even Rom 3:27; 7:20-25; 8:2; and Gal 6:2 are exceptions, as he claims.
39. See A. F. Segal, "Covenant in Rabbinic Writings," *SR* 14 (1985) 53-62.
40. See now the important study by R. B. Hays, *The Faith of Jesus Christ* (Chico: Scholars, 1983).
41. See G. Howard, *Paul: Crisis in Galatia* (Cambridge: Cambridge University Press, 1979), and his own earlier studies cited there.
42. Note how K. Barth translates *pistis* as "Treue" rather than "Glaube" at key points in his *Römerbrief* (Zürich: Evangelischer Verlag, 1940 [1918]).
43. Sanders, *Paul*. Cf. Wrede, *Paul*, and Schweitzer, *Mysticism*.
44. See the statistics in G. M. Taylor, "The Function of *PISTIS CHRISTOU* in Galatians," *JBL* 85 (1966) 58-76; and R. Scroggs, "Paul as Rhetorician: Two Homilies in Romans 1-11," *Jews, Greeks, and Christians* (eds. R. Hamerton-Kelly and R. Scroggs; Leiden: Brill, 1976) 271-98.
45. Since my understanding of the text developed over a period of years, sometimes the translation of a particular text differs from that of the same text cited in an earlier chapter.
46. It is difficult to give a literal translation at a time when contemporary English is shifting toward so-called "inclusive" language. Whatever be the case in English today, ancient Greek clearly made use of the generic singular (*BDF* 139). In such cases the subject has been translated as "one," while subsequent pronouns are masculine singular. Some words, when used in a technical and non-exclusive sense (e.g., 'sons') have been put between single quotation marks or, if a phrase, joined by hyphens. For example, the inclusive masculine plural of the root

adelph- avoids the correct but awkward "siblings" in favour of "brothers-and-sisters." Because of the importance of distinguishing between singular and plural in the second person, some archaic language has been deliberately retained in such cases.

NOTES TO CHAPTER ONE

1. R. R. Ruether, *Faith and Fratricide* (New York: Seabury, 1974) 228.
2. Even in Justin's *Dialogue*, the law is the main issue (chap. 10) and Christology is discussed later in the framework of Christian disregard of the Torah.
3. J. Wellhausen, *Prolegomena to the History of Ancient Israel* (Edinburgh: A. and C. Black, 1885) 425.
4. E. Schürer, *The Jewish People in the Time of Jesus Christ*, div. 2, vol. 2 (Edinburgh: T. and T. Clark, 1910) 124.
5. Ruether, *Faith*, 52. This is an important insight, but it may have nothing to do with the "Jewish Torah."
6. C. H. Dodd, *The Epistle of Paul to the Romans* (London: Hodder and Stoughton, 1932) 63, 179; cf. 43-45.
7. See P. Richardson, *Israel in the Apostolic Church* (Cambridge: Cambridge University Press, 1969), whom Ruether has misunderstood at this point.
8. Rom 1:3; 4:1; 9:3,5; 1 Cor 10:18.
9. She speaks (106) of those who "speak out of good intentions, but inaccurate exegesis." Cf. A. R. Eckardt, *Elder and Younger Brothers* (New York: Scribner's, 1967) 54-58; A. T. Davies, *Anti-Semitism and the Christian Mind* (New York: Herder and Herder, 1969) 102ff. K. Stendahl has hinted at but not yet expounded fully a more adequate understanding of these chapters.
10. G. F. Moore, *Judaism in the First Centuries of the Christian Era* (Cambridge: Harvard University Press, 1927-1930), 3:151.
11. H. J. Schoeps, *Paul: The Theology of the Apostle in the Light of Jewish Religious History* (Philadelphia: Westminster, 1961) 213, 198.
12. G. F. Moore, "Christian Writers on Judaism," *HTR* 14 (1921) 197-254. That a distorted understanding of the Jewish concept of Torah persists into the present is shown by chapter 3 in Charlotte Klein, *Theologie und Anti-Judaismus* (Munich: Kaiser, 1975).
13. G. Bornkamm, *Paul* (London: Hodder and Stoughton, 1971). The mask slips from the universalistic talk of a "church of Jews and Gentiles" when he speaks of "Gentiles" and "*former* Jews" in the church (209).
14. J. Munck, *Paul and the Salvation of Mankind* (London: SCM, 1959). W. Schmithals, *Paul and James* (London: SCM, 1965), reaches similar conclusions from a different perspective.
15. Generally accepted since W. G. Kümmel, *Römer 7 und die Bekehrung des*

Paulus (Leipzig: Hinrichs'sche Buchhandlung, 1929).

16. Cf. also U. Wilckens, "Die Bekehrung des Paulus als religionsgeschichtliches Problem," *ZTK* 56 (1959) 273-93; and K. Stendahl, *Paul among Jews and Gentiles* (Philadelphia: Fortress, 1976), especially chapter 2.
17. K. Stendahl, "The Apostle Paul and the Introspective Conscience of the West," *HTR* 56 (1963) 199-215, reprinted in the work mentioned in note 16.
18. C. G. Montefiore, *Judaism and St. Paul* (London: Goschen, 1914) 126. See also Schoeps, *Paul*, 213.
19. J. Klausner, *From Jesus to Paul* (New York: Macmillan, 1943); W. L. Knox, *St. Paul and the Church of the Gentiles* (Cambridge: Cambridge University Press, 1939).
20. S. Sandmel, *The Genius of Paul* (New York: Farrar, Straus, and Cudahy, 1958); E. R. Goodenough, "Paul and the Hellenization of Christianity," *Religions in Antiquity* (ed. J. Neusner; Leiden: Brill, 1968) 23-68.
21. L. Baeck, "The Faith of Paul," *Judaism and Christianity* (Philadelphia: Jewish Publication Society, 1958); W. D. Davies, *Paul and Rabbinic Judaism* (London: SPCK, 1948); Schoeps, *Paul*, 172ff.
22. W. D. Davies, "From Schweizer to Scholem: Reflections on Sabbatai Svi," *JBL* 95 (1976) 529-58.
23. See among others P. Schäfer, "Die Torah der messianischen Zeit," *ZNW* 65 (1974) 27-42; E. E. Urbach, *The Sages* (Jerusalem: Magnes, 1975) 297-302, 308-14.
24. Given the anti-Jewish environment of the Christian second century, the period when the text was subject to least control, there is also the possibility of interpolations contained in all the later MSS. Thus 1 Cor 15:56 is an interpolation (cf. the commentaries of Weiss and Moffatt) as is 1 Thess 2:13-16 (cf. B. Pearson in *HTR* 64 [1971] 79-94). If references to the fall of Jerusalem are indications of interpolation, this may also be true of Rom 10:9-10 and Gal 4:24-27. On Gal 3:19, see below, note 60.
25. E.g. in the RSV the begrudging "although" in Rom 3:21 and "yet" in Gal 2:16. Baur's presuppositions are contained in the translation of *peritomē* as "circumcision party" in Acts 11:2, Gal 2:12, Tit 1:10, and *gramma* as "written code" in Rom 2:27, 2 Cor 3:6.
26. E.g. because Rom 2:1ff deals with hypocrisy it is almost always understood as referring to Jews, in spite of the "therefore" connecting it with 1:18-32.
27. Schmithals, *Paul and James*.
28. See the complaint of M. Limbeck, *Die Ordnung des Heils* (Düsseldorf: Patmos, 1971) 50.
29. Davies, "Sabbatai Svi," 547.
30. On the centrality of this statement, cf. E. P. Sanders, "Patterns of Religion in Paul and Rabbinic Judaism: A Holistic Method of Comparison," *HTR* 66 (1973) 455-78.
31. "Man has his relationship with God only in his relationship with the Torah," Gutbrod, *TDNT* 4: 1055.
32. "Without commandments there could be no Torah. . . . God's first revelation to man is marked by the commandment (Gen 2:16-17)," Urbach, *Sages*, 315.

33. *M. T. Melakhim* 8, 11. On this text see especially S. S. Schwarzschild, "So Noachites Have to Believe in Revelation?," *JQR* 52 (1961-62) 297-308; 53 (1962-63) 30-65. On the reading "but" (*ella*) rather than "nor" (*velo*) in the last line, see also J. Katz, *Exclusiveness and Tolerance* (London: Oxford University Press, 1961) 175.
34. Note that Eliezer ben Hyrkanos calls the good deeds of the Gentiles sin "because they do them only to magnify themselves" (*B. Bat.* 10b).
35. The usual list comprises the prohibition of blasphemy, idolatry, adultery, murder, robbery, and eating flesh cut from a living animal, and the injunction to establish courts of justice (*Sanh.* 56a). Some have seen in the list an attempt to formulate a kind of natural law.
36. E. P. Sanders, "The Covenant as a Soteriological Category and the Nature of Salvation in Palestinian and Hellenistic Judaism," *Jews, Greeks and Christians* (ed. R. Hamerton-Kelly and R. Scroggs; Leiden: Brill, 1976) 15. With allowance made for difference of terminology, he shows that the same is true of Hellenistic Judaism. Whether or not 4 Ezra is to be considered an exception to the general rule depends on the degree to which one considers the work to be a drama, which for Israel receives its resolution in chapter 14.
37. Josephus, *Ant.* 20:17-48. In general, see N. J. McEleney, "Conversion, Circumcision and the Law," *NTS* 20 (1974) 319-41.
38. G. Klein, *Der älteste christliche Katechismus und die jüdische Propagandaliteratur* (Berlin: Reimer, 1909).
39. "The son who serves his father serves him with joy, saying, 'Even if I do not always succeed [in obeying the commandments], yet, as a loving father, he will not be angry with me,' while the Gentile slave is always afraid lest he may commit some fault and therefore serves God in a condition of anxiety and confusion" (*Tanḥuma*, Noach, 19). Those who have experienced both a Jewish Sabbath and a Puritan Sunday will understand.
40. M. Barth, *Ephesians* (Garden City: Doubleday, 1974) 244-48; "Die Stellung des Paulus zu Gesetz und Ordnung," *EvT* 33 (1973) 496-526. Among the more important corrections to the all pervasive false concept of Jewish legalism, see E. P. Sanders, "On the Question of Fulfilling the Law in Paul and Rabbinic Judaism," *Donum Gentilicium* (ed. E. Bammel, C. K. Barrett, W. D. Davies; Oxford: Clarendon, 1978) 103-26.
41. Moore, *Judaism*, 1:277. He points out that it was the teaching of the schools both of Ishmael and Akiba and therefore prior to both. For earlier parallels see note 48 below.
42. *Exod. Rab.* 5. 9 (Soncino, 86-87). Cf. Bar 4:1, "She [wisdom] is the book of the commandments of God and the law that endures forever. All who hold her fast will live, and those who forsake her will die," and the passages contrasting Torah as medicine of life and medicine of death in Billerbeck, 3:130f, 498f.
43. See C. Roetzel, "Diathēkai in Romans 9,4," *Bib* 51 (1970) 377-90. This tendency will have been influenced by the Aramaic *qeyama*, which means both covenant and promise.
44. D. Rössler, *Gesetz und Geschichte* (Neukirchen: Neukirchener Verlag, 1960), made a beginning. He dealt only with 4 Ezra and *2 Baruch*, on which see the

more thorough study by W. Harnisch, *Verhängnis und Verheissung der Geschichte* (Göttingen: Vandenhoeck und Ruprecht, 1969).

45. A. Nissen, "Torah und Geschichte in Spätjudentum," *NT* 9 (1967) 241-77; *Gott und der Nächste im antiken Judentum* (Tübingen: Mohr, 1974), especially 46-98. Why did Christian interpreters not learn this long ago from such classic works as S. Schechter, *Some Aspects of Rabbinic Theology* (New York: Macmillan, 1909) or A. Büchler, *Studies in Sin and Atonement* (Oxford: University Press, 1928), especially 1-118?
46. Sanders, "Covenant." He concludes, "salvation comes by *membership* in the covenant, while obedience to the commandments *preserves* one's place in the covenant" (41).
47. See L. Monsengwo Pasinya, *La Notion de Nomos dans le Pentateuque Grec* (Rome: Biblical Institute Press, 1973).
48. See pseudo-Philo, *LAB* 11:2, where God tells Moses, "You shall illumine my people through that which I have given into your hands, the eternal law, and according to it I will judge the whole world. For it will be for a testimony. For when men say, 'We have not known thee and therefore we did not serve thee,' for that reason I shall punish them because they did not acknowledge my law." Cf. also the Hebrew *Test. Naph.* 8-9, which may antedate the Christian era.
49. That Torah in the intertestamental period has been connected with the order of creation, so that it encompasses all creatures, has been shown by Limbeck, *Ordnung*.
50. Note how in the Targums especially, Adam was to keep all the commandments and he and his descendants were punished for not doing so, Gen 2:15 (*Neofiti*), 3:15 (*Ps.-Jon.*), 3:22 (*Pal.*).
51. So *Jub*, *Test XII Patr.*, *2 Bar*, Sir; cf. *MKid.* 4:4. Cf. J. P. Schultz, "Two Views of the Patriarchs: Noachides and pre-Sinai Israelites," *Texts and Responses* (ed. M. A. Fishbane and P. R. Flohr; Leiden: Brill, 1975) 43-59.
52. For the Torah as antidote to the sin of Adam and the evil impulse, see *Kid.* 30b, *B. Bat.* 16a, *Shab.* 146a, etc. "In any case death was due to Adam and deliverance from sin came by the Torah," Knox, *Gentiles*, 95. "Sinai had restored a proper relationship between God and Israel through the mediatorship of Torah," R. Scroggs, *The Last Adam* (Oxford: Blackwell, 1965) 38.
53. See also 4 Ezra 3:32-36; 5:28-29; 7:11, 37, 70-73, 79-82, 127-129; 8:12-13, 55-58; 9:10-13; 13:37-38; *1 Enoch* 5:4; 93:4; 99:6-7; *2 Enoch* 65:4-5; *2 Bar* 15:4-6; 48:40-43; 54:14-19; 82:3-9; *Jub* 15:26-31; *Visio Ezra* 63, etc.
54. On the significance of these see M. Hengel, *Die Zeloten* (Leiden: Brill, 1961) 204-11.
55. See J. T. Townsend, "I Corinthians 3:15 and the School of Shammai," *HTR* 61 (1968) 500-504; K. Haacker, "War Paulus Hillelit?" *Das Institutum Judaicum der Universität Tübingen 1971-1972*, 106-20; H. Hübner, "Gal 3,10 und die Herkunft des Paulus," *KD* 19 (1973) 215-31; see Davies, *Paul*, 66.
56. R. Bultmann, *RGG*[2], 4:1021; Schoeps, *Paul*, 168, 219; Bornkamm, *Paul*, 10-12.
57. The fundamental study is D. Georgi, *Die Gegner des Paulus im 2. Korintherbrief* (Neukirchen: Neukirchener Verlag, 1964). See also J. Collange, *Enigmes de la deuxième épître de Paul aux Corinthiens* (Cambridge: University Press, 1972).

58. At least I have not been able to find it, and the only person who claims that the phrase is "an inherited Jewish formula," E. Lohmeyer, *Grundlagen paulinischer Theologie* (Tübingen: Mohr, 1929) 142, is able to cite no passages outside the Pauline writings themselves (24ff). More characteristic are phrases like "take upon oneself the yoke of the Kingdom of God/ commandments/ Torah" or "come under the wings of the Shekinah."
59. In addition to the inclusive and exclusive uses, perhaps we shall have to call this usage the "hospital we" (pluralis sociativus), as in the nurse's "How are we this morning?" As an indication of how far Paul's identification with his congregations could go, see Phil 3:7.
60. Gal 3:19, according to the oldest MSS. "Added because of transgressions" in later MSS is an interpolation from Rom 5:20, where it makes sense, whereas it contradicts the context in Galatians (cf. 3:15).
61. The phrase does not appear in the Greek of Rom 2:12, which should be translated: "Those who have sinned godlessly will perish godlessly, while those who have sinned in [the status of] Torah will be judged on the basis of Torah." Cf. James 2:12.
62. The Torah as covenant and commandments is only for Israel and irrelevant for Gentiles. There are of course many passages where *nomos* is equivalent to Scripture, which was "written for our instruction" (Rom 15:4; 1 Cor 10:11). Torah as teaching remains valid also for Gentiles.
63. Cf. Scroggs, *Adam*, 76-82.
64. Cf. M. Hooker, "Adam in Romans 1," *NTS* 6 (1959-60) 297-306.
65. Cf. S. Lyonnet, "'Tu ne convoiteras pas' (Rom. vii 7)," *Neotestamentica et Patristica* (Leiden: Brill, 1962) 157-65.
66. That this is the sense of two key passages in Rom 3:21-31 and 10:4ff has been shown by G. Howard in two very suggestive studies in *HTR* 63 (1970) 223-33, and *JBL* 88 (1969), 331-37.
67. The concept is Eckardt's, *Elder and Younger*, 137-40.
68. The title of the epilogue of J. Parkes, *The Foundations of Judaism and Christianity* (London: Vallentine-Mitchell, 1960).
69. "To the Jew, all of Paul's theology is a dialogue with the Gentiles in which the Jew is assumed and is silent," A. Cohen, *The Myth of the Judeo-Christian Tradition* (New York: Schocken, 1971) 75. A close look at what Paul does *not* say makes his silences become very eloquent for the present time.

NOTES TO CHAPTER TWO

1. A very interesting exception is A. Vanhoye, "Un médiateur des anges en Ga 3, 19-20" *Bib* 59 (1978) 403-11. Combining Acts 7:53 and 38 to provide a "parallel," he argues that the mediator is a single angel who mediates for the

many angels (parallel to the one mediator Moses, who mediates for the many Israelites). But because the second half of the "schéma" is completely unexpressed and because his exegesis of Acts is problematic, his solution is not acceptable.

2. W. Barclay, *The Letters to the Galatians and Ephesians* (Edinburgh: St. Andrews, 1962) 31-32.
3. H. D. Betz, *Galatians* (Philadelphia: Fortress, 1979) 169.
4. See the article with this title by Judah Goldin in *Religions in Antiquity* (ed. J. Neusner; Leiden: Brill, 1968) 412-24.
5. P. Schäfer, *Rivalität zwischen Engeln und Menschen* (Berlin: de Gruyter, 1975) 43-51, 72.
6. It cannot be demonstrated here why a reference to the giving of the law would be inappropriate at this point in Hebrews; see R. Jewett, *Letter to Pilgrims* (New York: Pilgrim, 1981) 39.
7. See Aristides, *Apol.* 14:2; *Kerygma Petrou* in Clem. Alex., *Strom* 6.5.40; and M. Simon, *St. Stephen and the Hellenists* (London: Longmans, Green, 1958) 109f.
8. See G. Delling, *TWNT* 8:35, n11. In some passages (e.g., *Jub.* 6:22; 30:12) it seems that the Torah had been written down by the angel after God had revealed it orally to Moses; see L. Ginzberg, *An Unknown Jewish Sect* (New York: Jewish Theological Seminary of America, 1976) 173. Similarly, in the *Apocalypse of Moses*, the "story and way of life of Adam and Eve, the first created," while it was "taught by the Archangel Michael," was "revealed by God to Moses his Servant when he received the tables of the law of the covenant from the hand of the Lord" (K. von Tischendorf, *Apocalypses Apocryphae Mosis, Esdrae, Pauli, Joannis. . .* [Leipzig, 1866] 1).
9. Passages such as Acts 7:38, where a single angel replaces the God of the Biblical narrative, do not belong here; cf. J. Jeremias, *TWNT* 4:870, n209. Angels as mediators of revelation to a prophet or seer (Enoch, Ezra) should also not be confused with the giving of the law.
10. See H. A. Wolfson, *Philo* (Cambridge: Harvard University Press, 1962) 1:376; 2:38f.
11. Betz, *Galatians*, 169, modifying the translation of R. Marcus, who reads "messengers," i.e. prophets.
12. Ginzberg, *Unknown Jewish Sect*, 172.
13. Josephus, *J.W.* 1.378, in the earlier parallel passage.
14. Slightly modified from the translation of R. Marcus. See W. D. Davies, "A Note on Josephus, Antiquities 15.136," *HTR* 47 (1954) 135-40.
15. J. Abelson, *The Immanence of God in Rabbinical Literature* (London: Macmillan, 1912). Cf. also the almost despairing puzzlement with Christian writers of S. Schechter, *Aspects of Rabbinic Theology* (New York: Schocken, 1961) 21ff.
16. That there is no Jewish parallel to Paul's statement is asserted by such different scholars as J. Jeremias, *TWNT* 4:870, n210, and Ginzberg, *Unknown Jewish Sect*, 172-74.
17. Lines 276-80, 252-55. See T. F. Glasson, *Greek Influence in Jewish Eschatology*

(London: SPCK, 1961) 69-73.

18. F. M. Cornford, *From Religion to Philosophy* (1912, reprint, New York: Harper, 1957) is still a classic study.
19. Sir 17:17, Dan 12:1, *Jub.* 15:31f, *Heb. Test. Naph.* 8:3-9:4, *1 Enoch* 89:59; 90:22, 25, Philo, *Post.* 91, *Targum Ps.-J* Gen 11:7f; Deut 32:8f., ps. Clem. *Rec.* 2:42; 8:50, Irenaeus, *Haer.* 3, 12, 9, etc.; *Mekilta*, Shirata 2, etc. In general, for passages see J. Michl, "Engel," *RAC* 5:53-259.
20. G. Caird, *Principalities and Powers* (Oxford: Clarendon, 1956) 7f.
21. Cf. H. Ringgren, *Word and Wisdom* (Lund: Ohlssons, 1947); H. H. Schmid, *Gerechtigkeit als Weltordnung* (Tübingen: Mohr, 1968); M. Limbeck, *Die Ordnung des Heils* (Düsseldorf: Patmos, 1971); K. Hoheisel, *Das antike Judentum in christlicher Sicht* (Wiesbaden: Harrassowitz, 1978).
22. See on this especially, J. Marböck, "Gesetz und Weisheit: Zum Verständnis des Gesetzes bei Jesus Ben Sira," *BZ* 20 (1976) 1-21.
23. Cf. 4 Ezra 3:32-36; 5:28f., 7:11, 37, 70-73, 79-82, 127-29; 8:12f., 55-58; 9:10-13; 13:37f; *1 Enoch* 5:4; 93:4; 99:6f.; *2 Enoch* 65:4f.; *2 Bar* 15:4-6; 48:40-43; 54:14-19; *Jub.* 15:26-31; *Visio Ezra* 63.
24. *Mekilta*, Baḥodesh 5; cf. *Lam. R.* 3:1.
25. *Shab.* 88b; cf. *Exod. R.* 5:9.
26. *TSot.* 8:6; cf. *Sot.* 35b.
27. "Or, according to R. Jose the son of R. Halfta, these angels [of Ps 68:18] were the princely counterparts in heaven of the nations of the earth" (*Pes. Rab.* 21). "You find that in the hour that the Holy One, blessed be He, came down to Sinai, hosts and hosts of angels came down with him, as it is said: 'With mighty chariotry, twice ten thousand, thousands upon thousands, the Lord came from Sinai to the holy place' (Ps 68:18). From them the nations of the world chose for themselves gods. It is like a king who entered a city, and in his court were rulers and princes and generals. One chose for himself a ruler for a patron, another a prince, and again another a general. But a very clever man was there. He said to himself: all these are dependent on the king and cannot do anything against him as he can against them. I choose for myself only the king as patron, who can withstand them all. Thus it was also in the hour when the Holy One, blessed be He, revealed himself on Sinai and the nations of the world chose gods for themselves. One chose for himself the sun, another the moon, another stars and planets, and again another angels. But Israel said to the Holy One, blessed be He: out of all these gods we have chosen only you, as it is said: 'The Lord is my portion, says my soul'" (Lam 3:24) (*Midrash Tannaim*, ed. D. Hoffmann, 190-91). Cf. also Deut 2:34.
28. "That the whole law was revealed at Sinai to all nations and offered to them for their acceptance, but refused by all except Israel . . . was the teaching of both the great schools of the second century, the schools of Ishmael and Akiba, and is therefore presumably part of the earlier common tradition from which they drew" (G. F. Moore, *Judaism* [Cambridge: Harvard University Press, 1927] 1:277). Cf. also H. J. Schoeps, "Haggadisches zur Auserwählung Israels," *Aus frühchristlicher Zeit* (Tübingen: Mohr, 1950) 184-200. In pseudo-Philo, *LAB* 11:2, God tells Moses, "You shall illumine my people through that which I have

given into your hands, the eternal law, and according to it I will judge the whole world. For it will be for a testimony. For when men say, 'We have not known thee and therefore we did not serve thee,' for that reason I shall punish them because they did not acknowledge my law."

29. Fragment 4 (Funk-Bihlmeyer). M. P. Nilsson, *Geschichte der griechischen Religion* (2nd ed.; Munich: Beck, 1961) 2:569-78, shows how in the Hellenistic period the philosophic belief in "powers," the analogy of the universal monarchical state, and the need to come to terms with what would be called today religious pluralism produced what he calls a "Drang zum Monotheismus." Of particular interest to us is the fact that subordinate deities were sometimes called *mesitēs* (576-78), or, specifically in Anatolian inscriptions, a *theios angelos* or *angelikos* (577, 662). See F. Sokolowski, "Sur le culte d'Angelos dans le paganisme grec et romain," *HTR* 53 (1960) 225-29.
30. Hippolytus, *Ref.* 6.19.8.
31. Irenaeus, *Haer.* 1.23.3.
32. Irenaeus, *Haer.* 1.24.4; cf. Cerinthus (1.26.1), Menander (1.23.5), Carpocrates (1.25.1, 4), Saturnilus (1.24.1-2), Baruch (*Ref.* 5.26.11).
33. Hippolytus, *Ref.* 6.34.3.
34. (Codex II) 105:12-16. For other references see F. T. Fallon, *The Enthronement of Sabbaoth* (Leiden: Brill, 1978) 103-4, and B. Przybylski, "The Role of Cathedrical Data in Gnostic Literature," *VC* 34 (1980) 56-70.
35. That this is a Hellenistic commonplace can be shown by such a conveyer of commonplaces as Maximus of Tyre: "You see in the whole world one unanimous law and teaching, [viz.] that there is one god, the king and father of all things, and many gods, the children of god, the co-rulers of god. The Greek says this and the barbarian says it and the mainlander and the islander and the wise and the foolish" (*Orat.* 11, no. 4, p. 132, ed. Hobein).
36. There is a conscious confluence of Hellenistic and Biblical concepts concerning the administration of the angels of the nations in Origen, e.g. *C. Cels.* 5:25ff. See J. Daniélou, *Origen* (New York: Sheed and Ward, 1955) 220-45.
37. H. Schlier *Der Brief an die Galater* (Göttingen: Vandenhoeck und Ruprecht, 1951) 105-20.
38. B. Reicke, "The Law and This World According to Paul," *JBL* 70 (1951) 259-76.
39. On which see especially E. Schweizer, "Die 'Elemente der Welt' Gal 4,3.9; Kol 2,8.20," *Beiträge zur Theologie des Neuen Testaments* (Zürich: Zwingli, 1970) 147-63.
40. "The essential principle in the precepts concerning idolatry is that we are not to worship any thing created—neither angel, sphere, star, none of the four elements nor whatever has been formed from them" (*Mishneh Torah*, Book I, Treatise 4 [Idolatry], II, 1 [67a]).
41. Cf. also *Mos.* 1.96; 2.53; *Decal.* 52-3; *Spec.* 1.13-15.
42. N. Kehl, *Der Christushymnus im Kolosserbrief* (Stuttgart: Katholisches Bibelwerk, 1967), 145-61.
43. The shorter text of 3:19a ought to be seriously considered: "Why then the law of deeds, until the seed should come to whom [the promise] was promised?" (*ti*

oun ho nomos tōn praxiōn achris an, ktl.). 1. It is found in the earliest witness, P[46] 2. Irenaeus cites it thus twice, and in one passage (*Haer.* 3.7.2) where he analyses the grammar he must have had the text open in front of him. 3. The longer text contradicts the context (3:15, 22). 4. The source of the longer text is easily explained (Rom 5:20). 5. The shorter text is the *lectio difficilior* ("law of deeds"). In any case, one should not let the interpretation of 3:19b be determined by an uncertain text of 3:19a. See H. Eshbaugh, "Textual Variants and Theology: A Study of the Galatians Text of Papyrus 46," *JSNT* 3 (1979) 60-72.

44. J. B. Lightfoot, *St. Paul's Epistle to the Galatians* (London: Macmillan, 1869) 144.
45. That v 20a is not a general statement about mediatorship but explicative is argued by C. H. Giblin, "Three Monotheistic Texts in Paul," *CBQ* 37 (1975) 540-41.
46. That the genitive is a genitive of quality (*BDF*, 165) is argued by V. Stolle, "Die Eins in Gal 3, 15-29," *Theokratia II* (Leiden: Brill, 1973) 207-8.
47. E.g. according to H. Lietzmann, *Galater* (Tübingen: Mohr, 1971), ad loc., the law was "gar nicht unmittelbar von Gott gegeben, sondern durch die Engel, deren Vermittler dann *weiterhin* Moses gewesen ist."
48. H. J. Schoeps, *Paul* (Philadelphia: Westminster, 1959) 213-18.
49. This chapter was originally presented as a paper to the Fourteenth Quinquennial Congress of the International Association for the History of Religions at the University of Manitoba, 17-22 August 1980. Since that time, Lou H. Silberman, "Prophets/Angels: LXX and Qumran Psalm 151 and the Epistle to the Hebrews," *Standing before God* (ed. A. Finkel and L. Frizzel; New York: KTAV, 1981) 91-101, has also argued that there is no Jewish tradition which speaks of angelic mediation of the Torah to Israel.

NOTES TO CHAPTER THREE

1. Cf. now the exciting approach of a systematic theologian, P. van Buren, *Discerning the Way: A Theology of the Jewish-Christian Reality* (New York: Seabury, 1980).
2. G. Klein, "Römer 4 und die Idee der Heilsgeschichte" (1963), "Individualgeschichte und Weltgeschichte bei Paulus" (1964), "Exegetische Probleme in Römer 3, 21-4, 25" (1964) in *Rekonstruktion und Interpretation* (Munich: Kaiser, 1969) 145-69, 180-224, 170-79. There have been many reactions to his provocative theses, none of which I find adequate. Cf. U. Wilckens, "Zu Römer 3, 21-4, 25" (1964), in *Rechtfertigung als Freiheit* (Neukirchen: Neukirchener Verlag, 1974) 50-76; K. Berger, "Abraham in den paulinischen Hauptbriefen," *MTZ* 17 (1966) 47-89; H. Boers, *Theology out of the Ghetto* (Leiden: Brill,

1977) 74-104; E. Käsemann, "The Faith of Abraham in Romans 4," *Perspectives on Paul* (Philadelphia: Fortress, 1971) 79-101.

3. A. Jülicher on Romans in *Die Schriften des Neuen Testaments* (Göttingen: Vandenhoeck und Ruprecht, 1907) 2:249.
4. Klein, "Römer 4," 150f.
5. G. von Rad, *Old Testament Theology* (New York: Harper, 1962) 1:379.
6. G. von Rad, "Faith Reckoned as Righteousness" (1951), *The Problem of the Hexateuch and Other Essays* (New York: McGraw-Hill, 1966) 125-30, all quotations on p. 130.
7. F. Hahn, "Genesis 15:6 im Neuen Testament," *Probleme biblischer Theologie* (Munich: Kaiser, 1971) 107.
8. H. J. Schoeps, *Paul* (Philadelphia: Westminster, 1961) 213-18.
9. E. P. Sanders, *Paul and Palestinian Judaism* (Philadelphia: Fortress, 1977) 33-59.
10. C. Westermann, *Genesis: Biblischer Kommentar*, Vol 1, Part 2 (Neukirchen: Neukirchener Verlag, 1981) 263.
11. It was known to Calvin, who fatefully rejected it. "They also, no less skillfully, corrupt the text, who say that Abram is here ascribing to God the glory of righteousness, seeing that he ventures to acquiesce surely in his promises, acknowledging Him to be faithful and true; for although Moses does not expressly mention the name of God, yet the accustomed method of speaking in the Scriptures removes all ambiquity." (*Genesis* [London: Banner of Truth Trust, 1965] 406). Whether Calvin is apt to be more familiar with the "accustomed manner of speaking in the Scriptures" than Ramban is to be doubted. An isolated insight is a single sentence in G. A. F. Knight, *Deutero-Isaiah* (New York: Abingdon, 1965) 208: "The words of Gen 15:6 . . . mean literally, 'And he found himself firm upon Yahweh, and he counted it to him as saving activity.'"
12. Rashi had said: "The Holy One, blessed to be He, counted it to Abram for merit (the *zkw* of the Targum) and for righteousness because of the faith with which he believed in Him."
13. On the contrary, it is to this passage, 15:8, that later Rabbinic tradition appeals when it wants to speak of Abraham's lack of faith (*Ned.* 32a).
14. Cf. L. Perlitt, *Bundestheologie im Alten Testament* (Neukirchen: Neukirchener Verlag, 1969); O. Kaiser, "Traditionsgeschichtliche Untersuchung von Genesis 15," *ZAW* 70 (1958) 107-26; Westermann, *Genesis*; J. van Seters, *Abraham in History and Tradition* (New Haven: Yale University Press, 1975); and the literature reviewed by them. I have not been able to consult J. Hoftijzer, *Die Verheissungen an die drei Erzväter* (Leiden: Brill, 1956).
15. Van Seters, *Abraham*, especially 249-78.
16. Kaiser, "Genesis 15. "
17. J. Begrich, "Das priesterliche Heilsorakel," *ZAW* 52 (1934) 81-92; see also C. Westermann, "Das Heilswort bei Deuterojesaja," *EvT* 24 (1964) 355-73.
18. C. Westermann, *The Promises to the Fathers* (Philadelphia: Fortress, 1980) 15.
19. C. Westermann, *The Praise of God in the Psalms* (London: Epworth, 1965) 64.

20. von Rad, "Faith."
21. Cf. Seybold, *ḥšb*, *TWAT* 3:243-61.
22. It is interesting that J. Pedersen, *Israel: Its Life and Culture I-II* (London: Oxford, 1926) 530, citing from memory, thinks that Gen 15:6 does read "*hashabh le̱*!"
23. Especially helpful have been A. Schoors, *I Am God Your Saviour: A Form-Critical Study of the Main Genres in Is XL-LV* (Leiden: Brill, 1973), and F. V. Reiterer, *Gerechtigkeit als Heil: ZDQ bei Deuterojesaja*; *Aussage und Vergleich mit der alttestamentlichen Tradition* (Graz: Akademische Druck-und Verlagsanstalt, 1976). It is to be noted that Westermann does not include Isa 51:1-8 among the oracles of salvation but in a second category, related to the collective lament, which he calls "proclamation of salvation."
24. Is it because of that or the righteousness of God that the Targum interprets Isa 41:2 of Abraham rather than Cyrus? "Who brought Abraham quickly from the east, even the chosen of righteousness in truth."
25. It is not possible to discuss here the importance of Israel "pursuing righteousness" (v 1) and the Torah going out to the Gentiles (v 4) for understanding Rom 9:30ff. See Chapter 8.
26. The incorporation of the concept of blessing into a history seen under the perspective of the promises of God is called by Westermann "one of the most theologically significant innovations of the early history of Israel," *Blessing in the Bible and the Life of the Church* (Philadelphia: Fortress, 1978) 53. Cf. also van Seters, *Abraham*, 271-78.
27. So Reiterer, *Gerechtigkeit*, 59-69.
28. "It is not improbable that DI has in mind the story told in Gen xv.1-6, in which Abram is distressed because he is childless. Yahweh bad him 'Look (*habbêt*, cf. the repeated *babbîtû* in the present passage) at the heavens,' and promised him that his descendants would be as numerous as the stars," (*The Second Isaiah* [Oxford: Clarendon, 1964] 209).
29. Cf. Perlitt, *Bundestheologie*, 66f; Westermann, *Promises*, 130.
30. A later midrash connects in an interesting manner Abraham, righteousness (of God?), and justification (of Gentiles?): "Said the Holy One, blessed be He, to Abraham: 'Thou hast loved righteousness' (Ps 45:8); thou hast loved to justify my creatures" (*Gen. Rab.* 49:9).
31. R. E. Clements, *Abraham and David: Genesis 15 and Its Meaning for Israelite Tradition* (London: SCM, 1967) 69, who does not follow his own insight. Gen 15:1-6 "derives from a time in which the possession of the land began to be doubtful for Israel" (H. Gunkel, *Genesis* [Göttingen: Vandenhoeck und Ruprecht, 1966] 183); "emanates from the period when Israel's tenure of Canaan began to be precarious" (J. Skinner, *Genesis* [Edinburgh: T. and T. Clark, 1930] 284); "derived from a period when matters of faith were a problem" (G. von Rad, *Genesis* [London: SCM, 1972] 190). But surely even more important than the land is the threatened loss of peoplehood, as the reference to *many* descendants (Gen 15:5; Isa 51:2; cf. 54:1) indicates.
32. Cf. M. Anbar (Bernstein), "The Covenant between the Pieces—Gen 15" (Hebrew), *Shnaton Lemiqra* 3 (1978-79) 41.

33. "I am YHWH, who brought you from Ur of the Chaldeans," Gen 15:7.
34. "And he [Abram] trusted in YHWH," Gen 15:6.
35. "YHWH made with Abram a covenant," Gen 15:18.
36. "I give this land," Gen 15:18.
37. A similar list, with these names in a different order and with the addition of the Rephaim is found in Gen 15:20f; v 19 has three additional names.
38. "To your seed I have given," Gen 15:18.
39. "And he counted it to him righteousness," Gen 15:6.
40. LXX and the Greek tradition following it; Targum Neofiti; Peshitta.
41. Contrary to the overly subtle distinctions made by H. W. Heidland, "Logizomai," *TWNT* 4:287-95, cf. Seybold, *ḥšb*.
42. M. Black, *Romans* (London: Oliphants, 1973) 76, is one of the few to notice the significance of the *eis*: "The view that Abraham's 'faith' was 'reckoned to him' as *equivalent* to 'righteousness' is less convincing than to take 'for righteousness' as meaning that Abraham's faith was counted to his credit 'with a view to the receiving of righteousness.' "
43. It is probable that this is the understanding of Targum Onkelos, which not only has a preposition but also uses the word "merit" (*lzkw*). Such an understanding is also clear in *Jub*. 30, where the deed of Simeon and Levi against the Shechemites was "counted to them for righteousness," defined as "written down to them for righteousness" (v 18), "written for a blessing" (v 23); "they inscribe as a testimony in his favour on the heavenly tablets blessing and righteousness" (v 19); "until a thousand generations they will record it and it will come to him and to his descendants after him" (v 20).
44. Cf. A. Marmorstein, *The Doctrine of Merits in Old Rabbinical Literature* (New York: KTAV, repr. 1968); G. F. Moore, *Judaism* (Cambridge: Harvard University Press, 1927-30) 1:535-45; Sanders, *Paul*, 183-98.
45. That Abraham and his seed were the recipients of God's righteousness (= mercy), cf. *Jub*. 31:25, "And Isaac blessed the God of his father Abraham, who had not withdrawn his mercy and his righteousness from the sons of his servant Isaac."
46. Philo, *L.A*. 3.228, *Kai dikaios enomisthē*. For other passages where Philo cites Gen 15:6, cf. J. B. Lightfoot, *Galatians* (London: Macmillan, 1869) 158.
47. *Mekilta de Rabbi Ishmael*, Beshallaḥ 4 (Lauterbach, 1:220).
48. Marmorstein, *Merits*, 37.
49. Cf. R. B. Ward, "The Works of Abraham; James 2:14-26," *HTR* 61 (1968) 283-90.
50. So the reading of Alexandrinus, which may be original (Vaticanus and Sinaiticus follow LXX). The omission of the preposition (as in MT) seems to make it even clearer that it is a question of God's righteousness. At least the other examples cited in the context (Joseph, Phinehas, Joshua, Caleb, David, Elijah, Hananiah, Azariah, Mishael, and Daniel) all receive a later reward for their faithfulness, not a declaration at the time.
51. Translation according to M. Black, "Critical and Exegetical Notes on Three New Testament Texts, Hebrews xi.11, Jude 5, James i.27," *Apophoreta: Festschrift für Ernst Haenchen* (Berlin: Töpelmann, 1964) 39-45, which is

simpler than the textual emendation proposed by G. Zuntz, *The Text of the Epistles* (London: Oxford University Press, 1953) 16, 170.

52. Cf. N. Dahl, "The Story of Abraham in Luke-Acts," *Studies in Luke-Acts* (ed. L. E. Keck and J. L. Martyn; New York: Abingdon, 1966) 139-58.

53. G. Deissmann, *Paul: A Study in Social and Religious History* (London: Hodder and Stoughton, 1926) 169.

54. F. Mussner, *Der Galaterbrief* (Freiburg: Herder, 1974) 220. Berger "Abraham," begins his article, "In Gal 3 the salvation gift of the Christians, the Spirit which they received (3:2-5), is presented as the content of the promise to Abraham; the attainment of which was dependent on the same condition as the obtaining of the promise: by faith."

55. For an important beginning in this direction, see G. Howard, *Paul: Crisis in Galatia* (Cambridge: Cambridge University Press, 1979) 46-65. See also E. Jacob, "Abraham et sa signification pour la foi chrétienne," *RHPR* 42 (1962) 148-56.

56. On this important concept see H. Cremer, *Die paulinische Rechtfertigungslehre im Zusammenhang ihrer geschichtlichen Voraussetzungen* (Gütersloh: Bertelsmann, 1901); A. Schlatter, *Gottes Gerechtigkeit: Ein Kommentar zum Römerbrief* (Stuttgart: Calwer Verlag, 1959); E. Käsemann, "Gottesgerechtigkeit bei Paulus," *ZThK* 58 (1961) 367-78; P. Stuhlmacher, *Gerechtigkeit Gottes bei Paulus* (Göttingen: Vandenhoeck und Ruprecht, 1965); D. Hill, *Greek Words and Hebrew Meanings* (Cambridge: Cambridge University Press, 1967) 82-162; K. Kertelge, *"Rechtfertigung" bei Paulus* (Münster: Aschendorff, 1967); J. A. Ziesler, *The Meaning of Righteousness in Paul* (Cambridge: Cambridge University Press, 1972); F. Crüsemann, "Jahwes Gerechtigkeit im Alten Testament," *EvT* 36 (1976) 427-50; M. T. Brauch, "Perspectives on 'God's righteousness' in recent German discussion," in Sanders, *Paul*, 523-42.

57. According to modern interpreters *ṣdqh* refers to God's righteousness in the Torah only in Deut 33:21. Paul also hears God's righteousness proclaimed in Deut 30:11-14, although the word does not appear (Rom 10:6-8).

58. Cf. Berger, "Abraham," 50.

59. "The unexpressed premise of this argument (v 7) is that men become acceptable to God and heirs of the promise on the same basis on which Abraham was accepted" (E. D. Burton, *Galatians* [Edinburgh, T. and T. Clark, 1921] 155). "The unexpressed premise of the argument, necessary to make this passage (v 11) prove the preceding proposition, is that no one does, in fact, continue in all the things that are written in the book of the law to do them" (ibid., 164). It is the "unexpressed premises" that allow us to read our own theology into a text which does not contain it at all.

60. New Testament theology would have done much better to follow Barth's *Römerbrief* than Bultmann's *Theology* in this matter. Cf. F.-W. Marquardt, *Die Juden im Römerbrief* (Zürich: Theologischer Verlag, 1971) 39: "*Pistis* is the possibility, which has now been opened for Gentiles and is to be acknowledged by Jews, for Gentiles to be together with Jews under God's command and promise, in order to praise the one God."

61. J. Haussleiter, *Der Glaube Jesu Christi und der christliche Glaube* (Leipzig,

1891); H. Ljungman, *Pistis* (Lund: Gleerup, 1964) 38-40; E. R. Goodenough, "Paul and the Hellenization of Christianity," *Religions in Antiquity* (ed. J. Neusner; Leiden: Brill, 1967) 35-80; M. Barth, "The Kerygma of Galatians," *Int* 21 (1967) 131-63; G. Howard, "On the Faith of Christ," *HTR* 60 (1967) 459-84; "The 'Faith of Christ,'" *ET* 85 (1974) 212-15; J. J. O'Rourke, "Pistis in Romans," *CBQ* 34 (1973) 188-94.

62. "The Function of *Pistis Christou* in Galatians," *JBL* 85 (1966) 58-76.
63. The reference seems to be to one group, the justified Gentiles, as distinguished from another group called those *ek nomou* (Rom 4:14, 16), those *ek peritomēs* (Rom 4:12; Gal 2:12), those *ex Israēl* (Rom 9:6).
64. See E. Bammel, "Gottes *Diathēkē* (Gal. iii. 15-17) und das jüdische Rechtsdenken," *NTS* 6 (1959-60) 313-19.
65. *Mekilta*, Pisḥa 14 (Lauterbach, 1.111). This dating is already presupposed by the LXX and Josephus. See D. Daube, "The Interpretation of a Generic Singular," *The New Testament and Rabbinic Judaism* (London: Athlone, 1956) 438-44.
66. For the possibility that this is the promise Paul is claiming for his gospel, see the suggestive book by W. Brueggemann, *The Land* (Philadelphia: Fortress, 1977).
67. See Chapter 1 and J. A. Sanders, "Torah and Paul," *God's Christ and His People* (ed. J. Jervell and W. Meeks; Oslo: Universitetsforlaget, 1977) 132-40.
68. Cf. D. M. Smith, "*Ho De Dikaios Ek Pisteōs Zēsetai*," *Studies in the History and Text of the New Testament* (ed. B. L. Daniels and M. J. Suggs; Salt Lake City: University of Utah Press, 1967) 13-25; and H. C. C. Cavallin, "The Righteous shall live by Faith; A Decisive Argument for the Traditional Interpretation," *ST* 32 (1978) 33-43.
69. The righteousness of God is often contrasted with our unrighteousness in early Judaism; cf. Dan 9:16, "O Lord, according to all thy righteousnesses let thy anger and thy wrath turn away"; 1QH 4:30f, "I know that a human being has no righteousness . . . to the Most High God belong all deeds of righteousness" or the last petition of the *Avinu Malkenu* prayer, "be gracious unto us and answer us, for we have no [good] deeds; deal with us in righteousness and faithfulness, and save us."
70. This may provide a clue for translating the notoriously difficult v 1. Along with Zahn and von Hofmann I would understand the "we" of the initial verb as the subject of the following infinitive and translate: "What shall we say then that we have gained in Abraham, our forefather according to the flesh?"
71. Cf. R. B. Hays, "Psalm 143 and the Logic of Romans 3," *JBL* 99 (1980) 107-15.
72. "Romans 3:21-31 and the Inclusion of the Gentiles," *HTR* 63 (1970) 223-33. See also his "Christ and the End of the Law: The Meaning of Romans 10:4ff," *JBL* 88 (1969) 331-37.
73. Cf. U. Mauser, "Galater iii.20: Die Universalität des Heils," *NTS* 13 (1967) 258-70; on the importance of Abraham in this connection, pp. 263-65.
74. That this is the reference and not the resurrection of Jesus is said among others by D. Zeller, *Juden und Heiden in der Mission des Paulus* (Stuttgart: Katholisches Bibelwerk, 1973) 105.

75. That commentators should not become all too spiritual in thinking of Abraham's faith and should recognize also its sexual implications is argued by M. Barth, *Foi et salut selon S. Paul* (Rome: Biblical Institute Press, 1970) 59-63, as did Calvin (*Romans*, ad loc.) before him.
76. For a slightly different understanding, see Chapter 8. Insofar as the usual interpretation in terms of the justification of Abraham can be called "positively blasphemous even for non-Jewish ears" (G. Bornkamm, *Paul* [New York: Harper, 1971] 143), perhaps it would be better to give up the interpretation rather than to accuse Paul of blasphemy.
77. M. Barth, *Justification* (Grand Rapids: Eerdmans, 1971) 67, has come very close to my understanding of Gen 15:6 (and to Ramban's use of Gen 50:20) when he writes: "Seeing the faith of his chosen, God confirms his gracious decision: he 'plans' faithfully, viz. 'in righteousness,' to carry out his promise at the proper time."

NOTES TO CHAPTER FOUR

1. S. Sandmel, *Anti-Semitism in the New Testament*? (Philadelphia: Fortress, 1978) 7, his italics.
2. W. Barclay, *Galatians* (Edinburgh: St. Andrew Press, 1958) 20. A similar influential popular work, W. Bousset on Galatians in *Die Schriften des Neuen Testaments* (Göttingen: Vandenhoeck und Ruprecht, 1907) 2:47, gives as a heading for 2:19-21 "Bewusster Bruch mit dem Gesetz."
3. G. Klein, "Individualgeschichte und Weltgeschichte bei Paulus," *Rekonstruktion und Interpretation* (Munich: Kaiser, 1969) 180-224. This essay has been widely discussed but in my opinion not yet successfully refuted. Cf. K. Berger, "Abraham in den paulinischen Hauptbriefen," *MTZ* 17 (1966) 47-89; H. Boers, *Theology out of the Ghetto* (Leiden: Brill, 1971) 74-82; M. Barth, "Die Stellung des Paulus zum Gesetz," *EvT* 33 (1973) 496-526; W. G. Kümmel, "'Individualgeschichte' und 'Weltgeschichte' in Gal 2:15-21," *Christ and Spirit in the New Testament* (ed. B. Lindars and S. Smally; Cambridge: Cambridge University Press, 1973) 157-73; H. Gollwitzer et al., "Der Jude Paulus und die deutsche neutestamentliche Wissenschaft," *EvT* 37 (1977) 549-87; M. Barth, "St. Paul—A Good Jew," *Horizons in Biblical Theology* 1 (1979) 7-45.
4. H. J. Schoeps, *Paul* (Philadelphia: Westminster, 1961) 213-18.
5. E. P. Sanders, "Patterns of Religion in Paul and Rabbinic Judaism," *HTR* 66 (1973) 455-78; *Paul and Palestinian Judaism* (Philadelphia: Fortress, 1977).
6. H.D. Betz, *Galatians* (Philadelphia: Fortress, 1979) 116. In addition I have used the commentaries of E. D. Burton, F. Mussner, H. Schlier, R. Bring, A. Oepke, P. Bonnard and the following articles: R. Bultmann, "Zur Auslegung von Galater 2:15-18," *Exegetica* (Tübingen: Mohr, 1967) 394-99; M. Barth, "Jews

and Gentiles: The Social Character of Justification in Paul," *JES* 5 (1968) 241-67; U. Wilkens, "Was heisst bei Paulus: 'Aus Werken des Gesetzes wird kein Mensch gerecht'?" *Evangelisch-katholischer Kommentar zum NT. Vorarbeiten.* (Zürich: Benziger, 1969) 1:51-77; J. Lambrecht, "The Line of Thought in Gal 2:14b-21," *NTS* 24 (1978) 484-95.

7. Cf. especially Berger, "Abraham," 47-49.
8. With respect to the situation of Galatians, I assume that it was written during Paul's Ephesian period to the churches of North Galatia, which were completely Gentile. Many of these Galatian Christians were beginning to Judaize (not to convert to Judaism), probably along lines that are clearer in Colossians. Recognition of this situation is much more important than any attempt to identify "opponents." (In particular, the situation in Corinth, where the rival apostles are Jewish Christians but where Judaizing or the law are not an issue at all, is quite different and may not be used to cast light on Galatians.) While the troublemakers who try to get the Galatians to Judaize are probably themselves Gentile Judaizers, this is not crucial for understanding the situation. It is not sure whether they are members of the Galatian churches or come from outside. In any case, they are in no sense to be understood as coming from James. Paul's argument is not with Jewish Christians, in Antioch or Jerusalem, or with Jews, but with the Galatian Judaizers. He does not argue with his opponents, even at second hand, but only calls them names (Gal 5:10-12; 1:6-9) and urges that they be cast out (1:6-9; 4:30). All of Paul's arguments in Galatians must be understood as being directed to the Galatian Judaizers and not to those who "court zealously" (4:17) or "trouble" (1:7; 5:10, 12) or "compel" (6:12-13) them.
9. Betz, *Galatians*, 113-14.
10. "Table fellowship with Gentiles had become a serious transgression of the law" (Bring, *Galatians*, 84); "die Ubertretung einzelner Gebote, wie es sich Petrus in Antiochien hatte zuschulden kommen lassen" (Bultmann, "Auslegung," 398); "the statutes of the law which Paul had declared to be invalid" (Burton, *Galatians*, 130); "the Halakha which forbids Jews and Gentiles to eat together" (A. T. Hanson, *Studies in Paul's Technique and Theology* [London: SPCK, 1974] 28). The unconscious attempt to interpret Gal 2:11-14 in the light of Mark 7 is of course completely illegitimate. Nothing is said at all about the food eaten but only about the company. Acts 10:28; 11:3 reflect a similar misunderstanding. Cf. G. F. Moore, *Judaism* (Cambridge: Harvard University Press, 1927-1930) 2:75.
11. And some statements which presupposes it, e.g. *Ber* 7:1.
12. I would understand it in general accordance with B. Reicke, "Der geschichtliche Hintergrund des Apostelkonzils und der Antiochia-Episode," *Studia Paulina in honorem J. de Zwaan* (Haarlem: Bohn, 1953) 172-87; D. Bronson, "Paul, Galatians, and Jerusalem," *JAAR* 35 (1967) 119-28; R. Jewett, "The Agitators and the Galatian Congregation," *NTS* 17 (1970) 198-212; W. Schmithals, *Paul and James* (London: SCM, 1965); and G. Howard, *Paul: Crisis in Galatia* (Cambridge: University Press, 1979).
13. Cf. e.g. D. Zeller, *Juden und Heiden in der Mission des Paulus* (Stuttgart:

Katholisches Bibelwerk, 1973). This is of course the exact opposite of the thesis argued by Klein. Cf. also P. Richardson, *Israel in the Apostolic Church* (Cambridge: Cambridge University Press, 1969) 22-25.

14. See R. B. Hays, "Psalm 143 and the Logic of Romans 3," *JBL* 99 (1980) 107-15.
15. Note the conjunction of the two concepts in such passages as 1QH 4:30-31, "I know that a human being has no righteousness . . . to the Most High God belong all deeds of righteousness" or the last petition of the Avinu Malkenu prayer: "Be gracious unto us and answer us, for we have no [good] deeds; deal with us in righteousness and faithfulness (*ṣdqh wḥsd*), and save us."
16. J. B. Tyson, " 'Works of Law' in Galatians," *JBL* 92 (1973) 430.
17. 1QS 5:21; 6:18; *2 Apoc. Bar.* 57:2 contain close verbal parallels but are quite different in substance.
18. M. Barth, *Ephesians* (Garden City: Doubleday, 1974) 1:244-48.
19. Sanders, *Paul and Palestinian Judaism*, 33-59.
20. E. Lohmeyer, "Gesetzeswerke," *ZNW* 28 (1929) 177-207.
21. See R. Walker, "Die Heiden und das Gericht: Zur Auslegung von Römer 2, 12-16," *EvT* 20 (1960) 302-14.
22. See Chapter 6.
23. M. Barth, "Jews and Gentiles," 247.
24. E. g. Burton, *Galatians*, 130-31.
25. Probably also in 2 Cor 5:1; cf. J. A. T. Robinson, *The Body* (London: SCM, 1952) 76-77.
26. It is only by an illegitimate application of Rom 7:9-10 and 2 Cor 3:6 to Paul himself that interpreters can say of this verse that "the true purpose of the law is indeed to kill man" (Bring, *Galatians* 95; cf. R. Bultmann, *Theology of the New Testament*, [New York: Scribner's, 1954] 1:267).
27. So J. A. Bengel, *Gnomon* on Gal 2:19, "*per legem* fidei, *legi* operum. Rom 3:27. Non sum injurius in legem: lege nitor, non minus divina."
28. Bultmann, "Auslegung," 396. Note however that in Romans 7 Paul is speaking of Gentiles moving from sense 2 to sense 3.
29. If Paul were completely consistent in his use of prepositions, I would point to the use of *dia nomou* here as in 2:19 and not *ek nomou* as in 3:21 and 2:16 ter; 3:2, 5, 10, 18.
30. For a discussion of how Paul hears the promise of the expression of the righteousness of God for Gentiles in Gen 15:6, see Chapter 3.
31. Schoeps, *Paul*, 213-18.
32. See Chapter 1.
33. Deut 21:23 provides the scriptural basis for the statement that Christ became a curse for Gentiles in order that they might receive a blessing. It is an example of "interchange in Christ" (see M. Hooker, "Interchange in Christ," *JTS* 22 [1971] 349-61). It must be emphasized that this is not an historical description of the circumstances of Jesus' death, although such an understanding often unconsciously influences the way the Synoptic trial narratives are read.
34. One interesting answer to the question of why Paul speaks of the curses and not

the blessings of the covenant when writing to Gentiles is given by M. Wyschogrod, "The Law: Jews and Gentiles," *Speaking of God Today* (ed. P. D. Opshal and M. H. Tanenbaum; Philadelphia: Fortress, 1974) 3-14. If he were writing in another context, I cannot believe that Paul would not have affirmed the statement of *Pss. Sol.* 14:1-3, "Faithful is the Lord to them that love him in truth, to them that endure his chastening, to them that walk in the righteousness of his commandments, in the law which he commanded us that we might live. The pious of the Lord shall live by it forever."

35. For the proper translation of this important verse, see D. M. Smith, "HO DE DIKAIOS EK PISTEŌS ZĒSETAI," *Studies in the History and Text of the New Testament* (ed. B. L. Daniels and M. J. Suggs; Salt Lake City: University of Utah Press, 1967) 13-25; and H. C. C. Cavallin, "The Righteous Shall Live by Faith: A Decisive Argument for the Traditional Interpretation," *ST* 32 (1978) 33-43. Paul omits the genitive after *pistis* in order to allow his understanding in terms of the faithfulness of Christ established in 2:16, 20.
36. E. P. Sanders sees correctly that Paul's point here is not to contrast human believing and doing, but he does not note that the two references to "doing" put them into his category of "doing the law" (*Paul, the Law, and the Jewish People* [Philadelphia: Fortress, 1983]). He was probably misled by his assumption that in Rom 10:5 and Gal 3:12 "Paul is disagreeing with the statement of the law" in Lev 18:5 (p. 104 of his "On the Question of Fulfilling the Law in Paul and Rabbinic Judaism," *Donum Gentilicum* [ed. E. Bammel, C. K. Barrett, and W. D. Davies; Oxford: Clarendon, 1978] 103-26).
37. See especially E. Schweizer, "Die 'Elemente der Welt' Gal 4, 3.9; Kol 2, 8.20," *Beiträge zur Theologie des Neuen Testaments* (Zürich: Zwingli, 1970) 147-63.
38. See Chapter 2.
39. "Statt *graphē* könnte hier (Gal 3:8) auch *nomos* stehen," G. Friedrich, "Das Gesetz des Glaubens Römer 3, 27," *Auf das Wort kommt es an* (Göttingen: Vandenhoeck und Ruprecht, 1978) 119. Cf. also *gegraptai* in 3:10, 13; 4:22, 27.
40. H. Räisänen "Paul's Theological Difficulties with the Law," *St Bib* 3 (1978) 321-36; "Legalism and Salvation by the Law," *The Pauline Literature and Theology* (ed. S. Pedersen; Arhus: Aros, 1980) 63-83.
41. Sanders speaks of "Different Questions, Different Answers" in his *Paul, the Law, and the Jewish People*.
42. It has become customary to understand the contradiction between "the alleged aim of the law, that it has been given for life, and its alleged effect, that it creates sin and death" (H. Conzelmann, *An Outline of the Theology of the New Testament* [New York: Harper, 1969] 226) in an existential fashion: the one law means death for "man before faith" but life for the believer. To move from an existential to a *heilsgeschichtliche* distinction, from Bultmann to Schweitzer, would come much closer to Paul's intention. One could compare the Rabbinic phrase about the Torah being for Israel "an elixir of life" (*sm hmwt*); cf. T. W. Manson, "2 Cor 2:14-17: Suggestions Towards an Exegesis," *Studia Paulina in honorem J. de Zwann* (Haarlem: Bohn, 1953) 155-62.
43. To let one example stand for many: "The fact that he gave up his Jewish way of

life was also in conformity with his gospel, which did not include the observance of the Torah," H. D. Betz, "2 Cor 6:14-7:1: An Anti-Pauline Fragment?" *JBL* 92 (1973) 101.

44. R. J. Z. Werblowsky, "Paulus in jüdischer Sicht," *Paulus—Apostat oder Apostel* (Regensburg: Pustet, 1977) 135. For a general definition of apostasy in this sense, see E. P. Sanders, "The Covenant as a Soteriological Category and the Nature of Salvation in Palestinian and Hellenistic Judaism," *Jews, Greeks and Christians* (ed. R. Hamerton-Kelly and R. Scroggs; Leiden: Brill, 1976) 40-41; and for Rabbinic references see A. Nissen, *Gott und der Nächste im antiken Judentum* (Tübingen: Mohr, 1974) 44, 62.
45. *apostatēs tou nomou*, Irenaeus on the Ebionites in Eusebius, *Hist. eccl.* 3.27.4. Cf. H. J. Schoeps, *Theologie und Geschichte des Judenchristentums* (Tübingen: Mohr, 1949) 127-35; and G. Lüdemann, "Zum Antipaulinismus im frühen Christentum," *EvT* 40 (1980) 437-55.
46. W. L. Knox, *St. Paul and the Church of Jerusalem* (Cambridge: Cambridge University Press, 1925) 122-23.
47. W. D. Davies, *Paul and Rabbinic Judaism* (London: SPCK, 1955) 70.
48. F. C. Grant, *Roman Hellenism and the New Testament* (Edinburgh: Oliver and Boyd, 1962) 136.
49. "In the course of his work among Gentiles, Paul came more and more to internalize the Gentile point of view and identify himself with it," H. Räisänen, "Legalism and Salvation," 80.
50. Cf. also the use of "we" and "you" in 3:23-27 and probably in 4:26, 28.
51. Barth, "Jews and Gentiles," 246, 250.
52. The whole statement is strange, for while it is almost impossible to understand anything about Cephas' actions "compelling Gentiles to Judaize" (Schmithals, *Paul and James*, 68-72), it fits the Galatian situation perfectly (6:12).
53. P. Richardson, "Pauline Inconsistency: I Corinthians 9:19-23 and Galatians 2:11-14," *NTS* 26 (1980) 347-62.
54. There is nothing, least of all in Galatians, to justify Bring's statement that "Paul had come to the conclusion that when they became Christian Jews must become like Gentiles" (*Galatians*, 81).
55. See Chapter 7.
56. That the suggestion is not completely anachronistic might be shown by Barnabas, who warns against "being like certain people, in that you say (heaping up your sins): 'The covenant belongs both to them and to us (*hē diathēkē ekeinōn kai hēmon)*'" (4:6). (Unfortunately the manuscript tradition is not at all clear at this point.) Is it too fanciful to think that among the "certain people" Barnabas opposes are heirs of Paul and Ephesians?

NOTES TO CHAPTER FIVE

1. Note that the book of Revelation does not provide a parallel, for those who are referred to under the names of Balaam (2:14) and Jezebel (2:20) are not Jews but Judaizing Gentiles: they are people "who say that they are Jews and they are not (but they are lying)" (2:9; 3:9).
2. R. Ruether, *Faith and Fratricide* (New York: Seabury, 1974) 102f, 134f.
3. P. Richardson, *Israel in the Apostolic Church* (Cambridge: Cambridge University Press, 1969).
4. Note that there is a big difference between those who keep the law ("uphold the Torah") and may break certain commandments and those who conform to certain commandments but do not keep the law.
5. H. J. Schoeps, *Paul: The Theology of the Apostle in the Light of Jewish Religious History* (Philadelphia: Westminster, 1961) 213-18.
6. E. P. Sanders, *Paul and Palestinian Judaism* (Philadelphia: Fortress, 1977).
7. See Chapters 1, 2, and 4.
8. *Exod. Rab.* 5:9; cf. also *TSot.* 8:6; *Shab.* 88b; *Midrash Tannaim* (ed. D. Hoffman) p. 190f; *Lam. Rab.* 3:1; *Deut. Rab.* 2:34; *Pes. Rab.* 21.
9. I have used the following commentaries: J. B. Lightfoot, *St. Paul's Epistle to the Galatians* (London: Macmillan, 1869); J. Eadie, *A Commentary on St. Paul's Epistle to the Galatians* (London: Hodder and Stoughton, 1900); T. Zahn, *Der Brief des Paulus an die Galater* (Leipzig: Deichert, 1907); E. D. Burton, *A Critical and Exegetical Commentary on the Epistle to the Galatians* (Edinburgh: T. and T. Clark, 1921); H. Schlier, *Der Brief an die Galater* (Göttingen: Vandenhoeck und Ruprecht, 1951); R. Bring, *Commentary on Galatians* (Philadelphia: Muhlenberg, 1961); A. Oepke, *Der Brief des Paulus an die Galater* (Berlin: Evangelische Verlagsanstalt, 1973); F. Mussner, *Der Galaterbrief* (Freiburg: Herder, 1974); H. D. Betz, *Galatians* (Philadelphia: Fortress, 1979). Not available to me was M. McNamara, "'to de (Hagar) Sina oros estin en tē Arabia' (Gal 4:25a): Paul and Petra," *Mill Stud* 2 (1978) 24-41.
10. As cited in Zahn, *Galater*, 298.
11. Betz, *Galatians*, 245.
12. Ibid., 251; Bring, *Galatians*, 221, 232.
13. Betz, *Galatians*, 243.
14. Ibid., 247.
15. For example, W. M. Ramsay, *Galatians*, 431, 430, finds the passage "unnecessarily insulting and offensive to the Jews, weak as an argument, and not likely to advance his purpose"; indeed it "would probably outrage Jewish prejudice." Betz, *Galatians*, 246, calls it "one of Paul's sharpest attacks upon the Jews," and G. Klein ("Römer 4 und die Idee der Heilsgeschichte," *Rekonstruktion und Interpretation* [Munich: Kaiser, 1969] 168) says of it: "Eine brutalere Paganisierung vorgeblicher Heilsgeschichte lässt sich schwerlich noch vorstellen." It is unclear why Paul would want to make such an uncalled-for attack and even more unclear why some modern interpreters should rejoice in it.
16. J. C. O'Neill, *The Recovery of Paul's Letter to the Galatians* (London: SPCK, 1972) 62-64. M. C. Callaway, "The Mistress and the Maid: Midrashic Traditions

behind Gal 4:21-31," *Radical Religion* 2 (1975) 94-101, is also tempted to omit vv 24-27 but wisely refrains. Her stimulating article is very sensitive to the problems these verses cause.

17. "This is a part of the OT that Paul would have been unlikely to introduce of his own accord; its value from his point of view is anything but obvious, and the method of interpretation is unusual with him. It stands in the epistle because his opponents had used it and he could not escape it," C. K. Barrett, "The Allegory of Abraham, Sarah, and Hagar in the Argument of Galatians," *Rechtfertigung* (ed. J. Friedrich, W. Pöhlmann, and P. Stuhlmacher; Tübingen: Mohr, 1976) 10. Ramsay, *Galatians*, 432, even suggests that Paul is replying to a letter from the Galatians asking about Isaac and Ishmael.
18. Schoeps, *Paul*, 238.
19. There is a good recent discussion in A. T. Hanson, *Studies in Paul's Technique and Theology* (Grand Rapids: Eerdmans, 1974), esp. 91-94.
20. C. H. Dodd, "A Problem of Interpretation," *Bulletin of the SNTS* 2 (1951) 7-18, 11, 12.
21. Burton, *Galatians*, 261f.
22. It is then quite incorrect to state, as does R. T. Stamm ("Galatians," *Interpreter's Bible* [Nashville: Abingdon, 1953], 10:541), "The verb *systoichei* . . . is regularly used to draw comparisons and parallels."
23. Polybius, 10.23.7. The definition in LSJ is a bit too static: "To stand in the same rank or line, of soldiers." The passage is in fact much more lively: "They were to practice charging the enemy and retreating by every kind of movement, until they were able to advance at an alarming pace; provided only that they kept together, both line and column (*eph' hoson syzygountas kai systoichountas diamenein*), and preserved the proper intervals between squadrons" (trans. Shuckburgh). A frequent movement involves the whole squadron swinging around 90 degrees (*epistrophē*) so that they keep in formation but the rider in front of or next to any individual constantly shifts. *Systoichein* is in no sense a technical term, even if *zygein* (to stand in rank) and *stoichein* (to stand in file) are "used by the tactical writers" in a technical sense (F. W. Walbank, *A Historical Commentary on Polybius* [Oxford: Clarendon, 1967] 2:226). As the translation shows, the prefix has only to do with the riders keeping in formation moving together. This passage is of no help whatsoever in understanding Gal 4:25.
24. *haptetai, geitniazei* (Chrysostom), coniunctus est (Vulg.). Only Theodore of Mopsuestia seems to have something close to the modern definition (*isodynamei*), cf. Lightfoot, *Galatians*, 226.
25. R. A. Lipsius, *Brief an die Galater, Römer, Philipper* (Freiburg: Mohr, 1892) 55.
26. J. H. Thayer, *A Greek-English Lexicon of the New Testament* (Edinburgh: T. and T. Clark, 1901) 608.
27. Metaphysics 1:5 = 986a.23. On the Pythagorean tables of contraries, see W. K. C. Guthrie, *A History of Greek Philosophy* (Cambridge: Cambridge University Press, 1962) 1:239-51.
28. E. g. *tōn enantiōn hē hetera systoichia*, 1004b.27. Cf. 1054b.35; 1058a.13;

1066a.15; 1072a.31; 1096b.6.

29. Parts of Animals 3:7 = 670b.21.
30. *Mekilta* (Lauterbach, 2:234-35). Pseudo-Jonathan at Deut 33:2 reads: "The Lord was revealed at Sinai to give the law unto his people of Beth Israel, and the splendor of the glory of his Shekinah arose from Gebal to give itself to the sons of Esau; but they received it not. It shined forth in majesty and glory from mount Pharan, to give itself to the sons of Ishmael; but they received it not. It returned and revealed itself in holiness unto his people of Beth Israel, and with him 10,000 times 10,000 holy angels."
31. See G. F. Moore, *Judaism* (Cambridge: Harvard, 1927) 1:277; H. J. Schoeps, "Haggadisches zur Auserwählung Israels," *Aus frühchristlicher Zeit* (Tübingen: Mohr, 1950) 184-200; L. Ginzberg, *The Legends of the Jews* (Philadelphia: JPS, 1968 [1911]), 3:80-82. Cf. *LAB* 11:2.
32. See Chapter 1.
33. Ps 83:6, etc; *1 Enoch* 89:11, 13, 16 (wild asses); *Jub.* 17:14 (Nabateans); 20:12-13; Josephus, *Ant.* 1. 215, 221 (Nabateans). Cf. S. Sandmel, *Philo's Place in Judaism* (New York: KTAV, 1971) 44, 71; Schoeps, *Aus frühchristlicher Zeit*, 26, 186. For other peoples said to be descended from Abraham, cf. Malchus in Josephus, *Ant.* 1. 240-41 (Assyria, Africa), and 1 Macc 12:21; 2 Macc 5:9 (Spartans). Cf. G. Mayer, "Aspecte des Abrahambildes in der hellenistisch-jüdischen Literatur," *EvT* 32 (1972) 118-27, esp. 121-23; D. Georgi, *Die Gegner des Paulus im 2. Korintherbrief* (Neukirchen: Neukirchener Verlag, 1964) 63-69.
34. G. B. Caird, *Principalities and Powers* (Oxford: Clarendon, 1956) 7-8.
35. See R. le Déaut. "Traditions targumiques dans le Corpus Paulinum?" *Bib* 42 (1961) 37-43.
36. Cited from J. Bowker, *The Targums and Rabbinic Literature* (Cambridge: Cambridge University Press, 1969) 224. The version in *Gen. Rab.* 55:4 is as follows: "Isaac and Ishmael were engaged in a controversy: the latter argued, 'I am more beloved than thou, because I was circumcised at the age of 13'; while the other retorted, 'I am more beloved than thou, because I was circumcised at 8 days.' Said Ishmael to him, 'I am more beloved, because I could have protested and did not.' At that moment Isaac exclaimed: 'O that God would appear to me and bid me cut off one of my limbs! Then I would not refuse.' Said God: 'Even if I bid thee sacrifice thyself, thou wilt not refuse.'"
37. Cf. F. Stummer, "Beschneidung," *RAC* 2:159-69. Note that the descendants of Esau no longer (Jer 9:24f) practiced circumcision, cf. Josephus, *Ant.* 13. 257f.
38. As were the Arabs; cf. Josephus, *Ant.* 1.214.
39. Out of this promise and the plural "sons" in Gen 21:7 developed the interesting Agadah of Sarah suckling Gentile children, some of whom would be future proselytes, *BM* 87a; *Gen. Rab.* 53:9.
40. Eadie, *Galatians*, 369; cf. the similar reconstruction of what Paul should have written in Mussner, *Galater*, 320.
41. Betz, *Galatians*, 246.
42. See L. Hurtado, "The Jerusalem Collection and the Book of Galatians," *JSNT* 5 (1979) 46-62.

43. A great deal is said about the heavenly or future Jerusalem in the literature of early Judaism (including Isa 54:11-17) as a promise for the present Jerusalem (see the references in Betz, *Galatians*, 246, n. 81). Paul stands in this line but adds that Gentiles now, before the eschaton, are citizens of this heavenly Jerusalem.
44. Betz, *Galatians*, 244. On the various meanings of this term, see C. Roetzel, "Diathēkai in Rom 9:4," *Bib* 51 (1970) 377-90.
45. "The two covenants of which Paul speaks are concurrent and can be identified in the original situation," Richardson, *Israel*, 100; see also U. Luz, "Der alte und der neue Bund bei Paulus und im Hebräerbrief," *EvT* 27 (1967) 318-36.
46. See Chapter 2.
47. Since C. K. Barrett, "The Allegory," 12, says that Isa 54:1 had never been associated with Sarah before Paul (although it clearly was in the later Jewish tradition), perhaps one ought to search for examples. The best I can come up with is Lightfoot's claim, perhaps a correct one (*Galatians*, 196), that Philo has Sarah and Hagar in mind when he cites Isa 54:1 in *Praem*. 151.
48. On this translation, cf. Richardson, *Israel*, 74-84; Mussner, *Galater*, 415-17; and W. D. Davies, "Paul and the People of Israel," *NTS* 24 (1977) 10.
49. Mussner, *Galater*, 331-33. Rather than "shutting them out" in turn, it would be sufficient to expel their false gospel, their gospel of slavery, their Ishmael attitudes.
50. Le Déaut, "Traditions," interprets this in the light of the Targum as "quarrelling."
51. The thorough discussions of Lightfoot, *Galatians*, 189-190, and Mussner, *Galater*, 322-24 (his article in *ThQ* was not available to me), are very convincing. The longer reading is easily explained: *TO GAR SINA* → *TO AGAR SINA* → *TO DE* (or *GAR*) *AGAR SINA*.
52. On the wild improbability of this desperate solution, still commonly held, see H. Gese, "*to de Hagar Sina oros estin en tē Arabia* (Gal 4:25)," *Vom Sinai zum Zion* (Munich: Kaiser, 1974) 59. To connect the name Hagar with the city Hagra and to locate Sinai in that neighbourhood, as Gese does, is perhaps a bit more plausible but still only complete conjecture. If word play were involved, rather than to refer to Arabic which not even the Nabateans and certainly not the Galatians spoke, one could assume that Philo's Greek "translations" were known: Hagar = *paroikēsis*; Sarai = *archē*; Sarah = *archousa*. This would indeed fit Paul's point and also be in accordance with the later Rabbinic explanation that *śry* = a princess to her own people and *śrh* = a princess for all mankind (*Gen. Rab.* 47:1).
53. Verse 25a has often been considered a gloss; verse 25b would reflect a post 70 C.E. situation, as in the commentaries of Pelagius and Ephraem Syrus. It is then not correct to say that "only a completely anachronistic modern nationalism could see it as a reference to the political bondage of Judea under the Romans" (Hanson, *Studies*, 96).
54. H. Lietzmann, *An die Römer* (Tübingen: Mohr, 1971) 91. I have also used the following commentaries: W. Sanday and A. C. Headlam, *A Critical and Exegetical Commentary on the Epistle to the Romans* (Edinburgh: T. and T.

Clark, 1902); C. H. Dodd, *The Epistle of Paul to the Romans* (London: Hodder and Stoughton, 1932); A. Nygren, *Commentary on Romans* (Philadelphia: Muhlenberg, 1949); O. Michel, *Der Brief an die Römer* (Göttingen: Vandenhoeck und Ruprecht, 1957); C. K. Barrett, *A Commentary on the Epistle to the Romans* (New York: Harper, 1957); F. J. Leenhardt, *L'Epître de Saint Paul aux Romains* (Neuchâtel: Delachaux et Niestlé, 1957); J. Munck, *Christ and Israel* (Philadelphia: Fortress, 1967); M. Black, *Romans* (London: Oliphants, 1973); O. Kuss, *Der Römerbrief, dritte Lieferung* (Regensburg: Pustet, 1978); C. E. B. Cranfield, *The Epistle to the Romans*, vol. 2 (Edinburgh: T. and T. Clark, 1979); E. Käsemann, *Commentary on Romans* (Grand Rapids: Eerdmans, 1980); U. Wilckens, *Der Brief an die Römer*, vol. 2 (Neukirchen: Neukirchen Verlag, 1980).

55. Schoeps, *Paul*, 238.
56. E. P. Sanders, "The Covenant as a Soteriological Category and the Nature of Salvation in Palestinian and Hellenistic Judaism," *Jews, Greeks and Christians* (ed. R. Hamerton-Kelly and R. Scroggs; Leiden: Brill, 1976) 15.
57. Barrett, *Romans*, 175. Cf. Käsemann, *Romans*, 261, "Verse 6a answers a difficulty and mentions *indirectly* the basis of the complaint in vv 1f. Israel, the bearer of the promise, has rejected in unbelief the message of Christ which is the fulfillment of the promise"; Kuss, *Römer*, 715, "der Apostel zieht die Folgerung *formel nicht ausdrücklich*."
58. Wilckens, *Römer*, 186; cf. 191, "*Noch immer nicht* nennt Paulus das Problem bei Namen, um das es geht: Hat Gott das im Unglauben verharrende Judentum trotz der ihm als 'Israel' gegebenen Heilssatzungen vom Heil ausgeschlossen?"
59. Sanday and Headlam, *Romans*, 239, 238, 226.
60. Dodd, *Romans*, 174, even argues with Paul in his exposition of 11:1: "The general tendency of the foregoing argument has been to suggest that God has repudiated His People, the Jews, as a corporate whole. But Paul cannot accept this suggestion without further consideration." Cf. also 43, 63, 179, 182f for similar arguments with Paul for not being anti-Jewish enough.
61. K. Stendahl, "The Apostle Paul and the Introspective Conscience of the West," *HTR* 56 (1963) 199-215.
62. "The latter people [church] has snatched away the blessings of the former [the Jews], just as Jacob took away the blessing of this Esau," Irenaeus, *ad. Haer.* 4.21.2f. Cf. already *Barn.* 13:2-3.
63. Michel, *Römer*, 202. Much more cautious is Wilckens, *Römer*, 196.
64. Munck, *Christ*, 49; cf. Cranfield, *Romans*, 481; Käsemann, *Romans*, 266. There is no basis to speak, as does Lietzmenn, *Römer*, 91, and many others, of the "leibliche und geistliche Israel."
65. Cranfield, *Romans*, 485; cf. Barrett, *Romans*, 187, 190; Nygren, *Romans*, 371; ("Like Pharaoh in his day, Israel is now a 'vessel of wrath.'"); Munck, *Christ*, 49, 59.
66. Käsemann, *Romans*, 275.
67. Michel, *Römer*, 210; cf. Dodd, *Romans*, 155.
68. Sanday and Headlam, *Romans*, 257; Wilckens, *Römer*, 199, is wiser not so to identify his "konkrete Gegner."

69. Dodd, *Romans*, 155. Much better is Cranfield, *Romans*, 482.
70. The only exception would be 16:17f if this chapter was part of the letter to Rome. For the situation generally of the addressees see W. Schmithals, *Der Römerbrief als historisches Problem* (Gütersloh: Mohn, 1975).
71. For example, E. P. Sanders ("Patterns of Religion in Paul and Rabbinic Judaism: A Holistic Method of Comparison," *HTR* 66 [1973] 458) begins his discussion of "the Tannaitic pattern of religion" thus: "The beginning point is the election of Israel, which was firmly and universally maintained by the Rabbis. It is best summed up in the one sentence, 'All Israel has a share in the world to come' (*Sanh.* 10:1)"; Paul agrees (Rom 11:26). Important to Rabbinic theology is the much misunderstood concept of "the merits of the fathers"; Paul agrees (Rom 11:28); see Chapter 3.
72. G. Eichholz, *Die Theologie des Paulus im Umriss* (Neukirchen: Neukirchener Verlag, 1972) 296.
73. "Der Ganze Abschnitt Röm 9-11 handelt von der Treue Gottes. Die Summe des Ganzen war schon in Röm 3,3 angedeutet," M. Barth, "Das Volk Gottes. Juden und Christen in der Botschaft des Paulus," *Paulus—Apostat oder Apostel?* (ed. M. Barth, et al.; Regensburg: Pustet, 1977) 75. "We shall misunderstand these chapters, if we fail to recognize that their key-word is mercy," Cranfield, *Romans*, 448. Cf. Eichholz, *Theologie*, 292, "*charis* ist Schlüsselwort von Röm 9-11. "
74. We translate according to Barrett, *Romans*, 180f, and Black, *Romans*, 131, to achieve consistency in Paul's use of *sperma*. But the meaning is the same even with the more natural translation.
75. Michel, *Römer*, 200f.
76. G. Klein, "Präliminarien zum Thema 'Paulus und die Juden,'" *Rechtfertigung*, 235.
77. That Gentiles could be called "out of Israel" has to do with the concept of Abraham's universal fatherhood referred to above, note 33.
78. Cf. P. Volz, *Die Eschatologie der jüdischen Gemeinde* (Hildesheim: Olms, 1966 [1934]) 29, 83, 280, 380; M. Hengel, *Die Zeloten* (Leiden: Brill, 1961) 309; C. H. Hunzinger, "Babylon als Deckname für Rom und die Datierung des 1. Petrusbriefes," *Gottes Wort und Gottes Land* (ed. H. Reventlow; Göttingen: Vandenhoeck und Ruprecht, 1965) 69-71. The latter two suggest that the identification took place by way of the Idumean Herod, but this is not certain.
79. This is obscured by the strange mistranslations of v 9a. RSV reads "What then? Are we Jews any better off?" in the text and "at any disadvantage" in the margin. We should not make wild guesses according to our understanding of the context but stick to the known meaning of words, and then our understanding of the context may change. We should translate: "What then do we put up as a defence?" (omitting *ou pantōs*).
80. That this is the sense of the word *dynamis* here is argued by Cranfield, *Romans*, 487.
81. Cf. Sanday and Headlam, *Romans*, 267-69; U. Luz, *Das Geschichtsverständnis des Paulus* (München: Kaiser, 1968) 79. The image of the potter in Sir 33:13 also seems to deal with Jews and Gentiles. Wisdom 15:7, on the other hand,

represents quite a different usage (contra Cranfield, *Romans*, 491).

82. "It seems apparent that the ancient Egyptians and Canaanites merely served the author as symbols for the hated Alexandrians and Romans of his own day," D. Winston, *The Wisdom of Solomon* (Garden City: Doubleday, 1979) 45.
83. B. Gärtner, *The Areopagus Speech and Natural Revelation* (Uppsala: Gleerup, 1955) 239f.
84. That *thelōn* must be understood in a causal and not a concessive sense, see Lietzmann, *Romans*, 93; Michel, *Römer*, 212; Barrett, *Romans*, 189f; Käsemann, *Romans*, 270f; Cranfield, *Romans*, 493f.
85. See K. Berger, "Abraham in den paulinischen Hauptbriefen," *MTZ* 17 (1966) 77f.
86. See the references in D. Zeller, *Juden und Heiden in der Mission des Paulus* (Stuttgart: Katholisches Bibelwerk, 1973) 128f, although he himself does not interpret Rom 9:27-29 postively. Better is Käsemann, *Romans*, 276.
87. See Munck, *Christ*, 67f; C. H. Dodd, *JTS* 5 (1954) 247f; and A. T. Hanson, *The Wrath of the Lamb* (London: SPCK, 1957) 90-92, for tentative suggestions along these lines. Leenhardt, *Romains*, 146, believes that Paul has drawn his image of the potter from Isa 45:9-13, where Cyrus is an instrument of mercy.
88. Munck, *Christ*, 49-55.
89. See the very suggestive article by M. Borg, "A New Context for Romans xiii," *NTS* 19 (1973) 205-18.
90. M. Barth, "Volk Gottes," 88. On Rom 10:4 and the theme of the inclusion of the Gentiles see G. Howard, "Christ the End of the Law: The Meaning of Romans 10:4ff," *JBL* 88 (1969) 331-37; and P. W. Meyer, "Romans 10:4 and the 'End of the Law,'" *The Divine Helmsman: Lou H. Silberman Festschrift* (ed. J. L. Crenshaw and S. Sandmel; New York: KTAV, 1980) 59-78.

NOTES TO CHAPTER SIX

1. Very important in this respect is L. Monsengwo Pasinya, *La notion de Nomos dans le Pentateuque grec* (Rome: Biblical Institute Press, 1973).
2. See B. S. Jackson, "Legalism," *JJS* 30 (1979) 1-22.
3. H. Schlier, *Der Brief an die Galater* (Göttingen: Vandenhoeck und Ruprecht, 1951) 55, is one of the few to even ask the question: "Are they works which fulfil the law, or works which the law requires, or finally works which the law works?"
4. E. D. Burton, *A Critical and Exegetical Commentary on the Epistle to the Galatians* (Edinburgh: T. and T. Clark, 1921) 120.
5. H. D. Betz, *Galatians* (Philadelphia: Fortress, 1979) 116.
6. E. Lohmeyer, "Gesetzeswerke," *ZNW* 28 (1929) 177-207; reprinted in *Probleme paulinischer Theologie* (Darmstadt: Wissenschaftliche Buchgesellschaft, 1954) 33-74, the edition used here. J. B. Tyson, "'Works of law' in Galatians,"

JBL 92 (1973) 423-31, is little more than a summary of Lohmeyer's discussion.

7. "Thus the nature of this genitive remains grammatically unclear"(73).
8. He admits that *mṣwwt* and *opera praeceptorum* (*2 Bar* 57:2) are not true linguistic parallels, although he and most others continue to make the association. M. Barth, *Ephesians 1-3* (Garden City: Doubleday, 1974) 244-48, also argues that the Pauline phrase has no parallel in Jewish writings. He is right to ignore 1QS 5:21; 6:18, because of the preposition: *m'śyw btwrh*. In 4Q Flor 1.7 we should read "works of thanksgiving" (*twdh*); cf. Amos 4:5 and *RevQ* 7 (1970) 221.
9. This midrash, which I have not seen, is briefly described in *EncJud* 16: 1516.
10. Rom 2:13, 25; 10:5; Gal 5:3.
11. Gal 6:13; cf. Rom 2:26.
12. Rom 2:27; 13:8; Gal 5:14; cf. Rom 8:4; Gal 6:2.
13. Lohmeyer, "Gesetzeswerke," 69, 72. He does not follow up this insight.
14. Ibid., 74. But what if it were clearly definiable, as in notes 23-24 below?
15. The references given on p. 39 do not speak of "working the works of God," although they are blindly copied by Tyson, ("Works of Law," 424) to support just that.
16. 1 Cor 15:58; 16:10; Phil 1:6; cf. Eph 2:10.
17. *Aboth* 3:16.
18. Phil 2:12f; cf. also Ps 90:7; *Pss. Sol.* 16:9.
19. Lohmeyer, "Gesetzeswerke," 50.
20. Ibid., 57; cf. 65. This aspect of Lohmeyer's work is emphasized by Tyson, "Works of Law."
21. U. Wilckens, "Was heisst bei Paulus: 'Aus Werken des Gesetzes wird kein Mensch gerecht'?" and J. Blank, "Warum sagt Paulus: 'Aus Werken des Gesetzes wird niemand gerecht'?" *Evangelisch-Katholischer Kommentar zum Neuen Testament: Vorarbeiten* (Neukirchen: Neukirchener Verlag, 1969) 1: 51-77, 79-95, do not make use of any of Lohmeyer's insights. As a result they are not at all helpful for our question.
22. H. Cremer, *Die paulinische Rechtfertigungslehre im Zusammenhang ihrer geschichtlichen Voraussetzungen* (Gütersloh: Bertelsmann, 1900); A. Schlatter, *Gottes Gerechtigkeit* (Stuttgart: Calwer Verlag, 1935); E. Käsemann, "Gottesgerechtigkeit bei Paulus," *ZThK* 58 (1961) 367-78; S. K. Williams, "The 'Righteousness of God' in Romans," *JBL* 99 (1980) 241-90.
23. K. Barth, *Der Römerbrief* (Zürich: Evangelischer Verlag, 1940 [1921]); G. Howard, *Paul: Crisis in Galatia* (Cambridge: Cambridge University Press, 1979) 95.
24. G. M. Taylor, "The Function of *Pistis Christou* in Galatians," *JBL* 85 (1966) 58-76.
25. See R. B. Hays, "Psalm 143 and the Logic of Romans 3," *JBL* 99 (1980) 107-115.
26. See Chapter 4.
27. See Betz, *Galatians*, 278-81; and H. Braun, *Qumran und das Neue Testament* (Tübingen: Mohr, 1966) 1:212-14.
28. See Chapter 2.

29. I have found very stimulating here R. Walker, "Die Heiden und das Gericht," *EvT* 20 (1960) 302-14.
30. When the traditional assumption becomes unconscious, it can cause misunderstandings of other passages as well, as when R. Bultmann, *Das Evangelium des Johannes* (Göttingen: Vandenhoeck und Ruprecht, 1959 [1941]) 164, says of John 6:28, "*erga tou theou* are of course the works which God requires." The Johannine concept of working the works of God (e.g. 9:4), of Abraham (8:39), or of Satan (8:41) would repay further study.

NOTES TO CHAPTER SEVEN

1. F. W. Beare, "Jesus and Paul," *CJT* 5 (1959) 85.
2. The term "primitive" could be retained if that meant nothing more than the Jerusalem church contemporary with Paul but it will be dropped lest it imply that the church was primitive in comparison with Paul.
3. Cf. R. A. Kraft, "In search of 'Jewish Christianity' and its 'theology'; Problems of definition and methodology," *Judéo-Christianisme* (= *RSR* 60 [1972]) 81-92; A. F. J. Klijn, "The Study of Jewish Christianity," *NTS* 20 (1974) 419-31; S. K. Riegel, "Jewish Christianity: Definitions and Terminology," *NTS* 24 (1978) 410-15.
4. J. Daniélou, *The Theology of Jewish Christianity* (London: Darton, Longman and Todd, 1964).
5. H. J. Schoeps, *Theologie und Geschichte des Judenchristentums* (Tübingen: Mohr, 1949).
6. So the tradition from Irenaeus to H. Lietzman, *A History of the Early Church* (New York: Meridian, 1949).
7. Cf. G. Lüdemann, "Zum Antipaulinismus im frühen Christentum," *EvT* 40 (1980) 437-55.
8. The people who appealed to James in the second century may have had as little in common with the real James as many of the people who appealed to Paul had with the real Paul.
9. Cf. the statements by such different scholars as G. Strecker, *Das Judenchristentum in den Pseudoklementinen* (Berlin: Akademie, 1958) 214, and J. Munck, "Jewish Christianity in Post-Apostolic Times," *NTS* 6 (1960) 103-16. That the legend of the Pella flight cannot be used as a bridge has now been decisively demonstrated by G. Lüdemann, "The Successors of Pre-70 Jerusalem Christianity: A Critical Analysis of the Pella-Tradition," *Normative Self Definition, Vol I. The Shaping of Christianity in the Second and Third Centuries* (ed. E. P. Sanders; London: SCM, 1980) 161-73.
10. B. J. Malina, "Jewish Christianity or Christian Judaism: Toward a Hypothetical Definition," *JSJ* 7 (1976) 46-57.

11. Statements like: "They are not orthodox Jews, for they do not practice circumcision" (V. Corwin, *St. Ignatius and Christianity in Antioch* [New Haven: Yale University Press, 1960] 58) make it necessary to be explicit about this. Cf. my "Judaism of the Uncircumcised in Ignatius and related Writers," *Anti-Judaism in Early Christianity; Vol 2, Separation and Polemic* (ed. S. Wilson; Waterloo: Wilfrid Laurier University Press, 1986) 33-44.
12. My limitation is very close to that of R. N. Longenecker, *The Christology of Early Jewish Christianity* (London: SCM, 1970), but when he speaks of Matthew, John, Hebrews, James, 1-3 John, 1-2 Peter, Jude and Revelation as "addressed to Jewish Christians or to potentially interested Jews" (18), he introduces confusion by including writings which in the opinion of most go far beyond his own definition. By no stretch of the imagination can 2 Pet 1:4 be called "Jewish Christian!"
13. Cf. C. H. Dodd, *The Apostolic Preaching and Its Developments* (London: Hodder and Stoughton, 1936).
14. Cf. U. Wilckens, *Die Missionsreden der Apostelgeschichte* (Neukirchen: Neukirchener Verlag, 1961).
15. The fact that none (Mark 12:30, 33; Luke 10:27; Matt 22:37) can reproduce the *Shema* accurately is but part of the evidence for this.
16. My attempt to reconstruct one such tradition in *No Stone on Another* (Leiden: Brill, 1970), 244-365, has not seemed convincing to very many.
17. The only New Testament writings for which a convincing case can be made that they were written by and for Christian Jews or ex-Jews are Revelation, John, and 1-3 John, but in none is there an obvious connection with Jerusalem, and all come from a period somewhat later than Paul.
18. I am convinced in general by the thorough refutation of his thesis by two such differing scholars as J. Munck, *Paul and the Salvation of Mankind* (London: SCM, 1959), and W. Schmithals, *Paul and James* (London: SCM, 1965).
19. This principle is well enunciated by H. D. Betz, *Galatians* (Philadelphia: Fortress, 1979) 6, but not always adhered to in his commentary (see e.g. 116).
20. See D. Georgi, *Die Gegner des Paulus im 2. Korintherbrief* (Neukirchen: Neukirchener Verlag, 1964) and J. F. Collange, *Enigmes de la deuxième épître de Paul aux Corinthiens* (Cambridge: Cambridge University Press, 1972).
21. One must distinguish between breaking certain commandments and not keeping the law at all. I would agree then with the thesis of Munck, *Paul*, and others about the Judaizing Gentile Christians. The most careful discussion is by J. G. Hawkins, *The Opponents of Paul in Galatia* (Ph.D. dissertation, Yale University, 1971).
22. Cf. G. Bornkamm, "Die Häresie des Kolosserbriefs," *Das Ende des Gesetzes* (Munich: Kaiser, 1952) 139-56, and the recent commentaries by E. Lohse and E. Schweizer.
23. I have tried to show that this is true also of Gal 4:25f. in Chapter 5.
24. And they certainly did not call themselves "the poor"; cf. L. Keck, "The Poor among the Saints in the NT," *ZNW* 56 (1965) 100-129, and "The Poor among the Saints in Jewish Christianity and Qumran," *ZNW* 57 (1966) 54-78.
25. This shows how Paul can be used to identify such passages as Matt 16:17-19 as

traditions of the Jerusalem church.

26. See my *No Stone*, 65-243, and for Gal 6:10, L. Hurtado, "The Jerusalem Collection and the Book of Galatians," *JSNT* 5 (1979) 46-62.
27. That this passage does not indicate an antagonism between Paul and the Jerusalem church is argued by Schmithals, *Paul and James*, 79-84.
28. That these verses belong here, see L. Hurtado, "The Jerusalem Collection."
29. Cf. D. Georgi, *Die Geschichte der Kollekte des Paulus für Jerusalem* (Hamburg: Reich, 1965) and K. F. Nickle, *The Collection* (London: SCM, 1966).
30. It was hoped that the Gentiles would come of their own accord to Zion once the redemption of Israel was final and visible. The classic statement of the distinction between a "centripetal" and a "centrifugal" concept of mission is B. Sundkler, "Jésus et les païens," *Arbeiten und Mitteilungen aus dem neutestamentlichen Seminar zu Uppsala* 6 (1937) 1-38. See also J. Jeremias, *Jesus' Promise to the Nations* (London: SCM, 1958) and Munck, *Paul*.
31. I would understand it along the lines of Schmithals' *Paul and James*, 63-78.
32. I have used as a convenient summary and control over the passages chosen P. Vielhauer, *Geschichte der urchristlichen Literatur* (Berlin: de Gruyter, 1975) 9-57.
33. Because of its complexity I have not included the hymn of Phil 2:6-11 in this study, even though it was identified by E. Lohmeyer, *Kyrios Jesus* (Heidelberg, 1928), with the Eucharistic tradition of the Jerusalem church. He has not found many followers.
34. Cf. J. Jeremias, *The Eucharistic Words of Jesus* (London: SCM, 1966) 101-3.
35. I follow the recent study by J. Murphy-O'Connor, "Tradition and Redaction in 1 Cor 15:3-7," *CBQ* 43 (1981) 582-89.
36. Apart from himself, Paul names as Apostles Junia, Andronicus, Cephas, and probably Barnabas, James, and Silvanus. See W. Schmithals, *The Office of Apostle in the Early Church* (Nashville: Abingdon, 1969).
37. Cf. W. Popkes, *Christus Traditus: eine Untersuchung zum Begriff der Dahingabe im Neuen Testament* (Zürich: Zwingli, 1967).
38. W. Kramer, *Christ, Lord, Son of God* (London: SCM, 1966) 20-26; cf. Vielhauer, *Geschichte*, 13-16. Rom 10:9a, on the other hand, "we confess that Jesus is Lord," is a homologia, which has a different origin and function.
39. Cf. Wilckens, *Missionsreden*, 80-82. It may be that from this formula and from the speeches in Acts 14 and 17 we can derive a pre-Pauline pattern of preaching in the Gentile mission. It is related to many of the motifs of Wisdom 11 15. Cf. also Rom 2:4.
40. See Vielhauer, *Geschichte*, 29.
41. F. Bovon, "Une formule prépaulinienne dans l'épître aux Galates (Ga 1, 4-5)," *Paganisme, Judaïsme, Christianisme* (Paris: Boccard, 1978) 91-107. Cf. Betz, *Galatians*, 42f.
42. Cf. Gal 2:16, where justification is presented as a concept common to Cephas and Paul, who are "Jews by birth."
43. That it was not is argued by R. Bultmann, *Theology of the New Testament* (New York: Scribner's, 1954) 1:49, and Vielhauer, *Geschichte*, 30-31. That it was is

argued by E. Schweizer, "Röm 1, 3f. und der Gegensatz von Fleisch und Geist vor und bei Paulus," *Neotestamentica* (Zürich: Zwingli, 1963) 180-89, and H. Zimmermann, *Neutestamentliche Methodenlehre* (Stuttgart: Katholisches Bibelwerk, 1968) 192-202.

44. Kramer, *Christ, Lord, Son of God*; F. Hahn, *The Titles of Jesus in Christology* (London: Lutterworth, 1969). It seems that the title which is the subject of the sentence could be changed more naturally than the formula which begins with the relative pronoun.
45. Bultmann, *Theology*, 46-47; E. Käsemann, "Zum Verständnis von Römer 3, 24-26," *ZNW* 43 (1950/51) 150-54. The literature on this formula is extensive; cf. E. Käsemann, *Commentary on Romans* (Grand Rapids: Eerdmans, 1980) 91-92, and W. Wilckens, *Der Brief an die Römer* (Neukirchen: Neukirchener Verlag, 1978) 1:182.
46. Cf. Wilckens, *Römer*, 183-84, and S. K. Williams, *Jesus' Death as Saving Event* (Missoula: Scholars, 1975) 11-16.
47. The translation of this line is based on Williams, *Jesus' Death*, 46-51. The best alternative would refer to God's covenant faithfulness, as argued by A. Pluta, *Gottes Bundestreue: Ein Schlüsselbegriff in Röm 3, 25a* (Stuttgart: Katholisches Bibelwerk, 1969). There is no way grammatically to make the phrase mean "to be received by faith" as in the usual interpretations, even if it is a Pauline insertion.
48. The translation or paraphrase of this line is based on N. Dahl, "The Atonement—An Adequate Reward for the Akedah?" *The Crucified Messiah* (Minneapolis: Augsburg, 1974) 156. Williams, *Jesus' Death*, 27-34, makes a strong case for understanding this line with reference to the Gentile mission, in which case it would be a parallel to the expanded formula in 1 Thess 1:9f (cf. note 39). But I am not completely convinced.
49. Käsemann, "Verständnis," 153.
50. Käsemann, *Romans*, 100. Commentaries sometimes point to the contradiction between the forbearance of Rom 3:25 and the wrath of 1:18ff, but of course the latter has to do with the situation of idolators outside the covenant.
51. Cf. Wilckens, *Römer*, 197, and the references given there.
52. Cf. Käsemann, "Verständnis," and Pluta, *Gottes Bundestreue*.
53. Bultmann, *Theology*, 37-42.
54. E. P. Sanders, "Patterns of Religion in Paul and Rabbinic Judaism: A Holistic Method of Comparison," *HTR* 66 (1973) 455-78.
55. One function of footnotes is to list exceptions, in this case Rom 7:5; 1 Cor 15:17 (Rom 4:7; 11:27 are quotations).
56. Rom 4:7-8 is a quotation.
57. Here the exceptions are Rom 2:4; 2 Cor 7:9-10, 12:21.
58. Cf. Heb 6:2, and Schoeps, *Theologie*, 202-11.
59. Rom 11:27 is a quotation and 1 Cor 11:25 is from the Jerusalem tradition. I would argue that in 2 Cor 3:6, 14, both the "ancient" and the "renewed" covenant are the language of the opponents (see the works cited in note 20). The word does not mean covenant in Gal 3:15, 17; 4:24 (see note 23) nor in Rom 9:4 (see C. J. Roetzel, "Diathēkai in Romans 9, 4," *Bib* 51 [1970] 377-90).

60. Cf. the discussion in Kramer, *Christ, Lord, Son of God* 131-50.
61. "Nicht die von Moses eingeleitete Heilsgeschichte Israels, sondern die Welt des gefallenen und unter dem Gotteszorn befindlichen Adam ist für Paulus das Gegenüber des gegenwärtigen Kairos" (Käsemann, "Verständnis," 154).

NOTES TO CHAPTER EIGHT

1. Cf. F. Mussner, "Heil für Alle," *Kairos* 23 (1981) 207-14. To put this aspect at the centre of Romans rather than justification by faith means to follow the lead of Origen and not Augustine; cf. P. Gorday, *Principles of Patristic Exegesis* (Toronto: Mellen, 1983).
2. A partial parallel can be found in the American civil rights movement of the sixties. When people at that time cited the Declaration of Independance, "all men are created equal," concretely it meant "blacks are created equal."
3. Especially when combined with *pas*, as in 5:12 and 18; cf. 2:9 and 3:4.
4. Cf. H. W. Bartsch, "Die historische Situation des Römerbriefes," *Studia Evangelica* 4 (T.U. 102) (ed. F. L. Cross; Berlin: Akademie, 1968) 281-91; W. Schmithals, *Der Römerbrief als historisches Problem* (Gütersloh: Mohn, 1975).
5. S. K. Williams, "The 'Righteousness of God' in Romans," *JBL* 99 (1980) 241-90.
6. Cf. E. P. Sanders, *Paul and Palestinian Judaism* (Philadelphia: Fortress, 1977) 441, 445.
7. R. B. Hays, *The Faith of Jesus Christ* (Chico: Scholars, 1983).
8. G. Howard, "The Tetragram and the New Testament," *JBL* 96 (1977) 63-83.
9. Cf. A. Wire, "Pauline Theology as an Understanding of God: The Explicit and the Implicit" (Ph.D. dissertation Claremont, 1974); and the work of two of Dahl's students, H. Moxnes, *Theology in Conflict: Studies in Paul's Understanding of God in Romans* (Leiden: Brill, 1980), and J. M. Bassler, *Divine Impartiality: Paul and a Theological Axiom* (Chico: Scholars, 1982).
10. "Obedience to God's faithfulness attested in the gospel" is one possibility mentioned by C. E. B. Cranfield, *The Epistle to the Romans*, (Edinburgh: Clark, 1975) 1:66, although not adopted by him.
11. In the sense that the Jerusalem church began preaching before Paul's commissioning or that Sinai was before Golgotha. It certainly does not reflect the unhistorical picture of Paul's preaching in Acts, beginning always first in the synagogue.
12. So BAGD, s.v., 2.c.
13. Cf. D. M. Smith, "HO DE DIKAIOS EK PISTEŌS ZĒSETAI," *Studies in the History and Text of the New Testament* (ed. B. L. Daniels and M. J. Suggs; Salt Lake City: University of Utah Press, 1967) 13-25; and H. C. C. Cavallin, "The Righteous Shall Live by Faith: A Decisive Argument for the Traditional

Interpretation," *ST* 32 (1978) 33-43.

14. It is difficult to see how the alternative reading does not make our "righteousness" the result of our own action in believing.
15. Paul does not use the possessive of MT or LXX because when he takes up the subject again he will speak of God's righteousness being manifested through the faithfulness of Christ, 3:22.
16. H. Räisänen, *Paul and the Law* (Tübingen: Mohr, 1983), esp. 97-109; E. P. Sanders, *Paul, the Law, and the Jewish People* (Philadelphia: Fortress, 1983) esp. 123-35.
17. H. Boers, "The Problem of Jews and Gentiles in the Macro-Structure of Romans," *Neotestamentica* 15 (1981) 5.
18. J. C. Beker, *Paul the Apostle: the Triumph of God in Life and Thought* (Philadelphia: Fortress, 1980) 79-80.
19. J. M. Bassler *Impartiality*, 123-137.
20. W. Nauck, "Die Tradition und Komposition der Areopagrede," *ZThK* 53 (1956) 37-38.
21. In this sense C. H. Dodd, *The Epistle of Paul to the Romans* (London: Hodder and Stoughton, 1932) and A. T. Hanson, *The Wrath of the Lamb* (London: SPCK, 1957) are correct in their understanding of one aspect of *orgē*.
22. See Chapter 6.
23. Cf. Bartsch, "Situation," 287. Boers, "Problem," 6, even parallels 2:4 directly with 11:18!
24. Bassler, *Impartiality*.
25. For 2:17-29, see Chapter 9.
26. Cf. especially Williams, "Righteousness," and R. B. Hays, "Psalm 143 and the Logic of Romans 3," *JBL* 99 (1980) 107-15.
27. E. Käsemann, *Commentary on Romans* (Grand Rapids: Eerdmans, 1980) 81-82.
28. Räisänen, *Paul*, 99.
29. Cf. now N. Dahl, "Romans 3.9: Text and Meaning," *Paul and Paulinism: Essays in Honour of C. K. Barrett* (ed. M. D. Hooker and S. G. Wilson; London: SPCK, 1982) 184-204.
30. L. A. Keck, "The Function of Rom 3:10-18; Observations and Suggestions," *God's Christ and His People: Studies in Honour of Nils Alstrup Dahl* (ed. J. Jervell and W. A. Meeks; Oslo: Universitetsvorlaget, 1977) 146.
31. See Chapter 9.
32. See Chapter 2.
33. Sanders, *Paul*, 442-47.
34. Cf. G. Howard, "Romans 3:21-31 and the Inclusion of the Gentiles," *HTR* 63 (1970) 223-33, and S. K. Williams, *Jesus' Death as Saving Event: The Background and Origin of a Concept* (Missoula: Scholars, 1975).
35. Williams, *Death*, 19-34. Although I remain convinced that a pre-Pauline formula underlies much of v 25, I am not as confident as Williams (or Käsemann) in being able to isolate it with precision.
36. There is a possible parallel in a saying of Yohanan ben Zakkai: "Just as the sin-offering makes atonement for Israel so righteousness makes atonement for

the Gentiles'' (*BB* 10b). If this saying is older than its context, as J. Neusner, *Development of a Legend: Studies on the Tradition concerning Yohanan ben Zakkai* (Leiden: Brill, 1970) 103-4, argues, and if *ṣdqh* here means ''righteousness of God'' (a meaning attested in the Siddur), then the saying would be very close to Paul. But this is completely speculative.

37. This translation is based in part on R. B. Hays, '''Have we found Abraham to be our Forefather according to the flesh?': A Reconsideration of Rom 4:1,'' *NT* 27 (1985) 84.
38. See Chapter 3.
39. As it stands, v 14 is a blatant contradiction of v 16, and so along with Pelagius and M. Black, *Romans* (London: Oliphants, 1973) 78, I have inserted an ''only'' in understanding it. Also, while v 15 states two good Pauline principles, I do not see how they function in this context. G. Klein, ''Römer 4 und die Idee der Heilsgeschichte,'' *Rekonstruction und Interpretation* (Munich: Kaiser, 1969) 161, notes how Paul ''fast beiläufig und wic ctwas Selbstverständliches'' speaks here of Israel as the seed of Abraham.
40. So Cranfield, *Romans*, 237. Among the few to insist on the grammatical point are L. Cerfaux, ''Abraham 'Père en circoncision' des gentils (Rom. IV,12),'' *Receuil Lucien Cerfaux* (Gembloux: Duculot, 1954) 2:333-38; J. Swetnam, ''The Curious Crux at Romans 4,12,'' *Bib* 61 (1980) 110-15; and U. Luz, *Das Geschichtsverständnis des Paulus* (Munich: Kaiser, 1968) 175.
41. The chiastic structure was pointed out by R. B. Ward, in an as yet unpublished paper read to the Society of Biblical Literature at its meeting in San Francisco 1981.
42. Swetnam, ''Crux,'' points to 4:23, which logically should read *Egraphē de ou di' auton monon.*
43. T. Zahn, *Der Brief des Paulus an die Römer* (Leipzig: Deichert, 1910) 212-17; Hays, ''Abraham.''
44. Those who would like to see a *hēmas* as subject confuse Greek with Latin grammar, according to Zahn.
45. Moxnes, *Theology*, 108.
46. Ibid., 111. Cf. also A. Kolenkow, ''The Ascription of Romans 4:5,'' *HTR* 60 (1967) 228-30.
47. Cf. J. Jeremias, ''Die Gedankenführung in Röm 4. Zum paulinischen Glaubensverständnis,'' *Foi et salut selon S. Paul* (ed. M. Barth et al.; Rome: Institut Biblique Pontifical, 1970) 51-58.
48. Pace A. T. Hanson, *Studies in Paul's Technique and Theology* (London: SPCK, 1974) 52-66.
49. ''In Judaism *ho anomos* or *hoi anomoi* is a common term for the Gentiles,'' W. Gutbrod, *TDNT* 4:1087.
50. Cf. G. Howard, ''Romans 3:21-31 and the Inclusion of the Gentiles,'' *HTR* 63 (1970) 223-33, and R. Meir in *Sanh* 59a.
51. Incidentally, one must allow Paul the freedom to write a conditional *realis* and not dismiss the sentence by saying ''it is quite clear that Paul regards [it] as totally untrue,'' as does Cranfield, *Romans*, 228.
52. If modern readers limit the *Urgeschichte* which precedes the history of Israel

proper to Gen 1-11, it seems that Paul would include all of Gen 1-16.

53. When Paul writes *peritomēs* instead of *diathēkēs*, is he influenced by the common phrase *bryt mylh* ?

54. Cf. C. K. Barrett, "Romans 9.30-10.21; Fall and Responsibility of Israel," *Die Israelfrage nach Röm 9-11* (ed. L. De Lorenzi; Rome: Abtei von St. Paul vor den Mauern, 1977) 99-121. Among the few to recognize that this is not the topic of this section are B. Klappert, "Traktat für Israel (Römer 9-11)," *Jüdische Existenz und die Erneuerung der christlichen Theologie* (ed. M. Stöhr; Munich: Kaiser, 1981) 76; and M. Barth, *The People of God* (Sheffield: JSOT Press, 1983) 39.

55. For the use of race imagery here, cf., e.g., Barrett, "Fall and Responsibility," 106.

56. Insofar as the verb *phthanō* often retains some of its classical meaning, its usage here implies that Israel ought to have arrived first. In any case, it does not preclude Israel from arriving later. Cf. 1 Thess 4:15 for a similar usage.

57. It has been suggested, apparently independently, by A. Strobel, *Untersuchungen zum eschatologischen Verzögerungsproblem* (Leiden: Brill, 1961) 187; H. Ljungman, *Pistis: A Study of its Presuppositions and its Meaning in Pauline Use* (Lund: Gleerup, 1964) 103-4; and H. Hübner, *Gottes Ich und Israel; Zum Schriftgebrauch des Paulus in Römer 9-11* (Göttingen: Vandenhoeck und Ruprecht, 1984) 63-65. That the proem text is not explicitly cited is not without parallel; cf. E. E. Ellis, *Prophecy and Hermeneutics in Early Christianity* (Tübingen: Mohr, 1978) 159.

58. That this is the sense of *ṣdq* here, cf. F. V. Reiterer, *Gerechtigkeit als Heil: ZDQ bei Deuterojesaja; Aussage und Vergleich mit der alttestamentlichen Tradition* (Graz: Akademische Druck- und Verlagsanstalt, 1976) 56-75. For the somewhat different understanding of the LXX (*to dikaion*), see J. W. Olley, *'Righteousness' in the Septuagint of Isaiah: A Contextual Study* (Missoula: Scholars, 1979) 96-101.

59. The phrase "pursue righteousness" is found also in Deut 16:20; Prov 15:9; Sir 27:8, but only Isa 51:1 speaks of pursuing righteousness parallel to seeking YHWH.

60. This was argued in Chapter 3.

61. It is important to note that throughout these chapters, "works" are not contrasted with "faith" but with the action of God in electing; cf. 9:11-12; 11:6-7.

62. Cf. J. E. Toews, "The Law in Paul's Letter to the Romans: A Study of Rom. 9:30-10:13" (Ph.D. dissertation, Northwestern University, 1977), and P. E. Dinter, "The Remnant of Israel and the Stone of Stumbling according to Paul" (Ph.D. dissertation, Union Theological Seminary, 1980). I owe much to these two very stimulating works and wish they were published in more accessible form.

63. The only two words in common: *idou* and *Siōn* do not mean citation.

64. The testimony hypothesis assumes that Ps 118:22, which *is* interpreted Christologically, must be behind all stone references, but it has been added to

the Isa 8 or Isa 28 tradition for the first time in 1 Pet 2.

65. Barrett, "Fall and Responsibility," 112; Toews, *Law*; P. W. Meyer, "Romans 10:4 and the 'End' of the Law," *The Divine Helmsman* (ed. J. L. Crenshaw and S. Sandmel; New York: KTAV, 1980) 62.
66. Dinter, "Remnant."
67. See Chapter 9.
68. J. C. O'Neill, *Paul's Letter to the Romans* (Middlesex: Penguin, 1975) 169. C. W. Otto, *Commentar zum Römerbrief* (Glauchau, 1886), 2:209, called *Christos* "Epexegese" to *telos* and translated "Denn Gesetzes Ende, nämlich Christus, ist . . . " (cited in A. Lindemann, "Die Gerechtigkeit aus dem Gesetz: Erwägungen zur Auslegung und zur Textgeschichte von Römer 10:5," *ZNW* 73 [1982] 239).
69. *Telos* can mean concretely the winning-post, goal in a race; cf. Plato, *Republic*, 613c.
70. Meyer, "Romans 10:4," translates similarly: "For the intent and goal of the law, to lead to righteousness for everyone who believes, is (nothing different from) Christ" (p. 68). Also Cranfield, *Romans* (Edinburgh: Clark, 1979) 2:519, says that the sentence is "primarily a statement about the law."
71. Cf. G. E. Howard, "Christ the End of the Law: The Meaning of Romans 10:4ff," *JBL* 88 (1969) 331-37.
72. E. Käsemann, "The Spirit and the Letter," *Perspectives on Paul* (Philadelphia: Fortress, 1971) 156, writes "Christ and Moses are just as exclusively contrasted with one another as Christ and Adam in Rom. 5.12ff."
73. They seem not to note the incongruity of having Paul attack Torah here in the context of his assertion that the word of God has not failed (9:6).
74. It was I believe a regression when the new textus receptus, Nestle 26 = UBS 3, reverted to the old textus receptus. To use as a reason that it would be otherwise "non-Pauline" (B. M. Metzger, *A Textual Commentary on the Greek New Testament* [New York: United Bible Societies, 1971] 525) is of course to beg the question. Cf Lindemann, "Gerechtigkeit," who, however, agrees with Metzger. But that simply assimilates Paul to the LXX and leaves the pronouns without antecedents. We should of course not assimilate the text to Gal 3—it is precisely the differences in wording which show how Paul wants the text to be understood.
75. See the survey in Toews, "Law."
76. Cf. R. Meir, *Sanh* 59a, and the discussion in Howard, "Christ."
77. Cf. J. A. Fitzmyer, "The Use of Explicit Old Testament Quotations in Qumran Literature and in the New Testament," *NTS* 7 (1961) 297-333; and the fuller discussion in Toews, "Law," and Dinter, "Remnant."
78. See V. H. Neufeld, *The Earliest Christian Confessions* (Grand Rapids: Eerdmans, 1963), and P. Vielhauer, *Geschichte der urchristlichen Literatur* (Berlin: de Gruyter, 1975) 23-28.
79. Cf. W. R. Kramer, *Christ, Lord, Son of God* (London: SCM, 1966), and Vielhauer, *Geschichte*, 14-22.
80. G. Howard, "Tetragram." Also Toews, "Law," writing before Howard,

interprets theologically.
81. It is possible that what called this topic to mind now was the second half of Joel 2:32 LXX.
82. Cf. H. Windisch, *Paulus und Christus* (Leipzig: Hinrichs'sche Buchhandlung, 1934); L. Cerfaux, "Saint-Paul et le 'Serviteur de Dieu' d'Isaïe," *Receuil Lucien Cerfaux* (Gembloux: Duculot, 1954) 2:439-54; J. Munck, *Paul and the Salvation of Mankind* (London: SCM, 1959) 24-33.
83. Where the LXX (not MT) had the Tetragrammaton in Hebrew letters. This means that we must read "God" and not "Christ" at the end of v 17; cf. Howard, "Tetragram," 78-79.
84. It is possible that this passage was suggested to Paul by Isa 52:10. It is also possible that it had some influence on his decision to go to Spain.
85. E. Hennecke, *New Testament Apocrypha* (ed. W. Schneemelcher; Philadelphia: Westminster, 1965) 2:101.
86. See Chapter 9.
87. Cf. P. Richardson, *Israel in the Apostolic Church* (Cambridge: Cambridge University Press, 1969) 135, 212.
88. Cf. R. J. Karris, "The Occasion of Romans," *The Romans Debate* (Minneapolis: Augsburg, 1977) 94. Note also how 15:14-21 corresponds to 1:8-15.
89. The arguments of Schmithals, *Römerbrief*, 157-161, are important, even if his solution is too drastic.
90. Cf. Ljungman, *Pistis*, 48-54.
91. Käsemann, *Romans*, 384, calls it "Acceptance of the Gentiles as a Mark of Christ's Lordship."
92. So Cranfield, *Romans*, 742, and U. Wilckens, *Der Brief an die Römer: 3. Teilband Röm 12-16* (Neukirchen: Neukirchener Verlag, 1982) 106.
93. Käsemann, *Romans*, 385.
94. Wilckens, *Römer 3*, 106.
95. Käsemann, *Romans*; Wilckens, *Römer 3*.
96. Williams, "Righteousness," 285-89. He was anticipated briefly by J. Knox, "Exegesis of Romans," *The Interpreter's Bible* (New York: Abingdon, 1954) 9:638.
97. F. F. Bruce, *Commentary on Galatians* (Grand Rapids: Eerdmans, 1982) 141.

NOTES TO CHAPTER NINE

1. Cf. E. P. Sanders, *Paul and Palestinian Judaism* (Philadelphia: Fortress, 1977).
2. The best description I know of Paul's missionary practice is found in E. P. Sanders, *Paul, the Law, and the Jewish People* (Philadelphia: Fortress, 1983) 179-90.

3. This has been generally recognized since W. G. Kümmel, *Römer 7 und die Bekehrung des Paulus* (Leipzig: Hinrichs'sche Buchhandlung, 1929), reprinted in *Römer 7 und das Bild des Menschen im Neuen Testament* (Munich: Kaiser, 1974) ix-160.
4. This is the conclusion, for somewhat different reasons, also of G. Lüdemann, *Paulus und das Judentum* (Munich: Kaiser, 1983) 20-22.
5. This is emphasized by F. Mussner, *Der Galaterbrief* (Freiburg: Herder, 1974) and *Tractate on the Jews* (London: SPCK, 1984).
6. Cf. Sanders, *Law*, 17-29.
7. See Chapters 2, 4, and 5.
8. D. Georgi, *Die Gegner des Paulus im 2. Korintherbrief* (Neukirchen: Neukirchener Verlag, 1964). See also J.-F. Collange, *Enigmes de la deuxième épître de Paul aux Corinthiens* (Cambridge: Cambridge University Press, 1972).
9. See Chapter 10. Nothing need be said at all about 1 Corinthians except to note with J. Weiss, *Der erste Korintherbrief* (Göttingen: Vandenhoeck und Ruprecht, 1910) 380, and J. Moffatt, *The First Epistle of Paul to the Corinthians* (London: Hodder and Stoughton, 1938) 268-69, that 1 Cor 15:56 is a gloss.
10. Cf. H. Koester, "The Purpose of the Polemic of a Pauline Fragment (Philippians III)," *NTS* 8 (1961-62) 317-32.
11. F. W. Beare, *A Commentary on the Epistle to the Philippians* (London: Black, 1959) 102-12, who incorrectly entitles the section "Renunciation of Judaism."
12. Two recent thorough reviews of the literature on the question are R. F. Collins, "Apropos the Integrity of 1 Thess," *Studies on the First Letter to the Thessalonians* (Leuven: University Press, 1984) 96-135, and T. Baarda, "'Maar de toorn is over hen gekomen. . . ' (1 Thess. 2:16c)," *Paulus en de andere joden* (Delft: Meinema, 1984) 15-74. Both authors conclude that the passage is authentic.
13. O. H. Steck, *Israel und das gewaltsame Geschick der Propheten* (Neukirchen: Neukirchener Verlag, 1967) 274-78. To be sure, he treats the passage as Pauline.
14. We have seen no evidence in the epistles that it was in fact such a hindrance, even if the charge did lead to Paul's arrest.
15. F. Werfel has in fact imagined such a debate in his *Paul among the Jews (a Tragedy)* (London: Mowbrays, 1928).
16. J. C. O'Neill, *Paul's Letter to the Romans* (Harmondsworth: Penguin, 1975) 52.
17. H. Räisänen, *Paul and the Law* (Tübingen: Mohr, 1983) 99.
18. Sanders, *Law*, 129.
19. Although the terminology is not quite accurate, what is meant can be seen in P. Dalbert, *Die Theologie der hellenistisch-jüdischen Missionsliteratur unter Ausschluss von Philo und Josephus* (Hamburg: Reich, 1954).
20. Sanders, *Law*, 125
21. The story is told in Josephus, *Ant.* 18. 81-84. He uses the *hierosyl-* root to refer to robbery from the temple contributions of Jews from Asia in *Ant.* 16.45, 164, 168; to describe robbery from the Jerusalem temple itself in *JW* 1.654 (= *Ant.* 17.163), 5.562, and *Ant.* 12.359; and in referring to Manetho's accusation that Jews robbed Egyptian temples before the Exodus (*AgAp* 1.249, 318f).

22. Cf. L. H. Feldmann's note on Josephus, *Ant*. 18.83, and H. J. Leon, *The Jews of Ancient Rome* (Philadelphia: Jewish Publication Society of America, 1960) 17-20.
23. See Chapter 8.
24. Sanders, *Paul*, 552.
25. Sanders, *Law*, 19f.
26. Thus A. R. Eckardt, *Elder and Younger Brothers* (New York: Scribners, 1967) 56, says that only a "strained exegesis" can deny that in Romans 11 Israel has not been displaced by the church in "the present dispensation;" A. T. Davies, *Anti-Semitism and the Christian Mind* (New York: Herder and Herder, 1969) 104, speaks of "the inadequacy of Romans 9-11" in allowing Jewish self-definition; and R. Ruether, *Faith and Fratricide* (New York: Seabury, 1974) 106, says "contemporary ecumenists who use Romans 11 to argue that Paul does not believe that God has rejected the people of the Mosaic covenant speak out of good intentions, but inaccurate exegesis."
27. See Chapter 5.
28. G. Eichholz, *Die Theologie des Paulus im Umriss* (Neukirchen: Neukirchener Verlag, 1972) 296.
29. P. E. Dinter, "The Remnant of Israel and the Stone of Stumbling in Zion according to Paul (Romans 9-11)" (Ph.D. dissertation, Union Theological Seminary, 1980). According to Sanders, *Paul*, 242-57, this is true also of Qumran. Cf. "We the remnant of thy people shall praise thy name, O God of mercies, who has kept the covenant with our fathers. In all our generations thou hast bestowed thy wonderful favours on this remnant of thy people" (1QM 14:8-9), and "He raised up for himself men called by name, that a remnant might be left to the Lord, and that the face of the earth might be filled with their seed" (CD 2:11-12).
30. As is assumed by most translations, which want Paul to distinguish between Israel as a whole and the small number of Jewish Christians who are to be saved.
31. See Chapter 8.
32. Beare, *Philippians*, 117.
33. It is not necessary to think of a deliberate citation of either Ps 94:14 or 1 Sam 12:22.
34. To which one could perhaps add from 8:30: "and predestined and called and justified and glorified."
35. See Chapter 8.
36. The "remnant" (*leima*) of 11:5 is then quite different from the "remnant" (*hypoleima*) of 9:27
37. *Pōroō* is not the same word as that translated "hardened" (*sklērynō*) in 9:18 and not quite so sclerotic. The substitution of "spirit of stupor" for the "heart" of the Deut text also ameliorates the accusation. As Paul said in 10:2, their heart is in the right place, but they do not see what he sees. It should also be noted that Paul does not make use of Isa 6:9f, the passage which is so important for the displacement theology of the Gospels and Acts.
38. Note the addition of "for myself" to the 1 Kgs 19:18 citation.

39. There are problems with the citation of Ps 69:23-24, added because of the catchword "eyes not to see." I personally believe with Lipsius that it is a post 70 C.E. scribal interpolation, similar to 1 Thess 2:14-17. It is very suspect because it follows immediately on v 22, which is used in all the passion accounts, a fact known to Christian scribes but not to Paul. The problem is not just the ununderstandable "table," but also the harshness of "bow down their backs forever" just before v 11. Thus even if it was written by Paul, which I seriously doubt, he immediately corrects it.
40. Cf. F. Mussner, "'Ganz Israel wird gerettet werden' (Röm 11,26)," *Kairos* 18 (1976) 242.
41. O. Michel, *Der Brief an die Römer* (Göttingen: Vandenhoeck und Ruprecht, 1957) 249, has misled later interpreters by speaking of a three-line prophetic oracle in v 25b-26a; so U. Müller, *Prophetie und Predigt im Neuen Testament* (Gütersloh: Mohn, 1975) 225-32; and D. E. Aune, *Prophecy in Early Christianity and the Ancient Mediterranean World* (Grand Rapids: Eerdmans, 1983) 280-81.
42. As does P. Stuhlmacher, "Zur Interpretation von Römer 11:25-32," *Probleme biblischer Theologie* (ed. H. W. Wolff; Munich: Kaiser, 1971) 555-70. J. Jeremias, "Einige vorwiegend sprachliche Beobachtungen zu Römer 11, 25-36," *Die Israelfrage nach Röm 9-11* (ed. L. De Lorenzi; Rome: Abtei von St. Paul vor den Mauern, 1977) 193-205, objects that *kathōs gegraptai* is otherwise not preceded by a *houtōs* in Paul. But then this text is prophetically understood to contain a mystery, and here as otherwise (1 Thess 4:15 before 16-17) Paul gives his own paraphrase before citing the text.
43. And not in the so-called threefold oracle, of which lines 1 and 2 are recapitulation and line 3 is a commonplace of all "Palestinian Judaism."
44. K. Stendahl, *Paul among Jews and Gentiles* (Philadelphia: Fortress, 1976).
45. There is a good discussion in W. D. Davies, "Paul and the People of Israel," *NTS* 24 (1978) 4-39, who finally cannot come to a decision. Note also R. Scroggs, "Paul as Rhetorician: Two Homilies in Romans 1-11," *Jews, Greeks and Christians* (ed. R. Hamerton-Kelly and R. Scroggs; Leiden: Brill, 1976) 276, "One of the striking features throughout chapters 1-4, 9-11 (and in distinction from chapters 5-8) is the sparseness of explicit Christian language and content. It is God who is emphasized in these chapters, one might even say the 'Jewish God,' while the figure of Christ remains in the background."
46. P. Richardson, *Israel in the Apostolic Church* (Cambridge: Cambridge University Press, 1969) 128-29, notes that Paul does not go on to cite Isa 59:21b, which might misleadingly be understood to refer to Christians.
47. There is no reference to Jer 31:33 here or elsewhere in Paul; see C. Wolff, *Jeremia im Frühjudentum und Urchristentum* (Berlin: Akademie, 1976) 134-42. NEB is completely wrong to insert "I will grant," as pointed out by Davies, "Paul and Israel."
48. So H. Hübner, *Gottes Ich und Israel: Zum Schriftgebrauch des Paulus in Römer 9-11* (Göttingen: Vandenhoeck und Ruprecht, 1984) 115-16.
49. For the neat rhetorical balance, see P. Richardson, *Israel*, 127-28, from whom I have to depart somewhat.

50. *Echthros* in the NT is always active and never passive (hated, i.e., by God). That breaks a certain parallelism in the two halves of the verse, but so do the two different senses of *dia* ("for your benefit" and "because of"); see J. Jeremias, "Römer 11," 202.
51. Sanders, *Law*, 196, reads into these verses what is not there when he says that "It is God's intent to have mercy on all, but mercy has faith as its condition."
52. Cf., e.g., Rom 7:1-6. In general see H. M. Gale, *The Use of Analogy in the Letters of Paul* (Philadelphia: Westminster, 1964).
53. W.D. Davies, "Romans 11:13-24. A Suggestion," *Paganisme, Judaïsme, Christianisme* (Paris: Boccard, 1978) 140, 141.
54. E. Käsemann, *Commentary on Romans* (Grand Rapids: Eerdmans, 1980) 306.
55. Cf 11:1-2; J. Fitzmyer, "Romans," in *The Jerome Biblical Commentary* (London: Chapman, 1968) 2:324; and H. Thyen, "Das Heil kommt von den Juden," *Kirche* (ed. D. Lührmann und G. Strecker; Tübingen: Mohr, 1980) 175, who interpret both as subjective genitives.
56. Cf. Sir 10:21 for a comparable use of this word pair: "The fear of the Lord is the beginning of acceptance; obduracy and pride are the beginning of rejection."
57. Cf. F. J. Leenhardt, *L'Epître de Saint Paul aux Romains* (Neuchâtel: Delachaux et Niestlé, 1957) 161-62; N. A. Dahl, "The Future of Israel," *Studies in Paul* (Minneapolis: Augsburg, 1977) 151; J. Fitzmyer, "Romans," 323; D. G. Johnson, "The Structure and Meaning of Romans 11," *CBQ* 46 (1984) 98f.
58. That statement is, of course, a warning to Israel and not a prediction of the Gentile mission.
59. Cf. the lack of antecedent for "among them" in v 17.
60. Thus U. Luz, *Das Geschichtsverständnis des Paulus* (Munich: Kaiser, 1968) 34, speaks of a "paränetischen Exkurs." See also D. Zeller, *Juden und Heiden in der Mission des Paulus* (Stuttgart: Katholisches Bibelwerk, 1973) 217; S. K. Williams, "The 'Righteousness of God' in Romans," *JBL* 99 (1980) 252; F. Mussner, "Ganz Israel," 252; H. Hübner, *Gottes Ich*, 108-9.
61. C. Plag, *Israels Wege zum Heil. Eine Untersuchung zu Römer 9 bis 11* (Stuttgart: Calwer, 1969).
62. Also B. Mayer, *Unter Gottes Heilsratschluss; Prädestinationsaussagen bei Paulus* (Würzburg: Echter, 1974) 275, argues against Plag that the paraenetic section, which might imply Israel's conversion, is not characteristic of Romans 11.
63. See A. Marmorstein, *The Doctrine of Merits in Old Rabbinical Literature* (New York: Ktav, 1968 [1920]), and Sanders, *Paul*.
64. See E. P. Sanders, "Patterns of Religion in Paul and Rabbinic Judaism," *HTR* 66 (1973) 455-78.
65. Sanders, *Law*, 194.
66. Among those who insist strongly on this point are Davies, "Paul and Israel"; Mussner, "Ganz Israel"; and B. Klappert, "Traktat für Israel (Römer 9-11)," *Jüdische Existenz und die Erneuerung der christlichen Theologie* (ed. M. Stöhr; Munich: Kaiser, 1981) 58-137. See also U. Luz, *Geschichtsverständnis*, 294; B.

Mayer, *Prädestination*, 289f; and U. Wilckens, *Der Brief an die Römer; 2. Teilband Röm 6-11* (Neukirchen: Neukirchener Verlag, 1980) 252.

67. The phrase is usually associated with F. Mussner, who however now seems to want to partially retract it: "Gesetz—Abraham—Israel," *Kairos* 25 (1983) 200-220. Better would be perhaps the "Partizipationsmodell" proposed by B. Klappert, *Israel und die Kirche* (Munich: Kaiser, 1980).
68. On this see *Sanh.* 97b and G. Scholem, *The Messianic Idea in Judaism* (London: Allen and Unwin, 1971) 251-56.
69. One classic example is the relationship between F. Rosenzweig and E. Rosenstock-Huessy.
70. Cf. J. Munck, *Paul and the Salvation of Mankind* (Richmond: Knox, 1959) and R. D. Aus, "Paul's Travel Plans to Spain and the 'Full Number of the Gentiles' of Rom. xi.25," *NT* 21 (1979) 232-62.
71. The term is used for convenience's sake, with full knowledge that it is an anachronism.
72. Eckardt, *Elder and Younger*, 138.
73. The reverse is also true and is in fact what happened.
74. Again, see especially Eichholz, *Paulus*, Davies, "Paul and Israel," and Klappert, "Traktat."

NOTES TO CHAPTER TEN

1. E.g., *Contra Celsum* 6.70. For the history of interpretation of this phrase see B. Schneider, "The Meaning of St. Paul's Antithesis 'The Letter and the Spirit,'" *CBQ* 15 (1953) 163-207; and J. Kremer, "'Denn der Buchstabe tötet, der Geist aber macht lebendig;' Methodologische und hermeneutische Erwägungen zu 2 Kor 3,6b," *Begegnung mit dem Wort* (ed. J. Zmijewski and E. Nellessen; Bonn: Hanstein, 1980) 236-39.
2. P. Vielhauer, "Paulus und das Alte Testament," *Oikodome* (Munich: Kaiser, 1979) 219, in a slight paraphrase. For a similar accusation, see E. Grässer, *Der Alte Bund im Neuen* (Tübingen: Mohr, 1985) 77-95.
3. Vielhauer, "Paulus," 213.
4. E. Käsemann, "The Spirit and the Letter," *Perspectives on Paul* (Philadelphia: Fortress, 1971) 156.
5. H. Windisch, *Der zweite Korintherbrief* (Göttingen: Vandenhoeck und Ruprecht, 1924), an important commentary unfortunately not accessible to me at the time of writing.
6. S. Schultz, "Die Decke des Moses. Untersuchungen zu einer vorpaulinischen Überlieferung in II Kor 3:7-18," *ZNW* 49 (1958) 1-30. An important recent work, M. Theobold, *Die überströmende Gnade* (Würzburg: Echter, 1982)

201-8, continues to believe that it is possible to reconstruct the midrash of the opponents.

7. D. Georgi, *Die Gegner des Paulus im 2. Korintherbrief: Studien zur religiösen Propaganda in der Spätantike* (Neukirchen: Neukirchener Verlag, 1964). It has been translated as *The Opponents of Paul in Second Corinthians* (Philadelphia: Fortress, 1986), and page references to the translation will be given in parentheses.
8. Windisch, *Korinther*, 112.
9. Although I am in fact convinced by the analysis of G. Bornkamm, "Die Vorgeschichte des sogenannten zweiten Korintherbriefes," *Geschichte und Glaube; Zweiter Teil* (Munich: Kaiser, 1971) 162-94. For a convenient summary see D. Georgi, "Corinthians, Second Letter to the," *IDB(S)* 183-86.
10. Georgi, *Gegner*. For all its erudition, this seminal study remains suggestive rather than definitive. In terms of careful exegesis I have been much more helped by J.-F. Collange, *Enigmes de la deuxième épître de Paul aux Corinthiens: Etude exégétique de 2 Cor. 2:14-7:4* (Cambridge: Cambridge University Press, 1972).
11. The cautions of C. J. A. Hickling, "The Sequence of Thought in II Corinthians Chapter Three," *NTS* 21 (1974) 380-95, must be taken seriously.
12. M. Rissi, *Studien zum zweiten Korintherbrief* (Zürich: Zwingli, 1969) 25.
13. C. J. Roetzel, *The Letters of Paul: Conversations in Context* (Atlanta: John Knox, 1982).
14. See L. Williamson, "Led in Triumph; Paul's Use of *Thriambeuō*," *Int* 22 (1968) 317-32.
15. See T. E. Provence, "'Who Is Sufficient for These Things?' An Exegesis of 2 Corinthians 2:15-3:18," *NT* 24 (1982) 54-81.
16. See W. Baird, "Letters of Recommendation. A Study of 2 Cor. 3:1-3," *JBL* 80 (1961) 166-72.
17. It must be emphasised against many interpreters that there is no reference here or in v 6 to the new covenant promise of Jeremiah 31. See C. Wolff, *Jeremia im Frühjudentum und Urchristentum* (Berlin: Akademie, 1976) 117-30; H. Räisänen, *Paul and the Law* (Tübingen: Mohr, 1983) 242, 245; Grässer, *Alte Bund*, 245; U. Luz, "Der alte und der neue Bund bei Paulus und im Hebräerbrief," *EvT* 27 (1967) 322.
18. See J. Lambrecht, "Structure and Line of Thought in 2 Cor 2, 14-4,6," *Bib* 64 (1983) 344-80.
19. As does M. Rissi, *Studien*, 22. The translation of the harder text follows Collange *Enigmes*, 53.
20. Luz, "Bund," 322-23 sees a real problem in the transition to the tablets. Georgi, *Gegner*, 249 (ET 248) says that it is "the motif of the heavenly letter" which forms the bridge between letters of recommendation and the tablets.
21. For a discussion, see D. Patte, *Early Jewish Hermeneutic in Palestine* (Missoula: Scholars, 1975) 150-51; and B. Z. Wacholder, *The Dawn of Qumran* (Cincinnati: Hebrew Union College, 1983) 60-61.
22. See Chapter 7. One could perhaps also refer to Hebrews in this respect.
23. Cf. CD 8:21; 19:33; 20:12; 1QpHab 2:3. In 1QH 4 there is a very interesting

correlation between the motifs of covenant (5, 19, 24, 34, 35, 39) and illuminated faces (5-6, 27-29)!

24. That it was in fact the rival missionaries who introduced the theme of "new covenant" and "ancient covenant" is argued by Schultz, "Decke," 13; and Georgi, *Gegner*, 252, 265-73 (ET 250, 258-64).
25. Georgi, *Gegner*, 252-58 (ET 250-54), of course also sees *gramma* to be part of the vocabulary of the opponents.
26. Schneider, "Antithesis."
27. The most impressive statement of this interpretation is by Käsemann, "Spirit."
28. See B. Cohen, "Letter and Spirit in Jewish and Roman Law" and "Letter and Spirit in the New Testament," *Jewish and Roman Law* (New York: Jewish Theological Seminary of America, 1966) 1:31-57, 58-64.
29. See E. Kamlah, "Buchstabe und Geist. Die Bedeutung dieser Antithese für die alttestamentliche Exegese des Apostels Paulus," *EvT* 14 (1954) 277; and E. Käsemann "Spirit," 143.
30. See Collange, *Enigmes*, 65-66, and Kremer, "Buchstabe," 230-33.
31. See U. Luz, *Das Geschichtsverständnis des Paulus* (Munich: Kaiser, 1968) 123-34.
32. See R. Bultmann, *Theology of the New Testament* (London: SCM, 1952) 1:240.
33. D. Georgi, *Gegner*, 168-82 (ET 137-48). See also J. N. Lightstone, *The Commerce of the Sacred: Mediation of the Divine among Jews in the Greco-Roman Diaspora* (Chico: Scholars, 1984) 118-19.
34. E.g., the Aramaic characters in Josephus, *Ant.* 12.15; the Hebrew characters in *Ant.* 1.5; the Latin characters in *Ant.* 14.319; the Greek characters in *Ant.* 14.197; 20.263; and the Hebrew and Greek characters in *Ant.* 12.48.
35. For the translation cf. Collange, *Enigmes*, 72-73.
36. "If the new glory is so much greater than the old, surely this, too, will be too dazzling for human eyes to bear? If Moses was forced to cover his face with a veil, will not the Christian minister also need to cover *his* face—since now the irradiation hazard must be infinitely greater?" M. Hooker, "Beyond the Things that are Written? St. Paul's Use of Scripture," *NTS* 27 (1981) 298.
37. The concept of Moses held by the opponents rather than Paul may be reflected in two interesting passages in Clement of Alexandria: "And as in the case of Moses, from his righteous conduct and from his uninterrupted intercourse with God, who spoke to him, a kind of glorified hue settled on his face; so also a divine power of goodness clinging to the righteous soul, in contemplation and in prophecy and in the exercise of the function of governing, impresses on it something, as it were, of intellectual radiance, like the solar ray, as a visible sign of righteousness, uniting the soul with light, through unbroken love, which is God-bearing and God-borne. Hence assimilation to God the Saviour arises to the Gnostic, as far as permitted to human nature" (*Strom.* 6.12 [104, 1-2]). " . . . accustomed to gaze as the Hebrews on the glory of Moses, and the prophets of Israel on the visions of angels, so we also become able to look the splendours of truth in the face" (*Strom.* 6.15 [132,5]).
38. *Mos.* 2.69, 70. Cf. also pseudo-Philo, *LAB* 12:1, "And Moses came down. And when he had been bathed with invisible light, he went down to the place where

the light of the sun and the moon are; and the light of his face surpassed the splendour of the sun and the moon, and he did not even know this."

39. *Mos.* 2.158-9.
40. *Gig.* 54.
41. One example can stand for many: "R. Elezer [ben Hyrkanus] sat down and expounded. His face shone like the light of the sun and his effulgence beamed forth like that of Moses, so that no one knew whether it was day or night," *Pirké de Rabbi Eliezer* (trans. G. Friedlander; New York: Blom, 1971) 7. For the important parallels to Qumran, see J. A. Fitzmyer, "Glory Reflected on the Face of Christ (2 Cor 3:7-4:6) and a Palestinian Jewish Motif," *TS* 42 (1981) 630-44.
42. And also that he himself is not a charismatic speaker; cf. 10:10; 11:6.
43. J. H. Schütz, *Paul and the Anatomy of Apostolic Authority* (Cambridge: Cambridge University Press, 1975) 173.
44. See G. Kittel, "*doxa*," *TDNT* 2.250. Examples are Rom 5:2; 8:18, 21; 1 Cor 15:43; Phil 3:21.
45. For this translation, see E. Hill, "The Construction of Three Passages from St. Paul," *CBQ* 23 (1961) 296-301.
46. But typically in a tribulation list, 2 Cor 6:8, "in honour (*dia doxēs*) and dishonour."
47. The participle in 1 Cor 2:6 refers to "the transitory rulers of this age."
48. B. S. Childs, *The Book of Exodus: A Critical, Theological Commentary* (Philadelphia: Westminster, 1974) 621, invents without warrant a midrashic tradition to this effect.
49. That this conception is completely foreign to the text is emphasized by P. von der Osten-Sacken, "Geist im Buchstaben: Vom Glanz des Mose und des Paulus," *EvT* 41 (1981) 230-35; and E. Stegemann, "Der Neue Bund im Alten; Zum Schriftverständnis des Paulus in II Kor 3," *TZ* 42 (1986) 97-114.
50. The Targums to Deut 34:7 say that the glory remained on Moses' face up to his death. Luke 9:32 maintains that it was still there in the first century.
51. D. L. Balch, "Backgrounds of I Cor. vii: Sayings of the Lord in Q; Moses as an Ascetic *theios anēr* in II Cor. iii," *NTS* 18 (1972) 351-64, points out some important parallels between 1 and 2 Corinthians, including this one.
52. That this is the sense of "righteousness" in 3:9 is argued by I. Dugandzic, *Das "Ja" Gottes in Christus: Eine Studie zur Bedeutung des Alten Testaments für das Christusverständnis des Paulus* (Würzburg: Echter, 1977) 109.
53. Hooker, "Beyond," 298.
54. Ibid., 299.
55. C. Buck and G. Taylor, *Saint Paul: A Study of the Development of his Thought* (New York: Scribner's, 1969) 63.
56. W. C. van Unnik, "'With Unveiled Face;' An Exegesis of 2 Corinthians iii. 12-18," *NT* 6 (1963) 153-69, has some important things to say about this word, even if his connection of it with the veil via Aramaic is quite strained.
57. Hickling, "Sequence," 390.
58. Rissi, *Studien*, 33.
59. For the translation "goal," see ibid., 32-33; Provence, "Sufficient," 75. There is at least the possibility that Paul has chosen the word *telos* here as a kind of

word play because the rival preachers spoke of the mystery (*teletē*) behind the veil. Cf. the Philo text cited in note 40 above.

60. See J. Behm, *TDNT* 4.961, "always (apart from Phil. 4:7) *sensu malo*," and Collange, *Enigmes*, 90.
61. It is otherwise first found in Melito of Sardis, as quoted in Eusebius, *Hist. eccl.* 4.26.13-14.
62. Cf. what Georgi, *Gegner*, says about "the Old Testament as the archive of the Spirit," 265-73 (ET 258-64).
63. If so, it refers of course to something read in the Corinthian church and not, as almost all commentators assume, as part of the worship of the *synagogue*.
64. There is an interesting conjunction of Moses, *palaia* and *grammata* in Origen, *Contra Celsum* 3.46, "In the Acts of the Apostles Stephen testified to Moses' scholarship, no doubt basing his statement on ancient documents (*ta palaia grammata*) not accessible to the multitude."
65. As in the NEB paraphrase, "For that same veil is there to this very day when the lesson is read from the Old Covenant; and it is never lifted, because only in Christ is the Old Covenant abrogated."
66. Collange, *Enigmes*, 98-99.
67. R. Le Déaut, "Traditions targumiques dans le Corpus Paulinien," *Bib* 42 (1961) 28-48, finds a very similar generalization in the Palestinian Targum to Exod 33:7b.
68. Along with Collange, *Enigmes*, 103-4; J. D. G. Dunn, "2 Corinthians III. 17—'The Lord is the Spirit,'" *JTS* 21 (1970) 309-20; C. F. D. Moule, "2 Cor 3:18b, *kathaper apo kuriou pneumatos*," *Neues Testament und Geschichte* (ed. H. Baltensweiler and B. Reicke; Zürich: Theologischer Verlag, 1972) 231-37; V. P. Furnish, *II Corinthians* (Garden City: Doubleday, 1984) 216; R. P. Martin, *2 Corinthians* (Waco: Word, 1986) 70-71.
69. See Fitzmyer, "Glory," and J. Lambrecht, "Transformation in 2 Cor 3,18," *Bib* 64 (1983) 243-54.
70. Cf. Collange, *Enigmes*, 138-39; Martin, *2 Corinthians*, 80; and E. Richard, "Polemics, Old Testament, and Theology; A Study of II Cor., III,1-IV,6," *RB* 88 (1981) 359-61, who, however, adduces too many texts.
71. The word *epistrephō*, to turn to or convert (as opposed to repent) is used by Paul specifically of the Gentile mission (1 Thess 1:9); has this influenced his alteration of the Exodus 34 citation in 3:16?
72. As suggested by Moule, "2 Cor 3:18b," 234, and argued by R. Hanhart, "Das Neue Testament und die griechische Uberlieferung des Judentums," *Uberlieferungsgeschichtliche Untersuchungen* (ed. F. Paschke; Berlin: Akademie, 1981) 293-303. The problem is that no known Greek version of Isa 25:7 refers to the veil.
73. H. Ulonska, "Die Doxa des Mose," *EvT* 26 (1966) 385.
74. Ibid., 388.
75. See P. Richardson, "Spirit and Letter: A Foundation for Hermeneutics," *EvQ* 45 (1973) 208-18.
76. Contrast the views of M. Hooker, "'Beyond the Things that are Written': An Examination of 1 Cor. IV.6," *NTS* 10 (1963) 127-32, and A. Legault, "'Beyond the Things which are written' (1 Cor. IV.6)," *NTS* 18 (1971) 227-31.

INDEX OF REFERENCES

1. BIBLE

2. Apocrypha and Pseudepigrapha

3. Qumran Literature

4. Classical and Hellenistic Authors

5. Rabbinic Literature

6. Early Christian Writings

INDEX OF MODERN AUTHORS

INDEX OF SUBJECTS